W9-AQB-519

Engaging in Evaluation and Assessment Research

Engaging in Evaluation and Assessment Research

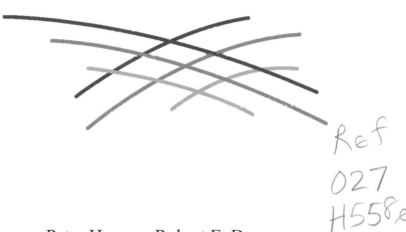

Peter Hernon, Robert E. Dugan,
and Danuta A. Nitecki

LIBRARIES UNLIMITED

AN IMPRINT OF ABC-CLIO, LLC
Santa Barbara, California • Denver, Colorado • Oxford, England

Library of Congress Cataloging-in-Publication Data
Hernon, Peter.
  Engaging in evaluation and assessment research / Peter Hernon, Robert E. Dugan, and Danuta A. Nitecki.
    p. cm.
  Includes bibliographical references and index.
  ISBN 978-1-59884-573-0 (pbk. : acid-free paper)—ISBN 978-1-59884-574-7 (ebook) 1. Libraries—Evaluation. 2. Public services (Libraries)—Evaluation. 3. Library administration—Decision making. 4. Library statistics. 5. Library science—Research—Methodology. I. Dugan, Robert E., 1952- II. Nitecki, Danuta A. III. Title.
  Z678.85.H46   2011
  027--dc22 2011010418

ISBN: 978-1-59884-573-0
EISBN: 978-1-59884-574-7

15 14 13 12 11   1 2 3 4 5

This book is also available on the World Wide Web as an eBook.
Visit www.abc-clio.com for details.

Libraries Unlimited
An Imprint of ABC-CLIO, LLC

ABC-CLIO, LLC
130 Cremona Drive, P.O. Box 1911
Santa Barbara, California 93116-1911

This book is printed on acid-free paper ∞
Manufactured in the United States of America

Contents

Illustrations

Figures

Tables

Preface

The separate literatures on evaluation and assessment continue to grow, but they tend to discuss each topic separately. Those literatures include some outstanding works that capture key concepts, their applications in various settings, and their connection to a planning process (from the setting of the mission, goals, and objectives to implementation of an ongoing process in which the library staff collects, analyses, and interprets data; links those data to program or service improvement; and begins the process anew by revisiting the goals and objectives). Relevant data might come from database vendors, the monitoring of simple activities, or the application of the formal research process, but those data must be linked to planning and the management of the library's infrastructure (facilities, collections, staff, and technology). In essence, evaluation might focus on library managers and the collection and use of assorted input, output, and impact metrics (e.g., those showing the percentage of satisfied or repeat customers, the number of questions customers pose at the reference desk in relation to other forums in which they ask reference questions) to document the extent of progress in meeting some library goals and to improve the delivery of services. For a more detailed discussion of metrics, readers should consult our *Viewing Library Metrics from Different Perspectives*.[1]

Much of the assessment literature focuses on student outcomes (e.g., graduation and retention rate) and student learning outcomes, and the expectations of external stakeholders, which view the library within an institutional context and want to know how well the library helps the institution meet its mission. Accreditation organizations, both regional and program, are examples of stakeholders concerned about the quality of the education that students receive and how different units of the institution work collaboratively to accomplish the overall mission. Government, ranging from local to national, wants to know how well academic institutions accomplish their mission and the extent to which students, their parents, and taxpayers receive value for money expended. Some of these same issues apply to public libraries, where library managers face increasing pressure to justify library services and to show what difference library programs and services make in the lives of the people who use them.

Metrics do not encompass all evaluation and assessment activities. Increasingly libraries must address questions of accountability, efficiency, effectiveness, and impact (the extent to which a program causes positive changes in the target population), and all of these issues are important to library managers and those to whom they directly report. With the increased interest in customer expectations and the concepts of service quality and customer satisfaction, some issues apply across service industries.[2] The focus of early research about service quality was to make comparisons across service industries. It is now possible, for instance, to compare libraries to other service organizations and to associate use with service quality and customer satisfaction. Some municipalities in the United States and other countries are doing so, as mayors and city managers ask, "Is the public more satisfied with the library or with other municipal departments?"

As evaluation and assessment issues become more complex, librarians will need to know how to conduct evaluation and assessment research while ensuring that the research is relevant to the needs of library managers and that the evidence gathered can be linked to accountability, decision making, and planning. After all, what good is the evidence gathered if it is not used for service improvement and to demonstrate accountability for resources expended?

We view assessment as a subfield of evaluation, but one that has its own nomenclature, stakeholders, and methods of data collection. Impact evaluation and assessment might involve the application of rigorous methods of data collection that go well beyond the comfort zone of many librarians, namely beyond the mere use of a simple survey. Regardless, the results must have application to use by management. After all, evaluation and assessment do not occur in a vacuum. Library managers should be open to problem solving, the process of identifying a discrepancy between an actual and a desired state of affairs, and taking action to resolve it. Evaluation and assessment research, and any metrics generated, can help managers identify that nontrivial discrepancy. Effective managers are not problem avoiders; they are problem solvers who rely on more than intuition in making decisions. The goal of evaluation and assessment is to ensure that library managers have access to a rich array of evidence that they can apply to planning and decision making.

As Peter Hernon and Ellen Altman pointed out in the late 1990s, there are eleven questions related to measurement, a tool in the evaluation or assessment process that enables managers to characterize library performance and thereby to make judgments. The questions might be treated separately or integrated. Some of the questions (how much?, how many?, how prompt?, how accurate?, how responsive?, how reliable?, and how courteous?) might be simpler to address, whereas others (how economical?, how well?, how valuable?, and how satisfied?) might be more complex. The how well question might involve the use of pre- and post-testing and experimental design and be related to other "how" questions.[3]

Engaging in Evaluation and Assessment Research covers these questions from the perspective of evaluation and assessment, but does so in terms of a cyclical planning process. This work also highlights relevant writings within and outside the discipline of library and information science and provides a detailed overview of the research process, an inquiry process that has clearly defined parameters and encompasses five activities:

1. Reflective inquiry (identification of a problem; conducting a literature search, in part to place that problem in proper perspective; the formulation of a theoretical framework and logical structure; and, as relevant, objectives, research questions, and hypotheses)

2. Adoption of appropriate procedures (research design, methodologies, and indicators of data quality)

3. The collection of data

4. Data analysis

5. Presentation of findings and a discussion of their implications

In the case of evaluation and assessment research, these activities take place within the context of what managers need to know. It is possible to construct a long list of topics meriting investigation, but many of these topics might not comprise organizational or institutional priorities. The first activity, reflective inquiry, must be framed within one of those priorities.

David R. Krathwohl views good research as those instances in which sound reasoning bonds each of the five activities together. There should not be a major conceptual or logical weakness in the bonding process.[4] To repeat, managers must be able to apply whatever evidence is collected from evaluation and assessment research to improve the quality of library programs or services, or to impact the infrastructure. Assessment findings must also be useful for demonstrating organizational and institutional accountability.

In twelve chapters, *Engaging in Evaluation and Assessment Research* covers evaluation and assessment as part of the research process (having five activities), while stressing how library managers can use evaluation and assessment results. This book is not another research methods textbook; the focus is on evaluation and assessment for managerial use—managerial decision making, planning, and communication with library stakeholders. In essence, why collect data if managers will not act on them? Taking effective action might be all the more reason for libraries to develop and use management information systems. We have added appendices for further clarification and demonstration of key aspects of the research and planning process and an overview of publication in peer-reviewed journals. The goal of this work is to add to the library manager's toolkit.

Anyone browsing the table of contents or the first page of a chapter will notice that we have not listed any one of us as the sole or principal author. Each of us drafted some of the chapters, and the other two authors made critical comments on those chapters. Before the book was finalized, all of us agreed on the content of each chapter; thereby we became joint authors of the entire book.

The target audience for this work includes practicing librarians and library school students interested in learning about the applied research process. With so many people now entering the workforce without the professional degree recognized by the American Library Association, we also provide an overview useful to them. As more libraries involve teams in gathering relevant metrics and evidence, knowledge about the research process will have to become more of a collective set of team skills. In this regard, libraries will have to connect the planning process and research to managerial leadership and ensure that the professional workforce has the necessary knowledge, skill set, and experiences. These individuals will also have to work with assorted stakeholders throughout the broader community. Futures such as those depicted in appendix A are not as extreme as they might seem at first; libraries continue to change during a time of great uncertainty, and some are already implementing some of the features of the scenarios depicted in that appendix. Maintaining critical stakeholder support as the library transforms and plays a larger institutional role will require strategic evidence gathered from metrics and from evaluation and assessment research. That evidence must be timely, relevant, of high quality, and understandable. Most likely, it will not be complete. Perhaps sufficient is a better word than complete; libraries lack the resources to produce complete findings, and social science research tends not to be definitive.

As Peter H. Rossi, Mark W. Lipsey, and Howard E. Freeman conclude, "ultimately, nothing teaches how to do evaluations [and assessments] as well as direct experience in designing and running actual evaluations [and assessments]. We urge all those considering entering the field of evaluation [and assessment] research to seek hands-on experience."[5] To this we add that novice researchers should seek knowledgeable mentorship, and more seasoned researchers should continue to add to their knowledge, abilities, and skill set. We see *Engaging in Evaluation and Assessment Research* as one of the foundation sources that will enable librarians to build a house of high-quality applied research—applied to meet local needs, demands, and expectations. Once again, managerial needs will guide the construction of that house, as this work amply shows. More than one type or style of house might be constructed.

NOTES

1. Robert E. Dugan, Peter Hernon, and Danuta A. Nitecki, *Viewing Library Metrics from Different Perspectives* (Santa Barbara, CA: ABC-CLIO, 2009).

2. For an introduction to different concepts, see Joseph R. Matthews, *The Evaluation and Measurement of Library Services* (Westport, CT: Libraries Unlimited, 2007); and, to a lesser extent, Peter Hernon and Joseph R. Matthews, *Listening to the Customer* (Santa Barbara, CA: ABC-CLIO, 2011); and Peter Hernon and Ellen Altman, *Assessing Service Quality: Satisfying the Expectations of Library Customers*, 2nd ed. (Chicago: American Library Association, 2010).

3. Peter Hernon and Ellen Altman, *Assessing Service Quality: Satisfying the Expectations of Library Customers* (Chicago: American Library Association, 1998), 51–55.

4. David R. Krathwohl, *Social and Behavioral Science Research: A New Framework for Conceptualizing, Implementing, and Evaluating Research Studies* (San Francisco: Jossey-Bass, 1985), 42, 49.

5. Peter H. Rossi, Mark W. Lipsey, and Howard E. Freeman, *Evaluation: A Systematic Approach*, 7th ed. (Thousand Oaks, CA: Sage, 2004), ix.

Acknowledgments

We wish to thank the American Library Association for permission to quote the following sources;

- Chapter 3: Marlu Burkamp and Diane E. Virbick, "Through the Eyes of a Secret Shopper," *American Libraries* 33, no. 10 (November 2002): 56–57.

- Chapter 12: Association of College and Research Libraries, *Value of Academic Libraries: A Comprehensive Research Review and Report*, by Megan Oakleaf (Chicago: Association of College and Research Libraries, 2010), 58.

- Appendix A: David J. Staley and Kara J. Malenfant, *Futures Thinking for Academic Librarians: Higher Education in 2025* (Chicago: Association of Research Libraries, 2010), 3, 21–22, accessed June 23, 2010, http://www.ala.org/ala/mgrps/divs/acrl/issues/value/futures2025.pdf.

Chapter 1

Planning

For a twenty-first-century library, accountability entails demonstrating, not merely claiming, its support of and contributions to the achievement of the institution's mission. Stakeholders want to know that the resources allocated to the institution are efficiently applied to meet the stated mission, as well as what indicators of effectiveness document progress in the achievement of institutional goals. Specifically, they are placing increased pressure on institutions of higher education to indicate what students learn at the program and institutional levels by applying assessment processes that replace traditional standards with less prescriptive ones.[1] Regardless of the stakeholder perspective, institutional effectiveness addresses

- infrastructure support (e.g., sufficient human, physical, and financial resources to support educational programs and to facilitate student achievement of learning goals),

- outputs (how much is accomplished),

- student outcomes (public accountability), and

- student learning outcomes (improvements in student learning and, to some extent, academic quality).[2]

Libraries are not immune from having to address institutional effectiveness and efficiency. As the need to measure accountability evolves beyond the use of self-reporting surveys and reliance on informally collected anecdotes, libraries must find new ways to demonstrate their value and effectiveness by focusing on efficiency and quality metrics.

Organizational planning enables the library to focus on the development and implementation of efficient and effective processes for both assessment and evaluation. Strategic planning takes a long-term view of what particular activities an organization should undertake to align its mission, vision, and values with its environment. It shapes the broader context, goals, and initiatives. Strategic planning, it should be noted, differs from tactical planning, which is analogous to setting annual goals and objectives and is used to implement the content of the strategic plan.[3] In brief, *planning* is the process of

- conducting a needs assessment of the organization by gathering and interpreting information on both external and internal environments,

- identifying and framing the key issues necessary to support the institutional mission,

- developing written goals and objectives,

- implementing services and activities to accomplish those objectives, and

- evaluating the overall quality and success of those services and activities based on the stated objectives.[4]

As part of their effort to demonstrate accountability through assessment, institutions often deploy a hierarchical framework with horizontal and vertical components to plan, gather, analyze, and report information, and to make changes to institutional and educational learning goals. When strategic planning is applied in educational institutions, however, the process can be hampered by the absence of clearly defined and reliably documented outcomes. Goals are set, alternative action plans are discussed, and a best course of action is selected. Nonetheless, the effectiveness of the selected plan is seldom evaluated against the educational outcomes implicit in the institutional mission. If the implemented strategic plan is evaluated, the criteria of success are likely aggregated outcomes related to financial health, student enrollments, and student retention, rather than the outcomes of student learning or community impact.[5]

Successful assessment and evaluation processes depend on the existence of clearly stated organizational and institutional mission statements as well as broader strategic plans that contain goals and measurable objectives on which to determine progress toward meeting objectives and their associated activities. Although one plan may encompass both assessment and evaluation processes, this chapter differentiates between the two because a library might place higher priority on one rather than the other.

THE DIFFERENCES BETWEEN ASSESSMENT AND EVALUATION

It is useful to think of evaluation and assessment as separate but connected concepts and processes. Evaluation, a broader concept, considers all aspects of an organization, a unit of that organization, or a program or service; those aspects relate to resources, staffing, operations, effectiveness, and efficiency. Assessment in higher education, on the other hand, describes processes used to examine student learning that results from exposure to academic programs. For public libraries, assessment may be associated with impact analysis for community services (e.g., summer reading programs and literacy programs). Assessment is an ongoing process aimed at improving learning,[6] while evaluation may be used to compare the data collected about the infrastructure to some standard for the purpose of judging worth or quality.[7]

Outcomes assessment might measure the contributions that the library or an academic program makes to the achievement of the institution's educational mission. By assessing formal student learning outcomes, the library wants to improve the effectiveness of its services through what Peggy L. Maki calls the "assessment cycle": Once learning outcomes have been developed, librarians, it is hoped in cooperation with program faculty members, gather and interpret evidence and, through a feedback loop, use that evidence to improve learning and the delivery of that learning.[8] It might be that the library and academic programs need to develop and refine methodologies as they move from informal to formal methods of data collection and thus better document learning changes that occur in the individuals.

ASSESSMENT

Assessment, a type of evaluation that gathers evidence from the application of evaluation research, is the ongoing process of

- establishing clear, measurable expected outcomes of learning;

- ensuring that learners have sufficient opportunities to achieve those outcomes;

- systematically gathering, analyzing, and interpreting evidence to determine how well learning matches stated expectations; and

- using the resulting information to understand and improve learning.[9]

As librarians, or anyone for that matter, begin to engage in assessment, they should reflect on the following questions:

- What is its purpose? Why is the campus or the municipality focusing on it?

- What level of assessment is desired? Who will be assessed?

- What is the focus of assessment? Will it have implications for individual learners, or will it deliver programmatic outcomes at the course, program, department, campus, or college/university level? Those conducting the assessment will have to make choices about research design (see chapter 3) and what they are trying to address (e.g., the range of knowledge (breadth and depth), skills (basic, higher-order, and career-related), attitudes, or behavior).

- What assessment resources are available?[10]

One purpose of assessment is to indicate the extent to which a program achieves its objectives and outcomes so that program faculty can use the findings to inform

- program planning,

- decision making to improve the quality of the program,

- revision of program objectives,

- resource allocation and budget requests,

- reporting on program progress, and

- accreditation.[11]

Assessment in higher education might focus on either program effectiveness or student learning outcomes. Academic institutions have reported outcomes for years. Student outcomes as representing program effectiveness and student learning outcomes, however, are not the same. Student outcomes refer to aggregate statistics on groups of students, and these quantitative performance indicators summarize assessment results of college performance that can be distilled down to numbers. Institutional performance indicators or student outcomes include student retention and transfer rates, graduate rates, student-to-faculty ratios, time to degree, and employment rates for a graduating class. These institutional-based outcomes are sometimes used to compare year-to-year institutional performance internally as well as to compare performance with other institutions.

Traditionally, libraries have also tended to rely on performance indicators, focusing on efficiency criteria involving input and output metrics (e.g., the number of items cataloged per day or the number of reference transactions completed per day). Goals and objectives from library long-term or strategic plans have focused on judging success in terms of efficient resource provision, or on whether the staff has completed certain tasks or set up specific activities, rather than on whether library services have had a discernible effect on users.[12] Librarians, however, must also consider effectiveness-related questions, such as the following:

- Is the library performing activities and offering the services that it should provide?

- Is library staff accomplishing organizational goals and objectives?

- How can staff ensure that the library offers high-quality services and activities?[13]

William Neal Nelson and Robert W. Fernekes identify library activities and programs applicable for viewing outcomes and impacts. In a support role, performance areas that contribute to institutional goals include the following:

- Services—provide a range of quality services and offer prompt and competent assistance to users; reasonable and convenient hours; reference assistance; and off-campus programs.

- Instruction—provide a variety of formal and informal instruction in use of library materials in all formats and integrate information literacy skills into instruction.

- Resources—provide varied, authoritative, and up-to-date resources in a variety of formats; maintain currency by weeding.

- Access to resources—provide access in a timely and orderly fashion; maintain a central catalog of library resources; and support distance learners with equivalent means of access.

- Staff—make a well-qualified and trained staff available in sufficient size and quality to meet programmatic and service needs of primary users.

- Facilities—have well-planned and secure buildings that are conducive to study and research and offer adequate space in a climate-controlled environment.

- Budget—meet reasonable expectations of users; support appropriate levels of staffing; and support an adequate collection of resources.[14]

Regional and program accreditation organizations expect an assessment of student needs and perceptions, an understanding of levels of student satisfaction, and a demonstration that the findings are actually used to make service improvement. As a result, academic libraries should be more concerned about the collection of quantitative and qualitative metrics that focus on the impact that the library makes in the lives of students, faculty, researchers, and others than they are with measuring traditional library inputs. Bonnie Gratch Lindauer finds that "probably the most direct contribution the library makes to institutional goals is its role in developing clear student learning objectives for information literacy skills; assessing the progress and achievement of these objectives; and showing how the outcomes are used to improve student learning."[15]

An assessment plan covering student learning outcomes discusses the systematic collection of information about student learning and how the time, knowledge, expertise, and resources available inform decisions about how to improve learning.[16] Closely tied to the educational mission of the institution and its campus-wide objectives, a learner-centered assessment plan for the library identifies the library's goals and objectives in support of campus outcomes and the areas in which the library will make its contribution (e.g., information literacy; information technology; course research requirements; point-of-need assistance; and graded tutorials, pathfinders, and quizzes).[17] In essence, the plan reiterates the institutional and library mission statements, the areas of activity (e.g., information literacy), the level of that activity (e.g., course or program), and the various stages of the assessment cycle.

Library Assessment Planning

According to Irene Rockman, "the changing nature of teaching, learning, and scholarship," combined with access to information becoming more complex and diverse, has been at the center of library transformation. Librarians are still trying to infuse information literacy throughout the curriculum. They might do so through the general education component of the undergraduate curriculum as they "weave information literacy into both lower- and upper-division courses, redesign services, reshape librarian roles and responsibilities, and revisit with discipline-based faculty members about course descriptions and student assignments to include information literacy principles."[18] Still, the focus of their efforts may not be at the program level as institutional accreditation organizations expect.

Library assessment planning begins with a review of the institution's strategic plan and vision and mission statements. Linkage to specific excerpts from the institution's mission, goals, and objectives should be clearly established in the library's mission statement and planning documents, and should be developed with input from library staff, classroom faculty, students, and administrators. Making this linkage is a key step in ensuring consistency among library activities, programs, and initiatives and the purpose and goals of the institution. It provides the foundation for the library to identify how its own goals and objectives contribute to those of the institution and how it measures the extent to which those goals and objectives are met.

Most library assessment plans include the usual types of input, process, and output performance metrics. A comprehensive library assessment plan, however, might contain an assessment of the library's contribution to relevant research and student learning. A variety of assessment methods ought to be employed, and some should be used on a consistent basis to generate longitudinal timeline data. Any plan should focus on assessing progress, since the goal of assessment is to improve rather than to demonstrate that the library has arrived at its final destination. When creating an assessment plan, it is important to consider the inclusion of the following general sections: purpose, objectives and outcomes, conducting an assessment, and results.

Purpose

The first section is a narrative that explains the purpose of the assessment plan and effort. In general, this section presents the library's needs for demonstrating accountability. This discussion can be facilitated by identifying the various internal and external stakeholders and then, from their perspective, addressing their information needs.

Accountability perspectives exist on several planes. One is to identify efficiency or effectiveness objectives and create outcomes based on those objectives. These objectives and their related outcomes support the stated mission and goals of the institution; thus, they provide an internal perspective. Process (efficiency) objectives include reviewing hours open or staff productivity workflow. Effectiveness objectives cover education-based outcomes (e.g., the impact the library has on its users). [19] The assessment process measures the progress the library makes toward meeting the objectives that emerge from the outcomes.

Another perspective is that of external stakeholders, such as parents, employers, and those monitoring the quality of higher education (namely the federal government, state governments, and the regional and program accreditation organizations). Interested in student learning outcomes, they want to know what skills, values, and behaviors students gain as they interact with members of the institution over time. Accountability therefore includes demonstrating to both internal and external stakeholders how the library and other units add value directly to a student's life. The assessment process includes analyzing the results of the assessment, sharing with or otherwise reporting them to others, and using the results to strengthen and improve performance by making changes to the manner in which learning occurs at the institution and in the classroom and in student contact with library resources and services.

Objectives and Outcomes

The second section identifies the plan's objectives and their related outcomes. Different types of objectives (e.g., program objectives, such as "the library's collection will improve in the physical sciences," or learning objectives, broad statements of what the program or institution wants students to be able to do or to know), are identified. Often these broad learning objectives serve as the framework that supports the institution's general education curriculum. As such, they are directly related to the stated goals of the institution's educational mission.

Outcomes, which are more detailed and specific statements derived from the program and learning objectives, specify what is wanted as a measurable end result of the library's efforts. There may be things the program wants students to know (cognitive), ways students may think (affective/attitudinal), or things students should be able to do (behavioral, performance, or psychomotor).[20] Objectives are assessed directly or indirectly by measuring specific outcomes related to them. In addition, information and the results gained from the assessment can be used to improve programs and services that impact learning.

Outcomes have specific characteristics. They are often measurable. There is little incentive for the library to engage in assessment unless an outcome is meaningful, that is, related to a stated objective. The assessment of an outcome provides the library with evidence that will help it in making decisions about the continuous improvement of the program, which is the basis for the particular objective and outcome.

In addition, the outcome must be written in a manner so that the assessor can determine when it has been achieved. This is particularly important for those outcomes that support student learning objectives. These outcomes should be written using action words; simply stated, "students will be able to [insert action verb] [insert some object]." Table 1.1 identifies various action verbs. The outcome must also be appropriate for the level of the program being examined. For example, the outcome based on an information literacy objective (e.g., evaluate sources that support a course-required research paper) differs when it is assessed at a general course level rather than for a particular academic discipline or specialty.

Table 1.1. Action Verbs

define	compare	modify	judge
explain	choose	contrast	formulate
solve	compose	defend	state
analyze	interpret	rank	change
construct	select	list	decide
design	evaluate	summarize	support
identify	demonstrate	use	discover
describe	paraphrase	distinguish	locate
apply	recognize	combine	differentiate

Student learning outcomes may also identify who is being assessed and where. For example, are all students or a group of them (e.g., freshmen, transfer students, or biology majors) the subject of assessment? Are the students being assessed at the course, program, or institutional level? At the course level, assessment in the form of student learning outcomes is formative and seeks to improve the educational experience for current and future students. Individual faculty might use the one-minute paper, which asks students to reflect on what was covered in class that day and to identify aspects that they still do not understand. Those aspects are revisited at the start of the next class. At the end of the course, the faculty member evaluates the final student projects, tallies scores from tests and assignments, assigns grades, and, it is hoped, uses the information for course improvement (perhaps based on a personally developed rubric). Assessment at the course level, therefore, is formative, and evaluation might be summative.

At the program level, faculty members outline the strengths and weaknesses of student work in relationship to departmental learning goals. Assessment may come from embedded course assignments, capstone experiences, field experiences, portfolios, or external tests. The department uses these and other data, such as those taken from student questionnaires, to inform decisions about curriculum and pedagogy and to identify areas for student improvement.

Finally, at the institutional level, evidence is gathered from a sample of students to reflect the student body in general and to demonstrate whether there is a progression in student learning. The institution may use a common college-wide assessment methodology (e.g., a portfolio, a published test of general education skills, or a capstone experience).

The number of outcomes found in this section of the planning document should be limited. Starting with few student learning outcomes—three or four—is a good idea when getting started. The number of outcomes may always be increased as a culture of evidence-based assessment builds from the success of the initial assessment effort.

Conducting the Assessment

This section of the plan discusses the collection of information about the stated outcomes. Specifically, for student learning outcomes, this section

- discusses the methods to collect information,

- identifies the measures and explains why these measures were chosen, and

- addresses how the assessment will be implemented.[21]

Some of the information may already exist in institutional documents, such as those found in an office for institutional research. Those documents may include data taken from questionnaires or interviews and might cover competency-based instruction, student and program placement, gate keeping (e.g., admissions tests), and campus and program evaluation from program reviews and retention studies.

As stated in the purpose of the assessment plan, however, the library is most interested in assessing student learning. Librarians should first look for whatever outcome-related information currently exists. If there is no such information, they may have to create an instrument to gather the information needed. Before doing so, they should search for available instruments; before using them, it is critical to check their reliability and validity and to determine the extent to which they cover what the librarians want to know.

As discussed in *Outcomes Assessment in Higher Education* and *Revisiting Outcomes Assessment in Higher Education*, there are two general types of evidence gathering that document student learning: *direct* and *indirect* methods. Direct methods require students, and for public libraries other learners, to display their knowledge and skills; indirect methods ask them (or someone else) to reflect on—rather than demonstrate—student learning.[22] To be as meaningful as possible, data should be collected using a multiplicity of direct or indirect methods at differing times in the student's life at the institution. Whenever possible, the assessment of student learning outcomes should be based on a direct examination of students' work, either formatively (while they are in process of learning) or summatively (at the end of the session, course, or program). In practice, there is an overdependence on the use of indirect methods for assessing student learning outcomes, namely asking students how much they have learned (perhaps by using a survey or extrapolating from student satisfaction data). Perceptions alone are not reliable indicators of learning. Satisfaction also has a tenuous relationship with learning; students reporting being satisfied with their experience in the program does not necessarily correlate with how much they learned. Asking students how much they have learned or grown as a result of their academic studies may yield some potentially useful information, but it is not until students demonstrate the extent of their learning that assessors can state that an outcome has been achieved.

Rubrics, which are a scoring guide that describes the criteria used to evaluate completed student assignments, are sometimes used to distinguish among levels of student performance or achievement when librarians and faculty directly assess student learning outcomes. To be effective, a rubric's performance descriptions must be clear and incremental, and the level of complexity must be appropriate for the concept being studied.

Other information in this section of the plan includes when the assessment will be conducted, by whom, and at what cost. A schedule for assessment may be established. The time frames may include upon matriculation; at the end of a specific semester; at the completion of a required set of courses; upon completion of a certain number of credits; upon program completion, graduation, or gaining employment; and a certain number of years after graduation (when examining lifelong learning).[23] Realistically, the library's opportunities for assessing student learning outcomes may be limited to a short time period at the end of an instruction session or during or at the end of a course when a librarian is embedded into the course or if a faculty member wants help in assessing learning outcomes. Another time frame may be set because of the need to provide a report by a certain date, such as when preparing a self-study report for accrediting purposes.

An ideal situation to ensure objectivity and to avoid bias is to use someone from outside of the assessment project to collect the information. However, it is often unrealistic for libraries to pay an outside evaluator.[24] Still, if an outside assessor is used, that person or persons should be well trained in using the methods and tools chosen.

Finally, the costs of assessment should be discussed in this section of the assessment plan. Even if only internal resources are used, there are related initial or continuing costs (time; financial, such as the costs for an externally developed measurement tool; and personnel costs).[25]

Results

This last section of the assessment plan describes how the results may be used. First, the data collected must be analyzed and interpreted. It is important to identify who will interpret the results, because those results inform teaching/learning (e.g., pedagogy) and decision making (e.g., budgeting and planning). Interpreters of the data are external assessors (representatives from agencies, faculty at other institutions, employers, and alumni) and internal assessors (librarians; student affairs representatives who assess portfolios compiled for general education; or members of interdisciplinary teams, assessment committees, the writing center, the academic support center, or the student affairs office).

The assessment plan should identify and explain how and with whom the library will share or otherwise report results to enhance institutional effectiveness and support accountability. Most often the *how* will be through one or more reports organized around issues. Those benefiting from the report(s) include the external and internal stakeholders identified in the purpose section of this plan: academic departments, institutional administrators and boards of trustees, and program and institutional accreditation organizations.

Because assessment is concerned with measuring the progress made toward meeting stated objectives and informing decision making for achieving objectives, assessment applies the results to inform decision making and make continuous improvements in course, program, and institutional quality. Too often an institution's commitment to assessing student learning is undertaken irregularly as a requirement for re-accreditation. Instead, the assessment process should be viewed as a cycle that

- identifies the mission, purpose, objectives, and outcomes;

- discusses the implementation of the assessment process for the purposes of compiling information and/or data;

- reviews and analyzes the information and/or data compiled;

- reports on the analysis; and

- explains how the analysis informs decision making and any changes in how the objectives will be reached (as measured by the outcomes).

Once the steps in this process have been completed, the assessment cycle begins again.

Barriers and Benefits to Assessment Planning

Effective and successful assessment programs must have continuous and ongoing intellectual and financial commitments from institutional leadership rather than having to rely on resources available on an irregular basis (occurring as episodic events). In addition to an ongoing commitment, barriers that libraries might encounter include the following:

- The perception that one cannot measure what the library does. It is difficult to assess the impact of the library on students and faculty and its larger organizational setting.

- Lack of leadership. There is a lack of understanding and vision of how the use of outcome metrics demonstrates the value and impact of the library. Libraries still depend too much on the traditional input and output metrics to explain their effectiveness.

- The assumption that the library does not control its own outcomes. Librarians suspect that the institution might use the evidence gathered against the library. Some data gathered from the application of outcomes, it is feared, may not cast the library in a positive light.

- Lack of expertise. Many library staff members do not have the skills needed to gather statistics and metrics and to analyze the data fully and correctly.

- Inertia. Often the staff prefers the status quo. Staff members are not interested in change and assume that "if it is not broken, there is no need to fix it."[26]

To this list, the assessment team at Columbia University Library adds

- insufficient time and support for analyzing and applying the data collected;

- the need to make data gathering routine and consistent;

- the lack of an organizational commitment to data-driven decision-making: such decision-making is perceived as neither an expectation nor a priority; and

- "survey fatigue."[27]

The benefits of planning for and undertaking assessment include the collection of data that can help the library to improve services, productivity (while lowering costs per transactions), and customer service. Studying the results from assessing student learning informs planning, budgeting, staffing, and programming as well as guiding the changes in the library's instructional effectiveness. Furthermore, the evidence of learning provided through assessment can be communicated to the various stakeholders, helping to build a case for the value and impact of the library. According to Joseph R. Matthews, "the value of the assessment plan is that it will help campus administrators to see libraries not merely as ends in themselves (self-contained units) but as strategic tools that can be used to achieve goals and objectives."[28]

The characteristics of a good assessment plan include getting positive answers to the following questions:

- Are student learning goals identified?

- Will the library's contribution to helping students achieve their goals be addressed by the assessment procedure?

- Are multiple assessment methods and metrics used?

- Does the plan identify the people (committees) involved and the processes that will be used?

- Are the results of assessment related to the planning process and likely to have a positive impact on students, faculty, and researchers?[29]

In summary, the following points remain essential to the assessment of impacts and outputs. First, in collaboration with other key constituent groups, a library assessment plan should focuses on performance indicators that contribute to those outcomes and outputs that the institution truly values. Second, librarians should find other assessment instruments and opportunities on campus or in the community in which aspects of library performance might be included (e.g., senior or alumni surveys). Third, as part of a culture of evidence gathering and managerial use, benchmark data should be established for appropriate performance indicators that measure progress, change, and achievement. Fourth, relevant, available institutional and library data should be inventoried and used to complement other data collection methods; the goal is adoption of a multimethod approach.[30]

EVALUATION

Evaluation is a systematic, objective process of identifying and collecting data and establishing criteria for determining the success, impact, results, costs, outcomes, or other factors related to a library activity, program, service, resource use, or policy. It addresses questions about whether and to what extent a program or service achieves its goals and objectives. Evaluation can be used to ensure that goals and objectives are met, improve programs and services during their development phase, compare competing programs and services, and contribute to the body of best practices about effective program or service design and implementation. Complicating matters, given the stagnation or decrease in funding resulting from the economic recession of 2008–2009 and its aftermath, there are increased constraints on a number of libraries to deliver service. As a result, more evaluation research now focuses on customer expectations about staff, collections, and the facility; the impact that the library has on its customers; and the outcomes that managers want the organization to meet. Rather than service improvement, survival becomes a key motivation for conducting evaluations and applying results to difficult decisions.

Evaluation is also a political and managerial activity, which provides insights for making policy decisions and resource allocations. It can be used to monitor operational effectiveness and provide evidence to distinguish among effective/efficient and ineffective/inefficient programs, services, and policies. The information gathered is useful for long- and short-term organizational planning when library managers decide whether or not to continue a program, service, or activity; to add or drop particular strategies and techniques; or to allocate resources among competing programs or services. Evaluation therefore is expected to have practical applications.[31]

Information resulting from evaluation research can be communicated to a variety of stakeholders and assist libraries in telling their story and demonstrating their effectiveness and value to their communities. The information also helps to explain what libraries do and for whom. Using the data gathered, library managers can highlight goals and report to senior decision makers (e.g., policymakers and advisory councils) and funders that reflect the impact and outcomes of their investments. The information can also be used to enhance the library's visibility, promote its services, and increase advocacy on its behalf.

Program Evaluation

While there are different types of evaluation, the most important distinction is between formative and summative evaluation. The former, which examines the implementation of the program or service, is used to develop or improve the design and delivery of a program or service. The latter uses the results from a program or service as an outcome or impact for judging value and quality. William M. K. Trochim, a professor in the Department of Policy Analysis and Management at Cornell University, further delineates types of formative evaluations as

- needs assessment, which determines who needs the program, how great the need is, and what might work to meet the need;

- evaluability assessment, which determines whether an evaluation is feasible and how stakeholders can help shape its usefulness;

- structured conceptualization, which helps stakeholders define the program or service, the target population, and possible outcomes;

- implementation evaluation, which monitors the fidelity of program or service delivery; and

- process evaluation, which investigates the process of delivering the program or service and considers alternative delivery procedures and processes.

Summative evaluation, he notes, is subdivided into

- outcome evaluations, which investigate whether the program or service caused demonstrable effects on specifically defined target outcomes;

- impact evaluation, which is broader and examines the overall or net effects (intended or unintended) of the program or service as a whole;

- cost-effectiveness and cost-benefit analysis, which addresses questions of efficiency by standardizing outcomes in terms of their dollar costs and values;

- secondary analysis, which reexamines existing data to address new questions or use methods not previously employed; and

- meta-analysis, which integrates the outcome estimates from multiple studies to arrive at an overall or summary judgment about an evaluation question.[32]

A specific type of evaluation of interest to libraries is program evaluation, which is a systematic study conducted periodically or on an ad hoc basis to determine how well a program works; help decision makers understand, verify, or increase the impact of products or services on users; and assist funding organizations in verifying that the service provider indeed helps its constituents. Program evaluation is also useful in improving delivery mechanisms and to make them more efficient and less costly. Evaluation research can identify program strengths and weaknesses, verify that what the service provider thinks it is doing is what it actually does, indicate that the program is really running as originally planned and merits replication as best practices elsewhere, and produce valid comparisons among programs to decide which should be retained (e.g., in the face of pending budget cuts).

Program evaluations can be formative or summative. Formative program evaluations are used to improve the program's implementation, and summative program evaluations help to determine the impact that the program has had on its intended audience as well as to judge the quality of the program. Although both formative and summative program evaluations are important, the next section, on planning for library evaluation, focuses on summative program evaluations because of their usefulness to libraries. The structure of a planning effort concerning formative program evaluation is similar to that of the summative evaluation, but it differs in when it would be conducted (before or during implementation versus at the end of a program or program cycle), how it would be conducted (the types of direct and indirect methods applied), and how the data are applied (by internal decision makers to improve the program versus using the resultant data to inform internal decision makers and for reporting to external stakeholders).

Planning for Library Evaluation

An evaluation plan describes the evaluation process. Regardless of the specific data elements that will be sought, a program or service evaluation needs to be planned. It does not just happen, and it is not a product of activities associated with a program or service.[33] The plan contains an introduction, a statement of purpose, the evaluation design, data collection and analysis, and results.

Introduction

In this section, the library addresses its readiness to conduct a summative evaluation. Unlike an outcomes assessment plan, which develops the goals and objectives around which to measure progress in the accomplishment of these objectives, a program or service evaluation has set clearly specified goals and objectives before an evaluation study takes place. If the program or service does not involve data collection, the evaluation process is difficult, if not impossible, to undertake.

Purpose of the Evaluation

In this section, the library states the purposes for the evaluation: what is being evaluated, why it is important for that to be evaluated, and what the evaluator wants to know. The purpose of the evaluation may be explained in the context of strategic planning related to the library's mission, goals, and objectives; the research addresses whether the program or service met its objectives. In addition, the evaluation may be conducted for decision making (e.g., to consider whether to continue, expand, or contract the program or service; and to increase, decrease, or cease the allocation of resources). Furthermore, the target audience (i.e., the stakeholders most interested in the results) is identified.

Evaluation Design

The overall design of the evaluation, which is presented here, examines the effectiveness and impact of the program or service and explains how well it is delivered. Librarians should carefully develop the evaluation study to select the design and methodologies that will produce the best information in a timely manner, in reportable formats that the intended audiences will understand. Narratives explain the decisions made about the design and

- identify what must be measured and what aspects of the program or service will be evaluated;

- note the kinds of respondents and how they will be selected;

- determine the type of questions to ask;

- specify the evaluation methods and the kinds of measurements used;

- select the data-collection techniques to deploy;

- plan the construction and/or purchase of any data collection instruments;

- determine when to conduct the evaluation;

- identify the resources available for the study, including budget and personnel;

- determine the time frame for data collection;

- plan data analysis; and

- describe the presentation/distribution and use of results.[34]

A logic model, which is developed during the planning phase of the program or service, may be useful when designing the evaluation. In its simplest form, such a model states that, if the library gets these resources (inputs) and applies them to conduct specific activities and deliver these services (throughput and outputs), the organization will accomplish stated outcomes.[35] Because of its linear arrangement, the logic model can be structured as a worksheet, with columns representing the resources, activities, outputs, and outcomes. If constructed during the planning phase, the model guides *what* could be evaluated. If a model is not created during the planning phase, the objectives for the program or service, if stated properly, could be used to create a logic-model worksheet for application during the evaluation.

Data Collection and Analysis

The evaluation plan gathers data about what has happened in the program or service or how much has been provided to users (in the form of inputs, processes, and outputs) and the impact on the users as well as on the library itself. In this section of the plan, the library identifies the sources of data, the data collection methods, data analysis, and who will collect and analyze the data.

The sources of information for this section comprise individuals or groups of users or library staff members, or a combination of both, and program documentation. The sources might include related literature, existing records and statistics, counts or transactions logs, observations or responses that have been self-reported or otherwise collected as input from participants, observations of the program or service, specialists or experts, and stakeholders. The frequency or intervals of data collection, as well as the date and time of data collection, are also specified in this section of the plan, if such information was not presented in the evaluation design.

Once collected, the data are organized, interpreted, and analyzed. The analysis is described in the context of the stated purpose of the evaluation and the findings, their rationale, or any explanations. The analysis may include narratives, charts, tables, graphs, and illustrations. Conclusions, including judgments and recommendations, are often stated as a narrative. The various individuals who will be responsible for gathering and analyzing the data and the sources used are identified. This may include the person or team responsible overall for managing the evaluation, members of the library staff, or outside consultants or evaluators.

The Results of the Evaluation

This section of the evaluation plan identifies the methods for disseminating the results, in what format, to whom, and the expected content. For example, a formal written report may be submitted to the library's governing body. The content of the report includes an executive summary (a one- to two-page, concise overview of findings and recommendations), the purpose of the report, what type of evaluation(s) was conducted, those decisions that the findings support, who is making the decision, and so on; the methodology (types of data/information collected), instruments used for collection, how the data were analyzed, and the limitations associated with the methodology used; interpretations and conclusions (derived from data analysis); and recommendations (about the decisions to make).[36] Depending on the intended stakeholder, a multiplicity of reports of varying content and different formats might be produced. For example, a one-page summary of the findings mounted as a Web page may satisfy the information needs of a particular stakeholder.

Benefits and Barriers to Library Evaluation

Evaluation is frequently carried out under constraints or limitations, which should be discussed as part of the planning process. A common argument is that undertaking the evaluation process draws resources from other services, especially in terms of time and cost. It is important that the evaluation be conducted at a time in which the data will be useful to decision makers and not provide outdated insights. These constraints, however, should be addressed as the scope of the evaluation is set: what is possible and affordable, and when the research should be conducted.[37]

Not only are there burdens concerning staff time and cost for conducting evaluation research, but the evaluation methodology, design, and analysis may be too complicated for staff to understand and effectively implement. A study sponsored by the Digital Library Federation found that, although respondents could frame research questions, they did not provide the same level of detail for the data needed to address those questions, the resources to carry out the study, and plans for using the findings for planning and better decision making. The respondents sometimes chose a research methodology in preparing and conducting the study that was not well suited to their skill sets.[38]

Two other common barriers concern the results of the evaluation. One is that the study might produce negative results—harmful to the program or service. Another is that stakeholders may not understand the results. To overcome this latter barrier, the library should focus on a means of communication and content that the stakeholders favor. The bottom line is to know the stakeholders, their expectations, and their preferred means of communication.

There are several benefits to conducting evaluation research. The process can provide objective evidence that demonstrates a program or service is effective and requires continued support from funding sources and the community. There are opportunities for program staff to share information with staff working in similar programs and peer libraries. In addition, demonstrating the effectiveness of programs through evaluation research can raise the profile of the library and promote the library by

- communicating program and service benefits to multiple stakeholders,

- demonstrating accountability and justifying funding needs to those allocating resources,

- determining which programs and services should be expanded or replicated, and

- helping to identify exemplary programs and services for recognition.[39]

CONCLUDING THOUGHTS

A multiplicity of stakeholders expect institutions as well as their libraries to be accountable for the resources they receive and the effectiveness and efficiency of their programs and services. Accountability includes not only the rationale for the expenditure of resources as inputs and for the usage of the resultant programs and services as outputs, but also the impact on the users (expressed in terms of outcomes). Stakeholders want to learn about the value received as a result of the resources invested, and they are no longer interested in just claims about value; they want evidence that can withstand scrutiny.

Assessment planning helps libraries to formulate goals, objectives, and outcomes that can be examined for effectiveness and impact and to make improvements in the delivery and content of programs and services. The intended result is to close the gap between the expected outcome and what is being realized. One effective type of outcome concerns student learning, and the assessment planning process can guide the library in creating measurable objectives that demonstrate progress toward meeting student learning objectives. Those outcomes focus on an increase in identified skills, abilities, and knowledge, as well as changes in behavior and attitudes.

NOTES

1. Robert E. Dugan and Peter Hernon, "Outcomes Assessment: Not Synonymous with Inputs and Outputs," *The Journal of Academic Librarianship* 28, no. 6 (November 2002): 377.

2. Peter Hernon and Robert E. Dugan, "Assessment and Evaluation: What Do the Terms Really Mean?" *College & Research Library News* 70, no. 3 (March 2009): 146.

3. Jo McClamroch, Jacqueline J. Byrd, and Steven L. Sowell, "Strategic Planning: Politics, Leadership, and Learning," *The Journal of Academic Librarianship* 27, no. 5 (September 2001): 372.

4. Peter Hernon and Charles R. McClure, *Evaluation and Library Decision Making* (Norwood, NJ: Ablex, 1990), 12.

5. Michael C. Choban, Gary M. Choban, and David Choban, "Strategic Planning and Decision Making in Higher Education: What Gets Attention and What Doesn't," *Assessment Update* 20, no. 2 (March–April 2008): 13.

6. The Mathematical Association of America, "Frequently Asked Questions," accessed January 21, 2010, http://www.maa.org/SAUM/faq.html#diffeval; Linda Suskie, *Assessing Student Learning: A Common Sense Guide*, 2nd ed. (San Francisco: Wiley, 2009), 12–13.

7. William Huitt, John Hummel, and Dan Kaeck, "Assessment, Measurement, Evaluation, and Research," in *Educational Psychology Interactive* (Valdosta, GA: Valdosta State University), accessed January 21, 2010, http://www.edpsycinteractive.org/topics/intro/sciknow.html.

8. Peggy L. Maki, *Assessing for Learning: Building a Sustainable Commitment across the Institution* (Sterling, VA: Stylus, 2004), 5; see also Peggy L. Maki, "Developing an Assessment Plan to Learn about Student Learning," *The Journal of Academic Librarianship* 28, nos. 1–2 (January–March 2002): 8–13.

9. Suskie, *Assessing Student Learning*, 4.

10. Joseph R. Matthews, *Library Assessment in Higher Education* (Westport, CT: Libraries Unlimited, 2007), 2–3.

11. Carrie L. Zelna, "Basic Assessment Plan Development," n.d., slide 8, accessed January 27, 2010, http://www.ncsu.edu/assessment/presentations/assess_process/basic_plan_devt.pdf.

12. Sharon Markless and David Streatfield, "Developing Performance and Impact Indicators and Targets in Public and Education Libraries," *International Journal of Information Management* 21, no. 2 (April 2001): 168.

13. Hernon and McClure, *Evaluation and Library Decision Making*, 7.

14. William Neal Nelson and Robert W. Fernekes, *Standards and Assessment for Academic Libraries: A Workbook* (Chicago: Association of College and Research Libraries, 2002), 12.

15. Bonnie Gratch Lindauer, "Comparing the Regional Accreditation Standards: Outcomes Assessment and Other Trends," *The Journal of Academic Librarianship* 28, nos. 1–2 (January–March 2002): 20.

16. Barbara E. Walvoord, *Assessment Clear and Simple: A Practical Guide for Institutions, Departments, and General Education* (San Francisco: Jossey-Bass, 2004), 2.

17. Nelson and. Fernekes, *Standards and Assessment for Academic Libraries*, 42–43.

18. Irene F. Rockman, "Strengthening Connections between Information Literacy, General Education, and Assessment Efforts," *Library Trends* 51, no. 2 (Fall 2002): 195.

19. Markless and Streatfield, "Developing Performance and Impact Indicators and Targets," 175.

20. Zelna, "Basic Assessment Plan Development," slides 15–16.

21. Walvoord, *Assessment Clear and Simple,* 10.

22. Peter Hernon and Robert E. Dugan, *Outcomes Assessment in Higher Education: Views and Perspectives* (Westport, CT: Libraries Unlimited, 2004); Peter Hernon, Robert E. Dugan, and Candy Schwartz, *Revisiting Outcomes Assessment in Higher Education* (Westport, CT: Libraries Unlimited, 2006). Direct methods might include student work samples, collections of student work in portfolios, capstone projects, course-embedded assessment, observations of student behavior, internal or external juried review of student projects, performance on problem and analysis (students explain how they solved a problem), performance on national licensure examinations, locally developed tests, and standardized tests perhaps used on a pre-test and post-test basis. Indirect methods might include alumni, employer, and student surveys and exit interviews with graduates.

23. Maki, "Developing an Assessment Plan to Learn about Student Learning," 11.

24. Authenticity Consulting, LLC, "How to Design Successful Evaluation and Assessment Plan," accessed January 23, 2010, http://managementhelp.org/misc/designing-eval-assess.pdf.

25. Megan Oakleaf and Neal Kaske, "Guiding Questions for Assessing Information Literacy in Higher Education," *portal: Libraries and the Academy* 9, no. 2 (April 2009): 276–83.

26. Matthews, *Library Assessment in Higher Education*, 6–7.

27. Columbia University Libraries, CUL Assessment Team, *Assessment Plan, Columbia University Libraries: 2007 through 2009* (February 1, 2007), 6, accessed January 23, 2010, https://www1.columbia.edu/sec/cu/libraries/bookmarks/img/assets/9436/CUL_Assessment_Plan.pdf.

28. Matthews, *Library Assessment in Higher Education*, 123.

29. Ibid., 127.

30. Bonnie Gratch Lindauer, "Defining and Measuring the Library's Impact on Campuswide Outcomes," *College & Research Libraries* 59, no. 6 (November 1998): 560.

31. Ronald R. Powell, "Evaluation Research: An Overview," *Library Trends* 55, no. 1 (Summer 2006): 118.

32. William M. Trochim, "Introduction to Evaluation," *Research Methods: Knowledge Base* (October 20, 2006), accessed September 7, 2010, http://www.socialresearchmethods.net/kb/intreval.htm.

33. Danuta A. Nitecki, "Program Evaluation in Libraries: Relating Operations and Clients," *Archival Science* 4, no. 1 (March 2004): 26.

34. Powell, "Evaluation Research," 114.

35. Susan Barnes and Maryanne Blake, *Measuring Your Impact: Using Evaluation for Library Advocacy* (Chicago: Medical Library Association, 2008), 39, accessed January 3, 2010, http://nnlm.gov/evaluation/workshops/measuring_your_impact/myi_slides.pdf.

36. Carter McNamara, "Basic Guide to Program Evaluation" (Authenticity Consulting, LLC, 2008), accessed January 2, 2010, http://www.managementhelp.org/evaluatn/fnl_eval.htm.

37. U.S. Bureau of Justice Assistance, Center for Program Evaluation, *Guide to Program Evaluation*, 11, accessed January 2, 2010, http://www.ojp.usdoj.gov/BJA/evaluation/guide/bja-guide-program-evaluation.pdf.

38. Denise Troll Covey, "Academic Library Assessment: New Duties and Dilemmas," *New Library World*, 103, nos. 1175/1176 (2002): 156–64.

39. Peggy D. Rudd, *Perspectives on Outcome Based Evaluation for Libraries and Museums: Documenting the Difference: Demonstrating the Value of Libraries through Outcome Measurement* (Washington, DC: The Institute of Museum and Library Services, n.d.), 20.

Chapter 2

Relevant Literature

As Peter H. Rossi, Mark W. Lipsey, and Howard E. Freeman point out, "the terms program evaluation and evaluation research are relatively recent inventions"; however, their antecedents date back several centuries.[1] Historically, program evaluation has been viewed in terms of social programs and their formative or summative evaluation. The goal was to create new programs and to revise existing ones to make them more effective and efficient. "Following World War II federal and privately funded programs were launched to provide urban development and housing, technological and cultural education, occupational training, [rural development, family planning, and improved nutrition], and preventive health activities."[2] "By the end of the 1950s," as they note, "program evaluation was commonplace." "During the 1960s, the number of articles and books about evaluation research grew dramatically," and, "in the early 1970s, evaluation research emerged as a distinct specialty field in the social sciences."[3]

Beginning with the 1970s, a number of textbooks and journals devoted to program and policy evaluation emerged.[4] For instance, the American Evaluation Association, which sees evaluation as "assessing the strength and weaknesses of programs, policies, personnel, products, and organizations to improve their effectiveness,"[5] publishes the *American Journal of Evaluation* and *New Directions for Evaluation*, a quarterly sourcebook. A number of textbooks cover evaluation research and program evaluation in general and specific disciplines and fields (e.g., education, health care, and speech pathology). Perhaps Sage Publications (http://www.sagepub.com/home.nav) is the major publisher of textbooks and other monographs relating to evaluation and research methods. *Evaluation: A Systematic Approach*, now in its seventh edition, first appeared in 1979.[6] Following are other examples of Sage books on this topic:

- *Program Evaluation and Performance Measurement*, which provides a conceptual and practical introduction to the topic from the perspective of public and nonprofit organizations[7]

- *Theoretical Frameworks in Qualitative Research*, which explains a critical component of reflective inquiry (see chapter 3) and offers examples, which, however, tend not to be applicable to LIS[8]

- *Reframing Evaluation through Appreciative Inquiry*, which portrays a type of evaluation associated with appreciative inquiry, "a group process that inquires into, identifies, and further develops the best of 'what is' in organizations in order to create a better future." Appreciative inquiry recognizes "the best in people"; acknowledges "those things that give life"; affirms "past and present strengths, successes, assets, and potentials"; and asks questions.[9]

Furthermore, Sage has introduced Sage Research Methods Online as a beta trial; it links the content of more than 500 interdisciplinary publications covering the research process to a search tool that enables searches to query specific content (http://srmo. sagepub.com/publicstart;jsessionid=C24218648C729CB1EB13E5FF9293A6BF?authRe jection=true).

EVALUATION IN LIBRARIES

In libraries, evaluation has been associated with collection evaluation, a component of collection development and collection management; the evaluation of indexes and other reference sources; library instruction or information literacy; information retrieval systems; and gathering and using performance or output metrics. One example is *Evaluating Bibliographic Instruction*, a handbook that introduces evaluation and applies it to research designs, methodologies, and statistical analyses. Its purpose is to encourage instruction librarians to engage in evaluation and to use the data collected to document that stated goals and objectives are met.[10]

Perhaps evaluation—when defined simply as the collection and use of statistics—dates back to 1906, when James Gerould at Princeton University started collecting statistics for selected college and university libraries, those that later formed the Association of Research Libraries (ARL). In 1961 ARL took over the collection and distribution of these statistics for its member libraries. These statistics largely focused on inputs and later added basic output metrics. In 1979 the Association of College and Research Libraries began a similar compilation, entitled *University Library Statistics*, which in 1998 evolved into *American Library Trends and Statistics*.

In 1977 F. W. Lancaster introduced *The Measurement and Evaluation of Library Services*, which summarized numerous research studies and introduced assorted methods of data collection.[11] One of the early textbooks that links evaluation to action research and the production of data for managerial decision making is *Evaluation and Library Decision Making*.[12] Since then, other textbooks have emerged. One reversed part of the title of the Lancaster work; *The Evaluation and Measurement of Library Services* provides an overview of evaluation processes, models, methodologies, and data analysis and the evaluation of the library and its services.[13] As a companion, Joseph R. Matthews produced *Library Assessment in Higher Education*.[14] Robert E. Dugan, Peter Hernon, and Danuta

A. Nitecki wrote *Viewing Library Metrics from Different Perspectives*, which presents a number of evaluation books and other writings that connect evaluation and assessment to assorted metrics of value to different libraries.[15] Their work, as well as that of Matthews, complements *Assessing Service Quality*, which provides an overview of evaluation and explores customer expectations expressed in the form of service quality and satisfaction.[16]

In addition to such works, numerous research studies directly and indirectly focus on formative and summative evaluation, address a wide assortment of services, and cover concepts such as effectiveness and service quality.[17] *Library Lit & Inf Full Text* and *Library Lit & Inf Science Retro* recognize "evaluation research" (more than 1,700 entries), "evaluation" (more than 32,000 entries), "service evaluation" (more than 2,000 entries), and "reference service evaluation" (more than 650 entries) as search terms. Limiting the search to "evaluation" and "up to 1990" produces more than 11,000 entries, many of which cannot be characterized as research studies. By focusing on peer-reviewed articles for the same time period, however, results in more than 3,000 entries. It is important to remember when reviewing these numbers that, for instance, reference service, as we now know it, did not emerge until the 1940s,[18] and the American Library Association's (ALA's) *RQ*, renamed *Reference & User Services Quarterly*, the official journal of ALA's Reference and User Services Association, began publication in 1960.

RELEVANT DATABASES FOR LOCATING EVALUATION AND ASSESSMENT STUDIES

When searching relevant literature, search engines such as Google and Yahoo! lead to numerous studies that are located on library Web sites but have not appeared in peer-reviewed journals. Of course, evaluators must review these works as they do any other literature, before relying on them. Still, some good studies and discussions might emerge that evaluators might otherwise miss.

The following databases focus on the literature of library and information science (LIS):

- Library Literature

- LISA Abstracts

- LISTA

These others include LIS as a social science discipline:

- Academic Onefile

- Academic Search Complete

- Dissertations and Theses-FullText

- Emerald (Emerald Management 120)

- Expanded Academic ASAP

- ISI Web of Knowledge

- Project Muse

- SAGE Journals Online

- ScienceDirect (Elsevier)

SAGE Journals Online, a database of Sage Publications, and ScienceDirect provide access to some journals devoted to evaluation as a scholarly field of study.

Many of the articles appearing in peer-reviewed journals focus more on research—action research—than evaluation per se. Perhaps the reason is that evaluation studies emphasize local problem solving; that is, they are institution or organization specific. The research is not cast in terms of problems important beyond a local situation. Still, good evaluation research should review all relevant research, whether or not it is narrowly cast.

Finally, the U.S. Government Accountability Office (http://www.gao.gov) is worth mentioning. In the congressional agency's site map, there is a heading for "Resources for the Auditing and Accountability Community" and a subheading for "Special Publications on Auditing, Evaluation Guidance and Other Topics," which leads to the category "evaluation and research methodology" (http://www.gao.gov/special.pubs/erm.html). The following guides are available as PDF files:

- *Case Study Evaluations*, PEMD-10.1.9 (1990)

- *Designing Evaluations*, PEMD-10.1.4 (1991)

- *The Evaluation Synthesis*, PEMD-10.1.2 (1992)

- *Performance Measurement and Evaluation: Definitions and Relationships*, GAO-05-739SP (2005)

- *Prospective Evaluation Methods: The Prospective Evaluation Synthesis*, PEMD-10.1.10 (1990)

- *Quantitative Data Analysis: An Introduction*, PEMD-10.1.11 (1992)

- *Using Structured Interviewing Techniques*, PEMD-10.1.5 (1991)

Despite the age of many of these guides, their content is still relevant for gaining a general understanding of the topics presented.

DIFFERENTIATING BETWEEN EVALUATION AND ASSESSMENT

Regional and program accreditation organizations expect institutions of higher education to determine the extent to which students make progress in achieving the educational mission of the college or university, and assessment shows how well these institutions advance student learning. Assessment therefore is a means by which institutions and their programs gather evidence to show how well they meet accreditation standards and address accountability. Librarians tend to discuss their engagement in assessment when, in fact, they are merely evaluating a program or service, presumably gathering evidence of effectiveness and insights into improvement. Assessment can exist at the course, program, or institutional level, but those conducting such studies must provide a baseline against which they document any improvement and can attribute any improvement to the learning goals of the course or program.[19]

As a general rule, evaluation might involve collaboration with a research team. Assessment, on the other hand, involves collaboration with stakeholders. For academic institutions the stakeholders might be faculty and program administrators, whereas public libraries might partner with members of city and county government to review literacy and other programs for their impact on the community and the extent to which participants actually learn and improve their skill set, perhaps significantly; the word *significantly* implies the use of inferential statistics.

Evaluation is linked to benchmarking when either of the following questions is addressed:

- In the context of a standard, goal, and objective, how good do we want to be with the services we offer?

- Does our performance meet, exceed, or fail to meet the standard?

If that standard is set by an accreditation organization, then the evaluation, in fact, comprises assessment. Best practices address three questions:

1. How do others do it?

2. Are others doing it better than we are?

3. How can we adapt our library to accommodate what others do?

Best practices become assessment when libraries factor into the answer the impact of their services on the communities served. In other words, the key question is: "What change has occurred in the community from its contact with the library and its infrastructure?" To answer this question most likely requires collaboration with stakeholders and ensuring that their perspectives are covered.

For instance, a library might "conduct regular surveys to assess the effectiveness of the online library catalog in allowing users to find resources;" "compare ILL [interlibrary loan] materials to peer benchmark libraries"; "periodically survey users to assess effectiveness of resources and services in meeting their needs"; "survey student library users regarding library materials"; "review contracts and cooperative agreements"; "compare staff, space, and funding to benchmarks"; and "survey faculty on the value of library instruction for improvement of their student research skills."[20] These activities actually comprise evaluation. Conceivably the last item—gauging faculty perceptions— might be regarded as an indirect indicator of learning. To call it assessment, however, requires some insights into student improvement throughout a course of study; in essence, some indication of what they knew at the beginning of the course and how much they learned by the course's conclusion. When libraries calculate the ratio of undergraduate students participating in library instruction sessions to the total undergraduate student population, they are compiling a student outcome, which is really a student-focused output.

The Assessment Literature

Some of the better assessment literature appears in fields other than academic and public libraries. One example is *Assessing for Learning: Librarians and Teachers as Partners*. Although the focus is on school media centers and meeting relevant standards, there is an excellent discussion of assessment tools, the difference between evaluation and assessment, and the role of libraries in the academic achievement of students.[21]

There has been increased interest in gauging the impact of library services on the community that public libraries serve and to work with various stakeholders to demonstrate the ongoing impact of library services.[22] The Institute of Museum and Library Services (IMLS) supports outcome-based evaluation and identifies the benefits for libraries.[23] The goal is to encourage libraries to determine the impact of their services and programs on the communities served. The Texas State Library and Archives Commission, for instance, supports the position of IMLS and notes:

> Outcome measurement is a systematic method of assessing the extent to which a program has achieved its intended result. It attempts to answer the questions, "What difference did the program make?" and, "How did the participant benefit?" Referred to by various names, including Outcome Based Evaluation (OBE) and outcomes assessment, it is useful as both a planning tool and an evaluation tool. Outcomes are beneficial changes for program participants that include changes in their skills, knowledge, behavior, attitude, status, or life condition.[24]

Much of the use of assessment in the literature of library and information science, even with those libraries having an assessment officer and department, focuses on evaluation and issues of effectiveness more than on issues of impact and improved learning: "knowledge leading to understanding but also abilities, habits of mind, ways of knowing, attitudes, values, and other disposition that an institution [or organization] and its programs and services assert they develop."[25] Do students and other members of the community really achieve the expectations set in the institutional and library mission statements and the goals specified in strategic plans?

Kenneth R. Smith, Eller Distinguished Service Professor of Economics and Faculty Associate to the Provost, University of Arizona, was one of the first to encourage librarians to abandon their traditional role in bibliographic instruction and to contribute to student learning. He advocated for them to work collaboratively with faculty to measure the impact of their teaching on student learning; in effect, he wanted to move the discussion from teaching to the impact on student learning.[26] Figure 2.1 provides examples of later writings that enlarge on Smith's perspective and link outcomes assessment to accreditation.

Hernon, Peter, and Robert E. Dugan, eds. *Outcomes Assessment in Higher Education: Views and Perspectives.* Westport, CT: Libraries Unlimited, 2004.

Hernon, Peter, and Robert E. Dugan. *Outcomes Assessment in Your Library.* Chicago: American Library Association, 2002.

Hernon, Peter, Robert E. Dugan, and Candy Schwartz, eds. *Revisiting Outcomes Assessment in Higher Education.* Westport, CT: Libraries Unlimited, 2006.

Maki, Peggy L. *Assessing for Learning: Building a Sustainable Commitment across the Institution.* Sterling, VA: Stylus Publishing, 2004, 2010.

Matthews, Joseph R. *Library Assessment in Higher Education.* Westport, CT: Libraries Unlimited, 2007.

Middle States Commission on Higher Education. *Developing Research & Communication Skills: Guidelines for Information Literacy in the Curriculum.* Philadelphia, PA: Middle States Commission on Higher Education, 2003.

Middle States Commission on Higher Education. *Student Learning Assessment: Options and Resources.* 2nd ed. Philadelphia, PA: Middle States Commission on Higher Education, 2007. The first edition was published in 2003.

Oakleaf, Megan. "The Information Literacy Instrument Assessment Cycle: A Guide for Increasing Student Learning and Improving Library Instructional Skills." *Journal of Documentation* 65, no. 4 (2009): 539–60.

Oakleaf, Megan. "Using Rubrics to Assess Information Literacy: An Examination of Methodology and Interrater Reliability." *Journal of the American Society for Information Science and Technology* 60, no. 5 (May 2009): 969–83.

"Outcomes Assessment." *The Journal of Academic Librarianship* 28, nos. 1–2 (January–March 2002): 1–46; 28, no. 6 (November 2002): 356–80.

Suskie, Linda. *Assessing Student Learning: A Common Sense Guide.* Bolton, MA: Anker Publishing, 2004; San Francisco: Jossey-Bass, 2009.

Figure 2.1. Some Key Readings on Assessment

When they discuss assessment, the writings in the literature of library and information science present course-level assessment, but they may not compare student knowledge, skills, and abilities from a *before* and *after* perspective—before the instruction was offered and after it was. Some exceptions include an article by Sara J. Beutter Manus, who described the role of a librarian embedded in a course devoted to instruction of first-year music undergraduates.[27] One of the more ambitious studies examines the information competency of students at California State University and the translation of these competencies into scenarios that directly measure student learning.[28]

IMPACT EVALUATION AND ASSESSMENT

Impact evaluation examines the extent to which a program or service produces changes in the desired direction. Implicit to it is having preexisting goals and criteria of success; *impact* means that there is movement or change toward achieving stated objectives. Impact assessment is similar, but it views change in the target population from the perspective of rubrics or whatever framework is in place to determine progress in meeting accreditation or other outside expectations. Both impact evaluation and assessment may involve the use of an experimental design, hypothesis testing, and inferential statistics.

In a survey of ARL member libraries, Zsuzsa Koltay and Xin Li conclude that "impact assessment is a field in its infancy for research libraries."[29] Turning to public libraries, based on 3,176 responses to a national telephone survey, 44,881 Web survey responses from customers of more than 400 public libraries, and 319 interviews, a project team from the University of Washington showed "that public libraries are a key element of America's digital infrastructure, and that large numbers of people are using libraries' public access services to meet their needs in health, education, employment, and other important areas."[30] In essence, they compiled and reported on a series of outcomes, mostly comprising evidence gathered from the use of indirect methods, but the compilation contains significant errors (e.g., the accuracy of the data respondents supplied and the vague wording of some questions). Nonetheless, the findings will be of interest to a number of public library stakeholders, and the data can be easily captured in dashboard form and reported in a series of persuasive stories that will appeal to stakeholders.

An example of impact assessment to measure the technological skills of undergraduate accounting students at the course level uses nonparametric statistics to measure learning and differences among the students. Those students "improved their perceived ability to use the computer to analyze a technical problem, to complete an unfamiliar project successfully, and to increase their understanding of various Internet sources."[31]

COPING WITH CHANGE

In *Beyond Survival*, Elizabeth J. Wood, Rush Miller, and Amy Knapp discuss academic libraries in transition and the challenges that they face.[32] Among the challenges for a number of ARL and other academic libraries is the sharp decline in the circulation of print books and questions posed at the reference desk, while at the same time, there is a dramatic increase in the use of digital reference services. Further, libraries are seeing a change in how the public uses space. Academic libraries, for instance, are replacing individual study carrels and expanding group study space, adding comfortable casual setting, and relaxing policies on the use of food and drink in the building. Ironically, the use of physical facilities increases at a time when the use of print material often dramatically declines. Coping with change and the challenges results in new literature that appears in peer-reviewed journals, monographs, conference presentations and proceedings, and library Web sites.

Joseph Branin, Frances Groen, and Suzanne Thorin, for instance, review "the changing nature of collection management in research libraries," and they call attention to the *Use of Library Materials: The University of Pittsburgh Study*, known as the Pitt Study.[33] Published in the later 1970s, this important study shows that any book purchased had a 50 percent chance of ever being borrowed. Furthermore, as books in the collection aged and did not circulate, their likelihood of ever circulating greatly diminished. Journal use, in general, did not fare much better. Today there is a major shift in collections from print to electronic sources, and patterns of use are also shifting. Figure 2.2 updates findings from the Pitt study, has broad implications for other libraries, and serves as a reminder that there are numerous topical areas in evaluation research to explore.

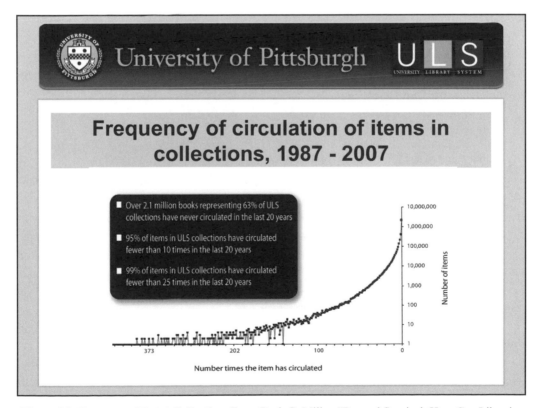

Figure 2.2. Turnover of Print Collection. From Rush G. Miller, "Beyond Survival: How Can Libraries Maintain Relevance in the Digital Age" (presentation at the ALAO conference, October 30, 2009).

CONCLUDING THOUGHTS

From the literature it appears there is great interest in evaluation and assessment, with some libraries creating an assessment officer and department, and conferences devoted entirely to the subject. Still, there is a tendency to confuse the terms and to use evaluation methodological tools to report outcomes. It is time to move beyond a discussion of course assessment and indirect methods of assessment—perceptions about learning—and determine what students and others have actually learned, or how much their knowledge, skills, and abilities have improved. As a guide to future challenges, Laura Saunders's dissertation should be required reading for anyone interested in assessment. It shows that neither librarians nor others have assumed the necessary leadership role to advance information literacy as a program or institutional outcome.[34] Coverage remains at the individual course level and the willingness of individual faculty to cooperative. Second, other challenges relate to transparency, accountability, and changing the organizational and institutional cultures. A key question is: "How do libraries use the evidence they gather to improve their role and effectiveness in student learning and enhance accountability?" At the same time, the Lib-Value Project (http://libvalue.cci.utk.edu/node/2, an IMLS-funded grant project) indicates that there is increased interest in placing the library within the broader institutional context and demonstrating its value and worth.

NOTES

1. Peter H. Rossi, Mark W. Lipsey, and Howard E. Freeman, *Evaluation: A Systematic Approach*, 7th ed. (Thousand Oaks, CA: Sage Publications, 2004), 2.

2. Ibid., 8.

3. Ibid., 9.

4. For a list of the journals, see ibid., 10.

5. American Evaluation Association, "About Us," accessed February 18, 2010, http://www.eval.org/aboutus/organization/aboutus.asp.

6. See Peter H. Rossi, Howard E. Freeman, and Sonia R. Wright, *Evaluation: A Systematic Approach* (Beverly Hills, CA: Sage Publications, 1979).

7. James C. McDavid and Laura L. Hawthorn, *Program Evaluation and Performance Measurement: An Introduction to Practice* (Thousand Oaks, CA: Sage Publications, 2006).

8. Vincent A. Anfana Jr. and Norman T. Metz, eds., *Theoretical Frameworks in Qualitative Research* (Thousand Oaks, CA: Sage Publications, 2006).

9. Hallie Preskill and Tessie T. Catsambas, *Reframing Evaluation through Appreciative Inquiry* (Thousand Oaks, CA: Sage Publications, 2006), 1, 3.

10. *Evaluating Bibliographic Instruction: A Handbook* (Chicago: American Library Association, Association of College and Research Libraries, Bibliographic Instruction Section, 1983).

11. F. W. Lancaster, *The Measurement and Evaluation of Library Services* (Washington, DC: Information Resources Press, 1977). He followed this work with similar writings, namely *If You*

Want to Evaluate Your Library . . . (Champaign: University of Illinois, Graduate School of Library and Information Science, 1988, 1993), and *The Measurement and Evaluation of Library Services* (Arlington, VA: Information Resources Press, 1991), coauthored with Sharon L. Baker.

12. Peter Hernon and Charles R. McClure, *Evaluation and Library Decision Making* (Norwood, NJ: Ablex, 1990).

13. Joseph R. Matthews, *The Evaluation and Measurement of Library Services* (Westport, CT: Libraries Unlimited, 2007).

14. Joseph R. Matthews, *Library Assessment in Higher Education* (Westport, CT: Libraries Unlimited, 2007).

15. Robert E. Dugan, Peter Hernon, and Danuta A. Nitecki, *Viewing Library Metrics from Different Perspectives: Inputs, Outputs, and Outcomes* (Santa Barbara, CA: ABC-CLIO, 2009).

16. Peter Hernon and Ellen Altman, *Assessing Service Quality: Satisfying the Expectations of Library Customers* (Chicago: American Library Association, 1998, 2010).

17. See, for instance, Thomas A. Childers and Nancy A. Van House, *What's Good? Describing Your Public Library's Effectiveness* (Chicago: American Library Association, 1993).

18. See Samuel Rothstein. *The Development of Reference Services through Academic Traditions, Public Library Practice and Special Librarianship* (Chicago: Association of College and Reference Libraries, 1955).

19. Georgetown College Library, "Assessment of the Library: Library Evaluation Plan, 1," accessed March 5, 2010, http://library.georgetowncollege.edu/Assessment.htm.

20. Ibid. 2.

21. Violet H. Harada and Joan M. Yoshina, *Assessing for Learning: Librarians and Teachers as Partners* (Westport, CT: Libraries Unlimited, 2005); 2nd ed. (Santa Barbara, CA: ABC-CLIO, 2010).

22. Rhea Joyce Rubin, *Demonstrating Results: Using Outcome Measurement in Your Library* (Chicago: American Library Association, 2006).

23. Institute of Museum and Library Services, *Perspective on Outcome Based Evaluation for Museums and Library Services* (Washington, DC: Institute of Museum and Library Services, n.d.), accessed February 18, 2010, http://www.imls.gov/pdf/pubobe.pdf. See also Texas State Libraries and Archives Commission, "Resources," accessed February 18, 2010, http://dev.texshare.edu/outcomes/resources.html.

24. Texas State Library and Archives Commission, "Outcome Measures," accessed March 6, 2010, http://www.tsl.state.tx.us/outcomes/. See also Florida Department of State, Division of Library and Information Services, Workbook: Outcome Measurement of Library Programs (Tallahassee, FL: Division of Library and Information Services, 2000), accessed March 6, 2010, http://dlis.dos.state.fl.us/bld/Research_Office/OutcomeEvalWkbk.doc.

25. Peggy L. Maki, *Assessing for Learning: Building a Sustainable Commitment across the Institution* (Sterling, VA: Stylus, 2004), 3.

26. Kenneth R. Smith, "New Roles and Responsibilities for the University Library Advancing Student Learning Through Outcomes Assessment," *Journal of Library Administration* 35, no. 4 (2002): 29–36.

27. Sara J. Beutter-Manus, "Librarian in the Classroom: An Embedded Approach to Music Information Literacy for First-Year Undergraduates," *Notes* 66, no. 2 (December 2009): 249–61.

28. Kathleen Dunn, "Assessing Information Literacy Skills in the California State University: A Progress Report," *The Journal of Academic Librarianship* 28, nos. 1–2 (January–March 2002): 26–35.

29. Zsuzsa Koltay and Xin Li, *Impact Measures in Research Libraries*, SPEC Kit 318 (Washington, DC: Association of Research Libraries, 2010), 12.

30. Samantha Becker, Michael D. Crandall, Karen E., Fisher, Bo Kinney, Carol Landry, and Anita Rocha, *Opportunity for All: How the American Public Benefits from Internet Access at U.S. Libraries* (Washington, DC: Institute of Museum and Library Services, 2010), iv, accessed October 29, 2010, http://www.gatesfoundation.org/learning/Documents/OpportunityForAll.pdf.

31. Sudip Bhattacharjee and Lewis Shaw, "Enhancing Skills through Technology: A Project for Advanced Accounting Students," in *An Action Plan for Outcomes Assessment in Your Library*, by Peter Hernon and Robert E. Dugan (Chicago: American Library Association, 2002), 180.

32. Elizabeth J. Wood, Rush Miller, and Amy Knapp, *Beyond Survival: Managing Academic Libraries in Transition* (Westport, CT: Libraries Unlimited, 2007).

33. Joseph Branin, Frances Groen, and Suzanne Thorin, *The Changing Nature of Collection Management in Research Libraries* (Washington, DC: Association of Research Libraries, 2002), accessed October 30, 2010, http://www.arl.org/bm~doc/changing-nature-coll-mgmt.pdf; Allen Kent, *Use of Library Materials: The University of Pittsburgh Study* (New York: M. Dekker, 1979).

34. Laura Saunders, "Information Literacy as a Student Learning Outcome: As Viewed from the Perspective of Institutional Accreditation" (PhD diss., Simmons College, 2010).

Chapter 3

The Components of an Evaluation and Assessment Research Study

Novice evaluators and other researchers in library and information science (LIS) often let the reflective inquiry of their study be shaped by the method of data collection they know best or *want* to use, but that methodology may not adequately address the problem statement, study objectives, and research questions. Furthermore, the research literature appearing in LIS for guidance in setting up a problem statement and other components of the reflective inquiry tends to cover these components poorly or to omit some of them. Much of the published literature, for instance, still lacks a problem statement and in some instances mischaracterizes the requisite conceptual base (e.g., customer expectations or information needs).

Assessment research, a type of evaluation research, contains the same components, but when academic and public librarians apply them, they tend to rely on surveys and other indirect methods of data collection. They might even use data collected from LibQUAL+® and mischaracterize the findings as conveying the extent of customer satisfaction or as applicable to outcomes assessment. Clearly there is a tendency to confuse evaluation with assessment and to equate course evaluation and student satisfaction as indicators of student learning; such methods do not indicate what students actually learned over time—the duration of a course or program of study. Course evaluation, the checking of bibliographic references in student papers, and the assignment of grades involve evaluation. The purpose of assessment is to gather data on a recurring basis and to move from reliance on indirect methods to the adoption of direct methods that provide insights into what was actually learned. Evaluation might also involve recurring data collection; library evaluators, however, often shift from one problem area to another depending on organizational priorities. Today, products such as the satisfaction survey of Counting Opinions provide a means to engage in continuous data collection. Perhaps satisfaction is one area in which libraries can abandon independent data collection and rely on LibSAT, produced by Counting Opinions (see chapter 6).

With the requirement that libraries monitor the impact of their programs and services, demonstrate accountability (organizational effectiveness and efficiency), and improve ongoing services, there is a need to understand the research process and carefully select those researchable problems that demand the greatest attention. It is no longer sufficient for library managers to assume they know their customers and make decisions about services based on intuition and what they learn from anecdotal evidence that frontline staff relays to them. Assessment, in particular, requires evidence that can withstand the scrutiny of others and shows the extent to which the library is effective and efficient and makes an impact on those it serves.

This chapter, which complements the readings listed in figure 3.1, highlights the components of an evaluation or any type of research study, which are reflective inquiry (problem statement, literature review, theoretical or conceptual foundation, logical structure, objectives, research questions, and hypotheses), procedures (research design and methodology), and data quality indicators (reliability and validity, or their qualitative equivalent: credibility, transferability, dependability, and confirmability).

REFLECTIVE INQUIRY

David R. Krathwohl views reflective inquiry in terms of a chain of reasoning that bonds one component with the others and integrates previous research. With evaluation, or for that matter any other type of research, it is important to settle on what the research will examine and not exceed that context and to ensure that each component of the study is well thought out.[1] That chain therefore should be logical and contain well-bonded links—similar to what we expect in a chain-link fence. With each component of reflective inquiry, the researcher reviews previous components and strengthens the bond between each component.

Problem Statement

Within any topical area (e.g., reference service effectiveness or the impact of the library on student learning or community literacy), numerous problems theoretically exist. The purpose of the problem statement is to show which aspect of that topical area will be investigated and that this aspect is both significant and unique. The problem statement, the first component of a proposed study, identifies the *problem* around which any proposed study in the social sciences is based. The problem must be clearly stated, specific, manageable, important, written to stimulate reader interest, and, in the case of evaluation and assessment research, actionable and applicable to planning and decision making.

There is no universal agreement across disciplines and fields of study about how to write a problem statement. Is it merely a question or a statement of purpose, or are more elements present? A mere question does not show conflict or that something is unsettled, perplexing, and in need of formal investigation that relies on all of the components

Dilevko, Juris. "Reading Literature and Literature Reviews," *Library & Information Science Research* 29, no. 4 (2007): 451–54.

Hernon, Peter. "Components of the Research Process: Where Do We Need to Focus Attention?" *The Journal of Academic Librarianship* 27, no. 2 (March 2001): 81–89.

Hernon, Peter, and Candy Schwartz. "Procedures: Research Design," *Library & Information Science Research* 31, no. 1 (2009): 1–2.

Hernon, Peter, and Candy Schwartz. "Reliability and Validity," *Library & Information Science Research* 31, no. 2 (2009): 73–74.

Hernon, Peter, and Candy Schwartz. "A Research Study's Reflective Inquiry," *Library & Information Science Research* 30, no. 3 (2008): 163–64.

Hernon, Peter, and Candy Schwartz. "What Is a Problem Statement?" *Library & Information Science Research* 29, no. 3 (2007): 307–9.

Hernon, Peter, and Candy Schwartz. "Writing an Abstract," *Library & Information Science Research* 32, no. 3 (2010): 173.

Nitecki, Danuta A. "Finalizing a Research Paper—Findings through Conclusion," *Library & Information Science Research* 32, no. 1 (2010): 1–3.

Figure 3.1. Readings Covering the Components of a Research Study

discussed in this chapter. A statement of purpose indicates what the study will accomplish, but does not place that statement in the context of a problem. One way to envision a problem statement therefore is to associate it with four elements:

1. Lead-in

2. Originality

3. Direction

4. Justification or study value

The first element provides transition from a background section to the problem statement and is aimed at setting up the next element, the claim of originality, which often centers on a knowledge void or on conflicting evidence. This claim declares the uniqueness of the proposed study, and the literature review supports that claim. Evaluation and assessment research encourages replication, whereas publication in peer-reviewed journals requires uniqueness. *Replication* refers to drawing repeated samples from the same population or repeated use of a research design or methodology over time. Evaluators and those engaged in assessment want to see if action based on previous data collection has led to service and program improvement.

The direction declares what the general focus of the study is, and it might contain a purpose statement or an all-encompassing research question or two that clarify the intent of the study. The audience therefore understands what the study will examine. The final element explains the value of the proposed research and its contribution to theory and/or practice.

The subsequent components of the reflective inquiry and procedures expand on this modest beginning—the problem direction—and further clarify and delimit the scope of the study. Explained differently, the researcher is beginning to build a chain of reasoning.

Literature Review

The literature review supports the problem statement and the declaration of originality. It also identifies, synthesizes, and applies research studies relevant to the problem direction. Once the studies have been identified, this section does not merely present their findings; rather, the goal is to relate these studies to the proposed one. Evaluators review the research designs, methodologies, and key variables used in those studies, and they identify what is relevant and what danger signs might exist. One danger sign might be low response rates to the questionnaires used in related research. With this knowledge evaluators should seek ways to offset a potential low response rate, assuming they plan to use a survey.

Novice evaluators and assessors might undertake a cursory literature review and want to rush to the procedures section. Because the procedures section emerges from the reflective inquiry, they should conduct a thorough literature review and see how other evaluators have investigated similar problems. Unless they do this, the proposal might contain some faulty links in the chain of reasoning.

In summary, one purpose of the literature review, especially by extending it to literature outside LIS, is to review the chain of reasoning that others have developed. As a result, a good literature review goes beyond mere identification and description of past research.

Theoretical Framework

Similar to other types of research, evaluation and assessment research applies one or more theories or concepts. Evaluators and assessors need to understand concepts such as customer satisfaction and service quality as well as impact assessment. (One function of validity is to ensure that researchers have an accurate understanding of relevant concepts and translate that understanding into effective methods of data collection, and another function is to confirm that study findings represent the theory or concepts discussed.) Adding to confusion, the LIS literature does not always provide an accurate depiction of concepts. For this part of a proposal, it may be critical to explore outside literatures and dissertations.

Logical Structure

The logical structure, which provides the framework within which the problem will be investigated, is a visual diagram that takes the problem *direction* and lays out relevant components and variables. The logical structure, which moves a study from an abstract presentation to an identification of the elements presented in the problem direction, clarifies the theories, concepts, critical variables, and knowledge implicit in the problem statement's direction. By articulating how all parts of the direction fit together, the logical structure provides the context for selecting study objectives, research questions, and, if relevant, hypotheses.

Evaluators use the literature review, in part, to add potential variables to the logical structure. The structure therefore might be compared to a restaurant menu, one that lists all of the food choices by category of foods (e.g., appetizers, main course, and dessert); there are no specials excluded from that menu. After a careful review of the menu, evaluators decide what to order, that is, to select. That decision becomes the study's objectives, which are translated into research questions and hypotheses, and these sections of reflective inquiry have implications for study procedures.

In summary, the visual diagram affords evaluators and other researchers an opportunity to search for weaknesses in the chain of reasoning they are trying to develop. For any weaknesses they uncover, it is imperative that they put in place ways to offset them.

Objectives

Working from the logical structure, researchers list the study objectives—those aspects of the menu they intend to investigate. Objectives provide the conceptual framework for the research questions and the formulation and testing of any hypotheses.

Every objective has two components: an action verb and the content or object of that verb. Evaluation studies typically involve *depicting* and perhaps *relating* (comparing and contrasting). Assessment studies might do the same; both might also involve testing the impact of an intervention. Objectives might be cast as follows:

- To describe (determine, identify, depict, etc.)

- To relate (compare or contrast)

- To test

Objectives examine each part of the logical structure specified in the problem direction. Evaluators start with one part of the problem direction and then move the other parts. At the same time, they might relate one part of the diagram to another part. For example, assuming the problem direction centers on the satisfaction of the elderly with library workshops, the logical structure, for instance, would specify the types of workshops as well as variables associated with the elderly. Sample objectives might be to

- identify the extent of satisfaction with technology workshops,

- identify the extent of satisfaction with the explanation of Boolean search operators,

- identify the extent of satisfaction with the exercise covering Boolean search operators, or

- compare the extent of satisfaction with a workshop between elderly working full-time and those who are retired.

Research Questions

The "to describe" objectives are converted into research questions.[2] One objective might require more than one question, and all of the questions must be clearly worded and define terminology as needed. Data collection focuses on addressing those questions, and the findings section of the final paper might be organized around those questions. Those questions, however, are condensed into headings such as "the extent of workshop satisfaction."

Hypotheses

Hypotheses, like research questions, flow from the logical structure, but they represent a narrowing of objectives and involve comparing, contrasting, and testing. Hypotheses are expectations about the nature of things based on generalizations about the assumed relationship between variables. Hypotheses enable evaluators, on the basis of sample data—the use of probability sampling—to determine whether or not something about the population is likely to be true or false. In so doing they involve statistical testing and determination of whether or not a relationship is statistically significant. In short, hypotheses reflect a highly sophisticated conceptual framework for the study, while research questions indicate a less sophisticated and more exploratory framework.

PROCEDURES

Procedures refer to the study design and the methods by which evaluators will investigate the problem and address stated research questions and hypotheses.

Research Design

Chapter 5 focuses on research designs. Suffice it to say here that evaluators need to answer questions such as the following:

- What is the population under investigation? (Can it be determined?)

- Will a sample be drawn from the population? Will that sample reflect some population characteristic? If yes, which one(s) from the logical structure?

- How large will that sample be?

- When and where will the study be conducted?

Methodology

Methodology is the means by which evaluators collect data. The means might involve quantitative or qualitative data collection or both types (see chapters 6–8). Chapter 9 focuses on statistics and data analysis.

DATA QUALITY

Data quality refers to reliability and validity; these issues apply to both the research design and methodology. Reliability seeks to determine the extent to which the data are consistent; consistency is the extent to which the same results are produced from different samples of the same population. Validity refers to the extent to which study findings are generalizable to a population (external validity) or to which the study accurately measures what it purports to measure (internal validity). Internal validity also asks whether evaluators have made the correct interpretation of the findings, or whether other factors, variables, or conditions have been considered or acknowledged. If the reliability and internal validity of the data are limited, so too is the degree to which the findings can be generalized outside a particular setting. In many instances, however, evaluators have little desire or interest in generalizing findings beyond a particular population or setting. External validity should be of less concern than ensuring that the study examines what it intends to study.

Course Evaluation

Course evaluation has been mistakenly characterized as relevant to both assessment and evaluation. For assessment, it has been erroneously called an indirect measure for gauging student learning.[3] With so much grade inflation and student expectations of a high grade in a course, course evaluation has limitations. It does not capture student satisfaction; the instruments typically are not set up to ascertain student satisfaction with the courses and the instructor—they neither ask satisfaction questions nor use a proper measurement scale. Furthermore, the instruments may have serious reliability and validity problems, and they do not capture what was actually learned. (Figure 3.2 is an example of an instrument that has been studied repeatedly and has a high degree of reliability and validity.)

EXAMPLE OF BOTH REFLECTIVE INQUIRY AND STUDY PROCEDURES

Mystery shopping tends to involve qualitative data collection and a subjective evaluation of the experience. It might be applied to the process of getting a library card; asking a question; attending a workshop or public meeting; or, in the case of academic libraries, the use of an information, learning, or knowledge commons.[4] Libraries might contract with a mystery shopping company to conduct a certain number of visits, perhaps for $25 per mystery shopper visit.

This section takes the topic of mystery shopping and offers a draft proposal that contains each of the components discussed above. Please note that this section could have been written in one of two ways: (1) as a local evaluation study or (2) as a research study with the intention of seeking publication in a peer-reviewed journal. If it were an evaluation study, both the background and problem statement sections would center on a particular library, and the originality component of the problem statement would be unnecessary. Because the purpose here is to best illustrate all of the components of a proposal, the focus is on a research paper intended for possible publication. One final observation is that this proposal could have addressed a different aspect of mystery shopping (i.e., a specific service as opposed to overall service provision); if it had, the focus of the research would have shifted.

Background

This section provides a context for understanding the problem statement and attracting potential readers. Typical readers of the literature library and information science peruse the titles and abstracts of papers, and, if they are still interested, turn to the first part of the published paper—the background.

Let us also assume that the title of the paper is "Using Undercover Agents for Service Evaluation."

Student Course Evaluation

Course: LIS _____   Section number: _____   Instructor: _____

Year: 20____   Semester (check one): ____ Fall   ____ Spring   ____ Summer

Number of students in the class (the instructor will supply this): _____

I am (check one): ____ a master's student ____ a doctoral student ____ auditing the course

I am (check one): ____ a full-time student ____ a part-time student

This course is (check one): ____ a requirement   ____ an elective

This form is intended to collect your opinions about the course. It takes about 10 minutes to complete. Please place a check mark in the box that best matches your opinion. The scale values range from "strongly agree" to "strongly disagree." NA means "not applicable." If you have specific comments on items 1–5, please make them in item 10.

	Strongly Agree	Agree	Neither Agree nor Disagree	Disagree	Strongly Disagree	NA
1. Course content matched the syllabus.						
2. Course/program outcomes were communicated clearly to the class.						
3. Course content was too advanced for me.						
4. The instructor						
a. communicated ideas and information clearly.						
b. explained assignments clearly.						
c. encouraged me to think critically.						
d. encouraged me to ask questions.						
e. graded fairly.						
f. presented course content in an organized manner.						
g. provided constructive feedback on graded assignments.						
h. provided that feedback in a timely manner.						
i. showed enthusiasm for class content.						
j. treated me with respect.						
k. was available during stated office hours.						
l. was approachable during stated office hours.						
m. was prepared for each class session.						
n. responded promptly to e-mails or phone calls.						
5. I understood course content better from the						
a. assigned readings						
b. assignments						
c. in-class discussion						
6. I contributed to the class by	Never	➡			Every class	
a. asking questions						
b. completing all the readings on time						
c. participating in discussions						
d. participating in group projects						

Figure 3.2. Student Course Evaluation

7. On average, how many hours per week did you spend:

    a.   doing class readings?   __0-3   __4-6   __7-9   __10-12 __13+

    b.   working on assignments?   __0-3   __4-6   __7-9   __10-12 __13+

    c.   other (please specify: _____)? __0-3   __4-6 __ 7-9 __10-12 __13+

8. Do you have any suggestions for

    a.   activities or assignments that would strengthen the value of the course for future students?

    b.   improving teaching in the course?

9. I would encourage others to take a course from this instructor (check one):

    ___yes   ___no

Why?

10. Other comments (including about your responses to the items on the previous page)

Figure 3.2. Student Course Evaluation (*Cont.*)

With increased attention to customer service in academic and public libraries for more than a decade, there is more interest in evaluating library programs and services, but from the customer's perspective. Such evaluations might use surveys or interviews, but for more than eight years, a technique borrowed from the business community (e.g., hotels, banks, restaurants, grocery and retail stores, job announcement Web sites, and the travel industry) has been applied to libraries, especially public libraries. The literature of library and information science notes that some public libraries in the United States (e.g., the Orlando [FL] County Library System, the Arapahoe Library District [Englewood, CO], and the Stanislaus [CA] County Free Library) have used this technique, known as mystery shopper evaluation. Such evaluation might rely on the individuals asking questions or observing the facilities or on the use of hidden video and audio equipment. The questions asked might be asked by telephone, e-mail, through the library or consortial homepages, or in person.

The literature hints that libraries use the data collected to improve service delivery, in particular staff training and commitment, and management follow up on the intended changes. One goal is to avoid experiences such as this:

> I decided to call the branch manager and complain, since my library-student status permitted me to be indignant! The manager's response: "Our librarians are trained in customer service. And our customer satisfaction ratings are consistently above 90%." I said, "I am trying to explain to you that I am not part of that 90%, and you have service problems." He apologized sincerely but indicated that he was still quite proud of the branch's satisfaction scores. He did not offer me any encouragement or incentive to want to re-visit the reference desk.
>
> There you have it. Assessment data used against the customer! Customers are overwhelmingly delighted with the branch's services. Customers with complaints must, therefore, be anomalies. Making extra efforts to satisfy expectations of a small minority of customers is not a particularly high priority for library management.[5]

Problem Statement

> For a research study, the problem statement contains four parts: the lead-in, originality, direction, and study value or justification. NOTE: For an evaluation or assessment study, the originality might be eliminated, but the value or justification section is expanded and has a local context.

Apparently some public libraries believe that mystery shopping is an excellent way to ensure that the customer has a voice in service evaluation; no study, however, has investigated whether and how the results of such an evaluation truly lead to service improvement. The purpose of this study is to fill that gap by examining what libraries do with the results. Do they use them to make any changes in the facilities or services, and have they determined if those changes actually led to improvements?

As libraries embrace a culture of managing with evidence (i.e., gathering and using data to make decisions), there is still a question about whether they actually use data they gather to make management decisions that improve the delivery of services. The findings will provide evidence about the existence of such a culture and indicate whether the findings are linked to planning. Such insights would be useful for libraries engaged in strategic planning and for workshops and conference programs addressing a culture of evidence gathering and managerial use.

Note: *What else should the justification/value section address?*

Literature Review

The literature review results in a synopsis of the current status of published knowledge related to the topic of inquiry, and it identifies relevant methodologies for data collection, reliability and validity issues, conflicting research findings, and empirical data. Specific studies are referenced and fully cited, but the review is not merely an annotated bibliography.

To find relevant literature on the topic, evaluators should search databases that cover library literature and the social sciences (see chapter 2). They should not ignore standard search engines and dissertations.

There is an extensive literature on mystery shopping outside library and information science (LIS) that identifies a number of companies that provide mystery shoppers on a fee basis. The literature of LIS is limited and tends not to be research based.

The Literature of Library and Information Science

Those writing about mystery shopping regard it as an impartial method that should be embedded in the organization's culture, because it describes the actual experiences of customers, some of which might be unsatisfactory, and identifies areas for improvement. Vanessa Czopek appears to have been the first to introduce the application of mystery shopping to libraries. In 1996 a representative of the Modesto Chamber of Commerce shopped the Stanislaus County Free Library system (with a main library located in Modesto, California). The "less than stellar" results were shared with the staff, and the protocol was refined and applied to all twelve branches in the library system.[6]

Joy Thomas encourages the use of this technique to examine issues such as whether staff members acknowledge the "presence of student[s] through smiling and/or open body language," initiate conversations with students "with a courteous greeting," acknowledge "others waiting for service," appear "unhurried during the reference transaction," "generally, . . . [face] student[s] when speaking and listening," and maintain or re-establish "eye contact with student[s] throughout the transaction." Some of the factors she examined, however, relate more to determining someone's information need than what mystery shopping legitimately examines.[7] At the same time, it is important to note that in some Asian and other cultures, it is impolite to maintain eye contact for a prolonged period of time.

A more complete overview of mystery shopping as a diagnostic technique appears in an article in *American Libraries*. The authors, Marl Burkamp and Diane E. Virbick, highlight its use at the Arapahoe Library District, as part of a year-long evaluation of services.[8] They discuss its purpose, the data collection process, whether staff was aware of the testing, the initial impressions of the shoppers, and the major areas examined: customer service, including such service delivered by telephone; circulation and checkout procedures, physical facilities, and staff attitude and appearance.

They explain that

- Evaluation criteria were tailored for each department. For example, shoppers tested [staff] regarding requests for job information and application procedures. Receptionists were rated on their telephone skills and ability to solve problems and appropriately refer patrons. The communications and marketing staff, who oversaw the secret shopper survey, were tested with typical patron calls and requests just like everyone else. Even the director was evaluated regarding the handling of calls, complaints, and questions.

- Shoppers recorded their initial impressions . . . on a three-point scale. They rated the cleanliness and orderliness of the aisles, shelves, rest rooms, and reference and circulation desks. They made a quick . . . [evaluation] of how busy the library seemed to be, how calm and hospitable the atmosphere was for patrons, and how bright or dim the lighting appeared.

- The secret shoppers similarly recorded their first impressions of staff, including whether they were visible, approachable, neat, and enthusiastic. Did staff immediately stop conversations with other employees when a patron approached? Did they demonstrate a desire to be helpful? Were they able to provide accurate and useful directions and assistance?

- Facilities outside each library were also judged. Was parking adequate? Was the landscape well-groomed? Was the bookdrop easily accessible? Were accommodations for handicapped or elderly people adequate?

- Other specific areas were examined using a five-point scale. We asked the shoppers to evaluate employees' ability to provide outstanding, friendly service while observing library policies—the challenge faced by staff every day. We also tested the staff's knowledge and ability to explain those policies, answer general questions, and solve specific patron problems. If the shoppers asked for a new library card, were they given appropriate information about using it? Did staff explain checkout periods, overdue fines, and renewal procedures? If the secret shoppers returned an overdue book, were the correct fines assessed and did the staff demonstrate a positive, non-judgmental attitude?

- Finally, did staff ask the shoppers if they found everything they were looking for? When the shoppers left, did staff thank them for visiting or invite them to return?

- The secret shoppers summarized their findings in two ways: an overall review provided general findings and recommendations in the areas of communications, physical site/safety issues, and staffing for items observed at most of the libraries. Results were also broken down by specific library.[9]

Felicity McGregor provides an overview of the use of mystery shopping at the University of Wollongong, Australia,[10] and Philip C. Calvert discusses its use in New Zealand.[11] McGregor tested staff friendliness and approachability, staff attentiveness to customers, the accuracy of the information staff provided, staff knowledge and skills, the appropriateness of any referrals, and the ability of staff to solve problems. In effect, some of these factors are more in line with unobtrusive testing than the use of mystery shopping. Mystery shopping is applicable to the testing of signage, facilities, the ease of finding services and identifying staff,[12] and impressions of the service provided.

Mystery shoppers might be employees of a commercial market research company or members of the community the library serves. Most of the studies, however, appear to favor the use of a commercial company, although they do not mention the Mystery Shopping Providers Association (http://www.mysteryshop.org/index-na.php), which draws attention to ethical companies and alerts readers to possible legislation regulating the use of mystery shopping.

Elizabeth Kocevar-Weidinger, Candice Benjes-Small, Eric Ackerman, and Virginia R. Kinman mention that mystery shopping has extended to academic libraries in the United States. They indicate the attributes that mystery shoppers probed (e.g., staff approachability, helpfulness, politeness, and use of jargon; the greeting of customers; and length of wait time).[13] Most important, they reproduce the evaluation form that the mystery shoppers completed; their form uses a three-point rating scale. The wording of the questions tends to be subjective, which underscores the need for shopper training before data collection begins. Such training most likely increases the cost of the study but produces more valid data.

The conclusion of these authors is that mystery shopping provides a useful form of evaluation, and other libraries should try it. By implication, these authors suggest that the libraries studied will be revisited in the future and that the libraries should use the data for service improvement and accountability.

Finally, it is possible to apply mystery shopping across libraries to examine a particular phenomenon, perhaps staff friendliness. Although she did not engage in mystery shopping, Mary Wilkins Jordan proposes a friendliness factor; she visited thirty libraries and asked questions to construct this factor.[14] The results might serve as a benchmark for any library exploring staff friendliness. (Similar constructs, with corresponding metrics, could be developed for other areas depicted in the logical structure.)

The Literatures of Other Disciplines

Numerous studies in different disciplines apply the technique to various service industries and discuss the benefits of engaging in mystery shopping. These writings present the data collection process, but most important, some of them explain the psychometric quality of the rating scales used in such studies.[15] There is a tendency to adapt the SERVQUAL instrument, which documents the discrepancy between customer expectations and perceptions of the service received; customers answer questions about both their expectations and their perceptions, perhaps by selecting a number from a ten-point scale. However, the studies discussed in the previous section do not rely on a ten-point scale, preferring a simpler scale. If mystery shoppers are asked to revisit the library over time, smaller point scales inhibit the ability of evaluators to document change, especially small change, over time. There is also a lack of discussion about how the findings are linked to strategic planning and service improvement.

Theoretical Framework

What is the conceptual base of the study? What exactly is the relevant concept (or concepts)? Note: The conceptual base here is less complex than many other topics. No conceptual model is involved in this instance other than participant observation.

Mystery shopping is associated with participant observation, whereby evaluators or their surrogates observe and interact with subjects in their work setting and record their accounts and observations. The data gathered serve as a check against participants' subjective reporting of what they say they do.[16] The observations are carried out with a case-study design that takes into account the organizational context.[17] Participant observation tends to involve qualitative data collection, but there can be a quantitative component, assuming the observers complete a form that applies some measurement scale to the questions asked.

Participant observation might also involve the use of unobtrusive testing, the process of asking service personnel questions for which answers have already been determined. Such testing has the following advantages:

[the] observation of staff members under operating conditions assumed to be normal, measurement of the success with which staff members answer various types of questions, and ability to conjecture why certain types of questions were answered incorrectly. Such an approach is especially appropriate when the ultimate objective is providing a high-level quality of performance.[18]

The critics of unobtrusive testing consider covert monitoring to be deceitful and point out that the method tends to be used for the purpose of conducting research rather than for service improvement.[19] Mystery shopping requires organizational buy-in to the testing and the generation of aggregate data from which staff members can learn. Still, it is possible that staff members might be informed of the instances in which they were shopped, or the time intervals between shops (e.g., once a month), as is often done in the retail trade.

Logical Structure

The visualization depicts the problem statement and lays out all of the areas in which the researchers will have to make decisions (e.g., whether to engage in probability sampling). At this stage of developing the study, the "how," "when," and "where" components are not defined: "how" is the methodology, and "when" and "where" are part of the research design. The methodology section presents the "how" component and introduces the data collection instrument.

Note: The diagram does not appear in any subsequent writing about the study. The purpose of that diagram is to review the emerging chain of reasoning and to see where problems might lead to a weak bond in that chain.

Figure 3.3 depicts the study's logical structure and reflects the areas in which the investigator must make decisions. The structure works with the problem direction, which is this case is

whether and how the results of such an evaluation truly lead to service improvement. The purpose of this study is to fill that gap by examining what the libraries do with the results. Do they use them to make any changes in the facilities or services, and have they determined if those changes actually led to improvements?

The diagram (or figure) has components for "study findings result in service improvements" and "facilities and service areas." For both components, evaluators list associated variables. The diagram also refers to "how," "where," and "when."

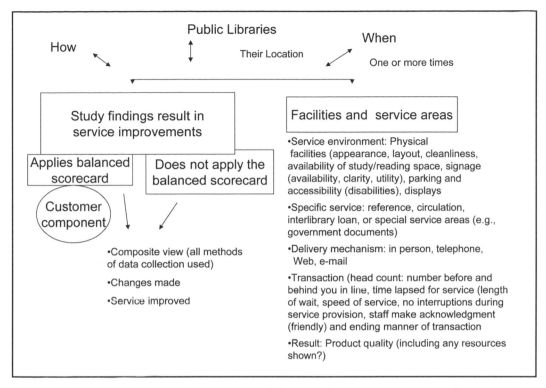

Figure 3.3. Study's Logical Structure

Objectives and Research Questions (Table 3.1)

Descriptive objectives (e.g., "to identify") generate research questions, whereas comparison or contrasting objectives require hypotheses. Objectives are derived from the selections made in the logical structure. Exploratory research tends to focus on descriptive objectives.

Table 3.1. Objectives and Research Questions

Objectives	Research Questions
To depict the quality of the facilities and service areas examined [The word "quality" needs definition.]	[The question addresses which facilities and/or service areas are probed.] Are any problems [with those facilities and/or service areas] noted?
To determine whether the findings gathered go unused	Are the findings, in total or in part, used to make service improvements?
To identify the uses the library makes of the results of mystery shopping	Are the results used to make any changes in services or the facilities? Are the results used to improve services or the physical facilities? What are the improvements? Are data collected to see if the changes lessen the call for improvements?
To identify whether the results of mystery shopping are linked to the balanced scorecard	In what ways, if at all, are results of mystery shopping shared? Are the results linked to a depiction of the balanced scorecard?
To identify if data gathered from mystery shopping are used in conjunction with other types of customer data for service improvement	How does the library use all of the data for service improvement? How do data from mystery shopping fit into the overall picture of service improvement? Does the library compile output metrics with the data? Do those metrics address customer satisfaction as documented by mystery shopping?

Hypothetical Hypothesis

Because no comparison or contrasting objectives were listed, the researchers would not engage in hypothesis testing. However, to aid reader understanding, a hypothetical hypothesis is offered.

Example: There is no statistically significant difference ($p = .05$) in the uses of the results of mystery shopping to improve physical facilities between those libraries using the balanced scorecard and those not doing so.

Research Design

Research design addresses practical matters about the execution of the study, including who will be asked to participate and where and when the study will be conducted. Key questions to address include the following:

- Will the investigation focus on a population or a sample? If it is a sample, is that sample drawn from probability or nonprobability sampling? What is the sample size?

- How often will data be gathered, and for what time span?

- Where and when will the study be conducted? Does the answer to this question involve the use of case studies?

Some public libraries link mystery shopping to the customer portion of the balanced scorecard, which recognizes that an organization's strategic directions evolve from more than a perspective on cost efficiency. The scorecard visually presents information that influences managerial decisions, with the aim of improving performance. Devised by Robert S. Kaplan and David P. Norton from research with companies at the "leading edge of performance measurement," the scorecard provides a detailed overview of organizational effectiveness.[20] The scorecard might include four strategic perspectives: (1) the customer (How do they see us?), (2) internal (What must we excel at?), (3) innovation and learning (Can we continue to improve and create value?), and (4) financial (How do we look to shareholders?).

Because not all public libraries engaged in mystery shopping link the results to a balanced scorecard, this study examines mystery shopping in the context of the use and nonuse of the scorecard. First the investigators attempted to determine the number of public libraries that have used mystery shopping in the past five years and to place those libraries regionally in the United States (according to http://www.census.gov/geo/www/us_regdiv.pdf). To do so, they reviewed the literature of LIS for public library use of mystery shopping, conducted searches in various search engines using the term "mystery shopping public libraries," and placed inquiries on public library director listservs. They also conducted the Public Library Association and the Urban Libraries

Council for additional suggestions. Next the investigators categorized the library, whether or not it links mystery shopping to the balanced scorecard. Table 3.2 displays the result of a hypothetical search of the Web for the South (South Atlantic, East South Central, and West South Central); this region therefore becomes the study population. (Before concluding that the table captures the population of libraries, the investigators will verify the list of libraries in these regions by checking with the directors of those libraries to determine that their library has indeed engaged in mystery shopping in the past five years, whether or not the library uses the balanced scorecard and links the results of such testing to the scorecard, and whether they know of other libraries in the region to add to the list.)

Table 3.2. Hypothetical Study Population*†

Name of Library	Uses the Balanced Scorecard	
Orange County Library System (Orlando, FL), http://www.ocls.info/about/balancedscorecard/default.asp	Yes	
Madison County Public Library (Berea, KY)		No?
XXX	Yes	
XXY	Yes	
XXZ	Yes	

*The South and its three divisions (South Atlantic, East South Central, and West South Central) include the states of Alabama, Arkansas, Delaware, Florida, Georgia, Kentucky, Louisiana, Maryland, Mississippi, North Carolina, South Carolina, Oklahoma, Tennessee, Texas, Virginia, and West Virginia, as well as the District of Columbia.

†This table is illustrative; we did not conduct a thorough investigation of different search engines.

Finally, once the institutional review board of the investigator's institution has affirmed the privacy protection plan for the libraries, data collection will begin in fall 2012. (It may be necessary to omit table 3.2 from the actual study and refer to individual libraries as A, B, and so on.)

Methodology

This section discusses how data will be gathered to address the study objectives and research questions. Will there be one or more methods of data collection? Will the method(s) be quantitative or qualitative based? What does the data collection instrument(s) look like? What is the actual process of data collection?

The investigators as a team will visit each library and meet with the director, other members of the senior management team, and departmental managers. They will use three methodologies: one-to-one personal interviews, focus group interviews, and an examination of documentation gathered (e.g., strategic planning reports and annual reports).

> Note: This section details each of these methods and the data collection instruments. For example, what questions will be asked and in what order during the focus group interview, how will the interviews be recorded, and so on?

Data Quality

> This section refers to reliability and validity and discusses the role of a pre-test and how that pre-test is conducted.

Since the Arapahoe Library District has engaged in mystery shopping, and staff members there have written an article about their experience (see note 8), that library serves as the pre-test site. The investigators will meet with the staff involved in overseeing the mystery shopping and reviewing the study questions (validity) to ensure that the questions on the data collection instruments are clearly worded (reliability). They will review any existing and relevant documentation with the staff and discuss how it applies to the study questions (validity) and how the data will be coded (reliability). They will also review and code the relevant documents and determine the extent of their consistency in their coding (interscore reliability).

CONCLUDING THOUGHTS

Appendix A, which focuses on the future of academic libraries, illustrates an entire study, with its reflective inquiry and procedures. As topics for evaluation and assessment will expand in the future, it is possible that readers might explore some of the possibilities that the scenarios suggest.

Before any proposal is finalized and the evaluators proceed with data collection, there is a need to review the research questions and any hypotheses to determine whether the findings will address all of them and whether they will be reported quantitatively or qualitatively. If the decision favors quantitative data collection, decisions about relevant descriptive and inferential statistics must be made. The next step, as the appendix indicates, is to collect the data, analyze them, and report them in the findings section of a paper or report. The discussion section addresses the implications of the findings and refers to relevant literature. The conclusion returns to the study's value and encourages the organization to take action that will improve service. Any oral presentation focuses on the findings and suggests actions to be taken. Managers then can reflect on the findings and relate the data to the strategic planning process.

NOTES

1. David R. Krathwohl, *Social and Behavioral Science Research: A New Framework for Conceptualizing, Implementing, and Evaluating Research Studies* (San Francisco: Jossey-Bass, 1985).

2. Depending on the study objectives, some sample questions for a workshop or public meeting are: "Could you find a seat?," and "Were you welcomed as you entered the room?"

3. Middle States Commission on Higher Education, *Student Learning Assessment: Options and Resources*, 2nd ed. (Philadelphia, PA: Middle States Commission on Higher Education, 2007), 29.

4. See Peter Hernon and Ronald R. Powell, *Convergence and Collaboration of Campus Information Services* (Westport, CT: Libraries Unlimited, 2008).

5. "Using Library Assessment Data against the Customer," Lib[rary] Performance Blog, April 7, 2009, accessed February 11, 2010, http://libperformance.com/2009/04/07/using-library-assessment-data-against-the-customer/.

6. Vanessa Czopek, "Using Mystery Shoppers to Evaluate Customer Service in the Public Library," *Public Libraries* 37, no. 6 (November/December 1998): 370–71.

7. Joy Thomas, "Mystery Shoppers at the Library: A Planning Report" (2000), 5–6, accessed February 11, 2010, http://www.csulb.edu/divisions/aa/grad_undergrad/senate/committees/assessment/dev/awards/documents/thomas_99.pdf.

8. Marlu Burkamp and Diane E. Virbick, "Through the Eyes of a Secret Shopper," *American Libraries* 33, no. 10 (November 2002): 56–57.

9. Ibid., 57.

10. Felicity McGregor, "Exploring the Mystery of Service Satisfaction" (Wollongong, Australia: University of Wollongong, Academic Services Division, 2005), accessed February 10, 2010, http://ro.uow.edu.au/cgi/viewcontent.cgi?article=1026&context=asdpapers; see also Proceedings of the 6th Northumbria International Conference on Performance Measurement in Libraries and Information Services, Durham, England, August 2005.

11. Philip C. Calvert, "It's a Mystery: Mystery Shopping in New Zealand's Public Libraries," *Library Review* 54, no. 1 (2006): 21–35.

12. McGregor, "Exploring the Mystery of Service Satisfaction," 5.

13. Elizabeth Kocevar-Weidinger, Candice Benjes-Small, Eric Ackerman, and Virginia R. Kinman, "Why and How to Mystery Shop Your Reference Desk," *Reference Services Review* 38, no. 1 (2010): 28–43.

14. Mary Wilkins Jordan, "What Is Your Library's Friendliness Factor?" *Public Library Quarterly* 24, no. 4 (August 2007): 81–99.

15. See, for example, Adam Finn and Ujwal Kayandé, "Unmasking a Phantom: A Psychometric Assessment of Mystery Shopping," *Journal of Retailing* 75, no. 2 (1999): 195–217; Adam Finn and Ujwal Kayandé, "Scale Modification: Alternative Approaches and Their Consequences," *Journal of Retailing* 80, no. 1 (January 2004): 37–52.

16. For an excellent overview of participant observation, see Family Health International, *Qualitative Research Methods: A Data Collector's Field Guide, Module 2: Participant Observation,* accessed February 12, 2010, http://www.fhi.org/NR/rdonlyres/ed2ruznpftevg34lxuftzjiho65asz7betpqigbbyorggs6tetjic367v44baysyomnbdjkdtbsium/participantobservation1.pdf.

17. A case-study design investigates a problem within its real-life context, the boundaries behind the problem and its context are not clearly evident, and multiple sources of evidence are used. Such a design allows for an in-depth analysis of a particular library and how it views mystery shopping for managerial purposes. For a discussion of the case-study design, see Robert K. Yin, *Case Study Research*, 4th ed. (Newbury Park, CA: Sage Publications, 2009).

18. Charles R. McClure and Peter Hernon, *Improving the Quality of Reference Service for Government Publications* (Chicago: American Library Association, 1983), 11–12.

19. See "Categorization of Critical Responses to McClure and Hernon, with a Brief Assessment of Each Assertion," in *Unobtrusive Testing and Library Reference Services,* by Peter Hernon and Charles R. McClure (Norwood, NJ: Ablex, 1987), 165–70.

20. Robert S. Kaplan and David P. Norton, "The Balanced Scorecard—Measures That Drive Performance," *The Harvard Business Review* 70, no. 1 (January–February, 1992): 71–79; Robert S. Kaplan and David P. Norton, *The Balanced Scorecard: Translating Strategy into Action* (Boston: Harvard Business School Press, 1996).

Chapter 4

Applicable Concepts and Language of Research

To understand researchable problems in library and information science (LIS), to assess their impact on libraries and their representative institutions, or to evaluate potential solutions for what the research finds, research often includes a conceptual framework that is relevant to the problem under study. As in other types of research, librarians and other information professionals ready to engage in evaluation and assessment research and to design a research study should be explicit about the framework within which they are undertaking their study. That framework addresses relevant theories and concepts that guide data collection and make connections to a broader theoretical underpinning.

Many practitioners, as well as students and other neophyte researchers, are surprised by the expectation that they should include a theoretical framework in their research and are disadvantaged by not using a logical structure to clarify the perspective they will pursue for their study (see chapter 3). Conducting an evaluation or assessment, or for that matter any type of systematic inquiry, without addressing the conceptual framework for the work is analogous to taking a journey without directions—if you do not know where you are going, then you cannot know if you get there.

This chapter introduces the neophyte researcher to conceptual frameworks and considers what they are, why they are important, and how to use them in planning and conducting an evaluation. This practical introduction is followed by brief discussions of some popular concepts found in LIS research that influence how the profession evaluates the exploration of library services and operations, and customer behaviors, perceptions, and opinions.

THEORETICAL AND OTHER CONCEPTUAL FRAMEWORKS

A theoretical framework consists of the variables and terms, as well as relationships among them, within which a problem is articulated and explored. It provides a perspective or focus to view the problem. An explicit theoretical framework used to develop an evaluation or assessment clarifies the problem as well as the rationale for excluding issues from the exploration. It is closely linked to the literature review, which in part helps to identify relevant theoretical frameworks, and the selected framework in turn may define the parameters of the literature review. Both "seek out and relate relevant knowledge to guide the conduct of the proposed study."[1] As Peter Hernon and Robert E. Dugan illustrate:

> For example, the staff might believe that library anxiety is an impediment to academic achievement and, therefore, seek to reduce anxiety as a factor inhibiting change in user behavior and performance. The theoretical framework discusses what library anxiety is and if certain variables are linked to it. The literature review, on the other hand, identifies and relates studies within library and information science that have examined library anxiety.[2]

A theoretical framework may be identified in a number of ways, with varying degrees of complexity. Most simply, a conceptual framework may be a set of *descriptive categories* that are used to guide exploration, without any expectation that they are an exhaustive set of descriptors. However, when a number of unique and independent categories together are necessary and sufficient to explain a phenomenon, the framework is a *taxonomy*. Categories, whether or not taxonomies, that are interconnected through a set of relationships form a *theoretical framework*.[3]

A number of benefits emerge from using an explicit theoretical framework in guiding a study. By systematically considering different perspectives on a problem (identified through a literature review) and narrowing a study's focus, the researcher better articulates surrounding issues, and the very process of doing so offers insights into understanding the problem. This process places the study within the broader research conversations about the problem and offers others a delineated inquiry to build upon in future research. Most practically, the identification of the theoretical framework guiding a study provides a focus for other steps in planning and executing the query. Existing frameworks relevant to the inquiry may be found through a review of the literature of the field or from adaption of structures from other disciplines. LIS research often adopts theories and perspectives on problems from other disciplines and fields, especially in the social sciences, business, marketing, psychology, leadership, and education.

Students new to undertaking research are typically puzzled by how conceptual frameworks form the bases for their study. They may expect to complete the requirement of using a theoretical framework by selecting one and discussing it as a separate step in their research. They reach an enlightened moment when they realize how useful conceptual frameworks are to help design their study. Several steps are recommended, including use of a logical structure (diagram) to depict major variables or categories as well as the relationships or interactions among them. Particularly useful at the early conceptualization stage of a study, this graphic process begins with identifying terms of interest and the relationships among them. Terms may be those used in the initial problem statement or may emerge from reading other research on the topic. Categorizing the terms helps the researcher think through the problem being addressed, selecting specific options to utilize in helping decide the study's focus (e.g., who the participants are, what variables relate to their activities or opinions). The logical structure also serves as a reminder to consider where, when, and how data will be gathered.

Interacting with the logical structure is a process of making choices about what to include and what to exclude from the study. The final structure should be simple, though in the formative process it may intentionally become complicated to enable the researcher to consider all perspectives and issues potentially related to the inquiry. The researcher's selection of elements to include in the study helps validate that the resulting choices reflect the problem and an appropriate approach to address it. A narrative describes the selected elements and justifies their relation to the study, assisting the reader in understanding what the research intends to do. The steps for preparing and using a logical structure include

1. identifying terms related to the topic of inquiry;

2. arranging the terms in categories central to the inquiry, with lines illustrating their relationships;

3. selecting those relevant to the problem of inquiry and deleting other terms;

4. writing or confirming a simple statement of direction for the inquiry to reflect the categories;

5. inserting a placeholder for the research design and methodology to address when, by whom, and how the study will be conducted; and

6. not including the logical structure diagram in the research report.

Practitioners may have little interest in an exhaustive review of theories related to the problem of evaluation or assessment. Nonetheless, an evaluator may use a theoretical framework to organize the parts of the problem to be examined. The logical structure may also be used by evaluators in discussion with library managers and staff to select what is realistic, relevant, and within budget to include in the evaluation. Figure 3.3 (p. 49) illustrates a logical structure used for an examination of how public libraries use study findings to improve service delivery. That study also includes a balanced scorecard to manage the library.

SOME RELEVANT CONCEPTS

Critical concepts applicable to LIS research include, among others, information-seeking behavior, service quality and satisfaction, effectiveness, economic efficiency, and return on investment. A perusal of dissertation research will indicate other relevant concepts.[4] This section merely provides an overview of selected concepts.

Information-Seeking Behavior

Several models of *information-seeking behavior* have emerged from research on the process by which people seek to satisfy their needs for information. These are distinguished from concepts surrounding *information retrieval*, which mostly focuses on technological tools to identify information that exists within a system. Information-seeking behavior concepts offer insight into understanding human behavior, while information retrieval frameworks typically inform design and performance of automated systems.

Applying communication research, Brenda Dervin and others have developed the concept of "sense making" since 1972, which has evolved in a wide range of applications, including to libraries and information systems. Core to this framework and its associated methodology for examining information-seeking behavior is the view that there is no distinction between information and knowledge. Rather than thinking of them as nouns, the model suggests these words are both verbs related to making sense in a world of gaps.[5] Two propositions emerge from work on this model:

> One is that it is rarely person attributes [traits and predispositions] or task or organizational attributes but rather how users conceptualize their movement through time-space and their gap bridging that predicts sense making and sense unmaking best. The second is that under those circumstances when noun-oriented characteristics such as status or demography or personality do predict best, it usually means there is a constraining force operating in the situation, a force which may need attention because it may be limiting sense-making potentials.[6]

Various sense-making studies have developed categories to describe human information-seeking and use behavior, for example, "found direction, got a new way of looking at things, got connected to information, got companionship and support, avoided a bad place, got pleasure and joy, arrived where I wanted to."[7] These and other facets of this framework may be useful in designing an evaluation of information-seeking behaviors relevant to creating or improving library services or information systems.

Another approach comes from Elreda Chatman's application of sociology and ethnographic research to her theories of information poverty, life in the round, and normative behavior. Her work offers propositions relating to how an individual's information-seeking behavior relates to the social environments in which he or she lives, conducting research in such worlds as retirement homes and prisons.[8]

From work in information literacy and school libraries, Carol Kuhlthau modeled the Information Search Process, with six stages of information seeking: initiation, selection, exploration, formulation, collection, and search closure.[9] This often cited model has also been applied in a wide range of disciplines. Humboldt State University Library has reproduced the model from Kuhlthau's 1993 book. In 2004 she updated her model; it provides more illustration of the stages of information seeking and data collection, especially within elementary and secondary education.[10]

Donald O. Case offers examples of studies on information needs and information-seeking behavior that occurs in others types of libraries.[11] Cheryl Metoyer-Duran studied information-seeking behavior among five ethnolinguistic communications: first-generation Korean, Chinese, and Japanese Americans; Latinos; and Native Americans. Her research has particular relevance for public libraries, in that members of these communities are likely to rely on formal and information gatekeepers to provide them with the information or knowledge needed rather than to visit libraries and other service organizations themselves.[12]

Information-seeking behavior is frequently found to be the underlying conceptual framework for evaluations of automated systems and electronic resources. For example, David Nicholas has conducted several studies using transaction log analysis to understand use of electronic resources.[13] An extensive study of the impact of e-journals on scholarly behavior among researchers in the United Kingdom (UK) concludes that computer usage logs "provide an accurate picture of online behaviour."[14]

Effectiveness

Measures of library performance were a popular focus of evaluation studies in the second half of the twentieth century, particularly among public libraries. Through a review of studies prior to 1970, Edward Evans, Harold Borko, and Patricia Ferguson compiled a group of "criterion concepts" in evaluating library effectiveness, as well as specific techniques to measure them. Their framework consisted of six basic categories (with illustration of their measures):

1. accessibility (ratio of services requested to services available)

2. cost (ratio of book budget to users)

3. user satisfaction (user satisfaction with services rendered)

4. response time (speed of services)

5. cost/benefit ratio (ratio of total service expenditures to users)

6. use (ratio of documents circulated to number of users)[15]

Nancy Van House and Thomas A. Childers conducted a thorough study to identify factors that described the effectiveness of the public library and developed a list of indicators.[16] Nancy Van House also coauthored another practical guide for use in evaluating academic library effectiveness.[17]

Others approach library effectiveness assessment in terms of inputs and outputs,[18] relating effectiveness to outputs. In this context, F. W. Lancaster suggests that "the overall criterion of effectiveness is the proportion of user demands that are satisfied."[19] Richard Orr addresses effectiveness of library management by distinguishing two questions: "How good is it?" and "What good does it do?" These questions focus on capacity and value, and they introduce the notion of benefit as an output.[20]

Joseph R. Matthews considers measuring a library's effectiveness, and by association, the director's success, in a political context. He suggests that selecting the factors to consider in designing an evaluation of a library's performance should include its customers and other stakeholders. By doing so, the identified set of performance measures will communicate the value of the library with maximum impact.[21]

Economic Efficiency

While evaluation of effectiveness gauges the outcome of library services or processes in meeting operational goals and user demand, assessment of efficiency measures how economically these operations are performed. The usefulness of cost efficiency evaluations is in improving operations and managing processes. Productivity becomes a goal for success.

Most common factors used to evaluate efficiency are measures of time and cost. Various standards of productivity have evolved to suggest norms of efficiency. These include, for example, monthly cataloging expectations of 250 to 400 titles by a cataloger and thirty to sixty minutes per item for original cataloging.[22]

One tool used to judge performance of nonprofit organizations, where there is no price on outputs, is the Data Envelopment Analysis (DEA). Wonsik Shim demonstrated that this tool is suitable to benchmark U.S. research libraries.[23] The DEA as an efficiency score is the ratio of the weighted sum of outputs to the weighted sum of inputs, where the weights are calculated by the DEA model. Those libraries characterized as fully efficient use the fewest input metrics for a given level of service or produce a maximum of outputs given their level of inputs. According to Gerhard Reichmann, the DEA "calculates the degree of relative efficiency of all other libraries in the sample and indicates which efficient library serves as a benchmark [peer] for inefficient libraries."[24]

Various software products (e.g., Frontier Analyst from BANXIA Software) handle the calculation of DEA efficiency scores. Selection of inputs and outputs is part of an evaluation's design and may include, for example, inputs of the number of full-time equivalent library employees, the number of book materials held, capital expenditures, and outputs of the number of serial subscriptions, total circulations, regular opening hours per week, and book materials added.[25] The result is benchmarking information on relative performance of libraries against best practice efficient libraries.

Service Quality

A number of models exist to evaluate, from the customer's perspective, what constitutes service quality. Most popular and influential in shaping service quality research over the past three decades is the Service Quality Gaps Model and SERVQUAL instrument developed by A. Parasuraman, Leonard L. Berry, and Valarie A. Zeithmal.[26] The Gaps model evolved as a conceptualization of five gaps to characterize the relationship between customers and a service organization, and it includes factors such as expected service, perceived service, actual service delivery, service standards, and external communications about the service. The five gaps (see figure 4.1) reflect a discrepancy between customers' expectations and management's perceptions of these expectations (Gap 1); management's perceptions of customers' expectations and service quality specifications (Gap 2); service quality specifications and actual service delivery (Gap 3); actual service delivery and what is communicated to customers about it (Gap 4); and customers' expected service delivery and the perceived service delivered (Gap 5). SERVQUAL is a measurement tool of one of the gaps that conceives of service quality as the difference between customers' expectations for excellent service and their perceptions of the service delivered by the evaluated operations. Implemented as a questionnaire requesting participants to rank expectations and perceptions, the tool utilizes statements about various facets of services. These dimensions have changed with extended research, but include the five dimensions of reliability, tangibles, responsiveness, assurance, and empathy as critical to customers' evaluation of service quality. The authors evolved this framework through research across many service industries and found that reliability was the most important factor affecting a customer's gauge of service quality, regardless of the nature of the service.

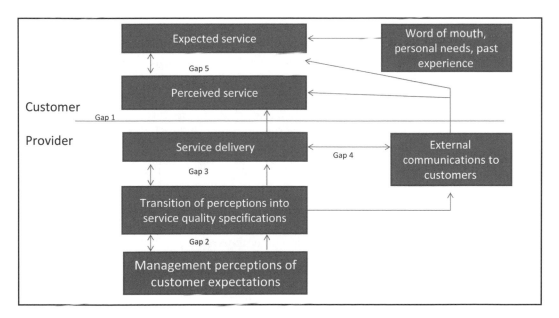

Figure 4.1. The Gaps Model of Service Quality. Adapted with permission from A. Parasuraman, Valarie A. Zeithmal, and Leonard L. Berry, "A Conceptual Model of Service Quality and Its Implications for Future Research," *Journal of Marketing* 49, no. 4 (fall 1985): 44.

Several studies used the SERVQUAL tool to evaluate service quality in libraries.[27] The framework was further expanded for application to libraries through the thorough development of the LibQUAL+® instrument.[28] Work among researchers at Texas A&M and the Association of Research Libraries created a tool over several years that has drawn over a million respondents who are customers of library services and who collectively offer insights into what is important for library users. Debates in the literature over the applicability of this framework to measuring library services have subsided, but illustrate the challenges to applying conceptualizations from other disciplines to problems in library and information science.[29]

Other frameworks beyond the marketing focus of the SERVQUAL offer different perspectives on service quality. Benjamin Schneider and Susan S. White discuss several of these through a review of research on the topic. They link the service climate of a workplace to delivery and experience of service quality, as well as approaches introduced by operations management research.[30]

Satisfaction

Library and information science researchers have joined others in trying to distinguish the concepts of service quality and satisfaction. Rowena Cullen summarizes the interrelationship between the two concepts as follows. Satisfaction may involve long- and short-term perceptions and a personal reaction to a service resulting from a number of customer transactions; those transactions are likely of varying quality. Furthermore, customer satisfaction at the micro level concerning an individual service contributes to the dimensions of service quality (namely, tangibles, reliability, responsiveness, assurance, and empathy). A macro (or global) view of service quality is "derived from all the services with which the customer has interacted," and integrating the five dimensions of service quality contributes to customer overall satisfaction with the organization.[31]

Peter Hernon and John R.Whitman offer a simple definition of satisfaction as "a sense of contentment that arises from an actual experience in relation to an expected experience."[32] Satisfaction is an emotional reaction to a specific service transaction, whereas service quality is a judgment by an individual based on numerous experiences with the service or a collective set of impressions among many to create a service's reputation of service quality.[33]

The evaluation of customer satisfaction tends to use open-ended questions of a global nature and aims to offer general areas in which customers may be more or less satisfied with a specific service, whereas service quality evaluations seek to identify specific problems requiring improvement.[34] Various frameworks exist to provide categories for aspects of satisfaction. Noriaki Kano, for example, offers a model for evaluating customer satisfaction based on four factors. He introduced an exploration of minimum standards through "basic or threshold attributes," based on his research to differentiate contributions to perceived quality of the product or service from the customer needs. These might include, for example, keyword search capability in development of an excellent online catalog. His model also highlights the "performance attributes" that increase customer satisfaction and that when removed create dissatisfaction (e.g., automatic spell checkers), the "attractive attributes" that create customer excitement or an "awe effect" but do not affect satisfaction if discontinued (e.g., the visual presentation of search results), and the "indifferent attributes" that do not affect customer satisfaction at all (e.g., the font style used in the catalog display).[35]

Return on Investment

Return on investment quantifies, in economic terms, benefits and the expenditures required to produce them. In turn, the tradeoff of the two translates into the value placed on the service. A study conducted by the Carnegie Library of Pittsburgh illustrates ways to discuss the value the library offers its community. Among the most valued contributions that its clients stated the library makes to its community are to promote literacy and learning, improve neighborhood quality of life, and provide activities for children and teens. Benefits are measured by one of three methods and provide some insight into what people value as a benefit of a service like a library: consumer surplus, contingent valuation, and cost of time. Because most library services are free, it becomes difficult to measure consumer surplus or to put a price on the services' value above their direct cost. The surplus value is sometimes estimated by determining, for example, how many books, DVDs, or downloaded articles are borrowed from the library compared to the number of these that the users would buy on the market from alternative sources. The contingency valuation approach involves asking what people are willing to pay for a service. Cost of time estimates the time users expend to access library services, which in turn they can gauge against the benefits they receive from the service.[36]

Interest in developing the concept of return on investment and methods to calculate it in library settings has grown in the United Kingdom in recent years. The British Library, for example, has posted reports of a commissioned economic impact study to assess both direct and indirect value of the library to the UK economy. The underlying concepts of the contingent valuation method used in this study covered the following questions, which offer a framework to design a return on investment evaluation:

- How much are clients willing to pay for the continuation of the library's services?

- What minimum payment would clients be willing to accept to forgo the library's existence?

- How much would they invest in terms of time and money to make use of the library?

- How much would they have to pay to use alternatives to the library, if such could be found?[37]

The American Library Association Research and Statistics Web site (http://www.ala.org/ala/research/librarystats/roi/index.cfm) offers a useful bibliography on return on investment that mostly addresses studies illustrating the value of public libraries.

CONCLUDING THOUGHTS

Evaluation and assessment research, like other types of research, is not created in a vacuum. It builds on previous work, whether to guide clarification of the problem being investigated or to design the methodology for gathering and analyzing data. An explicit conceptual framework provides the roadmap to undertake the journey of designing and executing an evaluation. It narrows the scope of the problem to a manageable inquiry. It defines the factors by which the evaluation is structured. The framework suggests the approach by which data will be gathered to draw insights, for example, on customer behavior, expectations, perceptions, satisfaction, judgments of quality, or on the library's performance in terms of efficiency, effectiveness, or return on investment.

But these are only a few possible perspectives on evaluating a library, its customers, its value, or its operations. The library as an organization or as a service provider might also be evaluated for its collaboration within an academic institution in affecting teaching, its leadership in transforming the role of the library as a learning enterprise, or its innovation in providing information literacy training. Different conceptual frameworks may offer grounding for the design of such evaluations. The evaluator, and the practitioners who will benefit from the results, are likely to identify terms and problem questions or which categories, taxonomies, or theories developed in other settings will be relevant. In turn, the results of the evaluation will present insights for future evaluations and research. The language of research is cyclic, and the road to discovery of new insights may intersect with other paths. A conceptual framework picked for a specific evaluation pulls the pieces together to structure the study and make the effort worthwhile for improving services and operations.

NOTES

1. Peter Hernon, and Robert E. Dugan, *An Action Plan for Outcomes Assessment in Your Library* (Chicago: American Library Association, 2002), 83.

2. Ibid.

3. See Daniel Cline's Web site for Graduate Students in Educational Leadership, accessed December 26, 2010, http://education.astate.edu/dcline/guide/framework.html.

4. See Gloria J. Leckie, Lisa M. Given, and John E. Bushman, *Critical Theory for Library and Information Science: Exploring the Social from Across the Disciplines* (Santa Barbara, CA: ABC-CLIO, 2011).

5. For more details about the concept, see Brenda Dervin, "Welcome to the Sense-Making Methodologies Site," a Web site that brings together work on the model; accessed December 29, 2010, http://communication.sbs.ohio-state.edu/sense-making/.

6. Brenda Dervin, "Sense-Making Theory and Practice: An Overview of User Interests in Knowledge Seeking and Use," *Journal of Knowledge Management* 2, no. 2 (December 1998): 39.

7. Ibid.

8. Elfrada Chatman, "A Theory of Life in the Round," *Journal of the American Society for Information Science* 50, no. 3 (1999): 207–17.

9. Carol C. Kuhlthau, "Accommodating the User's Information Search Process: Challenges for Information Retrieval System Designers," *Bulletin of the American Society for Information Science and Technology* 25, no. 3 (February/March 1999): 12–16.

10. Humboldt State University Library, "Kuhlthau's Model of the Stages of the Information Process," accessed December 28, 2010, http://library.humboldt.edu/~ccm/fingertips/kuhlthau.html; Carol C. Kuhlthau, *Seeking Meaning: A Process Approach to Library and Information Services* (Norwood, NJ: Ablex, 1993), 45–51; Carol C. Kuhlthau, *Seeking Meaning: A Process Approach to Library and Information Services*, 2nd ed. (Westport, CT: Libraries Unlimited, 2004).

11. Donald O. Case, *Looking for Information: A Survey of Research on Information Seeking, Needs, and Behavior* (New York: Academic Press, 2002, 2007).

12. Cheryl Metoyer-Duran, *Gatekeepers in Ethnolinguistic Communities* (Norwood, NJ: Ablex, 1993).

13. David Nicholas, Paul Huntington, and Hamid R. Jamali, "Diversity in the Information Seeking Behaviour of the Virtual Scholar: Institutional Comparisons," *The Journal of Academic Librarianship* 33, no. 6 (2007): 629–38; David Nicholas, Ian Rowlands, Paul Huntington, Hamid R. Jamali, and Patricia H. Salazar, "Diversity in the E-journal Use and Information-Seeking Behaviour of UK Researchers" *Journal of Documentation* 66, no. 3 (2010): 409–33; David Nicholas, D. Clark, Ian Rowlands, and Hamid R. Jamali, "Online Use and Information Seeking Behaviour: Institutional and Subject Comparisons of UK Researchers, *Journal of Information Science* 35, no. 6 (2009): 660–76; David Nicholas, Paul Huntington, Hamid R. Jamali, Ian Rowlands, Tom Dobrowolski, and Carol Tenopir, "Viewing and Reading Behaviour in a Virtual Environment: The Full-Text Download and What Can Be Read into It," *Aslib Proceedings: New Information Perspectives* 60, no. 3 (2008): 185–98.

14. David Nicholas, Peter Williams, Ian Rowlands, and Hamid R. Jamali, "Researchers' E-journal Use and Information Seeking Behaviour," *Journal of Information Science* 36, no. 4 (August 2010): 494–516. Abstract available at http://jis.sagepub.com/content/36/4/494 (accessed December 28, 2010).

15. Edward Evans, Harold Borko, and Patricia Ferguson, "Review of Criteria Used to Measure Library Effectiveness" *Bulletin of Medical Library Association* 60, no. 1 (January 1972): 102–10.

16. Nancy A. Van House and Thomas A. Childers, *The Public Library Effectiveness Study: The Complete Report* (Chicago: American Library Association, 1993); Thomas A. Childers and Nancy A. Van House, "Dimensions of Public Library Effectiveness," *Library & Information Science Research* 11, no. 3 (1989): 273–301.

17. Nancy A. Van House, Beth T. Weil, and Charles R. McClure, *Measuring Academic Library Performance: A Practical Approach* (Chicago: American Library Association 1990).

18. Rosemary R. DuMont, "A Conceptual Basis for Library Effectiveness," *College & Research Libraries* 41, no. 2 (March 1980): 103–11.

19. F. W. Lancaster, *If You Want to Evaluate Your Library . . .* (Champaign: University of Illinois, Graduate School of Library and Information Science, 1988), 5.

20. Richard M. Orr, "Measuring the Goodness of Library Services: A General Framework for Considering Quantitative Measures," *Journal of Documentation* 29, no. 3 (September 1973): 315–32.

21. Joseph R. Matthews, *The Evaluation and Measurement of Library Services* (Westport, CT: Libraries Unlimited, 2007).

22. P. M. Smith, "Cataloging Production Standards in Academic Libraries," *Technical Services Quarterly* 6, no. 1 (1988): 3–14, as cited in Matthews, *The Evaluation and Measurement of Library Services*, 188.

23. Wonsik Shim, "Assessing Technical Efficiency of Research Libraries," *Advances in Library Administration and Organisation* 17 (2000): 243–339. See also C. Kao and Y. Lin, "Comparing University Libraries of Different University Size," *Libri* 49 (1999): 150–58; T. Chen, "An Evaluation of the Relative Performance of University Libraries in Taipei," *Library Review* 3 (1997): 190–200.

24. Gerhard Reichmann, "Measuring University Library Efficiency Using Data Envelopment Analysis," *Libri* 54, no. 2 (2004): 136.

25. Ibid.

26. Valarie A. Ziethaml, A. Parasuraman, and Leonard L. Berry, *Delivering Quality Service Balancing Customer Perceptions and Expectations* (New York: The Free Press, 1990).

27. See, for example, Susan Edwards and Mairead Browne, "Quality in Information Services: Do Users and Librarians Differ in Their Expectations?" *Library & Information Science Research* 17, no. 2 (1995): 163–82; Francoise Hébert, "Service Quality: An Unobtrusive Investigation of Interlibrary Loan in Large Public Libraries in Canada," *Library & Information Science Research* 16, no. 1 (1994): 3–21; Danuta A. Nitecki, "User Expectations for Quality Library Services Identified through Application of the SERVQUAL Scale in an Academic Library," in *Continuity and Transformation: The Promise of Confluence. Proceedings of the 7th Association of College and Research Libraries National Conference*, ed. Richard AmRhein (Chicago: Association of College and Research Libraries, 1995): 53–66; Danuta A. Nitecki, "Changing the Concept and Measure or Service Quality in Academic Libraries," *The Journal of Academic Librarianship* 22, no. 3 (May 1996): 181–90; Marilyn D. White, "Measuring Customer Satisfaction and Quality of Service in Special Libraries" (unpublished final report to Special Libraries Association, September 1994); Danuta A. Nitecki and Peter Hernon, "Measuring Service Quality at Yale University's Libraries," *The Journal of Academic Librarianship* 26, no. 4 (July 2000): 259–73.

28. Association of Research Libraries, "Major Initiatives: LibQual+," accessed December 28, 2010, http://www.arl.org/major-initiatives/lq/index.shtml.

29. See Brian A. Quinn, "Adapting Service Quality Concepts to Academic Libraries" (Libraries Faculty Research Texas Tech University, 2007), accessed December 28, 2010, http://thinktech.lib.ttu.edu/bitstream/handle/2346/503/fulltext.pdf?sequence=1.

30. Benjamin Schneider and Susan S. White, *Service Quality Research Perspectives* (Thousand Oaks, CA: Sage Publications, 2004).

31. Rowena Cullan, "Perspectives on User Satisfaction Surveys," *Library Trends* 49, no. 4 (Spring 2001): 665.

32. Peter Hernon and John R. Whitman, *Delivering Satisfaction and Service Quality: A Customer-Based Approach for Libraries* (Chicago: American Library Association, 2001), 32.

33. Peter Hernon and Ellen Altman, *Assessing Service Quality: Satisfying the Expectations of Library Customers,* 2nd ed. (Chicago: American Library Association, 2010).

34. Ibid.; Peter Hernon and Danuta A. Nitecki, "Service Quality: A Concept Not Fully Explored," Library *Trends* 49, no. 4 (Spring 2001): 687–708.

35. The Kano model was first published in a Japanese-language article: N. Kano, N. Seraku, F. Takahashi, and S. Tsuji, "Attractive Quality and Must-Be Quality," *Hinshitsu Quality: The Journal of Japanese Society for Quality Control* 14 (1984): 39–48. See also "The Executive Fast Track: Customer Satisfaction Model (Kano)," *12 Manage,* accessed December 30, 2010, http://www.12manage.com/methods_kano_customer_satisfaction_model.html; Debapriya Chakraborty, "Kano Model: Tool for Measuring Consumer Satisfaction," accessed December 28, 2010, http://ayushveda.com/blogs/business/kano-model-tool-for-measuring-consumer-satisfaction/; Peter Hernon and Joseph R. Matthews, *Listening to the Customer* (Santa Barbara, CA: ABC-CLIO, 2011).

36. Carnegie Library of Pittsburgh, *Community Impact and Benefits* (April 2006), accessed December 31, 2010, http://www.clpgh.org/about/economicimpact/CLPCommunity ImpactFinalReport.pdf.

37. British Library, "Measuring Our Value," accessed December 31, 2010, http://www.bl.uk/pdf/measuring.pdf; http://www.bl.uk/about/annual/pdf/ar0304meas.pdf.

Chapter 5

Designing Evaluations and Assessments*

The goal of an evaluation or assessment research design is to produce a meaningful strategy that addresses the problem statement, research questions, and hypotheses, and operationalizes the logical structure (see chapter 3). That strategy answers who will be studied, how often data collection will occur, and when and where the study will be conducted. Turning to the logical structure, which is a part of reflective inquiry, the key components for now are who or what will be studied; in figure 3.3 (p. 49), this means the boxes for "study findings result in service improvements" and "facilities and service areas." Will the study focus on the entire target population or a portion of that population? If a portion, how will the sample be drawn, and will it be representative of that population?

Related questions that merit attention include the following:

- Are any variables or characteristics of the population important for selecting a sample?

- Should any of these variables be controlled (at what level and how)?

- Will any of the variables mask other variables?

How often raises the possibility of one-time or repeated data collection, and for both evaluation and assessment studies, *where* is most likely limited to the communities, or part of a community, that a particular library or information center serves.

Taking the time to resolve the above-mentioned aspects of research design is a critical step in considering the possible directions that evaluation or assessment research might take and settling on the design most relevant to the organization. Shortcuts or inattention to all of those aspects may result in invalid data collection and an inability to use the results for improving library services or operations. As this chapter explains, research design refers to the structure by which the study is organized and its components are related. It covers a broad category of research components, which might include sampling, either probability or nonprobability; case studies; types of design (experimental to descriptive); and criteria of relevance (reliability and validity). The chapter closes with sample decision points associated with research designs for some sample topics.

SAMPLING

Statistical sampling produces a sample that is representative of a universe. However, samples of a universe differ from one another as well as from the universe itself. Hence, there should be an objective measure of the possible variation between samples and of a sample's relationship to the universe. With this information, it is possible to determine the amount of error that arises because a sample does not correspond exactly to the universe. This is an important feature of statistical sampling, because evaluators can be precise about the amount of error introduced by the sampling process. They can then decide whether that error is tolerable when weighed against tradeoff factors such as the cost of obtaining a larger sample that produces less error.

Random Selection

The essence of statistical sampling is selecting a sample by some random (or chance) process. By randomizing sample selection, evaluators ensure that the sample represents the universe within the limits of sampling error. Sampling error, or precision, is a measure of the expected difference between the value found in a statistical sample and the value of the same characteristics that would have been found by examining the entire universe. Sampling errors are stated at a specific confidence level, the predetermined level at which a null hypothesis is not accepted.[1]

Random selection refers to the elimination of personal bias or subjective considerations from the choice of the sample items. Every item in the universe has an equal or known probability of being selected. Although the results obtained from drawing various random samples from the same universe differ, those differences stem from chance, not personal bias or other systematic factors.

The selection of a sample by some random method in order to draw conclusions about a universe is known as *probability sampling*. Regardless of the name used to describe the method, there are two key elements:

1. Each possible sample from the universe has a known chance of being selected.

2. The actual selection technique executes the random method.[2]

When the desire is not to generalize to a universe, but rather to limit conclusions merely to respondents or participants, sample selection relies on nonprobability sampling. Such sampling may be easier and cheaper to conduct, while still producing useful insights.

SAMPLING DESIGN

Sample design involves defining the universe, if possible, and the sampling units; choosing the sampling strategy and the type of sampling; and determining the size of the sample.

Defining the Universe and the Sampling Units

The universe is the entire collection or group of items to which estimates and inference apply. (If evaluators cannot determine the universe, statistical sampling does not occur; nonprobability sampling, however, can.) Once the universe has been defined, evaluators either obtain or develop a sampling frame. For example, it might be a list of undergraduate students majoring in political science or elementary school children enrolled in a summer reading program, or a database of bibliographic records for books added to a collection in a year.

The sampling frame has several characteristics. First, it permits the sampler to identify and locate the specific item that is to be drawn into the sample and to differentiate that item from all others in the sampling frame. The frame also contains all of the items in the universe. For example, if the universe is defined as the workforce of the library, the list of workers from which the sample is drawn includes all workers, professional and not, as of the date the study will be conducted; there are neither duplicate entries nor entries not found in the universe.

Evaluators may want to define subdivisions of the universe. One type of subdivision is the stratum, a subpopulation obtained by dividing the universe into two or more mutually exclusive groups or strata, which evaluators can do if they know in advance the number of sampling units in each stratum. Independent random samples are selected from each stratum in order to obtain more precise estimates or to emphasize certain portions of the universe, such as units with higher dollar expenditures.

Another type of universe subdivision is the domain of interest. This type of subdivision is necessary when separate estimates are needed for each class into which a universe may be divided. Thus, evaluators rely on the sample if they are to develop this information. An example of a domain of interest is students at the university who major in biology.

Sampling units are often defined as persons or things that evaluators want to study— the units of the universe about which they need information. Sometimes, however, because of the arrangement of the universe, the lack of a list of items they want to observe, and practical considerations, evaluators may select a sampling unit that is larger than the item about which they want to obtain data. An example is selecting a household in order to determine library use patterns of its members. In this example, the item of interest, the household member, is called the "secondary sampling unit," and the larger unit, the household, is the *cluster* or *primary sampling unit*. The primary sampling unit must be mutually exclusive and include the entire universe. This means that each unit being observed, the secondary sampling unit, must belong to one and only one primary sampling unit, and that the primary sampling unit must cover the entire universe.

Choosing a Sampling Strategy

The choice of a census (everything or everyone) and a sample is an important decision. Besides study objectives, factors such as cost, time, precision, and the feasibility of drawing certain kinds of samples must be considered. A census is appropriate when individual items in the universe are important in themselves, when the information to be obtained is critical, and the universe is so small that sampling is not needed. Also, when all the data are already in machine-readable form (e.g., in an Excel file), it may be no less efficient to analyze every item. However, some files may be too large to permit such an examination.

When a study objective is intended to draw conclusions about a universe of people or things, and when evaluators can list the universe, statistical sampling is the preferred method. (It is not necessary literally to list the universe. For example, it is possible to select randomly from the list of all conceivable telephone numbers without possessing a physical list of such numbers. Sometimes the list exists only in a conceptual sense.)

Statistical sampling, based on the theory of probability, enables evaluators to determine the sample objectively and to compare it to the universe. Using statistical sampling, a third party can repeat a study and expect to reach comparable conclusions about the characteristics of the universe being measured—assuming that party examines the same universe. Although the study results may be interpreted differently, there can be no questions about the facts. Likewise, statistical samples can be combined and evaluated even if different people take them. Evaluators working at different locations can participate independently in the same study, and the results from the several locations can be combined to develop one estimate. Further, a study started by one evaluator can be continued by another and, if evaluators decide to extend the sampling, they can do so easily and combine the results.

Determining the Type of Statistical Sampling

If a statistical sample is the choice, a further decision involves the type of sampling method: random, stratified, systematic, quota, or cluster.

Random Sampling

Random sampling, the simplest method of drawing a statistical sample, is the most common; however, sometimes, it is less efficient than other methods. One assumption underlying the use of this method is that the population is homogeneous. No attempt is made to segregate or separate any portion of the population into different groups before the sample is selected. As a result, each individual item in the universe has an equal chance of inclusion in the sample.

Random sampling ensures that the sample statistic is representative of the population parameter and that evaluators can determine the amount of difference between the two. The difference between the characteristics of a sample and those of the population from which the sample was taken is called *sampling error*. This error is a function of the size of the sample; the error is the greatest when the sample size is small. For random samples, evaluators can estimate sampling error.

Stratified Sampling

Stratified sampling refers to the situation in which the universe is divided into two or more parts and a sample is selected from each part. The parts may be selected in proportion to their numbers in the population itself. In some instances, evaluators might use disproportional stratified sampling. When defining parts (strata) and setting stratum boundaries, evaluators should remember certain rules. First, each sampling unit can be included in one, and only one, stratum. Second, the strata must not overlap. Third, the items in each stratum should be as similar as possible in relation to the characteristic being measured.

Because the universe is divided into two or more parts (strata) in this type of sampling, evaluators can use a different procedure to select the samples in the various sub-universes. Depending on the arrangement of the items in the sub-universes and the numbering system used, they might use random sampling in some of the strata and systematic sampling in others. For example, all undergraduates majoring in a social science discipline—the universe (population)—might be divided into departmental majors, and the selection of participants might be based on each department major. In this way, the sample enables the creation of a hypothesis that compares respondents to departmental majors.

Systematic Sampling

Systematic sampling may be used when the sampling units are not numbered or when it would be too cumbersome to attempt to match the sampling units against random numbers. With this type of sampling, evaluators do not select each member of the population independently. Once the first member of the population has been chosen, other members of the sample are automatically determined. This type of sample focuses on taking every nth person or thing; for instance, every tenth person entering or exiting the library. The sampling interval therefore becomes 10.

As an alternative, evaluators might take every fifth element from a list until the total list has been covered. If that list contains 500 names, the sampling interval is 5, the sampling ratio is 1:5, and the sample is 100. The list is viewed as circular in that the evaluator begins with the first nth value and continues through the list until the entire sample has been selected. As long as the list does not contain any hidden order, this sampling method is as good as the random sampling method. Its only advantage over the random sampling technique is simplicity.

Quota Sampling

Quota sampling recognizes that evaluators may want to select a proportion of the population according to certain characteristics. For example, evaluators might base their sampling on class level and take a proportion of undergraduate and graduate students at the university in such a way that they can make comparisons about the student population: undergraduate versus graduate students.

Cluster Sampling

This type of sampling involves the selection of groups of items (clusters) rather than individual items directly. Cluster sampling focuses on a naturally occurring group of individuals. Evaluators divide the population into subdivisions, clusters of smaller units. Some of these subdivisions are randomly selected for inclusion in the study. If library customers come from geographical subdivisions, this kind of sampling is known as *area sampling*. Examples of clusters are counties in a state, persons in a household, and particular parts of a city or town recognized by certain street boundaries.

Lynn S. Connaway and Ronald R. Powell provide an excellent introduction to cluster sampling.[3] The U.S. Bureau of the Census and other government agencies and private and not-for-profit sectors have produced computer maps of the United States; similar agencies and groups in many other countries have done the same. Depending on the level of privacy that exists in a country's data-gathering approach to those completing decennial census forms, and using supplementary geographically coded data that the private sector has collected, a wide assortment of datasets can be linked to the computerized maps (associated with geographic information systems). The result is that a more sophisticated type of area sampling is permissible.

An Alternative to Statistical Sampling: Nonprobability Sampling

When the population is unknown or unknowable (e.g., the population of users of a homepage or perhaps participants in a blog), evaluators might default to nonprobability sampling, for which the samples are drawn in such a way that evaluators cannot determine how representative the same units are of the population. Furthermore, when they need data quickly and cheaply, they might also consider such sampling. The sampling choices include the following:

- *Convenience* sampling, in which the selection of items is based on their availability (easily or economically available). For example, librarians offering instruction in information literacy might approach those faculty members whom they know will welcome assistance in the evaluation of written assignments or course assessment.

- *Typical item* sampling, in which the selection of items or units is based on some prior assumption that, because specific population units are "typical," they should be chosen for the sample. Often the decision about what is typical is an arbitrary one. For example, evaluation might focus on library use during a so-called typical day or week.

- *Quota* sampling, in which the selection might correspond to convenience. Unlike its counterpart discussed in the section on probability sampling, in this case the evaluators might decide that they want to study students from each of the four traditional class levels of university undergraduates. They decide arbitrarily to select twenty from each class level and design a method to find these eighty students quickly and conveniently—the first eighty students to volunteer for study inclusion.

- *Snowball* sampling, in which the selection of new participants comes from the identification of previous participants. Assume that library evaluators are conducting focus group interviews with *lost* customers, those who had a bad experience while using the library and now find other ways to gather needed information and materials to complete class assignments. At the end of a focus group interview, the moderator might ask participants to identify other lost customers who might be approached to participate in the next round of interviews. (Note that for privacy reasons, the moderator might request that participants approach lost customers known to them and ask these customers to contact the library.)

Determining the Sample Size

A determination of sample size involves four concepts: sampling error, precision, confidence level, and standard deviation. *Sampling error* is the extent to which the means, the arithmetical averages, of repeatedly drawn samples, deviate from each other and presumably from the population mean. By minimizing sampling error, evaluators increase the likelihood that the sample represents the population. *Precision* is the amount of sampling error that can be tolerated but that will still permit the results to be useful. This is sometimes called *tolerable error* or the *bound on error*. *Confidence level* is a measure of the degree of assurance that the estimate obtained from a sample differs from the universe parameter being estimated by less than the sampling error. The *standard deviation* is a measurement of the dispersion or scatter of a group of values around their mean. As is evident, determining the sample size is a complex matter. Fortunately there are some excellent sources to guide this decision.[4]

A CAUTIONARY NOTE ABOUT STATISTICAL SAMPLING

In setting up a study, the question arises about whether or not to engage in sampling. If the universe is small or the individual sampling units in the universe are very important, it is often advisable to examine every item in the universe. However, if the universe is large, a sample is preferred to a complete enumeration of the universe, because the information that is wanted can be obtained more cheaply, more quickly, often more accurately, and in greater detail. In some instances, only one of these benefits applies, and, in some extreme situations, none does. These points deserve some explanation.

Sampling is usually cheaper than a complete review of the universe because, by definition, it usually deals with only a small group selected from the universe. Engaging in data collection includes consideration of cost as a variable—the cost of examining individual items. By reducing the number of items to be examined, sampling permits a substantial reduction in cost. A good sampling plan, however, may add some costs that would not be present in a complete review. Although almost always much smaller than the savings, such costs should not be ignored. They usually cover developing the sampling plan, selecting the sample, monitoring the sample selection process, processing the data and calculating estimates and sampling errors, and providing special training or instruction necessary for completion of the previous steps.

With regard to speed, sometimes a recommendation must be prepared or a decision be made within a relatively short time. No matter how good the quality, information is useless unless it is received in time to be used in making a recommendation or arriving at a decision. The measurement or examination process takes time; so too does the summarization of results. Because a sample involves fewer items than a complete review, these processes can be done more quickly to make them more useful to planners and decision makers.

Sometimes an attempt will be made to obtain more information from the sample than the study was designed to provide. An example of this is taking a sample that was designed to evaluate the effectiveness of a library's information literacy program and then attempting to develop estimates for different domains of interest (e.g., classifying students by subject or class level). In some cases, attempts to use a sample for purposes other than those for which it was designed can lead to estimates with sampling errors as large as, or larger than, the estimates themselves.

Similarly, some people believe that sampling furnishes less accurate information than a census. In fact, the opposite view is probably more reasonable, because sampling may reduce the risk of measurement errors and the recording, processing, and reporting of data. Because sampling involves coping with fewer items, it frequently allows evaluators to use personnel who have been better trained to collect, process, and evaluate the data than would be practical in a complete examination of the universe.

By suggesting that sampling permits more detailed information to be obtained, we mean that if an attempt is made to measure all of the items in the universe, it may be possible to make only one or a few observations on each sample item. However, if sampling is used and fewer items are measured, it may be possible to collect much more data about each item and thus develop more in-depth information about the universe.

In sum, if statistical sampling is feasible and is carried out correctly, it usually has advantages over complete enumeration and nonstatistical sampling. Still, even if the evaluators avoid common sampling mistakes (e.g., selecting and applying a type of sampling method incorrectly) and design a study that meets all the requirements of good sampling, nonsampling errors might emerge. These are errors of measurement (e.g., response, coding, or interviewing errors). Total error, a function of sampling and nonsampling error, can only be substantially reduced if both types of errors are addressed, controlled, or minimized.

VARIABLES

Evaluation studies might explore relationships between (and among) variables. Variables, which are "any property of a person, thing, event, setting, and so on that is not fixed,"[5] exist in different forms:

- A *dependent* variable explains, or is used to measure, observable behavior (e.g., a change in attitudes). This variable depends on or is influenced by the independent variable.

- An *independent* variable, which is frequently equated with the treatment (e.g., instructional program or hours of service), is manipulated so that its effect on the outcome and dependent variable can be observed. The independent variable determines, influences, or produces the change. In those research designs dealing with a determination of causal relationships, the causes become independent variables, and the effects are dependent variables. When variables are not manipulated, a distinction between cause and effect becomes impossible.

- *Control* variables are held constant or randomized so that their effects are neutralized or controlled. Examples include gender and age.

CRITERIA OF RELEVANCE

Criteria of relevance refer to reliability and validity. Any evaluation research design, as well as the data obtained from an evaluation or assessment study, most likely contains inherent limitations and potential biases. By the use of random assignment to control and experimental groups, the employment of statistical analysis, and attention to issues of validity, these limitations can usually be minimized and their possible impacts reduced.

Internal validity, which concerns itself with the extent to which evaluators measure what they intend to measure, raises a key issue: valid for what purpose? As Lee J. Cronback points out, the measuring instrument is not validated. Rather, by using that instrument for a particular purpose, "one validates . . . an interpretation of data arising from a specified procedure."[6] External validity examines the generalizability of the design and findings to a population.

Internal Validity

Internal validity involves eliminating those variables that suggest alternate explanations or that prevent the identification of causal relationships. There are a number of possible threats to the internal validity of a research design:

- *History* raises the possibility that some factor, other than the independent variable, accounts for the change in the dependent variable. For example, the length of time between conducting the pre-test and post-test may have a detrimental effect.

- *Maturation* suggests that the change resulted from biological or psychological processes, which occurred over time, and not from the treatment itself. As with history, maturation becomes more of a concern the longer the period is between the pre-test and post-test.

- *Pre-testing* may affect the dependent variable; pre-testing may alert participants or educate them about the topic under investigation. If subjects are administered a post-test, their performance may reflect a marked improvement due to the fact that they were pre-tested; improvement may not be a result of manipulation of the independent variable. For this reason, some of the evaluation designs discussed later in the chapter either avoid the use of a pre-test or administer a pre-test to one control group but not another.

- *Measuring instruments* or observational techniques, rather than the treatment itself, might account for change in the dependent variable, if they are not sufficiently compatible. Further, the validity of the study findings may have been influenced by the fact that the evaluators as observers, raters, graders, interviewers, and coders gained experience, became tired, obtained a more complete understanding of the project, or lowered their expectations of test subjects.

- *Statistical regression* means that extreme scores obtained on a first test might move toward the mean on subsequent tests. The change may be interpreted as a consequence of the treatment used, when in fact the change results from statistical regression.

- A nonrandom assignment of *subjects* to groups might indicate that the groups were dissimilar from the beginning. Any change therefore might be attributed to the differential selection of subjects, rather than the actual treatment received.

- *Mortality* refers to the possibility that some subjects may have dropped out of the study after completion of the pre-test but before the administration of the post-test. In such instances, every effort should be made to identify common patterns or characteristics to ensure that any differences between a group's pre-test and post-test scores cannot be attributed to the loss of subjects.

- More than one of the above-mentioned threats might be active at the same time and produce an *interaction*. This is especially possible in those cases in which subjects were not randomly assigned to groups, and the evaluation was based on existing, intact groups.

Finally, three special types of internal validity merit noting:

1. *Content validity* is concerned with the representativeness of the measuring instrument in describing the content that it is intended to measure. This type of validity is more easily applied to practical considerations than to abstract or theoretical concepts. The central question is, "How well does the content of the instrument represent the entire universe of content that might be measured?" Face validity, which represents the evaluators' appraisal that the content reflects what they are attempting to measure, comprises a type of content validity. Face validity is also judgmental and subject to interpretation.

2. *Criterion-related validity* compares scores on the data collection instrument to certain criteria known or commonly believed to measure the attribute under study. The purpose is to determine the extent to which the instrument covers a criterion. A problem with the application of criterion validity is that many types of behavior cannot be converted into an appropriate criterion.

    There are two types of criterion-related validity: *predictive* and *diagnostic*. The purpose of the former is to estimate or predict a future outcome, while the latter type diagnoses the existing or current state of a subject. The central difference between the two relates to the time when the data depicting the criterion are collected. To qualify as predictive validity, the correlation between the test scores and the criterion comes at a later time. Diagnostic validity requires that the correlation not be delayed, but made at approximately the same time. The following example clarifies the distinction.

If evaluators administer a library skills test to students completing the required freshmen English course, diagnostic validity is determined by a correlation of test scores with, perhaps, the grade that the students received on a term paper that required the use of library resources. Predictive validity involves a correlation of their test scores with the grade from a term paper in a subsequent class. Longitudinal data gathered under a suitable design definitely aid the determination of predictive validity. (Grade inflation is a major weakness of basing a comparison on grades.)

3. *Construct validity*, which has the most generalized application of the three types of validity discussed here, questions whether the theoretical construct or trait is actually measured. For example, does a study of creativity, motivation, anxiety, or self-actualization actually measure that trait? One way that the question can be answered is to correlate items on locally produced tests to those on standardized tests. If the correlation is high, one assumes that the new instrument measures what it is intended to (the construct).

This discussion should not conclude with the impression that all validity issues can be reduced to the precision of statistical analysis. When evaluation and assessment focuses on a human component examined from the perspective of qualitative data collection, the investigator does not rely on statistical precision, and for this reason, it is important to consider issues of data trustworthiness, rigor (dealing with subjectivity, reflexivity, and the social interaction in the methodology), quality, and credibility or believability of the findings.

External Validity

External validity, which is concerned with the representativeness of the sample compared to the larger population, can be increased by the use of statistical sampling techniques that examine characteristics similar to those of the target population. Certain factors that threaten the external validity of a study can be grouped into population and ecological validity. The former is concerned with generalizability to subjects of other populations and whether the characteristics of the subjects receiving a particular treatment inhibit generalizations to other groups. For example, some library programming and workshops might be more effective for people of a certain grade, educational, or reading level, or for people with certain abilities and skills.

Population validity is an important concern in those instances in which the population from which evaluators select subjects differs from the population to which they want to generalize. For example, evaluators in public libraries might test programmed instruction on high school students but want to generalize the findings to all user groups. To display wider generalizability, the instruction would have to be tested on different user groups.

Ecological validity addresses the generalizability of study findings to other environmental conditions (e.g., changes in physical setting, time of day, or evaluators). Threats to this type of validity exist when

- insufficient insights into the design and procedures of a study exist to permit replication,

- participants' awareness that they are receiving special treatment encourages them to either perform better than they normally might or to respond in a certain way (known as the Hawthorne effect), and

- the perception of a treatment as new or unusual influences participant motivation and performance.

Change resulting from the treatment may decline as the novelty of that treatment decreases. Further, a pre-test may facilitate learning, increase participants' awareness of the problem under investigation, or give subjects an opportunity to reflect on the issue.

Reliability

Reliability is the extent to which the same results are produced on different samples of the same population. It is concerned with replication and the consistency, stability, or accuracy from measurement to measurement. Common methods used to test for reliability include test and retest, alternative form, and split half. For *test and retest*, the same test is administered to the same individuals or groups after a certain period of time. Based on the two sets of scores for each person, a correlation coefficient is computed. A high correlation between the two indicates data reliability. The problem, though, is that threats to internal validity (e.g., history, pre-testing, and maturation) may arise.

With the *alternative form*, the same people encounter two testing situations. Approximately two weeks after the completion of the initial test, they may be given an alternative form of the same test. Since the same test is not administered both times, a person's recall of the original test situation is lessened. The problem with this method is that it is difficult to construct two parallel forms of the test having the same purpose.

Unlike the other methods, the *split-half* method can be conducted on one occasion. One approach is to have two or three questions that measure the same variable on one test and then, from all of the responses, determine the degree to which each person answered those two or three questions correctly. This way, evaluators can have reliability estimates on different variables on the same test.

Another approach is to divide the total number of test items in half, with the correlation of the scores between the two halves, offering the estimate of reliability. The division of a test into half is comparable to the development of an alternative form of the same test. To use this method, however, data collection measures one variable. When a class receiving instruction in information literacy is administered a set of 10 questions related to knowledge of Boolean searching, a correlation between the first and second set of five questions for each student indicates reliability of the test scores.

The methods discussed in this section examine *internal consistency*, or the interrelationships among the components of a data collection instrument. If different people score a test or code the data collection instrument for computer or manual analysis, a purpose of reliability is to determine that they did, in fact, score or code in a similar manner. Specific statistical tests (e.g., Cronbach's alpha and Kuder-Richardson formula 20 and 21) test for reliability.

Summary

Reliability and validity apply to both the research design and the methodology. Standardized tests might have a history in which different researchers over time have investigated the reliability and validity of the test. In the case of course evaluation, there are ample discussions in the literatures of psychology and higher education about what such evaluation measures, a representative set of questions, and how to improve the wording of the questions asked. Another method is to define key concepts using standard definitions. For reliability, evaluators might pre-test the questions on a small group and elicit feedback on the wording of the questions. The goal is to improve the wording so that questions are not open to varied interpretation. Evaluators might also repeat a question and compare both sets of answers for the purpose of reliability. If, for instance, an evaluator applies content analysis—a systematic analysis of the occurrence of words, phrases, concepts, and so on in books and other types of materials—this person might randomly select a few documents, develop instructions to guide data collection, ask some colleagues to code those documents, and compare the results. This process is known as *scorer* or *interscore reliability*.

CASE STUDY

A case study can be a type of research design for learning about a complex instance, based on an extensive description and analysis of that instance taken as a whole and in its context. A case study appears in six forms:

1. *Illustrative*, meaning that the descriptive case study adds depth to whatever information is already available about a program, service, or practice.

2. *Critical instance*, meaning that a single instance provides a unique but important perspective on a program, service, or practice.

3. *Exploratory*, meaning that the description leads to the formulation of hypotheses.

4. *Program implementation*, meaning that the evaluator studies operations at several sites.

5. *Program effects*, meaning that there is an examination of causality and often the use of multisite, multimethod evaluations.

6. *Cumulative*, meaning that findings from many case studies collectively provide detailed insights into study questions.

Of the six forms, the first two are the most commonly used.

There are three general bases for selecting instances, or case study sites: convenience, purpose, and probability (see table 5.1). Only rarely is convenience a sound basis for instance selection; probability sampling is generally not feasible in such a circumstance. As a result, instance selection on the basis of the purpose of the study is the most appropriate in many designs.

For case studies, it is important to achieve measurement validity, which can be accomplished by using multiple sources of evidence and building a solid chain of reasoning. Part of this chain relates to the sequence of activities for data collection and drawing conclusions, and that sequence may involve an audit trail that others can follow to verify the results.

Table 5.1. Instance Selection in Case Studies*

Basis of Selection	When to Use and What Questions It Can Answer
Convenience	Is this site selected because it was expedient for data collection, what is happening, and why?
Purpose	
Bracketing	What is happening at extremes? What explains such differences?
Best cases	What accounts for an effective program?
Worst cases	Why is the program not working?
Cluster	How do different types of programs compare with each other?
Representative	In instances chosen to represent important variations, what is the program [or service] like, and why?
Typical	In a typical site, what is happening, and why?
Special interest	In this particular circumstance, what is happening, and why?
Probability	What is happening in the program [or service] as a whole, and why?

*Adapted from U.S. General Accounting Office, Program Evaluation and Methodology Division, Case Study Evaluations, Transfer Paper 10.1.9 (Washington, DC: General Accounting Office, 1990), 23.

EVALUATION DESIGNS

This section emphasizes the use of experimental, quasi-experimental, and descriptive designs, but does not detail or diagram any of them using statistical terminology. The purpose is to present each simply so that library staff can make comparisons and determine which might have the most application to their situation. Both experimental and quasi-experimental designs have great application to assessment and monitoring of, for instance, the improvement in learning over time.

The designs discussed in this section examine impact evaluations and assessments and whether an intervention or treatment produced its intended effect. The designs look at the impact of the treatment, or independent variable, once all confronting effects have been removed or controlled. *Confronting effects* are those masking the true effects of an intervention and competing with the intervention measures to explain any changes in the population that occurred after the program began.

Formative and summative evaluation may require different designs, because one provides feedback to modify or improve a program or service in operation, and the other examines the effectiveness or efficiency of a completed activity. Depending on the particular set of objectives, the evaluation design might lead to a survey for measuring opinions, attitudes, or perceptions; an experiment for gauging the impact learning; correlations for investigating the amount of variation between similar factors; or a comparison whereby evaluators observe consequences and examine the data for plausible causation.

The choice of an appropriate design also depends on constraints of time, finances, human and material resources, and political concerns. Based on the evaluators' review of the constraints, they select the design most appropriate to the problem statement, objectives, and level of available expertise.

Experimental and quasi-experimental designs frequently require the use of a control group. A control group consists of subjects who either do not receive the treatment or intervention or receive the usual or standard treatment, while the experimental group receives special treatment. Control groups perform a useful purpose: they invite comparison to the group receiving the treatment and offer support about whether observed change resulted from the treatment and not the normal maturation process that occurs with individuals and organizations (or comparison to other validity threats as well). Incidentally, in some instances there might be an insufficient number of participants to permit the use of a control group.

Instead of using a control group, evaluation studies might employ a comparison group, which seeks to determine whether a particular treatment produced the desired outcome more effectively, or more efficiently, than an alternative method. The purpose is to test and compare different methods and to see which is the most effective or efficient. Depending on the particular objectives, a third type of group might be used. Two groups having different competencies, attitudes, or perceptions might be selected and contrasted.

Experimental Design

An experimental design aids in ruling out rival explanations and extraneous variables and is the most likely to protect against threats to internal validity. For an experimental design, subjects must be assigned to control, comparison, or contrasting groups randomly;

evaluators manipulate the independent variable (intervention), observe its effect on the dependent variable (subjects), and set the timing of the observation or measurement.

Randomization ensures that the groups under study are similar and that any difference between them is due to the treatment (independent variable) and not to the participants themselves (e.g., their gender, age, or level of education). Randomization may be achieved by either random selection or random assignment. In the former, each person in the population has an equal chance of being selected to participate in the study, whereas the latter involves the random placement of subjects in a control or treatment group.

Randomized experiments are costly and time-consuming to conduct, require extensive controls on selection and treatments, may not have significant generalizability, and require knowledge of complex research designs and inferential statistics. Yet such research is the flagship of evaluation and assessment and produces the best insights about impact. In essence, *impact* is the net outcome or result attributed to the intervention minus confounding factors (extraneous variables that obscure or exaggerate the actual effects of an intervention). These factors involve threats to reliability and validity. It is also important to address the effects of chance, random fluctuations, and measurement error.

Instead of using randomization, evaluators might achieve equivalence by systematic assignment from serialized lists, provided that the ordering of these lists does not produce bias. By this method, students might be assigned to a group based on whether their college identification number ended in an odd or even digit. Prior to using this method, however, evaluators would have to determine that the institution did not assign numbers to students in a biased way. For example, they would want to ascertain prior to adopting this method that female students did not receive odd numbers and male students even ones.

Figure 5.1 characterizes how the impact of a study using an experimental design is determined. The outcome for either the experimental or control group might be determined by measuring the differences between the scores on the pre-test and post-test and then taking into account threats to validity, chance, and measurement error. Having this depiction in mind, evaluators can decide whether the experimental method and its requirements are most appropriate, the type of experimental design to use, and the need to control threats to validity and determine the amount of fluctuation attributed to chance.

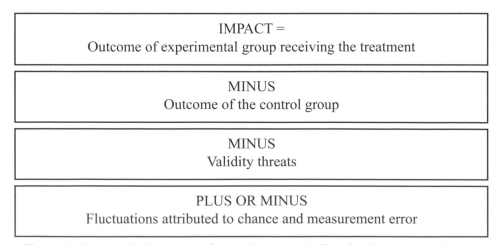

Figure 5.1. Impact of a Program or Service Involving the Use of an Experimental Design

Various types of experimental designs exist and have potential application to libraries and information centers. These designs either adopt a combination of a pre-test and a post-test or bypass the use of a pre-test in preference for a post-test. They may also use one or more control and experimental groups and vary the types of tests given to each.

In the *pre-test-post-test design*, evaluators randomly assign subjects to a control and experimental group and administer a pre-test to both groups. Some time after the experimental group has received the treatment, they give the post-test to both groups. The outcome—expressed as the mean scores for both groups, plus or minus the factors listed in the figure—indicates the extent of program or service effectiveness (or learning over time). Mortality, whereby participants drop out, is probably the major potential problem (see figure 5.2, part A). Evaluators must ensure that both the pre-test and post-test are administered in the same way, and that both groups have minimal contact with each other.

A variation of this design is to have both groups receive different treatments, but not to use one group as a control group. The differential effects of both forms of the treatment would be compared (see figure 5.2, part B).

Evaluators wanting to use a control group might be interested in a variation of the first design. Because pre-tests may affect participants' behavior or attitudes in some way, the pre-test/post-test design can be modified so that the control group only receives either the pre-test or post-test (figure 5.2, part C). It is also possible that neither the control nor the experimental group would take the pre-test. The two groups might even be exposed to different forms of the same treatment, with the measurement being in the form of a post-test.

The Solomon four-group design is based on the premise that the pre-test sensitizes participants to the treatment. If this premise has merit, study results cannot be generalized (external validity), and the treatment could not be administered to people who have not received the pre-test (internal validity). With this design, subjects are randomly assigned to four groups. Two of these groups receive the treatment and the post-test, but not the pre-test. A third experimental group benefits from the treatment and completes both the pre-test and post-test. A control group receives both tests as well (figure 5.2, part D), but not the treatment. This design controls for threats to internal validity.

Another option is a *pre-test-post-test design for many groups*, wherein subjects are randomly assigned to three or more groups. Each group receives the pre-test, a treatment, and the post-test (figure 5.2, part E). Again, variations in the administration of the pre-test and post-test are possible. There might be a comparison of the original program and a naturally evolving version of it. Program participants could be divided into two subgroups, "one of which remains stable and the other of which is encouraged 'to improve continually' on the basis of best option."[7] As noted by Carol H. Weiss,

> The experimental method does not require a stable program. It can be used even when the program meanders. If there is interest in the effects of a program under developmental conditions or in its usual nonstandardized form, randomized designs are perfectly suitable for studying outcomes.[8]

PART A: Pre-test/Post-test Design (with Control Group)

	Pre-test	Treatment	Post-test
Experiment	Yes	Yes	Yes
Control	Yes	No	Yes

The impact of the program or service is the difference between the post-test and pre-test scores for the experimental group and the difference between the post-test and pre-test scores for the control group. Evaluators need to consider threats to internal validity, chance, and possibly measurement error.

PART B: Pre-test/Post-test Design (without Control Group)

	Pre-test	Treatment	Post-test
Experiment 1	Yes	Yes	Yes
Experiment 2	Yes	Yes	Yes

The impact of the program or service is the difference between the post-test and pre-test scores for experimental group 1 and the difference between the post-test and pre-test scores for experimental group 2. Evaluators need to consider threats to internal validity, chance, and possibly measurement error.

PART C: Pre-test/Post-test Design (with Control Group)

	Pre-test	Treatment	Post-test
Experiment	Yes	Yes	Yes
Control Group	Maybe	No	Maybe

(The control group received either the pre-test or the post-test, but not both.)

The impact of the program or service is the difference between the post-test and pre-test scores for experimental group 1 and a comparison of this score to the post-test and/or pre-test scores for the control group. Evaluators need to consider threats to internal validity, chance, and possibly measurement error.

PART D: Solomon Four-Group Design

	Pre-test	Treatment	Post-test
Experiment 1	No	Yes	Yes
Experiment 2	No	Yes	Yes
Experiment 3	Yes	Yes	Yes
Control Group	Yes	No	Yes

The impact of the program or service is determined from a comparison of pre-test and post-test scores, as well as a comparison of the four post-test scores. Evaluators need to be sensitive to threats to internal validity, chance, and possibly measurement error.

PART E: Pre-test/Posttest Design (for Many Groups)

	Pre-test	Treatment	Post-test
Experiment 1	Yes	Yes	Yes
Experiment 2	Yes	Yes	Yes
Experiment 3	Yes	Yes	Yes

The impact of the program or service is determined from a comparison of the three pre-test and post-test scores, as well as the post-test scores by themselves. Evaluators need to be sensitive to threats to internal validity, chance, and possibly measurement error.

Figure 5.2. Types of Experimental Designs

Additional experimental designs are possible; however, these involve the use of more sophisticated statistical measures (factorial and repeated measures). Their sophistication, both in terms of design and statistical manipulation, may well be beyond the budget, time constraints, and skills of many librarians.

As this section has stressed, experimental designs most typically require the random assignment of subjects to groups. For some problems confronting evaluators in library and information science (other than those relating to the preservation of library materials), randomization is not feasible. Instead, evaluators must work with intact groups or place participants in groups by matching them on some attribute. With matching, however, evaluators can only be certain that the participants in each group are similar to the characteristic matched. Further, the threats to internal validity increase. For these reasons, evaluators must carefully select the appropriate design and be aware of its strengths and weaknesses.

Quasi-Experimental Design

When the random assignment of subjects to a group does not occur, and increased validity threats are potentially present, evaluators might engage in quasi-experimentation. They probe, but do not prove, causal relationships. Inferences presume that a particular interpretation of the data is the most plausible. If relevant theory has been applied and sound procedures have been followed, the likelihood of alternative explanations has been greatly reduced. A causal relationship is accepted as provisionally true, until or unless a better explanation emerges.

Where the quasi experimental design is weak, the findings are subject to varied interpretation. In such instances, especially for summative evaluation of a program or service, evaluators might adopt a multiple-methods approach and rely on different methods of data collection.

In quasi-experimental designs, evaluators match groups so that the groups share some similar characteristics. Matching is done on either an individual or aggregate basis. The former is usually preferable, because greater attention is given to the characteristics matched; greater knowledge about individuals and their characteristics, however, is required. Matching on an individual basis, therefore, becomes more time-consuming and costly.

Matching is not a substitute for randomization. Misleading results may emerge when the participants represent different populations. The possibility of statistical regression becomes a major threat to internal validity. Another danger is self-selection, or letting people choose to participate or enter a particular group. Self-selection is likely to produce people dissimilar from others in the population.

If matching is not feasible, evaluators use intact groups (e.g., classes). Those groups should be as similar as possible, with the similarities verified by a pre-test. Still, evaluators must remember various threats to internal validity (e.g., pre-testing) and compensate for them.

The description of experimental designs in figure 5.2 is also applicable here. The impact of the program or service is determined from the outcome minus the validity threats, the measurement error, and the fluctuations attributed to chance. As has been emphasized, the likelihood of an outcome being influenced by threats to validity and chance increases with quasi-experimentation or the descriptive designs presented later in the chapter. Experimental designs tend to have high validity, whereas quasi-experiments have moderate validity, and other designs tend to have limited validity.

Quasi-experimental designs frequently use pre-test and post-test measures in a time series so that treatments are removed or reintroduced at different times. Similar to the pre-test-post-test control group, described in the section on experimental designs, the *nonequivalent control group* compares two similar groups before and after the exposure of one group to a treatment (figure 5.3, part A). Although the groups are intact and participants are not randomly assigned to a group, evaluators can randomly assign a treatment to one group.

Evaluators might take intact groups and randomly assign participants to two subgroups, each of which received a different treatment. They might investigate one group prior to the introduction of the treatment. Both groups receive the treatment, but only the one that was not pre-tested is measured or observed after the treatment has been completed.

Measures such as selection and statistical regression offset the major threats to internal validity. The intent is to make the comparison group as similar to the experimental group as possible. The greater the number of similarities (e.g., enrolled in alternative sections of the same course taught by the same instructor, or performing in a similar fashion on a pre-test), the better is the comparison between the groups. Any lack of similarity between the groups understates or overstates the program outcome and should be incorporated in the analysis of study findings.

A *time-series design* involves the taking of repeated observations or measurements before and after each treatment has been given (figure 5.3, part B). In this way, any change in the dependent variable is observed over time, and evaluators have access to longitudinal data. Repeated testing serves as a check to some threats to internal validity, namely maturation, testing, and statistical regression, but not to history; some factor other than the treatment might have been the change agent.

There are a number of variations of the time-series design. Many do not require the use of a control group; however, the presence of such a group reduces threats to internal validity. For example, prior to and after the initiation of one treatment, evaluators draw repeated measurements in order to document any change in the dependent variable. Evaluators either periodically reinstate the same treatment or follow it with subsequent treatments. Furthermore, after they apply the first treatment, evaluators might administer the second one without removing the first treatment.

An interrupted time-series using *switching replications* enhances external validity and controls for most threats to internal validity. Two nonequivalent groups thereby receive the treatment at different times. By continuing the process and rotating treatments between the two groups, each group at different points serves as the control group.

Figure 5.3, part C, suggests that evaluators might compare the effectiveness of different treatments through the use of both a pre-test and post-test. Because this design does not use a control group, evaluators are more interested in an analysis of different treatments than in a comparison of treatments to a control group that did not receive a treatment.

PART A: Nonequivalent Control Group

	Pre-test	Treatment	Post-test
Experiment	Yes	Yes	Yes
Control	Yes	No	Yes

The impact of the program or service is determined by finding the difference between post-test and pre-test scores for the experimental group and comparing this score to the difference between the post-test and pre-test scores for the control group. Evaluators need to consider threats to internal validity, measurement error, and chance.

PART B: Time-Series Design

	Pre-test	Treatment	Post-test	Pre-test	Treatment	Post-test	Etc.
Experiment	Yes	Yes	Yes	Yes	Yes	Yes	. . .
Control Group	Yes	No	Yes	Yes	No	Yes	. . .

The impact of the program or service is determined by giving the experimental group and the control group repeated pre-tests and post-tests, and then comparing the scores of both groups. Evaluators need to consider threats to internal validity, measurement error, and chance.

PART C: Pre-test/Post-test Design

	Pre-test	Treatment	Post-test
Experiment 1	Yes	Yes	Yes
Experiment 2	Yes	Yes	Yes
Experiment 3	Yes	Yes	Yes
Experiment 4	Yes	Yes	Yes

The impact of the program or service is determined by taking the post-test and pre-test scores for each group, determining the differences, and comparing them. Evaluators need to consider threats to internal validity, measurement error, and chance.

Figure 5.3. Depiction of Quasi-Experimental Designs

Descriptive Design

The *pseudoexperimental design*, a type of descriptive design that lacks built-in control, cannot rule out rival explanations for change, or the lack of change, in the dependent variable. This design does not provide satisfactory controls to minimize threats to internal validity. For small projects for which quickly and inexpensively gathered data are needed (especially those comprising formative evaluation), this design, however, may have some merit. If the project is important and summative, and if there is sufficient time to collect and analyze the data, evaluators might use one of the aforementioned, more rigorous designs.

Three examples of pseudoexperimental designs are the *one-shot case study*, *one-group pre-test and post-test*, and *intact-group comparison*. The first design is descriptive, exposes a group to a treatment, and measures the impact. The two problems with this design are the absence of a control or comparison group, and that evaluators must surmise the attitudes, competencies, and so on of the group before the treatment.

With the one-group pre-test and post-test, observations are made before and after the group received the treatment. Although this design is an improvement over the previous one, it neither offers a control group nor satisfactorily minimizes threats to internal validity, As a result, rival explanations for the change, or the lack thereof, in the dependent variable are not eliminated.

The intact-group comparison involves the location of two intact groups, the administration of a treatment to one group but not the other, and the administration of a pre-test and post-test to both groups. The control group might receive only the pre-test or post-test. The weaknesses of this design are twofold: (1) subjects are not randomly assigned to groups, and (2) the groups may not be equivalent. If change in the dependent variable occurs, rival interpretations are not excluded.

Many descriptive designs employ case studies. Evaluators can take the results gathered from case studies and see if the interpretation made applies to other situations. When this approach is used, evaluators nonetheless should be cautious about applying inferences to other groups.

Finally, *ex post facto* studies, which are used when experimental designs are not possible, require caution in the interpretation of results. Nonetheless, in some instances evaluators might examine services and programs that were previously implemented before the library introduces a new service or program. Before that service or program begins, they might examine any historical records in an effort to determine if the experiment had been successful—or if not, why?

EXAMPLES

This section takes selected topics and identifies decision points relating to research design (see figure 5.4). Before librarians review their choices and make their decisions, they should have conducted a literature review and, among other things, seen how others have approached a similar problem. For instance, assume that evaluators want to conduct a usability test of the library's homepage and see how undergraduate students navigate

This figure views research design in isolation from the problem statement, objectives, research questions, and the rest of the procedures section.

Exploring Satisfaction with the Learning Commons

A learning commons located in library is a collaborative partnership that "brings together library, technology, and other campus services in an environment that fosters informal, collaborative and creative work, and social interaction."[a] Decision points for the research design form around the service and seating areas studied, the process of selecting survey participants (including the type of sample to use and the sample size), the time of the day or week for conducting the survey (will this be a one-time data collection or longer?), the degree of external validity sought, and associated reliability and validity threats.

Exploring the Public's Use of Playaways

A playaway comes with preloaded digital content, a battery to make it play, and earbuds to listen. Assuming that a library has circulation records indicating who uses playaways and how often, the section on research design might discuss the population and a probability sample. That sample might involve a random sampling or stratified random sampling, with each stratum representing different frequencies of use; evaluators might also consider the use of nonprobability sampling. Research design also covers sample size and how the selection of subjects will be made. The research design is followed by methodology and issues of reliability and validity.

Assessment of Political Science Students and Their Development as Information-Literate Undergraduates

Assuming the study focuses on course-level assessment—measuring student learning throughout the school term—the evaluators concentrate on a class, an intact group of students; they do not random sample students in a course, and they do not compare different sections of the same course.[b] Further, they do not have a control group, and they cannot withhold a type of instruction from part of the class. Evaluators might develop a set of scenarios, each of which corresponds to a core competency for information literacy,[c] and administer them as a pre-test (early in the course prior to working on relevant class assignments) and post-test (toward the end of the course). Is there a statistically significant improvement from pre-test to post-test scores ($p = .05$)? Since statistical sampling was not used to select which students are enrolled in the class, there are threats to internal validity that need to be addressed; for instance, there is mortality. However, dealing with the threats moves from research design to data quality. Data quality also involves certification of the scenarios as addressing a particular core information literacy competency.

Now, assuming the study focuses on program-level assessment—measuring student learning over the duration of the program—the evaluators might select some undergraduate students at different points in the program, by means of statistical sampling, and compare their performance—perhaps in working with the set of scenarios or completing a standardized test. Sampling involves the selection of students, the sample size and its determination, and the frequency of data collection. As an alternative, there might be an assessment week each academic year or term, during which all students complete the scenarios. If scenarios are used, they might take different forms (see the section of the chapter on reliability).

[a]University of Massachusetts, Amherst, W.E.B. Du Bois Library, "UMass Amherst Learning Commons," accessed January 19, 2010, http://www.umass.edu/learningcommons/.

[b]See, for instance, Sudip Bhattacharjee and Lewis Shaw, "Enhancing Skills through Technology: A Project for Advanced Accounting Students," in *An Action Plan for Outcomes Assessment in Your Library*, ed. Peter Hernon and Robert E. Dugan, 170–82 (Chicago: American Library Association, 2002).

[c]Kathleen Dunn, "Assessing Information Literacy Skills in the California State University: A Progress Report," *The Journal of Academic Librarianship* 28, nos. 1–2 (January–March 2002): 28. Dunn discusses the use of the scenarios in the context of achieving external validity.

Figure 5.4. Decision Points for Sample Topics

the site to find information. In a review of the literature, they may identify the number of individuals usually tested, how to attract them, the amount of time observation takes, whether or not incentives are required, and when during the semester they should request participation. In shaping their decisions, they may review study objectives and decide whether or not to seek generalization to a population. If so, do they study a small population or use a type of probability sampling to draw a representative sample? As an alternative, they might use a nonprobability sample, as usability studies tend to do.

As evaluators make decisions about research design, they work on the methodology and explain which one(s) to use and the process of data collection, and match study questions to problem statement *direction* and the objectives. Realizing that data quality applies to the entire procedures section, they discuss training of the observers, inter-score reliability, and the pre-test (covering the questions to be asked and the process of data collection).

CONCLUDING THOUGHTS

When evaluators engage in assessment, they might apply a type of experimental design and probability sampling to generalize across sections of a course or a program of study. When libraries develop a culture of evidence-based evaluation and assessment and use data for service improvement and accountability, they need to abandon the view of data collection as merely supporting preexisting beliefs and biases. They need objectively gathered data that adhere to basic principles of social science research, especially when they examine the impact (outcomes) of programs and services, and that demonstrate the difference that library programs, collections, and services truly make within an institutional or program context.

NOTES

*Parts of this chapter are derived from Chapter 5, "Evaluation Designs and Data Collection Techniques," and Chapter 6, "Sampling," in *Evaluation and Library Decision Making*, ed. Peter Hernon and Charles R. McClure (Norwood, NJ: Ablex, 1990); U.S. General Accounting Office, Program Evaluation and Methodology Division, *Case Study Evaluations*, Transfer Paper 10.1.9 (Washington, DC: General Accounting Office, 1990).

1. The confidence level is an arbitrarily chosen probability that is used to decide whether a given sample is likely to have come from a given population. The most commonly used levels are .05 and .01. The .05 level corresponds to the .95 level of confidence, and the .01 is the same as the .99 level of confidence. By setting the level at .05, the findings do not support the null hypothesis if the probability is more than .05; the probability level is reported as $p < .05$, with p standing for probability and the symbol < meaning "less than"; the symbol > means "more than."

Evaluators select the confidence level prior to data collection after they have reviewed the consequences of making a Type I error (not supporting a true null hypothesis) or a Type II error (supporting a false null hypothesis as true). The final determination also reflects the purpose of data collection (e.g., publication) and the margin of error that evaluators are willing to accept.

2. For a discussion of random assignment and experimental design, see U.S. Government Accountability Office, *Program Evaluation: A Variety of Rigorous Methods Can Help Identify Effective Interventions*, GAO-10-30 (Washington, DC: Government Accountability Office, 2009), accessed January 11, 2010, http://www.gao.gov.

3. Lynn S. Connaway and Ronald R. Powell, *Basic Research Methods for Librarians* (Westport, CT: Libraries Unlimited, 2010), 125–26.

4. Ibid., 128–32. See also Robert Swisher and Charles R. McClure, *Research for Decision Making Methods for Librarians* (Chicago: American Library Association, 1984), 103–28. Searching "Determining Sample Size Statistics" on various search engines will also produce relevant results; however, be sure to determine the credibility of the Web page and Web site.

5. Joanne G. Marshall, *An Introduction to Research Methods for Health Sciences Librarians* (Chicago: Medical Library Association, Courses for Continuing Education, 1989), 17. See also Connaway and Powell, *Basic Research Methods for Librarians*.

6. Lee J. Cronback, "Test Validation," in *Educational Measurement*, ed. Robert L. Thorndike, 447 (Washington, DC: American Council for Education, 1971).

7. Carol H. Weiss, *Evaluation Research: Methods for Assessing Program Effectiveness* (Englewood Cliffs, NJ: Prentice-Hall, 1972), 65.

8. Ibid.

Chapter 6

Getting Engaged in Evidence Gathering and Managerial Use

As discussed in chapter 1, libraries use assessment studies and data to aid their decision-making efforts related to the improvement of services and programs and meeting outside standards and requirements (e.g., those set by accreditation organizations). They apply the evaluation process to gather and analyze data that indicate how well their programs and services align in support of the stated organizational and institutional missions, goals, and objectives. Assessment and evaluation support organizational and institutional accountability and demonstrate a library's value to numerous and diverse stakeholders.

ASSESSMENT AND EVALUATION

Implementation of a library's assessment plan involves the selection of appropriate assessment metrics or research problems, then gathering and analyzing relevant assessment data. The plan indicates, for instance, when and how the assessment will take place, how the study will be conducted, and who will collect and analyze the data. Implementation of either assessment or evaluation research should not overwhelm a library's resources (e.g., funding, time, and the staff) and the current capabilities of the staff.

What Is Being Assessed and Evaluated

As part of assessment, academic libraries most often concentrate on the identification of the extent of students' use and the degree to which such use leads to academic growth and success. A 1999 study discovered eight areas of interest for library assessment studies:

user satisfaction, market penetration, ease and breadth of access, library impact on teaching and learning, library impact on research, the cost-effectiveness of library operations and services, library facilities and space, and organizational capacity.[1] Some of these areas actually relate to evaluation, not to assessment, as some stakeholders view assessment in terms of outputs and outcomes that reflect the library's impact on student learning. A later study found that more than 80 percent of the library respondents assess areas that directly affect their users' experience with the library: the Web site, the online public access catalog (OPAC); the facilities; reference services; and the collections and how they are acquired, used, and managed. Those library functions examined less often were the nonpublic operations of finance, human resources, administration, staff development, information technology infrastructure, and preservation.[2] However, again the tendency is to confuse assessment and evaluation.[3]

A major difference between assessment and evaluation is whether librarians in cooperation with faculty and perhaps others want to determine the impact of their services and programs; if students and others improved their knowledge, abilities, and skills over time due to their exposure to library instruction; and if students underwent a change in mindset. Measuring user satisfaction involves both assessment and evaluation. When assessment standards call for a determination of satisfaction, it becomes an output. Libraries most often approach satisfaction, however, as part of evaluation. Either way, customer satisfaction is important for libraries to monitor and meet (or exceed), as it encompasses the entire infrastructure: satisfaction with collections, facilities, staff, and technology.

An academic library's contributions to student learning are the most frequently discussed aspects of assessment in the literature of library and information science. In support of student learning, a library can identify a set of desired information skills and abilities about which to monitor improvement and the means of delivering them (e.g., synchronous instruction and asynchronous online tutorials). In addition, a library's assessable contribution to student learning may include a demonstration of

- student achievement of learning outcomes,

- the educational impact of instruction services,

- the reach and quality of library instruction (beyond the course level and integrated into programs and all institutional courses),

- the quality of library instruction, and

- the integration of library and information skills instruction throughout the curriculum.

A comprehensive type of evaluation focuses on the internal performance of the organization and staff. The purpose of an organizational evaluation is to identify important issues related to understanding the mission and goals of the organization and the organization's culture, climate, and values. Furthermore, such evaluation determines how goals are set, communicated, and achieved, thereby revealing the barriers to the successful use of libraries. The goal is to develop a plan that addresses issues and problems so that the organization becomes more efficient, streamlined, productive, and service oriented.

Organizational issues that might be examined include the following:

- staff (professional and support staff expertise in meeting current and projected program and service requirements, and the capability of in-service training)

- communication and cooperation (communication across the campus, and working relationships between the library and other institutional units)

- administration (effective use of library resources, a standing library advisory committee, and adequate provision of services to distance learners)

- budget (support appropriate to accomplish library objectives, the reasonable expectations of library users, and appropriate levels of staffing)[4]

Conducting an Assessment Study

Based on the library's assessment plan, conducting an assessment study includes collecting, analyzing, interpreting, and reporting data collected. An evaluation study, on the other hand, focuses on the accomplishment of the goals and objectives specified in the strategic plan. A library must decide what will be assessed; when the assessment will occur; and if it will be a single event, ongoing, or periodic. If the assessment study relates to student learning, the level of assessment (course, program, or institution) must also be resolved before proceeding. A library must also determine if the study will be formative or summative, whether any metrics will be gathered, whether the means of data collection will be direct or indirect, and whether the evidence gathered will be qualitative or quantitative. Direct methods of assessing student learning are performance based and focus on the actual work that students produce, while indirect methods ascertain the perceived extent or value of learning experiences. Indirect methods provide information that may enrich or illuminate aspects of what the direct methods suggest about students' academic achievement.

The tendency is to rely on indirect methods of data collection (e.g., those related to use of surveys that produce self-reports on learning). Still, there are ways to complement data collection that occurs through the application of the research process and to draw inferences. Statistics, for instance, might be gathered from the counts and reports available from the library's integrated library system. Transaction logs are also a useful tool for gathering counts, including frequency, date, time, and even by whom (e.g., undergraduate student, faculty) and from where (e.g., Internet Protocol [IP] address). Data may be compiled using a statistical data information system (SDIS), also known as a management information system, which is briefly discussed elsewhere in this chapter. Both the SDIS and the other methods discussed here, however, focus on outputs, those that stakeholders might appreciate.

Student Learning Outcomes

Developing an assessment plan (see chapter 1) involves designing learning objectives and outcomes that align with the institution's stated educational mission, often stated as general education objectives, and that support program or departmental education goals and course learning objectives. Aligning program or departmental outcomes and objectives can also help to customize library instruction to address specific disciplinary information needs and requirements.

Student learning outcomes should be *student focused*, which means that they center on what students learn rather than merely on what instructors impart; learning outcomes focus on the learning resulting from the activity rather than the activity itself. Such outcome statements articulate what students should know, understand, believe, and be able to do as a result of their course experience. Academic libraries often limit their involvement in outcomes assessment to information literacy and its multiple facets. The level of assessment might be the individual student, a course, a program, a department, or the institution. Course-level assessment ascertains how well students mastered learning outcomes associated with specific course learning objectives and outcomes. Course outcomes that are well aligned with program outcomes can be generalized to the program level. Assessment activities at the department level determine the degree to which groups of students master the materials presented in required and elective courses. Institution-level assessment allows the campus to see how well learning in the general education program generalizes to learning throughout the institution.

After determining the level at which assessment will occur and whether to use an experimental design, and settling on study objectives, another decision involves the selection of the method(s) of evidence gathering and to find, develop, or modify appropriate instrument(s). Direct methods may include capstone experiences and the use of faculty-developed scoring rubrics to rate student work products included in portfolios; standardized or locally developed tests; certification and licensure examinations; scenarios; essay questions that are blind scored by faculty across the department, division, school, or college; internal and external juried reviews of comprehensive senior projects; or external evaluation of performance during internships based on stated program objectives.

Indirect methods, on the other hand, include surveys of alumni, employers, or student perceptions of their own learning; the examination of graduate student publications, fellowships, and post-doctorates; enrollment trends/transcript analyses; and exit interviews of graduates. There might also be an effort to collect data related to student outcomes (e.g., persistence, retention, transfer, graduation rates and the length of time to degree, and job placement).

Other methods to measure student learning directly and indirectly include the following:

- A review panel to rate the quality of papers submitted by students. This may include student peer review and faculty members from other departments.

- A departmental comprehensive examination. The advantage of a departmental examination is that the curriculum for that department will not be properly assessed if a national examination is used.

- The professional viewpoint, which attempts to assess the outcomes of a college education that are relevant to a profession or professional school. Assessment tools include, for instance, the Law School Admission Test (LSAT) and Medical College Admission Test (MCAT).

- Inviting both external evaluators and internal interdisciplinary teams of readers to assess capstone projects, thereby maximizing the credibility and utility of assessment results for departmental faculty.

- An internally developed, two-part information literacy competency examination that includes multiple choice questions and contains questions requiring students to access, find, evaluate, and document information resources appropriate for academic research.[5]

- An externally developed testing program, such as those offered by the Educational Testing Service (ETS, http://www.ets.org/), that uses scenarios and problems instead of multiple-choice methods to measure students' capabilities to define, access, manage, integrate, evaluate, create, and communicate information in a technological environment. Students must demonstrate their knowledge as they interactively solve real-world academic or workplace problems.[6]

- Student journal entries or diaries that document the research processes they used.[7]

Most institutions and their libraries depend on traditional methods of pre- and post-tests, undergraduate surveys, or longitudinal surveys to measure the skills of students in selected academic departments. Tests are used to gather information on the status of knowledge or the change in status of knowledge over time. There are three basic types of tests. *Norm-referenced tests* indicate how the test-taker performs against a reference group or normative population. *Criterion-referenced assessments* reflect the extent to which important skills have been mastered, but they are not as useful as norm-referenced tests in gauging the test subjects' standing relative to their peers. A variant on the criterion-referenced approach is *proficiency testing*, which shows the level of skill attainment, but addresses standards of performance at varying levels of proficiency, typically using a point scale ranging from *below basic* to *advanced* performance. Tests provide objective evidence on what test-takers know and can do, and tests can be constructed to match a given curriculum or set of skills. They can be scored in a straightforward manner and are credible indicator of learning.[8]

Although various response options (e.g., multiple choice or true/false) can be used to establish benchmarks of knowledge or to provide a snapshot of performance at a certain point in a student's academic career, they are not necessarily linked to performance objectives and do not demonstrate how well students have actually learned the defined information literacy skills to find, evaluate, use, and apply information to meet a specific need.[9] As a result, it is important to have more than one method of assessment, if possible. Cecilia López finds that most department/discipline-specific assessment programs use multiple methods, at least one of which is a direct method (e.g., a standardized or faculty-developed comprehensive examination or a capstone course as the culminating experience of the major or degree program) and one of which is an indirect method (e.g., a senior, alumni, and/or employer survey).[10]

An example of an academic library using multiple methods is the Education and Instruction Group at George Washington University's Gelman Library, which relies on the following:

- Library Research Attitudinal Pre- and Post-Test, which asks students to rate their current research skills and answer behavioral questions while they engage in an activity.

- Observational Assessment Form, which instruction librarians use to observe student research behavior during hands-on practice in an electronic classroom.

- Faculty Assessment Survey, an end-of-semester form completed by faculty members after all student assignments, papers, and projects are submitted. It asks faculty members to reflect on and document changes in the quality of research and variety of sources that appear in student work as well as to reflect on their own learning when they received library instruction.

- Note Card Worksheet, which accompanies a One-Minute Note Card evaluation. Instruction librarians pass out and collect note cards on which students jot down three things learned during the session, as well as one thing that is still unclear. Afterward a worksheet is used to synthesize the feedback from all one-minute note cards of an entire class. Ideally, instruction librarians document substantial repetition in the learning outcomes and what students report learning.[11]

Megan Oakleaf cautions users of internally or externally developed fixed-choice tests. She finds that the popular fixed-choice information literacy tests (multiple-choice, matching, or true/false) have limitations: they do not assess higher-level thinking skills and do not provide an authentic assessment of student learning. These tests typically create an artificial situation that does not really test how learners react in a real-world situation. Instead, librarians may use a performance assessment approach such as the ETS *iCritical Thinking*™ (http://www.ets.org/icriticalthinking/about), which replaced the ETS iSkills test, or they may develop their own performance assessment procedure based on the observation of student behavior or an examination of student work samples. These *performance assessments* reinforce the concept that what students learn is transferable outside the classroom.[12]

In the past decade technology has been increasingly available and applied to measure student learning outcomes. One applied technology is classroom response systems or "clickers." Librarians use them to gather student demographic information (e.g., first time visiting the library) as well as for students to use to respond to projected test questions that can be compiled for analysis as a learning outcome metric. Another technology includes synchronous and asynchronous course management systems (CMS), which frame the mechanics of a course (e.g., an online container for the course syllabus, course announcements, as well as student chat sessions) and can facilitate rich data analysis. The instructor critiques student work in the developmental stage or when it is submitted as a final product; that same work may also be critiqued by a peer audience of students analyzing each others' work. In addition, a CMS is useful for student reflective journaling, an indirect method involving student self-assessment of learning. Simultaneously, the instructor assesses students' depth of understanding and decision-making processes, both in terms of identifying issues to share as well as describing their own responses and actions. The instructor can also analyze students' progress over the duration of a semester or longer.[13]

The application of rubrics to student learning outcomes is increasingly popular. A rubric is a descriptive scoring guide that articulates, in writing, the various criteria and standards in a list or chart used to evaluate or grade completed student assignments. A rubric translates informed professional judgment into numeric or category (e.g., *meets expectations* or *below expectations*) ratings on a scale, and two or more reviewers may review the same product or behavior. Assessments using well-designed rubrics are likely to be reliable, valid, and actionable, and can be helpful when assessing complex products or behaviors efficiently.[14]

Table 6.1 provides a rubric for information literacy. A reviewer or a group of reviewers could apply the rubric to assess students' skills in evaluating information resources critically. Rubric users could agree on assigning numeric or grade ratings for each of the columns and could apply weights to the skills assessed. The result is a numeric or grade rating for each student assessed. If reviewers consistently apply the rubric, the ratings or grades are comparable between individuals and could be aggregated for a cohort summation, and the aggregated sum is comparable among cohorts.

Applying the information gained through assessment research enables librarians and others to gauge progress toward meeting stated educational objectives, compare the results to institutional or inter-institutional standards and benchmarks, improve the content and pedagogy at the course and program levels, and relate the insights gained to the planning process.[15] As Chris A. Portmann and Adrienne J. Roush state:

> The effects of library instruction approach can be classified as summative assessment. That is, this approach provides data analysis intended to summarize or document student learning as the result of exposure to library instruction. However, summative findings can be used to evaluate the effectiveness of library instruction and in the end serve as a perspective for shaping future instruction: formative assessment. When used in this way, the effects of library instruction approach yield more meaningful findings than the student satisfaction approach. [16]

As a result of the work done on student learning outcomes and information literacy, some best practices have emerged. First, an important part of information literacy program planning is ensuring integration of findings with academic and other campus partners.[17] Second, limiting instruction to two or three learning objectives per session is best.[18] Third, assessment efforts produce the most useful results if skills are measured through performance-based demonstrations, if both the instruction and the assessment programs are based on clearly stated objectives, and if students have opportunities to practice skills before they are assessed.[19] Fourth, accreditation practice and procedures underscore the need for multiple assessment gathering and reporting strategies. Fifth, student learning should include both direct and indirect methods, and assessment findings should be compared (triangulated) with baseline data, benchmarked data, or data gathered over time. Sixth, the assessment of library learning outcomes should occur in a structured fashion whereby results are used to document learning and shape service, pedagogy, and policy.

Table 6.1. Students Will Evaluate Information Sources (Outcome)

Objective 4: Evaluate information and information sources critically

Skills	Below Expectations	Meet Expectations	Exceed Expectations
4.1: summarize the main ideas to be extracted from the information gathered	- is unaware of the criteria that may be used to judge information quality	- makes judgments about information to keep and discard - can judge relevance	- multiple and diverse sources of information and viewpoints of information are compared and evaluated
4.2: determine the scope, audience, purpose (e.g., government; business; individual) and currency of the information found in any source	- little effort is made to examine and thereby judge the information retrieved	- checks dates for information found - understands that not all information is trustworthy	- can use specific criteria to discern objectivity/fact from bias/propaganda - can distinguish gradations of relevancy
4.3: determine the authority, credibility (e.g., sources cited), accuracy, reliability (e.g., scholarly or popular), and objectivity of sources	- evaluation was merely an assertion of credibility without evidence to support claim - cannot judge relevance - accepts all information found - does not check for timeliness of information	- employs evaluation strategies to determine credibility - analyzes information from various sources to assess accuracy, authority, and timeliness	- selects the most up-to-date information depending upon topic - recognizes content bias and provides other research to balance that bias
4.4: distinguish point of view (e.g., ideological positions, assumptions, prejudices, biases), claims being advanced (including deceptions or manipulations), and forms of substantiation being used	- shows no evidence of source evaluation - cannot distinguish between facts and opinions	- examines and compares information from various sources to evaluate reliability, validity and timeliness, authority, and point of view or bias - distinguishes between facts and opinions	- analyzes quality information from various sources to assess accuracy, authority, and timeliness
4.5: analyze the relevance of information against the information need		- analyzes resources and makes conscious decisions about how each resource supports the development of the topic	- recognizes prejudice, deception, or manipulation

The Use of the Evidence Gathered

The purpose of assessment is to influence managerial processes, including budget and performance review cycles, vendor contract renewals, reorganizations and team building, strategic and facilities planning, technology/systems conversions, project management, and accreditation.[20] When librarians were asked about the impact that assessment evidence had on their organizations, the most frequently mentioned change was to the library's Web site and/or OPAC, followed by changes in collection (print to electronic), hours, and staff. Other areas included aspects of customer service, access services, instruction and outreach, and reference services.[21] Interestingly, there was no change in learning content and how it is conveyed.

Assessment data are frequently applied to staff training. In a survey of members of the Association of Research Libraries (ARL) conducted in mid-2007, respondents reported that library staff wanted hands-on training in the basics of assessment as well as training on specific tools and methods. Fewer than 17 percent of respondents agreed that "staff development in assessment is adequate."[22] In addition to adequate staff training, Sarah M. Pritchard has found that factors for undertaking a successful assessment include the availability of technical support and systems; internal and external communications; focusing on processes and services, not individuals; choosing the right metrics; having a realistic scope and schedules; gaining support from senior leadership; involving stakeholders in planning; and using the results so that both library staff and users see the changes.[23]

EVALUATION

Evaluation is a broader concept than assessment because it considers all aspects of a program or service, including resources, staffing, organization, operations, and efficiency. The results from an evaluation study are also used to compare data to a standard and to judge worth or quality. Once the goals and objectives of a program or service have been identified, libraries specify the major activities or processes they will undertake to accomplish them. One component of measuring the effectiveness of a program or service is to determine whether activities were actually implemented as planned. If activities were not implemented as planned, there is no reason to believe that they produced the desired results, namely that they accomplished stated objectives.[24]

Evaluation provides evidence needed for decision making or planning to address the performance of stakeholders or questions of effectiveness, efficiency, and impact. It is also possible to examine organizational performance, make comparisons to standards or benchmarks, and calculate value creation. A selected list of library programs, services, and operations that provide opportunities for evaluation includes

- collection development (met/did not meet specified goals);

- collections (digital libraries, the value of a journal, database usage, print book versus electronic book usage, status of the physical collection [age and physical shape, e.g., worn; needs binding; needs preservation]);

- customer service (e.g., library use/nonuse, customer expectations, hours open, signage, cleanliness of the facility, and customer use);

- facilities (the alignment of library space with user needs and expectations);

- ILL (turnaround time, fill rate, costs, requested items versus owned items, and document delivery, which is not always the role of ILL);

- internal library operations (e.g. effectiveness, efficiency, and responsiveness);

- networks (resource sharing and shared services such as cataloging);

- online library services (integrated library system, e.g., extent the system performs to specifications as outlined in the original contract, OPAC as a discovery tool, electronic reserves usage, and use and usability of library Web site);

- outsourced library services (e.g., deliverables of contracted staff training)

- public service points (evaluate the merger of two public service points [reference and circulation] to determined if the merger met expectations);

- reference services (e.g., the extent of reference desk use compared to the use of virtual reference; the nature of queries posed and the time needed to respond);

- staff (diversity, character of organizational structure [flat versus tall; team versus hierarchy]);

- library instruction (seating adequacy, appropriateness of pedagogical methods, number of students reached, and faculty–librarian relationships);

- student learning (achievement of learning outcomes, individual student progress on questions posed, and student demonstration of information literacy skills);

- technical services (time, costs, workflow, quality, accuracy);

- technologies (equipment use);

- workflows (productivity and effectiveness); and

- other (marketing strategies and public relations, advocacy, external collaboration efforts, effectiveness of the library's planning processes and existing plans, and the usefulness of library standards for benchmarking).

Designing the Evaluation Approach

Before undertaking an evaluation study, it is best to choose the program or service to evaluate. Then, based on the resources available (e.g., staff time), the library often limits the study to selected activities of that program or service. Identifying which user groups will be included in the study is another step in determining the scope of the evaluation. Based on these decisions, the library considers who is indirectly affected by the service (i.e., other stakeholders) and whether outputs and outcomes will be addressed.[25] Next, the library chooses an evaluation methodology. From the perspective of the library, there are different methods for evaluating programs, services, and operations. These might include a quantitative evaluation and the counting of numerical variables. One example of quantitative evaluation is input measurement, which includes the number of volumes held, the amount of money remaining in the budget, and the number of staff members. Another example is output measurement, which examines the use of facilities and equipment, the circulation of materials, document delivery time, reference service use, subject search success, and the availability of materials. Use is portrayed simply and one-dimensionally. Customer satisfaction can also be a quantitative measure. By themselves, these counts are merely measurements and do not really reflect quality, because they do not usually demonstrate a relationship between a program or service and its impact.[26] A library's evaluation of its quality requires interpretation of these measures using judgments in the context of the relationship of inputs or outputs, meeting goals, or changing lives.

Programs and services are established to meet one or more specific goals, which are often described in planning documents. *Program evaluation*, also referred to as goals-based evaluation, involves the collection of evidence to determine if programs have been implemented and/or are operating according to expectations. Program or goals-based evaluation involves the collection of evidence about the extent to which a program meets its goals and objectives, while performance metrics portray project activities, services delivered, and the products of those services.

Process evaluation is designed to understand and/or closely examine the processes in a program, service, or function, and it is more often used to evaluate the efficiency of internal work processes and procedures than the products of those activities. A process evaluation answers questions about program effort, identifies processes or procedures used to carry out the functions of the program, and addresses program operation and performance. A process evaluation tries to answer the following questions:

- What is required of staff in order to deliver the program or service?

- How well is the staff trained in the delivery of the program or service?

- What do users see as the strengths of the program or service?

- What does the staff see as strengths of the service or program?

- What do staff and/or users recommend as service or program improvements?[27]

A process evaluation might be concerned with the activities of an acquisitions department and how materials are acquired and prepared for shelving; the focus is not on how many books are ultimately used, but on how efficiently and accurately they were made available for use. In an academic library, process indicators might relate to staff training and development, knowledge of the curriculum, and participation in assignments and grading. Process evaluation is also useful for learning how a program or service operates so that it can be replicated elsewhere.

Outcomes are benefits to users from participation in the program and are often stated in terms of enhanced learning (knowledge, perceptions/attitudes, or skills) or conditions (e.g., increased literacy skills or self-sufficiency in finding information). *Outcomes-based evaluation* determines the impact of the library's programs and services on the users and how those impacts support the institution's stated mission. Questions might include the following:

- Has the program or service been developed in response to an identified need?

- Is impact on the end user a major goal of the project?

- Are those providing the program or service concerned more with the impact than with the amount of use of that program or service?

- Are those providing the program or service more concerned with the impact on the end user than with internal library operations?

- Are those providing the program or service concerned more with effectiveness or efficiency?

- Are those providing the program or service focused more on benefits to users than on their satisfaction?[28]

Evaluation might involve the use of standards and benchmarks. *Standards* refer to a set of guidelines or recommended practices, developed by a group of experts, which serve as a model for good library service. General types of standards include technical standards (e.g., cataloging codes), performance standards, input and output metrics, and qualitative and quantitative standards. *Benchmarking* uses standards to which internal operations can be evaluated and compared. The data from performance benchmarking are usually derived from analyses of organizational processes and procedures. Benchmarking helps to establish best practices, identify changes needed to improve services, evaluate user opinions and information needs, identify trends, exchange ideas, and develop staff. Candidates for benchmarking include the services or products of an organization, internal work processes, internal support functions, and organizational performance and strategy.

A useful framework for organizing an evaluation study design is a logic model, which visually represents the inputs, activities, outputs, and outcomes of a program and proposes the causal links among these entities. Having a framework helps to focus the study on the evaluative information or data needed (e.g., identifying customers and those indirectly affected by the service or program and the extent to which an objective for a planned program or service has been reached [goal-based evaluation]). Project, program, or service inputs are the various funding sources and resources that support that project, program, or service. The inputs and activities—the services, materials, and actions that are the focus of that project, program, or service—produce outputs, usually something that can be counted. It may also be possible to capture data concerning short-term impacts, the immediate changes as a result of the library implementing the activities. Long-term outcomes are the broader and more enduring impacts on the system.

Using the Findings

The findings support accountability; communicate the library's efficiency, what the library does, and how well—its value and effectiveness—to stakeholders; and promote its ongoing efforts to secure and maintain funding as well as find allies willing to advocate on behalf of the library. Depending on the study, the findings may be useful for benchmarking against performance standards and, if cost-based, for cost analysis and possibly as return on investment (ROI). The evaluation may become a case study if the report is constructed to inform others about the methodology, process, and findings.

Benchmarking

A benchmark is a point of reference against which something may be measured. Internally, benchmarking may be applied to evaluate services against performance standards. As an example, a library may conduct a quantitative study of internal processes concerning ILL, with the focus of the evaluation on the turnaround time for filling a user request via ILL. The performance standard that the library might establish is a two-day processing time for a user-requested monograph. The study, let us assume, found that it took an average of seven days to turn the user request into a loan request sent to another library. A manager may now use this benchmark to review and improve the ILL process in order to close the gap between the benchmark and the standard. Externally, with the collaboration of other libraries, benchmarking to similar services handled elsewhere identifies best practices. In this instance, the library could learn how other libraries comply with the performance standard of two-day turnaround for a monograph via ILL. A challenge of benchmarking is to clearly define the start and stop of the comparable process; for example, is "turnaround time" a measure of the library's internal processing of a request or the duration of time the user waits to receive the item sought?

Case Studies

The results reported in case studies are useful for their potential to be replicated in other libraries and for the applied methodologies and findings that could become best practices. Three examples follow. First, Leanne M. VandeCreek studied a university library's e-mail reference service through an electronic survey of users of the service. Six of the seven questions were closed-ended (multiple choice), solicited information about use of the service and satisfaction with the answer(s) received and response time, and produced an overall rating of the service. The seventh item was open-ended and encouraged respondents to offer positive or negative feedback or any suggestions they might have for improving the service. Survey results informed the library's decision to select and purchase chat software, and the pilot chat reference program began its planning phase. As a best practice, the author advises other libraries to involve customers in the planning stages before a new system or service is designed and implemented. In this specific instance, asking users how they see reference services, what they want from reference staff and collections, how they want reference information delivered, and how to best market reference services provided insights that ultimately saved the library time and expense.[29]

Second, Elizabeth Henry, Rachel Longstaff, and Doris Van Kampen examined how a library critically analyzes its collection in order to determine how well it supports the mission of the university. An inventory of the existing collection indicated that the bibliographic records analyzed were in the OCLC system. The library then contracted with OCLC to use its WorldCat Collection Analysis tool. The evaluation study reviewed total holdings, ILL statistics, and publication dates; compared e-book and print book collections; examined the print collection using *Books for College Libraries* and *Choice Outstanding Academic Titles*; and compared the print collection to the holdings of selected peer institutions. As a result of the data collected, it was possible to illustrate the value of the library's print and e-book collections and to demonstrate strengths, weaknesses, and imbalances in the overall collection. The analysis also revealed that the print collection was aging; somewhat unbalanced; and, in some disciplines, inadequate. Furthermore, the collection development policy needed to be updated. By using peer group comparisons, it became clear that some of the problems with the collection were widespread among comparable libraries and are not unique to this library. The peer group analyses showed that the average age of most collections was thirty to forty years, and that the titles were purchased at a time when library budgets were larger and focused primarily on print materials. The library found that OCLC's WorldCat Collection Analysis was an excellent tool for learning how to perform collection analysis and that it provided accurate data that graphically illustrate the library's holdings by subject. In addition, the analysis tool revealed collection strengths, weaknesses, uniqueness, overlap, source age, and format. As a best practice, the library found that ensuring the inclusion of its e-book holdings in OCLC was critical to a thorough analysis of the collection.[30] Libraries with aggregated e-book collections may not report title-by-title bibliographic information to OCLC.

Finally, Merrill Stein and others describe a multiple-methods approach to examining and enhancing the quality of walk-in service points at a university library. The study looked at public service delivery areas to ensure that the services provided effectively met the needs of library users in ways that are suitable and accessible to them and explored whether the physical layout of the public service delivery areas is conducive to providing the services that the community needs and desires effectively and efficiently. This study used nine data collection tools:

1. Quality walk: The study team began thirty yards outside the library main entrance and walked into and through the library, visiting each service point. Each team member took a customer perspective and jotted down possible improvements.

2. Suggestions from staff: These were gathered from staff, both in person and through e-mail, throughout the process.

3. Focus group interviews: A facilitator conducted three focus group interviews to discuss work process improvement and to explore the vision, mission, values, goals, leadership, and strategic direction.

4. Survey data: Using a convenience sample, customers were asked to complete a survey while in the library.

5. Transactional data: Circulation and library usage statistics were collected. In addition, a database contained the verbatim questions asked of library staff, the staff member's responses, information on when and where the question was asked, and how long it took to answer the question at service delivery points.

6. Mystery shopping: Nine secret shoppers were given written assignments to complete four to five specific tasks within a two-hour time period, such as locating reserve material, accessing a book through ILL, or finding and photocopying a journal article. Each secret shopper completed a standardized form immediately upon completion of each task. The form included items such as, "If you needed help, where did you find it? (What service point?)"; "How helpful was the guidance you received?"; "What, if any, problems did you experience?"; and "What made your experience easier?"

7. Direct observation using activity mapping: Eight different service points were identified. Nine trained observers used standardized forms to record the number of customers at these service points as well as the number of library staff at each service point. The data were analyzed and use patterns graphically displayed.

8. Benchmarking/site visits/best practices: Library staff on the study team visited six libraries, observed operations, and talked with colleagues. In addition, a call for best practices was disseminated on a librarian discussion list. A third function was to identify best practices via a literature review that looked for noteworthy models.

9. Scenario analysis: The study team held two all-day sessions, analyzed data, and reviewed recommendations. The team also created a set of scenarios for providing services and weighted the strengths and limitations of each scenario. The scenarios embodied best practices and included factors such as a print center, bolder signage, and a one-stop shopping service model.

This study consumed considerable resources, especially in the use of direct observation and activity mapping; getting expertise in instrument design, customized computer programming, and statistical analysis; and the amount of time spent in data collection. Offering advice for libraries wanting to replicate the study, the authors project that the quality walk, suggestions from staff, scenario analysis, and customer survey are within the capability of most libraries.[31]

Costs and Values

Libraries often use evaluation studies to help determine, examine, and understand costs, and they have always collected cost data as an input (budget) and an output (expenditure). In response to increasing demands for accountability, they are also analyzing costs in relation to the benefits and values of the services and programs provided and are sharing the information with their various stakeholders. Two evaluative processes include benchmarking and valuation through cost analysis and ROI.

As discussed previously, one application of benchmarking is as a measuring device to evaluate performance against a standard. Two evaluative benchmarks are the balanced scorecard and data envelope analysis. The *balanced scorecard* is a strategic planning and management system that aligns business activities with the vision and strategy of an organization, improves internal and external communications, and monitors organization performance in relationship to strategic goals. This framework for performance measurement adds strategic, nonfinancial performance metrics to traditional financial metrics, and it provides managers with a *balanced* view of organizational performance.

The balanced scorecard, which is ideal for the evaluation of strategic plans, can be used to demonstrate accountability by collecting and comparing performance information to internally developed objectives serving as standards.[32] From the perspective of a library, G. Stevenson Smith explains the four performance objectives covered in the balanced scorecard:

1. **Financial:** Targets ensure the library is financially viable. Evaluators may include government monies received, the number of customers, any increase in budget funding from the previous year, the total cost of operations and the number of customers, and total cost of operations and the total number of books in the collection.

2. **Customer:** Metrics of service quality and customer satisfaction. Evaluators may include the number and trend of customers using the library, satisfaction index scores based on a customer survey, the number and trend of complaints, and the number and trend of overdue books.

3. **Internal processes:** Performance metrics. Evaluators may include administrative cost and the total appropriation, new books and the total collection, dollars spent on new technology, and administrative cost per employee.

4. **Learning and growth of staff:** Employees must be adequately trained and skilled. Evaluators may include the number of hours of technology training per employee, satisfaction index scores on an employee work survey, the number of part-time employees and the total employees, and employee turnover rate.[33]

Matthews converts the four objectives into five objectives. At the bottom of his scorecard, the financial perspective addresses what financial resources are required to be successful. The core values are budget, value, and accountability, and the performance metrics are inputs. Upward is the organizational readiness perspective, which deals with customer satisfaction and service quality, and the capability of staff and the infrastructure to deliver services. The core values are staff skills, innovation, and the availability and reliability of tools and how these relate to the library's infrastructure. The performance metrics are inputs, process, and outputs. At the third level are two side-by-side perspectives: information resources and internal process. The information resources perspective includes print and electronic collections, selected quality Web links, ILL, and document delivery. This perspective examines whether the information resources provided satisfy customer expectations. Its core values are accessibility, quality, depth, programs, and staff training. The goal of the internal process perspective is to understand the processes and activities critical to enabling the library to meet the needs and satisfy the expectations of its customers and to add value that is visible to the customers. This perspective usually includes costs, quality, throughput, productivity, and time issues.

Staff use the available tools provided by the financial perspective in an efficient manner (internal process perspective) to provide access to collections (information resources perspective). The combination of organizational readiness, information resources, and efficient internal processes delivers a mix of products and services upward to the top of the balanced scorecard, which is the customer perspective. The customer perspective addresses what the library and its services will resemble to achieve the stated vision. The core values are purpose, service, and quality.[34]

Data envelopment analysis (DEA), the other evaluation benchmark, measures the relative efficiencies of organizations with multiple inputs and outputs as opposed to other techniques (e.g., ratio or regression analysis). Individual organizations, teams, or units are called decision-making units (DMUs). The inputs or outputs that the DMUs control are called standard or discretionary variables (e.g., total circulation, reference transactions, library visits, interlibrary loans, online searching, and the provision of information). Nondiscretionary variables (e.g., population density, area size, resident population, nonresidential borrowers, and socioeconomic indices) are beyond the control of library administration.[35] The basic purpose of DEA is to identify the efficient frontier (line on a graph) in some comparative set of DMUs. All units on the line presumably operate at 100 percent efficiency. A unit is evaluated by comparing its performance with the best performing units of the sample. DEA, therefore, provides an efficiency score for each inefficient unit and a benchmark set of efficient units.[36]

Costs and usage are important input and output metrics, but are unfortunately inadequate evaluative metrics when libraries are increasingly expected to demonstrate their impact on or value to users and to provide that information to the various stakeholders. Librarians can discover the costs for implementing a service or program as well as determining the amount of use. Through benchmarking, they can learn if the program or service performs as planned. These metrics, however, do not inform library decision makers or stakeholders about the impact of the service or program on users and the value that they place on that program or service.

There are various approaches to measure library value. One of the simplest that has been used for centuries is *money* and *time*. A library saves users' money by acquiring information resources on their behalf. For example, a user may borrow, read, and later return a recreational book for another person to use. The price is such that users could buy the book, but would rather use the library's copy and save their personal funds. In another example, a library resource that customers cannot afford or obtain is used. They may not be able to afford an expensive resource, or the resource (e.g., a loose-leaf taxation service or journal article) is not directly available to individuals. A library saves users' time by helping them find information faster than they could otherwise. This particular value includes reference services, in which librarians find information and do so faster than can users who are unfamiliar with the various information resources available. Saving money and time can be quantitatively evaluated from the library's perspective by applying *use* as a proxy. For example, the library reports that it circulated *X* number of books worth an average of Y dollars per book, saving users Z dollars. The money and/or time saved as valued from the users' perspective, however, are often not as well quantified.

In order to capture this customer perspective, librarians must learn how users value the library. A frequently sought-after value is customer satisfaction, and a popular data-gathering instrument is the customer survey. Libraries often use satisfaction surveys to capture customer satisfaction and to learn how customers value the library. Another set of popular values is *potential and actual. Potential value* refers to the resources that the library provides and makes available for use. *Actual value* is when those resources are used.

An often-used evaluative method is the cost-benefit analysis. In its simplest form, a cost-benefit analysis is a cost calculation or a ratio of the dollar value of expected benefits compared to the dollar value of costs. A cost-benefit analysis has three parts. First, all potential costs that will be incurred by implementing a proposed action are identified. Second, the analysis identifies all anticipated benefits (as valued in dollars) associated with the potential action. Third, managers subtract all identified costs from the expected benefits to determine whether the positive benefits outweigh the negative costs. If the results of this comparative evaluation method illustrate that the overall benefits associated with a proposed action outweigh the incurred costs, library managers will most likely implement the program or service. While the benefits necessary for a cost-benefit analysis are quantitative, the value of an identified benefit may have to be converted into a quantifiable form through a calculation, if the cost for the benefit is unknown.

Cost-benefit analysis as a means of evaluation is usually conducted prior to implementing a program or service. Ronald R. Powell, however, has found that cost-benefit studies can also justify the existence of a library activity by demonstrating that the benefits outweigh the costs.[37] A cost-benefit analysis that is conducted to demonstrate the benefits of an existing program in relationship to its costs is often referred to as an ROI. An ROI can be applied to calculate the dollar value of benefits gained for the dollar value of costs. There are two ways of reporting the results of an ROI. One is as a ratio that calculates value as the result of benefits divided by costs. The second is as a total sum of the value (benefit) of services that customers received. The difficulty is converting tangible and intangible benefits into a dollar value as well as ensuring that all costs are quantified.

There are several methods for converting benefits into dollar values. One is to determine purchase or exchange value, which is the cost that a customer is willing to pay for library services in terms of money, time, or effort. Another method asks users to estimate an alternative cost or the price they would pay if the library ceased to exist. Value has also been defined as the production of a commodity. In the case of a library, value equals the quantity of the commodity produced times the price unit of the commodity.[38] A variant of this formula recognizes the value of a library benefit (resource or service) as evidenced by its use:

value of usage = measured output of a service multiplied by the assigned price per unit

A calculated value of usage could, as an example, be the number of articles downloaded times the price per article. The output is measured by a counter, and the price per unit may be assigned by the library, the user, or an accepted benchmark. If 10,000 articles were downloaded, and the assigned price was $15.00 per article, the value of usage to the user would be $15,000. While the assigned value of the usage cannot be used to evaluate the library's quality, it can be applied as a proxy for one financial measure of the library's use, alongside the aforementioned concepts for saving the user *money* and *time*.

An important source describing in detail the use of cost-benefit analysis to calculate a library's ROI is *Measuring Your Library's Value*, which is essentially an instruction manual. This work applies user-based market value substitution based on contingent valuation analysis that asks survey respondents questions about their willingness to pay for the replacement of a no-longer-provided library service (e.g., borrowing books). Donald S. Elliott, Glen E. Holt, Sterling W. Hayden, and Leslie E. Holt list a library service, its substitute, the price range, the average price, and the assigned survey price— the conservative market-available alternative service cost (e.g., a bookstore).[39]

One of the major purposes of conducting a cost-benefit analysis is to make a statement such as "for each dollar spent on the library, the community receives $___ in benefits from library service." A 2010 report from the Division of Library and Information Services of the Florida Department of State found that, for every tax dollar received, Florida public libraries in 2008 provided $8.32 in value. Value was calculated for the following:

- **Revenue investment:** Revenues received by the public libraries, including federal, state, and local funds; fees and fines; cash gifts and donations; and funding for multitype library cooperatives.

- **User investment:** Investment that customers make (e.g., in their time, travel, purchases) necessary to use public libraries or specific services.

- **Cost to use alternatives:** Estimated costs to use alternatives to the public libraries should they cease to exist, and should users decide to pursue alternatives (measured in terms of time and other expenditures).

- **Total net benefits to users:** Cost to use alternatives minus the user investment.

- **Community economic benefits:** Benefits that result from the public library's presence in the community (e.g., library spending with vendors and contractors in the state; revenues generated by vendors and contractors in the library, such as copying, coffee shop, and gift shop; and spending that occurs as a result of library use, such as restaurants, stores, and coffee shops).

- **Lost use benefits:** Benefits derived from use that would be lost if the public library did not exist.

- **Economic return:** Results of public library use that can be expressed in economic terms.[40]

The Fels Institute of Government at the University of Pennsylvania analyzed a different set of library roles when determining the economic value of the Free Library of Philadelphia. The report calculated the economic value of library services that help residents learn to read and acquire working skills (literacy), locate job opportunities and develop career skills (workforce development), and develop or enhance businesses (business development). A fourth, unique measure examined how home values are affected by their proximity to a library; homes within a quarter mile of a library are worth, on average, $9,630 more than homes greater than a quarter of a mile away, thereby increasing home values, which, in turn, generates additional property taxes.[41]

Some academic libraries have studied ROI. Paula T. Kaufman reports on a landmark 2007 study that sought to develop a quantitative procedure for recognizing the library's value in support of the university's strategic goals, specifically using grant income generated by faculty when they use library materials. The study found that each $1.00 invested in the library returned $4.38 in grant income.[42] The Mildred F. Sawyer Library at Suffolk University (Boston, MA) calculated its ROI based on the following services provided during fiscal year 2009 (July 1, 2008–June 30, 2009): students borrowing laptops and books, printing in the library, database use from off-campus, and database use when the library was physically closed. Calculations were based on the number of occurrences (service outputs) multiplied by an informal and conservative market value of the occurrence to calculate a summed value for the services. The summed value was then divided by the sum of the Sawyer Library's personnel and operating expenditures. It was found that, for every dollar expended by the Sawyer Library, at least $8.65 was returned for the services identified.[43, 44]

Library value calculators help individuals to learn the value they personally receive from the library. An example is the Value of Library Service Calculator, a Web-based calculator provided by the Massachusetts Library Association, which is an application of the *value of usage* mentioned previously in this chapter and which lists library services (e.g., borrowing books and using ILL). Users enter the number of times they use each service, and the calculator returns the overall value based on the estimated value for each service. A link to another Web page explains how the services were valued. The sum of the value of the services is the "value of YOUR library use."[45]

The previously mentioned 2010 Florida study also includes a "personal economic Return On Investment (ROI)" calculator, based on data about each of the state's counties. Using the per visit revenue investment for each county as the cost of having a public library and then comparing that statistic to the per visit economic return as the benefit, the calculator allows users to enter the number of times they visit the library annually to discover their personal benefit. The calculator then returns the "Revenue per Visit in dollars," the "Economic Return per Visit in dollars," and the "ROI per Visit in dollars." Total revenue investment, the money spent by the county on the library, was turned into per visit revenue by dividing the total revenue by the number of visits. Total economic return, the dollar benefit that a customer receives by using a public library instead of having to buy the information, became a per visit number in the same way.[46]

From the library's perspective, the Sawyer Library's aforementioned ROI was to generate a figure relative to the university's investment. The library has also reported a student ROI annually (since fall 2002). The library calculates the per FTE contribution to the library from full-time students and a conservative market or substitution value for ten of the most-used services (e.g., borrowing reserve books or asking a reference question). The dollar sum of the services received by the student exceeds their contribution. A student using a minimum level of services realizes a savings—a personal return on investment—from using the library. [47]

A best practice is to be as conservative as possible when assigning a market value to a library service as an institutional or personal return on investment is developed. For example, the Mildred F. Sawyer Library assigns a value for a book borrowed from its general collection. First, the average cost for an academic book is found in *The Bowker Annual*. The library takes that cost and reduces it by 80 percent to reflect the cost of a used book. For the student ROI, the assigned value of a circulating book is 20 percent of the average cost of a new book.[48]

The academic library's value, impact, and contributions to research, service, and teaching have been frequently studied. Bonnie Gratch Lindauer maintains that

> rather than continuing to generate potentially irrelevant data, librarians, in collaboration with faculty in the disciplines and other academic staff, need to define for their institutions the key functions and resources perceived to be directly (or indirectly) linked to valued outcomes, such as student learning, teaching, and scholarly activity. Moreover, librarians need to specify indicators of performance that would generate needed and acceptable data and other forms of documentation.[49]

Similarly, Joseph R. Matthews states that determining "the value of the library's contribution to an institution's research environment will require considerable effort, but determining and communicating this value is becoming increasingly important for the academic library."[50] In *Value of Academic Libraries*, Oakleaf writes that the purpose of the report

> is . . . to provide Association of College and Research Libraries (ACRL) leaders and the academic community with 1) a clear view of the current state of the literature on value of libraries within an institutional context, 2) suggestions for immediate "Next Steps" in the demonstration of academic library value, and 3) a "Research Agenda" for articulating academic library value. It strives to help librarians understand, based on professional literature, the current answer to the question, "How does the library advance the missions of the institution?" The report is also of interest to higher educational professionals external to libraries, including senior leaders, administrators, faculty, and student affairs professionals.[51]

Figure 6.1, which is reproduced from that report, summarizes some of the key areas of library value. From a broader institutional perspective, there are multiple indicators of faculty research productivity that academic libraries could support (e.g., the number and value of grants secured and the number of publications, presentations, research reports,

Student Enrollment
- Recruitment of prospective students
- Matriculation of admitted students
- Recommendation of current students

Student Retention & Graduation
- Fall-to-fall retention
- Graduation rates

Student Success
- Internship success
- Job placement
- Job salaries
- Professional/graduate school acceptance
- Marketable skills

Student Achievement
- GPA
- Professional/educational test scores

Student Learning
- Learning assessments
- Faculty judgments

Student Experience, Attitude, & Perception of Quality
- Self-report engagement studies
- Senior/alumni studies
- Help surveys
- Alumni donations

Faculty Research Productivity
- Number of publications, number of patents, value of technology transfer
- Tenure/promotion judgments

Faculty Grants
- Number of grant proposals (funded or unfunded)
- Value of grants funded

Faculty Teaching
- Integration of library resources and services into course syllabi, websites, lectures, labs, texts, reserve readings, etc.
- Faculty/librarian collaborations; cooperative curriculum, assignment, or assessment design

Institutional Reputation & Prestige
- Faculty recruitment
- Institutional rankings
- Community engagement

Figure 6.1. Value Areas. From *The Value of Academic Libraries: A Comprehensive Research Review and Report*, prepared by Dr. Megan Oakleaf, Syracuse University (Association of College and Research Libraries, September 2010), 19. Used with permission from the American Library Association. See also Robert E. Dugan, Peter Hernon, and Danuta A. Nitecki, *Viewing Library Metrics from Different Perspectives: Inputs, Outputs, and Outcomes* (Santa Barbara, CA: Libraries Unlimited, 2009), 251–310.

creative works, and patent applications). Until libraries establish a clear link between the use of the print and electronic resources and the output of researchers, the value of academic libraries will not be fully recognized. Any metrics produced indirectly convey the value of the library. Matthews encourages libraries not to forget output metrics and how they indirectly reflect the library's contribution to teaching and research; such metrics might include the

- percentage of courses using the reserve reading room,

- percentage of students enrolled in those courses who actually checked out reserve materials,

- percentage of courses requiring term papers based on materials from the library,

- number of students who checked out library materials,

- percentage of faculty who checked out library materials,

- percentage of courses using reading packets based on materials photocopied from the library's collection,

- number of references cited in faculty publications from materials contained in the library collection,

- percentage of courses requiring students to use the library for research projects,

- number of items checked out of the library by undergraduates,

- percentage of library space occupied by students,

- number of pages photocopied by students, and

- percentage of freshmen students not checking out a library book.[52]

In summary, the literature concerning the impact and value of libraries is still developing. Researchers and practicing librarians are finding it difficult to determine the impact and value of the library, its services, and its programs, in large part because the results of interacting with library resources are intangible. For instance, how can the impact of reading a library book be evaluated, and how can value be evaluated when it differs from person to person? Value is subjective and based, in part, on the perspective held by the person at the time. Despite these difficulties, researchers and practitioners are exploring and experimenting with impact and value, and new knowledge and conceptual frameworks will likely emerge.

Addressing Problems in Conducting Evaluation Studies

Denise Troll Covey identified several problems revealed in surveys of, and discussions with, members of the Digital Library Federation concerning libraries and evaluation. Many respondents to her survey reported difficulty in deciding what data to gather and how to do so, and some of them expressed concerns that the most readily available data might not be the most valuable. Respondents reported instances of data being difficult or impossible to analyze and interpret because the research instruments were poorly designed and inadequately tested, while focus group questions were imprecise and ill suited for a study's evaluative purpose. The surveys also revealed that data were gathered but never analyzed, and data were analyzed but never used. Furthermore, even when data were carefully analyzed and interpreted, member libraries struggled with how to organize and present them to an audience for consideration in decision making and strategic planning. Respondents also reported underestimating the time it takes to accomplish steps in the research process. Problems in implementing any step in the research process complicated the development of subsequent steps. As a result, evaluations of library use presented an incomplete picture of what users actually do when they need information and what they do with the information they find.[53]

Many of the survey respondents expressed a belief that staff training would result in more effective data gathering, analysis, interpretation, presentation, and application. Libraries need to reduce the cost of trial-and-error efforts as they replicate the data-collection practices of other institutions. Further, they need to leverage the investment that many institutions have already made in staff training and development and to develop guidelines, best practices, and standard instruments that are both reliable and valid. Toward this end, they might develop how-to manuals and workshops that

- describe the advantages and disadvantages of various evaluation methods;

- provide instruction in how to develop data-collection instruments and gather and analyze the data;

- include sample data-collection instruments that have been successful in field-testing (an example is some of the instruments included in the Spec Kits available from the Association of Research Libraries, http://www.arl.org/resources/pubs/spec/complete.shtml);

- include sample quantitative and qualitative results, along with how they are interpreted, presented, and applied to realistic library problems;

- include sample budgets, timelines, and workflows derived from real experience; and

- design and standardize new methods of data collection appropriate for libraries in the hybrid environment of traditional and digital resources.[54]

The overall goal in conducting an evaluation study is to get the most useful evidence to key decision makers in the most cost-effective and realistic fashion. In doing so, it is critical to determine matters such as what information is needed to make decisions about a service, program, or process; how to collect, analyze, and interpret the data; the degree of data accuracy; whether complementary data should be collected; who will conduct the research and the extent of training these people will need; and what credible evidence will be reported to stakeholders and in what form.

Principles of Good Evaluation

The principles for good evaluation tend to focus on the following factors:

- Evaluation must have a purpose; it must not be an end in itself.

- Without the potential for action, there is no need to evaluate.

- Evaluation must be more than descriptive; it must address relationships among operational performance, users, and organizations.

- Evaluation may involve a communication process between staff and library customers.

- Evaluation should not be sporadic, but rather be an ongoing and continual means for monitoring, diagnosis, and change.

- Ongoing evaluation should be dynamic, reflecting new knowledge and changes in the environment. [55]

To this list we might add that stakeholders should be involved or represented, and that it is important to allocate adequate time for each step of the evaluation process, critically review the process from beginning to end, identify the benefits that will arise from future evaluation projects, and set the planning context so that the process itself can be improved.

CONCLUDING THOUGHTS

Libraries conduct assessment and evaluation studies, in part, as a response to the increasing demands for accountability, gauging the progress made toward meeting measurable objectives; to use the results to improve services, programs, and processes to decrease the gap between the expected and the observed; to demonstrate the library's value through its contributions to achieving the mission of the institution; and to inform interested stakeholders. Assessment and evaluation do not come naturally to librarians, who for the most part are unskilled in designing assessment and evaluation studies; choosing the appropriate data collection tools; gathering, compiling, organizing, and analyzing the data collected; and interpreting the results of the processes. Librarians have been collecting input, process, and output information for decades, and past practice has been that budgets, expenditures, staff size, collection holdings, usage, and other indirect indicators served as proxies for quality and value. It is not that librarians are unenthusiastic about conducting assessment and evaluation research. It may be that they are not comfortable with the reality that they may not have the background necessary to conduct more complex research that involves experimental design, hypothesis testing, and the use of inferential statistics to compare sample data to a population.

To overcome this limitation, librarians may want to partner with others in the institution who possess the needed research background, abilities, and knowledge. Ellysa Stern Cahoy and Loanne Snavely suggest strategies for the library to partner with the appropriate institutional members:

- Locate the offices and individuals responsible for assessment on the campus and explore what they do and how they do it.

- Determine what information is wanted and set goals.

- Make appointments with the appropriate people. Talk about the library's need for information in the context of what they do. Do not expect them to do something outside their scope or mission. Emphasize the usefulness of the data for all parties and for overall institutional assessment.

- Plan and be patient. It will likely take months for planning, gathering input on possible questions, developing the actual questions, and getting in the queue to administer the study, receive the results, and analyze the data.

- Work with experts to design clear, unambiguous questions. Avoid the use of library jargon and listen to the advice of your institutional partners.

- When finished, if the study was not exclusively related to the library, have any outside partners join you in presenting the results.

- Use the results to improve performance, implement new services, and inform the library's strategic directions.[56]

Despite the difference between assessment and evaluation, there are at least two overlapping practices applicable to both: using an internal management information system and benchmarking. A management information system (MIS) or decision support system (DSS) supports both assessment and evaluation activities. The design of the system should reflect the need for critical information to be readily available, easily accessible, and retrievable by all involved in making decisions. Meaningful data included in the system should be routinely input, harvested, and updated. Those data can be collected from numerous sources (see chapter 7) as well as the research in which the library invests. With the availability of low- and no-cost spreadsheets and graphics software to organize, sort, and filter data for interpretation and analysis, as well as the visual representation of results for communicating with stakeholders, librarians have statistical data, transactions, observations, and comments that can be effectively stored and available through the system.[57]

Although all libraries have sources of data and information, and many have created internal management information systems, it is difficult to gauge the use and usefulness of these systems for assessment and evaluation. Useful available data may not be collected, and the data that are collected may not be effectively applied to inform decision making. Although much of the information collected is locally produced, one must be wary of vendor-supplied data that depend on definitions, such as a page view or login, which, despite the efforts made to create standards such as through COUNTER (http://www.projectcounter.org/about.html), may differ from e-resource to e-resource and from vendor to vendor. Furthermore, libraries may focus on insufficient quantitative data and may need qualitative information (e.g., the actual comments that customers make as they use libraries and their programs and services). It may be more powerful to assemble qualitative data into stories that create powerful images. Still, the collection of quantitative data should remain a priority.

Despite these issues, libraries should create internal management information systems to help organize assessment and evaluation data. In addition, external third-party information services (e.g., Counting Opinions of Toronto, Canada) can provide them with externally administered management information systems that, when populated with local quantitative and qualitative data, can organize, sort, and filter the information. Librarians can create reports, perhaps some that rely on the graphical depiction of data, to inform decision making and to share with stakeholders.

A second best practice and a common use of assessment and evaluation data is benchmarking. Benchmarks are used for internal and external comparisons. Internally, benchmarks can be used to compare a recently calculated metric with the expected or desired measure or performance standard. For example, assume that when librarians assess student learning outcomes, only half of the students correctly answer a question about the evaluation of a Web source, and that the performance standard set is 80 percent. The internal benchmark might be used to alter the library's instructional approach and to reach the desired performance standard.

Externally, libraries conduct assessment or evaluation benchmarking by comparing services and processes with other institutions, learning from peers about best practices and then altering their practices to make internal improvements. Benchmarking is most appropriately applied to quantitative data. Libraries might compile peer institution benchmarks (e.g., the number of circulating print monographs per FTE student from each peer institution). The benchmarks are then reviewed during the library's planning or annual budgeting processes. Although benchmarking is often effective, libraries should remember that there are differences in the availability of resources from library to library and in institutional missions and organizational cultures. Peer comparisons, as a result, have limitations, and a discovered or imported best practice may not produce the desired results.

NOTES

1. Steve Hiller and James Self, "From Measurement to Management: Using Data Wisely for Planning and Decision-Making," *Library Trends* 53, no. 1 (Summer 2004): 139.

2. Stephanie Wright and Lynda S. White, "Library Assessment in North America," slides 6–7 (January 11, 2008), accessed February 16, 2010, http://www.libqual.org/documents/admin/WrightWhite.ppt.

3. Peter Hernon and Robert E. Dugan. "Assessment and Evaluation: What Do the Terms Really Mean?" *College & Research Libraries News* 70, no. 3 (March 2009): 146–49.

4. William Neal Nelson and Robert W. Fernekes, *Standards and Assessment for Academic Libraries: A Workbook* (Chicago: Association of College and Research Libraries, 2002), 83, 100, 103, 106.

5. Shaun Jackson, Carol Hansen, and Lauren Fowler, "Using Selected Assessment Data to Inform Information Literacy Program Planning with Campus Partners," *Research Strategies* 20, nos. 1–2 (2004): 49.

6. Mary M. Somerville, Gordon W. Smith, and Alexius Smith Macklin, "The ETS iSkillsTM Assessment: A Digital Age Tool," *The Electronic Library* 26, no. 2 (2008): 160–61.

7. Nelson and Fernekes, *Standards and Assessment for Academic Libraries*, 21.

8. Joy Frechtling, *The 2002 User Friendly Handbook for Project Evaluation* (Washington, DC: National Science Foundation, 2002), 55–57, accessed March 7, 2010, http://www.nsf.gov/pubs/2002/nsf02057/nsf02057.pdf.

9. Irene F. Rockman, "Strengthening Connections between Information Literacy, General Education, and Assessment Efforts," *Library Trends* 51, no. 2 (Fall 2002): 193.

10. Cecilia L. Lopéz, "Assessment of Student Learning: Challenges and Strategies," *The Journal of Academic Librarianship* 28, no. 6 (November 2002): 366.

11. Avril Cunningham, "Using 'Ready-to-Go' Assessment Tools to Create a Year Long Assessment Portfolio and Improve Instruction," *College & Undergraduate Libraries* 13, no. 2 (2006): 76–77.

12. Megan Oakleaf, "Dangers and Opportunities: A Conceptual Map of Information Literacy Assessment Approaches," *portal: Libraries and the Academy* 8, no. 3 (July 2008): 234, 238, 239, 247.

13. Lesley S. J. Farmer, "Using Technology to Facilitate Assessment of Library Education," *Teacher Librarian* 32, no. 3 (February 2005): 13.

14. Mary J. Allen, *Assessing General Education Programs* (Bolton, MA: Anker Publishing Company, 2006), 171.

15. See Peggy L. Maki, *Assessing for Learning: Building a Sustainable Commitment Across the Institution* (Sterling, VA: Stylus, 2004).

16. Chris A. Portmann and Adrienne J. Roush, "Assessing the Effects of Library Instruction," *The Journal of Academic Librarianship* 30, no. 6 (November 2004): 462.

17. Jackson, Hansen, and Fowler, "Using Selected Assessment Data to Inform Information Literacy Program Planning with Campus Partners," 51.

18. Carolyn J. Radcliff, Mary Lee Jansen, Joseph A. Salem Jr., Kenneth J. Burhanna, and Julie A. Gedeon, *A Practical Guide to Information Literacy Assessment for Academic Librarians* (Westport, CT: Libraries Unlimited, 2007), 41.

19. Rockman, "Strengthening Connections between Information Literacy, General Education, and Assessment Efforts," 192–93.

20. Sarah M. Pritchard, "No Library Is an Island: Finding Ground in the Culture of Assessment," slide 12, accessed January 21, 2010, http://www.sla.org/Presentations/sldc/sarah_LAB2002pp.ppt.

21. Wright and White, "Library Assessment in North America," slide 20.

22. Ibid., slides 17–18.

23. Pritchard, "No Library Is an Island," slide 13.

24. U.S. Bureau of Justice Assistance, Center for Program Evaluation, *Guide to Program Evaluation*, 19, accessed January 2, 2010, http://www.ojp.usdoj.gov/BJA/evaluation/guide/bja-guide-program-evaluation.pdf.

25. Joan C. Durrance and Karen E. Fisher, *How Libraries and Librarians Help: A Guide to Identifying User-Centered Outcomes* (Chicago: American Library Association, 2005), 34.

26. Ronald R. Powell, "Evaluation Research: An Overview," *Library Trends* 55, no. 1 (Summer 2006): 105–6, 110.

27. Carter McNamara, "Basic Guide to Program Evaluation," Authenticity Consulting, LLC (2008), accessed January 2, 2010, http://www.managementhelp.org/evaluatn/fnl_eval.htm.

28. Durrance and Fisher, *How Libraries and Librarians Help*, 85–86.

29. Leanne M. VandeCreek, "E-Mail Reference Evaluation: Using the Results of a Satisfaction Survey," *The Reference Librarian* 45, no. 93 (2006): 99, 101–2, 104–6.

30. Elizabeth Henry, Rachel Longstaff, and Doris Van Kampen, "Collection Analysis Outcomes in an Academic Library," *Collection Building* 27, no. 3 (2008): 114–16.

31. Merrill Stein, Teresa Edge, John M. Kelley, Dane Hewlett, and James F. Trainer, "Using Continuous Quality Improvement Methods to Evaluate Library Service Points," *Reference and User Services Quarterly* 48, no. 1 (Fall 2008): 78–81, 84–85.

32. Joseph R. Matthews, *Scorecard for Results: A Guide for Developing a Library Balanced Scorecard* (Westport, CT: Libraries Unlimited, 2008), xv.

33. G. Stevenson Smith, *Managerial Accounting for Libraries and Other Not-for-Profit Organizations*, 2nd ed. (Chicago: American Library Association, 2002), 211, 224.

34. Matthews, *Scorecard for Results*, 56, 65.

35. Stancheva Nevena and Vyara Angelova, "Measuring the Efficiency of University Libraries Using Data Envelopment Analysis," *Proceedings from INFORUM 2004* (May 25–27, 2004), accessed October 16, 2010, http://www.inforum.cz/pdf/2004/Stancheva_Nevena.pdf.

36. Shim Wonsik, "Applying DEA Technique to Library Evaluation in Academic Research Libraries," *Library Trends* 51, no. 3 (Winter 2003): 312–13. For examples of DEA, see Robert E. Dugan, Peter Hernon, and Danuta A. Nitecki, *Viewing Library Metrics from Different Perspectives: Inputs, Outputs, and Outcomes* (Santa Barbara, CA: Libraries Unlimited, 2009), 64–66.

37. Powell, "Evaluation Research," 112.

38. Association of College and Research Libraries, *Value of Academic Libraries: A Comprehensive Research Review and Report*, by Megan Oakleaf (Chicago: Association of College and Research Libraries, 2010), 20–21.

39. Donald S. Elliott, Glen E. Holt, Sterling W. Hayden, and Leslie E. Holt, *Measuring Your Library's Value: How to Do a Cost-Benefit Analysis for Your Public Library* (Chicago: American Library Association, 2007), 75–79.

40. University of West Florida, Haas Center for Business Research and Economic Development, *Taxpayer Return on Investment in Florida Public Libraries* (Tallahassee: Florida Department of State, Division of Library and Information Services, May 2010), 13. Studies of return on investment on libraries have also been conducted in Indiana, Pennsylvania, South Carolina, Vermont, and Wisconsin since 2005. See Florida Department of State, Division of Library and Information Services, *Return on Investment Study,* accessed October 16, 2010, http://dlis.dos.state.fl.us/bld/roi/2004-ROI.cfm.

41. University of Pennsylvania, Fels Institute of Government, Fels Research and Consulting, *The Economic Value of The Free Library in Philadelphia* (October 21, 2010), 3–6, accessed January 22, 2011, http://www.freelibrary.org/about/Fels_Report.pdf.

42. Paula T. Kaufman, "The Library as Strategic Investment: Results of the Illinois Return on Investment Study," *LIBER Quarterly* 18, nos. 3–4 (December 2008): 424, 433.

43. Suffolk University, Mildred F. Sawyer Library, "FAQ: Has the Library Calculated Its Return on Investment (ROI)?," accessed October 17, 2010, http://www.suffolk.edu/sawlib/faq.htm#anchor40210.

44. See also "Lib Value," accessed February 1, 2011, http://libvalue.cci.utk.edu/. Carol Tenopir is investigating "Value, Outcomes, and Return on Investment of Academic Libraries (Lib-Value)." She addresses academic librarians' growing need to demonstrate the ROI and value of the library to the institution and guides library management in the redirection of library funds to important future products and services. Lib-Value provides evidence and a set of tested methodologies and tools to assist academic librarians in these areas.

45. Massachusetts Library Association, "Value of Library Service Calculator," accessed October 16, 2010, http://69.36.174.204/value-new/calculator.html.

46. University of West Florida, Haas Center for Business Research and Economic Development, *Taxpayers Return on Investment in Florida Public Libraries: Survey Results Site Navigation [by County],* accessed October 16, 2010, http://haas.uwf.edu/library/county_data/escambia.htm.

47. Suffolk University, Mildred F. Sawyer Library, "FAQ: How Can I Get My Tuition Money's Worth from the Library?," accessed October 17, 2010, http://www.suffolk.edu/sawlib/faq.htm#anchor13268. See also Dugan, Hernon, and Nitecki, *Viewing Library Metrics from Different Perspectives*, 146–48.

48. Suffolk University, Mildred F. Sawyer Library, "Value of Services at the Mildred F. Sawyer Library: Academic Year 2009–2010 Based upon FY 2010 Expenditure Information," accessed October 17, 2010, http://www.suffolk.edu/files/SawLib/value_of_library_services__2010.pdf.

49. Bonnie Gratch Lindauer, "Defining and Measuring the Library's Impact on Campuswide Outcomes," *College & Research Libraries* 59, no. 6 (November 1998): 559.

50. Joseph R. Matthews, *Library Assessment in Higher Education* (Westport, CT: Libraries Unlimited, 2007), 111.

51. Association of College and Research Libraries, *Value of Academic Libraries*, 11.

52. Matthews, *Library Assessment in Higher Education*, 120.

53. Denise Troll Covey, "Academic Library Assessment: New Duties and Dilemmas," *New Library World* 103, nos. 1175/1176 (2002): 157–60.

54. Ibid., 160–61.

55. Powell, "Evaluation Research: An Overview," 104–5.

56. Ellysa Stern Cahoy and Loanne Snavely, "Maximizing Local and National Assessment for Evidence-Based Librarianship," *Reference and User Services Quarterly* 48, no. 3 (Spring 2009): 222.

57. Hiller and Self, "From Measurement to Management," 129–30.

Chapter 7

Quantitative Data Collection for Evaluation Research

Many academic librarians might associate quantitative data collection for reporting to the national government with the biennial Academic Library Survey (ALS), which the U.S. Census Bureau collects for the National Center for Education Statistics (NCES). It provides a comprehensive picture of the status of collections, transactions, staff, service per typical week, and library operating expenditures in postsecondary institutions (see http://nces.ed.gov/surveys/libraries/academic.asp). There is also the IPEDS (the Integrated Postsecondary Education Data System) survey, conducted annually, of all colleges, universities, and technical and vocational institutions that participate in the federal student financial aid programs. IPEDS data provided by the NCES, U.S. Department of Education, are available at http://nces.ed.gov/ipeds/. Furthermore, on a subscription basis, Counting Opinions (Toronto, Canada), in a partnership with the Association of College and Research Libraries, offers data from the ALS back to 2000, so that libraries have trend data and can use the input and output statistics for peer benchmarking, planning, and advocacy (see http://www.acrl.metrics.com/).

Public libraries, on the other hand, are more likely to view data collection in terms of the input and output metrics they assemble and provide to the Institute of Museum and Library Services (IMLS, http://harvester.census.gov/imls/data/pls/index.asp); the *Public Library Data Service (PLDS) Statistical Report*, collected annually by ALA/PLA, which "reports data from more than 900 public libraries across the United States and Canada on finances, library resources, annual use figures and technology";[1] *Hennen's American Public Library Ratings*, which is now based on data reported to the IMLS; or the *LJ Index*, which describes library service outputs, such as visits, circulation, public Internet computer usage, and program attendance.

If academic libraries participate in formal data collection involving the surveying of students and faculty, a number rely on LibQUAL+® or abbreviated versions known as LibQUAL® Lite, a series of services that libraries use to solicit and monitor user opinions of service quality. These services are offered by the Association of Research Libraries. The centerpiece is a Web-based survey bundled with training and the analysis of results to enable libraries to measure service quality and create national and international service norms. Since 2000, more than 1,000 libraries have participated in that survey. Librarians use LibQUAL+® to evaluate "and improve library services, change organizational culture, and market the library."[2]

In addition to LibQUAL+®, there is LibSAT (Counting Opinions, Toronto, Canada), which focuses on customer satisfaction and enables "libraries and library systems to collect, review, approve and report on the quantitative aspects (performance metrics) of Library performance."[3] The satisfaction survey provided enables customers of a central library and the branches—be they public or academic libraries—to complete it online or by means of a pencil-and-paper form, the responses to which staff then has to key in. The company takes the completed surveys and provides ways to prepare visual displays of findings and options to drill down to the written comments.

Unlike LibSAT which continuously records customer satisfaction and customer perspectives, LibPAS another product of Counting Opinions, enables libraries to collect, review, approve, and report on the quantitative aspects (performance metrics) of their performance, providing real-time and on-demand access to data for operational and advocacy purposes.

QUANTITATIVE DATA COLLECTION

Data collection, as discussed in this chapter, is associated with measurement, a specialized form of description that assigns numbers to specify differing characteristics of a variable. It provides a means for quantifying variables and making comparisons among them.[4] In *Assessing Service Quality*, Peter Hernon and Ellen Altman identify eleven questions that encompass the different "hows" of measurement: how much?, how many?, how economical?, how prompt?, how accurate?, how responsive?, how well?, how valuable?, how reliable?, how courteous?, and how satisfied? The last question might be rephrased, "How well does the library meet or exceed customer expectations?"[5] Still, evaluation research might investigate a problem in which the results cannot be simply cast in terms of input, output, or performance metrics.

MEASURING CUSTOMER EXPECTATIONS

Customer expectations are desired wants—the extent to which customers believe a particular attribute is essential for an excellent service provider. Such perceptions are a judgment of service performance. Customer expectations might be expressed in one of two ways: service quality and satisfaction. Service quality and satisfaction adhere to the Gaps Model of Service Quality, which posits five gaps, one of which reflects a discrepancy between customers' expected services and perceived service delivered.[6] This gap, the fifth one, is the basis of a customer-oriented definition of service quality that examines the discrepancy between customers' expectations for excellence and their perceptions of the actual service delivered (see figure 4.1, p. 63).

Satisfaction is a sense of contentment that arises from an *actual* experience in relation to an *expected* experience. The degree to which expectations conform to or deviate from experience is the pivotal determination of satisfaction. Measures of service quality also look at actual versus expected experience, but the focus here is to compare objectively what one wishes as an idealized service attribute with the current condition of that attribute. The process of making such a comparison involves an objective comparison between an ideal possibility and its present reality. By contrast, customer satisfaction measures a customer's immediate and subjective experience with a specific service encounter—a uniquely personal and internalized experience that generates a spontaneous perception based, consciously or subconsciously, on expectations, or an overall reflection of that customer's experiences with the service provider.[7]

LibQUAL+®

LibQUAL+® is a twenty-two-item questionnaire that measures perceptions of *service affect* (nine items such as "willingness to help users" and "employees who deal with users in a caring fashion"), *information control* (eight items such as "a library Web site enabling me to locate information on my own" and "making information easily accessible for independent use"), and *library as place* (five items such as "library space that inspires study and learning" and "a getaway for study, learning, or research"). There is also an opportunity for respondents to provide open-ended comments and for the library to insert some statements of local value. For example, here are three general satisfaction statements/questions presented with a nine-point scale:

- "In general, I am satisfied with the way in which I am treated in the library."

- "In general, I am satisfied with library support for my learning, research, and/or teaching needs."

- "How would you rate overall quality of the service provided by the library?"

There is also a claim that five statements address information literacy outcomes:

1. "The library helps me stay abreast of developments in my field(s) of interest."

2. "The library aids my advancement in my academic discipline or work."

3. "The library helps me to be more efficient in my academic pursuits or work."

4. "The library helps me distinguish between trustworthy and untrustworthy information."

5. "The library provides me with the information skills I need in my work or study."

Its developers claim that it takes approximately thirteen minutes to complete the instrument either online or, upon request, in paper form.

Libraries might participate in the survey on a regular basis (e.g., annually or biennially) or on an irregular basis. They might also follow up on key findings with focus group interviews and use the collective findings to institute new services, reallocate space, or improve workflow and operations.[8] Based on a random drawing, they might offer incentive prizes (e.g., gift certificates to a local bookstore) for survey completion.

The satisfaction statements are no substitute for conducting a formal satisfaction survey such as the versions that Counting Opinions provides. Although some librarians associate LibQUAL+® with assessment, it is a tool for evaluation. Some librarians have referred to it as a satisfaction survey and have included the results in institutional assessment reports, thereby confusing satisfaction with service quality. The above-mentioned five outcomes statements are superficial; are not associated with outcomes that faculty and librarians develop at the course or program level; and do not reflect a change in student behavior, abilities, or skills over time.

Counting Opinions

In contrast to LibQUAL+®, a survey that libraries use for a limited time period, Counting Opinions' online survey, LibSAT, provides academic and public libraries with continuous data collection that addresses reports of customer satisfaction with a library and its infrastructure: staff, collections and service, facilities, and technology. The survey also places library use in the context of other information providers and reflects customer preferences for types of resources.

The core measures included with LibSAT are available in different versions, enabling respondents to select from a short (two to three minutes), regular (five to seven minutes), or in-depth version (typically requires, on average, more than sixteen minutes to complete). Each version includes increasingly more aspects of service and additional opportunities for specific open-ended feedback. Results are available to libraries immediately upon their capture, and the online reporting tools provide various perspectives on the data, with ease of drill-down, custom report generation, and repurposing of results for various applications.

DIFFERENT METHODOLOGIES

With LibQUAL+® and LibSAT, libraries obtain prepackaged surveys that they can still tailor for local use, strategies for data collection, and an analysis and visual presentation of findings. In addition, for librarians wanting to initiate data collection, going beyond service quality and satisfaction, this chapter, together with chapter 8, highlights quantitative data collection expressed through the application of surveys, standardized tests, citation and content analysis, observation, sweeping study, transactional log analysis, and usability testing. Chapter 8 focuses on qualitative data collection, and chapter 6 reviews methods applicable to assessment. Together, these chapters cover a rich landscape of methodologies and relevant literature. Figure 7.1 identifies some studies in library and information science that use quantitative methodologies, but it downplays surveys, given their widespread use. Figure 7.2 offers some supplementary readings on mystery shopping, an emerging source of vital information about customer expectations and experiences in using a library or one of its services; Chapter 8 expands on the discussion of mystery shopping presented in this chapter. Figure 7.3 complements the first table by identifying some research studies on selected topical areas.

Citation Analysis

Brock, Enger K. "Using *Citation Analysis* to Develop Core Book Collections in Academic Libraries." *Library & Information Science Research* 31, no. 2 (April 2009): 107–12.

Kousha, Kavvan, and Mike Thelwall. "Google Book Search: Citation Analysis for Social Science and the Humanities." *Journal of the American Society for Information Science and Technology* 60, no. 8 (August 2009): 1537–49.

Levitt, Jonathan M., and Mike Thelwall. "Citation Levels and Collaboration within Library and Information Science." *Journal of the American Society for Information Science and Technology* 60, no. 3 (March 2009): 434–42.

Payne, Nigel, and Mike Thelwall. "Longitudinal Trends in Academic Web Links." *Journal of Information Science* 34, no. 1 (2008): 3–14. This Webometrics study examines the relationship between university inlinks and research productivity.

Content Analysis

Aharony, Noa. "Librarians and Information Scientists in the Blogosphere: An Exploratory Analysis." *Library & Information Science Research* 31, no, 3 (2009): 174–81.

Leeder, Christopher. "Surveying the Commons: Current Implementation of Information Commons Web Sites." *The Journal of Academic Librarianship* 35, no. 6 (November 2009): 533–47. This study evaluated the content of seventy-two academic library Web sites for information commons using content analysis, quantitative assessment, and qualitative surveys of site administrators.

Park, Jung-ran, Caimei Lu, and Linda Marion. "Cataloging Professionals in the Digital Environment: A *Content Analysis* of Job Descriptions." *Journal of the American Society for Information Science and Technology* 60, no. 4 (April 2009): 844–57.

Staines, Gail. "Toward an Assessment of Strategic Credibility in Academic Libraries." *Library Management* 30, no. 3 (2009): 148–62.

Delphi Technique

Jerabek, J. Ann, Lynn M. McMain, and James L. Van Roekel. "Using Needs Assessment to Determine Library Services for Distance Learning Programs." *Journal of Interlibrary Loan, Document Delivery & Information Supply* 12, no. 4 (2002): 4–61.

Focus Group Interviews

Jerabek, J. Ann, Lynn M. McMain, and James L. Van Roekel. "Using Needs Assessment to Determine Library Services for Distance Learning Programs." *Journal of Interlibrary Loan, Document Delivery & Information Supply* 12, no. 4 (2002): 52–53.

Mystery Shopping and Unobtrusive Testing

Burkamp, Marlu, and Diane E. Virbick. "Through the Eyes of a Secret Shopper: Enhance Service by Borrowing a Popular Business Technique." *American Libraries* 33, no. 10 (November 2002): 56–57.

Figure 7.1. Some Relevant Writings Appearing in Library and Information Science

Calvert, Philip C. "It's a Mystery: Mystery Shopping in New Zealand's Public Libraries." *Library Review* 54, no. 1 (2005): 24–35.

Hernon, Peter, and Charles R. McClure. *Unobtrusive Testing and Library Reference Services*. Norwood, NJ: Ablex, 1987.

Kocevar-Weidinger, Elizabeth, Candice Benjes-Small, Eric Ackermann, and Virginia Kinman. "Why and How to Mystery Shop Your Reference Desk." *Reference Services Review* 38, no. 1 (2010). Available from Emerald Management Xtra 175.

McClure, Charles R., and Peter Hernon. *Improving the Quality of Reference Service for Government Publications*. Chicago: American Library Association, 1983.

Whitlatch, Jo Bell. "Evaluating Reference Services in the Electronic Age." *Library Trends* 50, no. 2 (Fall 2001): 207–17.

Observation*

Dinkelman, Andrea, and Kristine Stacy-Bates. "Accessing E-books through Academic Library Web Sites," *College & Research Libraries* 68, no. 1 (January 2007): 45–58. This study involves direct observation of the library Web sites.

Standardized Tests

Gross, Melissa, and Don Latham. "Undergraduate Perceptions of Information Literacy: Defining, Attaining, and Self-Assessing Skills." *College & Research Libraries* 70, no. 4 (July 2009): 336–50. This mixed methods study uses both interviewing and a standardized test for information literacy.

Surveys

Nitecki, Danuta A., and Peter Hernon. "Measuring Service Quality at Yale University's Libraries." *Journal of Academic Librarianship* 26 (July 2000): 259–73.

Sweeping Study

Given, Lisa M., and Gloria J. Leckie. "'Sweeping' the Library: Mapping the Social Activity Space of the Public Library." *Library & Information Science Research* 25, no. 4 (2003): 365–85.

Transactional Log Analysis

Asunka, Stephen, Hui Soo Chae, Brian Hughes, and Gary Natriello. "Understanding Academic Information Seeking Habits through Analysis of Web Server Log Files: The Case of the Teachers College Library Website." *The Journal of Academic Librarianship* 35, no. 1 (January 2009): 33–45.

Connaway, Lynn Silipigni, and Clifton Snyder. "Transaction Log Analysis of Electronic (E-Book) Usage." *Against the Grain* 17, no. 1 (February 2005): 85–89. Preprint is available at http://www.oclc.org/research/publications/library/2005/connaway-snyder-atg.pdf (accessed December 31, 2009).

Figure 7.1. Some Relevant Writings Appearing in Library and Information Science (*Cont.*)

Knievel, Jennifer E., Heather Wicht, and Lynn Silipigni Connaway. "Use of Circulation Statistics and Interlibrary Loan Data in Collection Management." *College & Research Libraries* 67, no. 1 (January 2006): 35–49. This study analyzes the holdings, circulations, and interlibrary loan borrowing requests of an English-language monograph collection.

Meert, Deborah L., and Lisa M. Given. "Measuring Quality in Chat Reference Consortia: A Comparative Analysis of Responses to Users' Queries." *College & Research Libraries* 70, no. 1 (January 2009): 71–84. This study evaluates assessing transcripts of chat sessions using in-house reference quality standards.

Page, Jessica R., and Kuehn, Jennifer. "Interlibrary Service Requests for Locally and Electronically Available Items: Patterns of Use, Users, and Canceled Requests." *portal: Libraries and the Academy* 9, no. 4 (2009): 475–89. This study uses interlibrary loan and document delivery transactions.

Usability Testing

Battleston, Brenda, Austin Booth, and Jane Weintrop. "Usability Testing of an Academic Library Web Site: A Case Study." *The Journal of Academic Librarianship* 27, no. 3 (May 2001): 188–98.

Hepburn, Peter, and Krystal M. Lewis. "What's in a Name? Using Card Sorting to Evaluate Branding in an Academic Library's Web Site." *College & Research Libraries* 69, no. 3 (May 2008): 242–50. This article presents a card sorting usability study.

Kwak, Seung-Jin, and Kyung-Jae Bae. "Ubiquitous Library Usability Test for the Improvement of Information Access for the Blind." *The Electronic Library* 27, no. 4 (2009): 623–39.

Lehman, Tom, and Terry Nikkel. *Making Library Web Sites Usable: A LITA Guide.* New York: Neal-Schuman, 2008.

Reeb, Brenda. *Design Talk: Understanding the Roles of Usability Practitioners, Web Designers, and Web Developers in User-Centered Web Design.* Chicago: Association of College and Research Libraries, 2008.

Stephen, Elizabeth, Daisy T. Cheng, and Lauren M. Young. "A Usability Survey at the University of Mississippi Libraries for the Improvement of the Library Home Page." *The Journal of Academic Librarianship* 32, no. 1 (January 2006): 35–51.

"Website Usability: Research and Case Studies." *OCLC Systems & Services* 21, no 3 (2005) (entire issue).

Mixed Methods

Fidel, Raya. "Are We There Yet: Mixed Methods Research in Library and Information Science." *Library & Information Science Research* 30, no. 4 (December 2008): 265–72.

Kwon. Nahyun. "A Mixed-Methods Investigation of the Relationship between Critical Thinking and Library Anxiety among Undergraduate Students in Their Information Search Process." *College & Research Libraries* 69, no. 2 (March 2008): 117–31. This study combines the use of standardized survey instruments and analysis of the contents of student essays on critical incidents of their library use experience.

*See Bureau of Justice Assistance, Center for Program Evaluation, *Guide to Program Evaluation*, accessed January 2, 2010, http://www.ojp.usdoj.gov/BJA/evaluation/guide/bja-guide-program-evaluation.pdf.

Figure 7.1. Some Relevant Writings Appearing in Library and Information Science (*Cont.*)

Allison, Pamela, Denver Severt, and Duncan Dickson. "A Conceptual Model for Mystery Shopping Motivations." *Journal of Hospitality Marketing & Management* 19, no. 6 (2010): 629–57.

Beck, Jeff, and Li Miao. "Mystery Shopping in Lodging Properties as a Measurement of Service Quality." *Journal of Quality Assurance in Hospitality & Tourism* 4, nos. 1/2 (2003): 1–21.

Finn, Adam, and Ujwal Kayandé. "Unmasking a Phantom: A Psychometric Assessment of Mystery Shopping." *Journal of Retailing* 75, no. 2 (1999): 195–217.

WARC. "Data Collection Techniques: Mystery Shopping." (2010). Accessed January 7, 2010. http://www.warc.com/LandingPages/Generic/Results.asp?Ref=854.

Wilson, Alan M. "The Use of Mystery Shopping in the Measurement of Service Delivery." *The Services Industries Journal* 18, no. 3 (1998): 148–63.

Figure 7.2. Some Relevant Writings on Mystery Shopping

Collection Use

Oliver, Astrid. "Tracking Repetitive Use of Electronic Reserve Items: Using Electronic Reserves Repetitive Use Information to Help Gauge Copyright Compliance." *Library Hi Tech* 27, no. 1 (2009): 106–17.

Schlosser, Melanie. "Unless Otherwise Indicated: A Survey of Copyright Statements on Digital Library Collections." *College & Research Libraries* 70, no. 4 (July 2009): 371–85.

Institutional Repository Use

St. Jean, Beth, Soo Young Rieh, Elizabeth Yakel, and Karen Makey. "Unheard Voices: Institutional Repository End-Users." *College & Research Libraries* 72, no. 1 (January 2011): 21–42.

Library as Place

Ludwig, Logan, and Susan Starr. "Library as Place: Results of a Delphi Study." *Journal of the Medical Library Association* 93, no. 3 (2005): 315–24.

Pomerantz, Jeffrey, and Gary Marchionni. "The Digital Library as Place." *Journal of Documentation* 63, no. 4 (2007): 505–33.

Shill, Harold B., and Shawn Tonner. "Does the Building Still Matter? Usage Patterns in New, Expanded, and Renovated Libraries, 1995–2002." *College & Research Libraries* 65, no. 2 (2004): 123–50.

Reference Service

Chat

Arnold, Julie, and Neal K. Kaske. "Evaluating the Quality of a Chat Service." *portal: Libraries and the Academy* 5, no. 2 (2005): 177–93.

Figure 7.3. Topical Coverage of Some Research Studies

Horowtiz, Lisa R., Patricia A. Flanagan, and Deborah L. Helman. "The Viability of Live Online Reference: An Assessment." *portal: Libraries and the Academy* 5, no. 2 (April 2005): 239–58.

Mon, Lorri, Bradley W. Bishop, Charles R. McClure, Jessica McGilvray, Linda Most, Theodore P. Milas, and John T. Snead. "The Geography of Virtual Questioning." *The Library Quarterly* 79, no. 4 (October 2009): 393–420.

Pomerantz, Jeffrey, Lili Luo, and Charles R. McClure. "Peer Review of Chat Reference Transcripts: Approaches and Strategies." *Library & Information Science Research* 28, no. 1 (2006): 24–48.

Ruppel, Margie, and Jody Condit Fagan. "Instant Messaging Reference: Users' Evaluation of Library Chat." *Reference Services Review* 30, no. 3 (2002): 183–97.

Ward, David. "Measuring the Completeness of Reference Transactions in Online Chats: Results of an Unobtrusive Study." *Reference and User Services Quarterly* 44, no. 1 (Fall 2004): 46–56.

White, Marilyn D., Eileen G. Abels, and Neal Kaske. "Evaluation of Chat Reference Service Quality: Pilot Study." *D-Lib Magazine* 9, no. 2 (February 2003). Accessed January 7, 2010. http://www.dlib.org/dlib/february03/white/02white.html.

Interactive Real-time

Foley, Marianne. "Instant Messaging Reference in an Academic Library: A Case Study." *College & Research Libraries* 63, no. 1 (January 2002): 36–45.

Kloss, Louise, and Yin Zhang. "An Evaluative Case Study of a Real-Time Online Reference Service." *Electronic Library* 21, no. 6 (2003): 565–75.

Text Messaging

Pearce, Alexa, Scott Collard, and Kara Whatley. "SMS Reference: Myths, Markers, and Modalities." *Reference Services Review* 38, no. 2 (2010): 250–63.

Profit, Steven K. "Text Messaging at Reference: A Preliminary Survey." *The Reference Librarian* 49, no. 2 (2008): 129–33.

Public Library Internet Use

Bertot, John C., and Denise M. Davis. "Public Library Public Access Computing and Internet Access: Factors Which Contribute to Quality Services and Resources." *Public Library Quarterly* 25, nos. 1/2 (2006): 27–42.

D'Elia, George, Corinne Jorgensen, Joseph Woelfel, and Eleanor Jo Rodger. "The Impact of the Internet on Public Library Use: An Analysis of the Current Consumer Market for Library and Internet Services." *Journal of the American Society for Information Science and Technology* 53, no. 10 (2002): 802–20.

Figure 7.3. Topical Coverage of Some Research Studies (*Cont.*)

Pettigrew, Karen E., Joan C. Durrance, and Kenton T. Unruh. "Facilitating Community Information Seeking Using the Internet: Findings from Three Public Library-Community Network Systems." *Journal of the American Society for Information Science and Technology* 53, no. 11 (2002): 894–903.

Prabha, Chandra, and Raymond Irwin. "Web Technology in Public Libraries: Findings from Research." *Library Hi Tech* 21, no. 1 (2003): 62–69.

Social Network Use

Jacobson, Terra B. "Facebook as a Library Tool: Perceived vs. Actual Use." *College & Research Libraries* 72, no. 1 (January 2011): 79–90.

Usage Statistics (Database Vendors)

Duy, Joanna, and Liwen Vaughan. "Usage Data for Electronic Resources: A Comparison between Locally Collected and Vendor-Provided Statistics." *The Journal of Academic Librarianship* 29, no. 1 (January 2003): 16–22.

Shim, Wonsik, and Charles R. McClure. "Data Needs and Use of Electronic Resources and Services at Academic Research Libraries." *portal: Libraries and the Academy* 2, no. 2 (2002): 217–36.

Shim, Wonsik, and Charles R. McClure. "Improving Database Vendor's Usage Statistics Reporting through Collaboration between Libraries and Vendors." *College & Research Libraries* 63, no. 6 (2002): 499–514.

Stemper, James A., and Janice M. Jaguszewski. "Usage Statistics for Electronic Journals: An Analysis of Local and Vendor Counts." *Collection Management* 28, no. 4 (2003): 3–22.

Web Site Accessibility (Disability)

Hernon, Peter, and Philip C. Calvert, eds. *Improving the Quality of Library Services for Students with Disabilities.* Westport, CT: Libraries Unlimited, 2006. This study examines service quality and is not confined to Web site accessibility.

Lilly, Erica B., and Connie Van Fleet. "Measuring the Accessibility of Public Library Home Pages." *Reference & User Services Quarterly* 40, no. 2 (Winter 2000): 156–65.

Providenti, Michael. "Library Web Accessibility at Kentucky's 4-year Degree Granting Colleges and Universities." *D-Lib Magazine* 10, no. 9 (2004). Accessed January 7, 2010. http://www.dlib.org/dlib/september04/providenti/09providenti.html.

Samure, Kristie, and Lisa M. Given. "Digitally Enhanced? An Examination of the Information Behaviours of Visually Impaired Post-Secondary Students." *Canadian Journal of Information and Library Science* 28, no. 2 (2004): 25–42.

Spindler, Tim. "The Accessibility of Web Pages for Mid-Sized College and University Libraries." *Reference & User Services Quarterly* 42, no. 2 (Winter 2002): 149–54.

Figure 7.3. Topical Coverage of Some Research Studies (*Cont.*)

Administration of Standardized Tests

Everyone is familiar with the battery of standardized tests that school students periodically take and that those planning to attend college must pass with a high score. The advantage of such tests is that their reliability and validity have been studied and certified.[9] Standardized tests exist for a number of topics (e.g., management, leadership, and information literacy). At the same time, standardized tests might be locally developed. In the case of information literacy, some institutions have created tests that measures student learning and ability to apply what they learned over a period of time, perhaps from freshmen to senior years.

Citation Analysis

Citation analysis is a component of bibliometrics, which is defined as the quantitative study of literatures as reflected in bibliographies or, more specifically, discourse emerging from a study of authorship, publication, reading, and citations. Citations do not occur "in a void;" they "are not separated from the contexts and conditions of their generation."[10] Furthermore, they are part of scholarly communication—the part associated with the reward and recognition of scholars and researchers for their work—but by themselves they reflect neither use nor the motivation behind referencing a particular work or author. Anyone studying citation patterns might examine who wrote the works, the form of publication (e.g., in a peer-reviewed journal, or digital or print), the class of the material (primary, secondary, or tertiary), language, subject, and age. In some instances, researchers might go beyond the citations and determine the purpose for which works were cited (e.g., substantiation, refutation, and provision of additional information). Insights into these matters indicate how scholarly, current, research-focused, and interdisciplinary the cited literature is, as well as who wrote that literature and in what form it is most likely to appear.[11]

Citation analysis gives rise to metrics associated, for instance, with half-life—the range of years in which half of the citations to a particular journal or publisher, for example, are cited—and impact factor, which divides the number of current citations a journal receives to articles published in the previous two years by the number of articles published in that journal in the same time frame. Metrics might cover digital publishing, the references found on a Web site, and hot links to a Web site—what other sites reference the particular site. Relevant output metrics might even lead to the identification of the electronic journals receiving the most mention, and these might be labeled the *most prestigious* e-journals.

Content Analysis

Such an analysis might involve either quantitative or qualitative data collection; for a complementary discussion see chapter 8. For quantitative data collection it classifies textual or visual material, reducing it to more relevant and manageable bits of data. That reduction leads to the calculation of descriptive statistics, which convert raw data into indices that summarize or characterize datasets; such statistics comprise a set of procedures for organizing, describing, and summarizing observations. Content analysis looks at word choice, frequency, and sequencing; the intensity of feelings or expression; key words in context; or typologies or categories used. For example, researchers interested in studying course and program assessment might examine library blogs, wikis, and social networks for mention of such assessment, the commitment of faculty, problems encountered, and whether librarians play a leadership role. For program assessment, investigators might probe the self-studies that college and universities submit to program and regional accreditation organizations.[12]

Observation

Observation takes different forms, two of which are unobtrusive and obtrusive testing. In the former the participants are unaware that they are being tested, and in the latter they are aware of being tested. Unobtrusive testing shares some similarities with mystery shopping, both of which are field-based methods of using independent auditors or proxies as customers to gather information about a shopping experience or the extent of engagement of library staff in answering questions. Mystery shopping tends to involve qualitative data collection, with subjective evaluation of the experience (see chapter 8). It might be applied to the process of getting a library card, asking a question, attending a workshop or public meeting, or, in the case of academic libraries, the use of an information or learning commons.[13]

Unobtrusive testing is a quantitative method whereby the proxy approaches a staff member (perhaps someone at the reference desk) and asks a pre-tested question. One purpose might be to test the question negotiation ability of the staff member: Did he or she determine what the proxy needed to know? For example, the proxy might ask a general question and see if the staff member identified that the proxy wanted a digital government publication.

Researchers or library managers might combine both mystery shopping and unobtrusive testing into a single methodology. Figure 7.4 indicates what each method tends to examine, and evaluators can review those choices as they decide which are most relevant to their study objectives.

Obtrusive testing is a methodology to evaluate the use of a particular service, during which the user or provider of the service knows that data collection centers on the ability to answer questions. For instance, the investigator might give reference staff or students a set of reference questions to answer in a given time period and score them on the accuracy of the answer and their ability to negotiate a question.

Mystery Shopping
- Head count—number using the service:
    - Number before you
    - Number behind you
- Time elapsed for service
    - Length of wait
    - Speed of service
    - Staff member devoted attention to the question—no interruptions
- Appearance and layout: physical environment
    - Availability of study/reading space
- Displays
- Acknowledgment (the transaction)
    - Friendly
    - Eye contact (not always a good thing)
- Ending (manner concluding the transaction)
- Cleanliness of the location
- Signage
    - Availability
    - Clarity
    - Utility
- The result: "product quality"
    - Including what resources shown
- Parking and accessibility (disabilities)

Unobtrusive Testing
- Accuracy of answer given
    - Method of delivery (by telephone, in person, or virtually)
- Reasons for incorrect answers
- Time spent (reference interview to conclusion)
- Referral
    - Offered
    - Result—accurate answer?
- Demeanor of staff member
- Location
    - Did the staff member leave the desk—if yes, they went where?

Figure 7.4. Mystery Shopping and Unobtrusive Testing. See also Welsh Library Service Mystery Shopper, *Mystery Shop Report*, produced for the Wrexham County Borough Council (Twelfth Man Ltd., 2009), accessed November 3, 2010, http://wales.gov.uk/docs/drah/research/091101Mystery ShopperReporten.pdf.

Surveys

Surveys can be administered by mail, by e-mail (as an attachment), via the Web (offering a URL where people can complete the entire survey), or by telephone; they can be distributed in-house to library users, or in person; or they can be placed on or linked from homepages for anyone to fill out or placed at service points for customers to pick up and complete (e.g., as comment cards). One of the more interesting surveys available on a library's homepage is the satisfaction survey provided by Counting Opinions and used by both academic (e.g., Drexel University Libraries, see http://www.library.drexel.edu/) and public libraries (e.g., the San Francisco Public Library, see http://sfpl.org/). At one time a visitor to the homepage of the San Francisco Public Library would have found the upper right-hand corner of the initial Web page unfolding and revealing the customer survey.[14]

From an examination of the literature of library and information science, it appears that many investigators settle for a low response rate—well under 50 percent—and might assume that the responses are representative of a given population, for instance students in their freshmen year of college. Many colleges and universities, however, have a diverse student population, for example, in terms of race, sexual orientation, or disability. Taking just students with disabilities, in 2008 this population "represented nearly 11 percent of all postsecondary students. Moreover, this population appears to have grown."[15] Claims of representativeness must be supported with some statistical analysis comparing respondents to subsets of the population. Representativeness is a matter of degree, and a student population should not be judged merely in terms of age, class level, and discipline. Another caution relates to self-reporting, in which the accuracy of the responses cannot be verified. Furthermore, there is likely no control over who responds; such a circumstance inhibits the generalizability of study findings.

Many researchers have examined the effect of providing a variety of monetary incentives and nonmonetary ones (token gifts such as small packages of coffee, ballpoint pens, or participation in a raffle or lottery) to subjects. Generally some form of an incentive is most effective when it is enclosed with the survey; the promise of an incentive for a returned questionnaire is not as effective in increasing response. Monetary incentives might encourage participation when survey respondents are asked for lengthy responses to open-ended questions. Furthermore, such incentives might lead to fewer skipped questions or "N/A" type answer choices. Nonetheless, offering sizable incentives can create a bias effect among respondents, where there is a sense of obligation and respondents feel more positive about the topic (e.g., their satisfaction with library services). This feeling of obligation can skew data by mistakenly reflecting a higher degree of positive feedback. Though it is important to establish data significance by reaching a threshold of response quantity, it is even more important to ensure response quality.

As an alternative or a companion to the use of incentives, libraries or survey companies can embed widgets, which are text or visuals placed on a Web page, blog, or social network, to invite participation or to poll users on one or more questions. Respondents might be informed where they can go on the Web site to view study results. The use of widgets may improve response rates.

Another issue is one of questionnaire construction, including the sequencing of questions and the appropriate scale for registering survey responses. Fortunately there are a number of good guides to help the novice researcher. As discussed in chapter 2, Sage Publications is a leading publisher of such works. Sage also publishes journals in the social sciences that address issues of concern to this section of the chapter; for example, Paula Vicente and Elizabeth Reis, "Using Questionnaire Design to Fight Nonresponse Bias in Web Surveys." *Social Science Computer Review* 28, no. 2 (May 2010): 251–67. In addition, online resources (e.g., SurveyMonkey, http://www.surveymonkey.com/) provide excellent guidance and enable evaluators to create visually appealing text and to insert skip patterns.

Transaction Log Analysis

A *transaction log* is an electronic record of interactions that have occurred between a system and users of that system. These log files can come from various computers and systems (i.e., library Web sites, online public access catalogs, or, for that matter, any application that records user–system–information interactions). Transaction log analysis is the associated methodological approach for quantifying content in those files.[16]

Among other things, transaction log analysis presents domain names of users (e.g., .com, .edu, and .gov) and a portrait of the Web browsers used, hits, time spent at a particular place (e.g., a Web page), time downloading and material downloaded, and errors or problems encountered during use. For instance, an analysis of errors might indicate the types of spelling mistakes users make.

Usability Testing

Usability testing is a broad term that applies to *inquiry*, *inspection*, and *formal usability* testing. When staff members inquire about customer preferences, expectations, and experiences, they use focus group interviews, one-to-one interviews, and surveys. When they engage in interviewing, they can ask follow-up questions and, in the case of focus groups, get participants to interact with the comments that others make. The *inspection method* encompasses heuristic evaluation, a systematic inspection of a user interface design for usability, and *cognitive walkthroughs*, a review of a sequence of actions in which reviewers check specific characteristics (e.g., conventions for spelling variables versus procedure calls) and determine that there is no violation of systemwide procedures. In the inspection method, the designers of a Web site, database, or information system, and perhaps other specialists, often substitute for users and perform tasks in which they navigate the site, database, or system. Inquiry and formal usability testing involve actual users, but for different purposes. In formal usability testing, participants are observed as they perform given tasks. The goal is to improve the appearance, layout, and navigation of information contained on that site, database, or system.

A review of the literature shows that the number of test questions should not exceed twelve. During formal usability testing, the steps that participants take to answer questions are recorded, synthesized, and used to diagnose problems, but not to test subjects' knowledge of libraries and information literacy skills.[17] As well, comments they make during and after the session might be captured, analyzed, and used in the ongoing improvement of the site, database, or system.

Summary

"According to a Chinese adage, even a thousand-mile journey must begin with a first step. The likelihood of reaching one's designation is much enhanced if the first step and the sequent steps take the traveler in the correct direction. Wandering about here and there without a clear sense of purpose or direction consumes, time, energy, . . . resources[,]"[18] and prevents the creation of a solid chain of reasoning throughout the inquiry process. That initial step does not involve a decision about methodology! Methodological decisions result from addressing the previous stages of proposal writing, namely the reflective inquiry and research design.

Appendix C summarizes each of the methodologies discussed in this chapter and in chapter 8 and lists some of their advantages and disadvantages. No methodology offers only advantages. Evaluators need to seek the one (or ones) that have the best application for examining the study's problem statement, objectives, research questions, and hypotheses, and find ways to offset any major disadvantages. Table 7.1 shows which methodologies, in general, are appropriate to a given topical area.

Table 7.1. General Topical Areas and Associated Quantitative Methodologies

Collection analysis/use	Citation analysis, observation, record analysis (circulation, downloading, interlibrary loan)
Customer and noncustomer (lost, never gained, unwilling to be a customer) opinions/expectations	Survey
Determining one's knowledge, personality, abilities	Standardized testing
Ease of navigation: Web site, databases	Usability testing
Examination of scholarly communication	Citation analysis, observation, survey
Occurrence of words, phrases, concepts, and so on in some text	Content analysis
Search behavior	Observation, survey, usability testing
Staff performance	Obtrusive and unobtrusive testing
Traces of actual use	Observation, sweeping study, transaction log analysis

CONCLUDING THOUGHTS

This discussion of methodologies is not comprehensive. Readers should supplement the list by conducting a literature review to see which methodologies others investigating similar problems have used. The literature often suggests how successfully those methodologies were carried out. When published reports identify weaknesses in a methodology, evaluators should find ways to offset them.

Still, as evaluators develop their methodologies and data-collection instruments, they must be sure they understand the underlying theoretical concepts. For example, if someone wants to investigate service quality, that person should understand the Gaps Model and how that model translates into questionnaire development. As for other examples, there are different conceptualizations of effectiveness, economic efficiency, and so on, and a responsible evaluator selects the concept (i.e., the theoretical framework—see chapter 3) that is most applicable to the problem statement, objectives, research questions, and hypotheses, and views data collection as the basis of that concept. Many librarians, however, may avoid the use of hypotheses, even if they are relevant to the study, because they are unfamiliar with inferential, parametric, and nonparametric statistics.

NOTES

1. American Library Association, Public Library Association, *Public Library Data Service Statistical Report* (Chicago: Public Library Association, 2009), accessed December 30, 2009, http://www.ala.org/ala/mgrps/divs/pla/plapublications/pldsstatreport/index.cfm.

2. "LibQUAL+®: Charting Library Service Quality" (Washington, DC: Association of Research Libraries, 2009), accessed December 21, 2009, http://www.libqual.org/home.

3. Counting Opinions, accessed December 21, 2009, http://www.countingopinions.com/.

4. Measurement involves decisions about measurement scale and how to frame the response scale. For an excellent guide, see Delbert C. Miller, *Handbook of Research Design and Social Measurement* (Thousand Oaks, CA: Sage Publications, 1991).

5. See Peter Hernon and Ellen Altman, *Assessing Service Quality: Satisfying the Expectations of Library Customers*, 2nd ed. (Chicago: American Library Association, 2010).

6. Valarie Zeithaml, A. Parasuraman, and Leonard L. Berry, *Delivering Quality Service: Balancing Customer Perceptions and Expectations* (New York: The Free Press, 1990).

7. See Hernon and Altman, *Assessing Service Quality*.

8. For a list of the survey statements, see Joseph R. Matthews, *The Evaluation and Measurement of Library Services* (Westport, CT: Libraries Unlimited, 2007), 353. Hernon and Altman, *Assessing Service Quality*, provide a detailed overview of the survey and data presentation. The claim about outcomes appears in University of Texas at Austin, *LibQUAL 2008 Survey* (Austin: University of Texas at Austin, 2008), 35, accessed January 9, 2010, http://www.lib.utexas.edu/sites/default/files/vprovost/2008_LibQUAL_Institution-Results.pdf. See also Martha Kyrillidou, "Item Sampling in Service Quality Assessment Surveys to Improve Response Rates and Reduce Respondent Burden: The LibQUAL+® Lite Randomized Control Trial (RCT)" (PhD diss., University of Illinois, Graduate School of Library and Information, 2009). As Kyrillidou notes, the survey instrument is available in the form used at different institutions in a variety of places. The appendix to her dissertation (pp. 253–70) has two versions as well.

9. For a good, but dated, introduction to the use of standardized tests, see Rolland H. McGiverin, *Educational and Psychological Tests in the Academic Library* (New York: Haworth Press, 1990). Numerous tests and their certification histories are available on the Web and can be accessed through the use of search engines.

10. Blaise Cronin, *The Citation Process: The Role and Significance of Citations in Scientific Communication* (London: Taylor Graham, 1984), 86.

11. For more discussion about the value of citations and what they indicate, see ibid.

12. Laura Saunders, "Information Literacy as a Student Learning Outcome: As Viewed from the Perspective of Institutional Accreditation" (PhD diss., Simmons College, 2010).

13. Sample questions include: "Did you have any trouble using the computer equipment?"; "Was help available if needed?"; "Did the computer resources meet your needs?" For the workshop or public meeting, two relevant questions are "Could you find a seat?" and "Were you welcomed as you entered the room?"

14. Hernon and Ellen Altman, *Assessing Service Quality*, 145–47.

15. Peter Hernon and Philip Calvert, *Improving the Quality of Library Services for Students with Disabilities* (Westport, CT: Libraries Unlimited, 2006).

16. For an excellent overview, see Bernard J. Jansen and Isak Taksa, "Research and Methodological Foundations of Transaction Log Analysis," accessed December 31, 2009, http://www.igi-global.com/downloads/excerpts/8282.pdf; and Thomas A. Peters, "The History and Development of Transactional Log Analysis," *Library Hi Tech* 11, no.2 (1993): 41–66.

17. See University of Washington, University Libraries, "Ask Us! Usability How-to Guides, Web Links, and Books" (Seattle, WA: University Libraries, 2008), accessed January 5, 2010, http://www.lib.washington.edu/usability/howto.html; and John Kupersmith, "Library Terms Evaluated in Usability Tests and Other Studies" (2009), accessed January 5, 2010, http://www.jkup.net/terms-studies.html.

18. U.S. Government Accounting Office, *Designing Evaluations*, GAO/PEMD-10.1.4 (Washington, DC: Government Accounting Office, 1991), 6.

Chapter 8

Qualitative Study

Qualitative study is not merely a group of methodologies used to gather data, nor is it simply an alternative to undertaking research for those who are averse to statistics. Qualitative research shares with quantitative research the rigor of systematic inquiry, but differs in the purpose of the study, type of questions addressed, role of participants and investigators, data analysis, and meaningfulness of generalizing (or *generalizability* of) results. Qualitative studies, also called phenomenological and naturalistic inquiries, investigate phenomena in specific contexts and natural settings. Such research is considered by some who hold strong commitment to the longer established paradigms of scientific research to be a *soft*, less valued, and less seriously taken approach, one that is common to the social sciences and other applied disciplines. Library and information science (LIS) research, as well as practice, have been quick to adopt many of the methodologies evolved over the past quarter-century, but on occasion without full appreciation for the strengths and limitations of qualitative research. As one skeptic notes,

> For better or worse, librarians have discovered qualitative research. For better, because naturalistic inquiry has much to offer librarianship. For worse, because librarians probably will use it as yet another excuse for avoiding mathematics in general and statistics in particular.[1]

This chapter offers an overview of the research paradigm that distinguishes qualitative research; reviews several qualitative data-gathering methods commonly used in studies of libraries and information services; and introduces issues to consider in the analysis, presentation, and use of data gathered through application of these methods. The chapter does not intend to create qualitative researchers out of its readers, but hopefully will strengthen their ability to read critically reports of qualitative research and evaluate the usefulness of results of such studies.

DISTINGUISHING QUALITATIVE RESEARCH

Yvonna S. Lincoln and Egon G. Guba,[2] among the early researchers who undertook and popularized qualitative research methods, offer a helpful comparison of factors that distinguish studies within qualitative and quantitative frameworks. They suggest the comparison can be summarized by a review of seven factors that offer insights helpful for developing or reviewing academic library studies. Those factors are discussed below.

Type of Research

Fundamental to the differentiation of the two frameworks is that qualitative research is exploratory, whereas quantitative research is descriptive and sometimes predictive. Qualitative studies seek understanding, for example, of what contributes to the selection of electronic resources or reasons for seeking assistance from a librarian. Such exploration might also delve further into responses identified in a quantitative study in order to uncover further insights into reasons for the responses or to clarify interpretations of response categories. Associated with qualitative investigations are ethnographic, anthropological, observational, and field studies, all of which are important for studying a problem in natural settings where human activity occurs.

Object of Research

Assumptions about the reality that is being studied differ between the two frameworks. Qualitative research emphasizes the importance of people's views or behaviors in understanding the world, whereas quantitative research assumes that the world consists of structured events. One framework seeks perceptions and opinions; the other looks for factual occurrences.

Type of Questions

Questions addressed in qualitative studies are open ended, posed without preconceived categories of responses. In contrast, quantitative studies address questions that are formulated to be measurable, often building on the results of exploratory queries undertaken in qualitative studies. For example, a study of customer satisfaction with library services could include the following types of questions, illustrating the two approaches to research questions:

Qualitative types of questions:

- What about the library's services is important to you?
- Why do you not use the library's Web site?
- How do you imagine an outstanding library facility will look in ten years?

Quantitative types of questions/instructions:

- Please indicate the extent of your agreement or disagreement that each of the following library services is important to you:

	Strongly agree						Strongly disagree
	↓						↓
Reference assistance	1	2	3	4	5	6	7
Interlibrary loan	1	2	3	4	5	6	7
Reserve circulation	1	2	3	4	5	6	7

- Indicate the reasons why you do not use the library's Web site [check all that apply]:

    ___ Unattractive

    ___ Difficult to find what I need

    ___ No idea

- From the following images, select the one that best illustrates the ideal library of the future and explain why you think so:

Comparing these types of questions suggests the nature of the inquiry that qualitative and quantitative research makes. One produces messy, disorganized data, but potentially richer in its very diversity, while the other offers responses that may be counted (measured) to summarize patterns of opinions.

Number of Respondents

Typically, qualitative research involves a small number of participants, whether to tease out opinions or to observe behavior. In contrast, quantitative research often requires a sampling of a population; the purpose is to have a large number of participants who provide representative responses from which to draw conclusions.

Interviewer Qualifications

Much qualitative research requires a specialized knowledge of the focus of study that can be incorporated into the process of gathering data. Whether an interviewer delves into a question, driven by the respondent's answer, or an observer records selected elements of behavior from subjective viewings of a situation, the creative, engaging, and flexible qualifications of the data gatherer are an important contribution to the success of the study. No such adaptable qualifications are needed in the more mechanical and prescribed steps required for gathering of quantitative data, though knowledge of the focus of study may be applied in the design of the study instruments prior to data gathering. One approach is subjective and requires the interviewer to be an integral part of the investigation; in the other, the investigator is removed by the design of objective methods to provide information about descriptions, comparisons, and predications.

Analysis

Once data are collected, different approaches to their analysis are appropriate, depending on the research premises. Qualitative analysis is subjective, highly iterative, and time consuming, repeatedly reviewing data to develop patterns, reconsider them, and create new insights. Quantitative research typically applies objective statistical analysis to data. With use of computer processing and software tools, the time needed to review massive amounts of responses is only a minor imposition on the investigator, who reviews statistical test results to draw conclusions; software, however, is available to assist in the management of qualitative research data as well.

Generalizations of Results

Qualitative researchers often are not interested in generalizing the results of their research due to their motivation to understand the human context of phenomena. The researcher uses the details of collected data to build rich descriptions from the participants' viewpoints. Rich data, gathered from multiple individual perspectives, are organized into general themes that frame the interpretation the researcher brings to the understanding of the phenomena. This culminating presentation differs from that of quantitative research results, where statistical processing of data creates generalizable projections from the sample to the population it represents. With specifiable degrees of confidence, the quantitative researcher generalizes insights gained to a larger population, and, in some research designs, can predict future behaviors. In contrast, the qualitative researcher's focus is limited to the setting studied. Qualitative descriptions can offer context for quantitative generalizations. Some research guides urge novice investigators to experience the context of the activities they will study, through some initial qualitative techniques, before embarking on quantitative analysis. Others place qualitative research at the end of the quantitative inquiry as a way to interpret and better understand the results of statistical analysis. Whenever it is done, the benefit of complementing one approach with the other, known as *triangulation*, results in a deeper understanding of the human endeavor under study.

DATA GATHERING FOR QUALITATIVE RESEARCH

Qualitative data are not numeric and are gathered in a wide variety of ways. Sources for such data fall into three broad categories: interview, observation, and documentation. Regardless of the specific methodology used to gather the data, they share in common human engagement and thus subjective interpretation to capture and analyze the information. This characteristic raises concerns among some researchers about the validity of qualitative data. Traditional criteria used to judge quantitative research include attention to internal and external validity, reliability, and objectivity. These are concerned with the degree to which data are *true* to reality. Within the qualitative paradigm, however, truth lies in the perceptions that individuals have, and thus there is no external reality against which to measure whether data are true or false. This fundamental difference over what is measured does not give qualitative data gathering a pass on judgments of how sound the research is. In the course of human interaction, most of us ask questions of others, notice behaviors, and read newspapers or view televised accounts related to surrounding activities. The greater familiarity with these ways of gathering data and inductively drawing insights, rather than systematically counting and running statistical tests, gives some the false impression that qualitative data-gathering methods simply involve the compilation of notes about some daily encounters.

Alternate criteria for judging the *soundness* of qualitative research exist and require execution of tested methodologies, with protocols as thoughtfully evolved as those found in quantitative research methods. Lincoln and Guba provide four criteria (credibility, transferability, dependability, and conformability) as alternatives to the quantitative criteria of internal and external validity, reliability, and objectivity, respectively.[3] *Credibility* is a gauge of how believable the results of the research are, and given the qualitative research paradigm, it asserts that the participants perceive the phenomena to exist; research participants are the only ones to judge the credibility of results. This is typically done after the raw data are analyzed and the *story* or description is developed; participants—those interviewed or observed—may be invited to review and comment on how well the research captured their perceptions.

Transferability refers to the degree to which results apply to contexts other than the setting in which the research was conducted. Qualitative researchers can enhance their work to meet these criteria by describing thoroughly the context and assumptions of the research setting. The judgment of whether results make sense in another context is the responsibility of the next researcher wishing to make the transfer. *Dependability* is a concept offered as an alternative to measuring reliability in quantitative research. Reliability assumes that repeated measures of *reality* produce the same replicable results, and various hypothetical models are used to estimate the reliability of actual samples taken. In the qualitative approach, the assumption is that *reality* does not have a single presence, and that multiple measures actually are of different phenomena. In addressing this criterion, the responsible qualitative researcher accounts for changes in the research setting and describes how these affect the research approach to the study.

Confirmability is the major concern for objectivity. Qualitative research by its nature assumes that researchers bring unique perspectives, and therefore the data they gather are subjective and not *real*. To improve confirmability, researchers can undertake and document a number of strategies, for example, repeatedly checking data, subjecting results to a critique by another researcher, searching and describing instances that contradict findings, and auditing data-gathering procedures to judge potential bias.[4]

DIFFERENT DATA-GATHERING METHODOLOGIES

LIS researchers have embraced qualitative research methods to study topics that inform practice and contribute to theory. Early traditions of research in the discipline used quantitative methods to measure resource inputs and service outputs, as well as the information relevance of results that portray information seeking. That research informed the design of automated systems and production workflows. In the past quarter-century or so, as academic and public libraries have become more self-consciously identified as service organizations, the perspective of those served has become a more important influence on managing improvement. Not only satisfaction, but the concept of service quality, as introduced through researchers in marketing and business management, are topics of inquiry among LIS practitioners and researchers. The popularity of such tools as LibQual+® triggered greater awareness of methodologies for gathering data about customers' perceptions and opinions. Furthermore, the idea of stakeholders and the importance of their perspective in evaluating the value of libraries and information systems have become commonplace. A modest amount of training in the skills needed to apply qualitative research methodologies has surfaced through the literature, conferences, workshops, tutorials for using instruments, and general topics for discussion via blogs and other channels of communication.

This section of the chapter highlights key methodologies practiced among LIS professionals, with note of their advantages and disadvantages for gathering data useful to the evaluation and assessment of libraries. Although at least twenty different design types have been identified, methods are grouped by resulting interview, observation, and documentation data.[5] Appendix C, which covers the methodologies discussed in this and the previous chapter, should help evaluators select the appropriate method of data gathering.

Interview Methods

Interviews involve interactive communications with participants in the phenomenon under study. They may be conducted individually or with groups. They may be structured (scripted with predetermined questions) or unstructured (giving interviewers freedom to explore topics depending on answers given and their knowledge of the topic). Interviews may be conducted face to face, by telephone, or via the Internet (e.g., through the use of Skype). The data capture may be recorded verbatim through audio or visual devices, or through note taking, ranging from stenographic detail to selected or interpreted responses to structured questions. Participants may be asked to respond to questions or descriptions; they may engage in dialog or be invited to react to props (e.g., lists of factors, descriptions of scenarios, or visualizations). All these strategies require an interviewer as the key instrument to solicit opinions, perceptions, or other responses from another person (or persons) who has a relationship with the phenomena being studied. Interviewers should be knowledgeable about the topic, attentive to information given and nuances in meaning, solicitous and unbiased, and respectful of the respondent. These traits and skills are important in their ability to administer outlined questions in structured interviews or freely move conversations in directions useful for exploring the topic in detail.

Focus group interviews are a methodology for gathering data wherein participants offer responses and the discussion among them may generate insights and additional data. Focus groups exist for a single focused purpose and then disband, and except for the duration of their interview, they do not have a continued relation with the library. Such interviews should be set up in advance through invitation, with clarity of purpose and time commitment, and be followed by appropriate thanks for participation. Effective focus groups are not large, most effectively numbering between six and ten persons. Participants are selected for their familiarity with the setting and activity under review; they may be gathered based on convenience and need not represent a probability sample, as would be selected for quantitative research. The reasons for conducting focus group interviews are diverse. They may be a valuable way to invent the future by brainstorming ideas about services or products; a library, for example, may find it useful to float an idea for creating teaching spaces with a group of faculty in order to gauge the expected use of equipment or configuration of furniture. Understanding responses to a satisfaction survey may be another reason for conducting a focus group interview; library users may clarify the nuances of factors that contribute to dissatisfaction with staff behavior or navigation of the library's Web site, for example. Perceived value, such as the balance between required effort to locate materials and the resulting value of the information found, might be the library's equivalent to testing pricing with a focus group. A group discussion may trigger ideas about ad hoc problems or testing new services (e.g., Web site interfaces or instructional tutorials). Detailed discussions of how to conduct focus group interviews, written for librarians, are widely available.[6]

Advantages

Interviews provide an immediate response, with the opportunity for an effective interviewer to probe for appropriate details and clarity, resulting in rich and ample data about a topic relatively quickly. Group interviews offer the added advantages of saving time (instead of conducting multiple individual interviews), relying on multiple participants to make comments, and building on the recall that may easily occur when someone hears about activities from another member of the group. The dialog among group members generates broad coverage, and it is likely that the topic is well covered.

Disadvantages

Interviews generate a lot of data that have to be sorted, analyzed, and reanalyzed to formulate results. It may be costly and time-consuming for the interviewer to conduct repeated interviews. The success of interviews depends on the skills and effectiveness of the interviewer; if these are lacking, the opportunity to gather data is lost—nothing can be salvaged if the questions are not posed well or responses are not probed. Focus group interviews are typically conducted in artificial settings and do not offer observation in a natural context. Interviews provide insights into what people think, but they do not identify what they actually do.

Observation Methods

Methodologies involving observations generally do not rely on direct conversation with participants, although any dialog may be observed. LIS research seldom involves participation observation, in which the researcher becomes a participant in the context being observed; some methodologies, however, use participants to conduct and record their own observations. For example, studies on use of learning environments have asked students to photograph and describe favorite places where they engage in specified learning behaviors. Data are identified and selected for inclusion by participants, who have insights not apparent to an outside researcher.[7]

More common to observation methods are protocols, wherein direct observations are conducted by a researcher who is not a participant; aims to be detached from the activity; and is focused on specific people, behaviors, settings, or situations germane to the topic under study, rather than trying to be a part of the entire context. Among the more popular observation methods used in the evaluation of libraries and information systems are mystery shopping, ethnographic observation, sweep study, and verbal protocols.

Mystery Shopping

Originally developed for retail and marketing research, mystery shopping is a method by which unidentified persons pose as normal customers and conduct specified tasks to gather information on the shopping experience and behavior of service providers, sometimes in staged test situations. It appears unobtrusive to the employees because they are unaware of being observed, while providing feedback on the organization's service performance. Although practiced for decades in the commercial sector to check on the courtesy and integrity of staff, this practice has only begun to appear in nonprofit agencies, including libraries, over the past decade.[8] The reliance on this method and recognition of associated ethical issues in conducting it are illustrated by the evolution of standards surrounding the practice. Widely used guidelines are offered as part of an International Organization for Standardization (ISO) standard adopted in 2006 for conducting marketing and social research.[9] The American Medical Association has adopted the practice of using mystery shoppers for educational purposes, and in 2007, its Council on Ethical and Judicial Affairs concluded a study of the use of "mystery patients" in evaluating performance of health care and hospital services. The study recommended continued use of the method, which might similarly apply to behavior of library staff:

> Physicians have an ethical responsibility to engage in activities that contribute to continual improvements in patient care. One method for promoting such quality improvement is through the use of secret shopper "patients" who have been appropriately trained to provide feedback about physician performance in the clinical setting.[10]

There is even an international trade association, Mystery Shopping Providers, dedicated "to improving service quality using anonymous resources. [It has] over 150 member companies worldwide," and tens of thousands of professional mystery shoppers are certified annually.[11]

Advantages

This method can involve a relatively simple exercise and can uncover data about the service delivery and appearance of the library from the customer's perspective, without engaging actual customers. It may be a proactive evaluation technique to check on performance.

Disadvantages

There is some discomfort with the method's use of scarce resources and vulnerability to scams. This form of evaluation must be conducted in a political and social environment, and its use should be known by participants, but without tipping them to a specific exercise.

Ethnographic Observation

The University of Rochester Library engaged an anthropologist to work with staff to conduct research to understand behaviors of their constituents, both the study habits of students[12] and the interaction of faculty with digital tools and organizing work in virtual and physical workspaces.[13] Ethnographic methodologies known as work-practice study were used in this research. In an earlier study, researchers went to faculty offices and videotaped while the faculty members worked, asking them questions about how they discovered items and disseminated their work to others. In addition, telephone interviews and a review of gathered documents were conducted. The videotapes were transcribed and then reviewed by a trained anthropologist as well as by committee members, who individually and through brainstorming identified more than 150 ideas. These were grouped and analyzed to construct insights useful for the design and promotion of an institutional repository.

The later Rochester investigation, of the study behaviors of undergraduate students, involved a variety of methods to gather data. In addition to the work-practice study techniques used in the faculty study, the team of anthropologist and library staff engaged students in imaginative ways. Flipcharts were placed around the library building inviting responses to questions about why they liked coming to an area and what was missing. Charrette-style workshops were held for students to participate in drafting solutions to design problems; food and token payments were given as incentives. Drawings identifying the ideal library from the student perspective were produced. They emphasized flexibility, comfort, technology tools, staff support, and access to information resources.

Advantages

Repeatedly, librarians engaging people who visit libraries and use their resources and services acknowledge the discovery of unexpected insights. Viewing the library as a component of a community rather than an imposed entity leads to better understanding of its impact on the culture of its users. Using ethnographic techniques of observation and engagement identifies perspectives and interactions that form stories about phenomena and take advantage of the benefits of qualitative research.

Disadvantages

There is a challenge to gain entrée without creating a sense of intrusion when conducting ethnographic studies. There is also the risk of observing only a subset of the community and possibly missing the interests and perspectives of a major portion of the population that may be affected by changes made as a result of the research.

Sweeping Studies

Other ethnographic methods are finding application in the study of the library's "social activity space." The interactions of people with their environment, considering also power and other relationships in the space, have been studied by researchers in a variety of disciplines, including anthropology, geography, sociology, urban planning, environmental psychology, and architectural and interior design. The researchers apply various methods, such as location inventories, spatial mappings, location diaries, and observations. One methodology that has a small following among LIS researchers is the sweeping study, wherein systematic observations are made of furniture occupancy, characteristics of occupants, or activities and behaviors.[14] Based on a clear set of research questions, the researcher conducting a sweeping study identifies factors to observe, either a priori or emerging from recorded data. Typically, a floor plan is prepared with space to record notations about the location of factors discovered, and/or a chart is created to document the amount and placement of factors. For example, a sweep of a library's study areas might register what a student brings (e.g., phone, computer, iPod, books, and/or snacks) and places where the items are seen. Analysis of data includes counting the frequency of the appearance of factors, and sometimes in exploratory studies, identifying and categorizing the factors under study.

Advantages

If carefully executed, this is an unobtrusive method that generates a lot of data about what occurs in a physical space. An analysis of the data offers insights into the behaviors of occupants and detailed descriptions of the setting for these activities.

Disadvantages

It is difficult to remain unobtrusive when walking around with a clip board and making notations from observations. There are ethical issues about balancing maintaining people's privacy with the objective of observing and recording what they do.

Verbal Protocols

Gathering and analyzing verbal data contribute to a method introduced over a century ago to understand a person's thinking, learning, or cognitive processes such as reading. Such introspective techniques lost popularity for a few decades in the mid-twentieth century, but emerged again around the 1960s in educational and experimental psychology studies. Toward the end of the twentieth century, researchers used verbal protocol analysis to gain insights into internal processes that take place when completing tasks. Around this time, the methods began to appear in LIS research, particularly in research about searching the card catalog, followed by the online catalog, and later usability testing of the Web and other system interface design.[15]

This methodology consists of individuals talking aloud to express their thoughts, their decisions, or their behaviors while completing a task. Data are collected while participants are performing a task; researchers typically ask the subject to verbalize thoughts that occur or describe the rationale for taking actions. As in most qualitative research, researchers should not become involved with the subject's work or opinions expressed. They might prod the subject if there is an irregular or long silence, and preferably should remain out of the subject's view. It is important that the main focus of the person's activity be the task performed, not its explanation. Once recorded, verbal data are analyzed in much the same labor-intensive manner as other qualitative data, with multiple and repeated reviews and emerging or theorized coding.

Advantages

This approach, which provides rich data about cognitive processes, offers data collected over time, which is particularly helpful when assessing the impact of an intervention or change in knowledge. For example, a think-aloud verbal protocol for conducting a Web search in response to specific problems posed by the researcher may offer insights into the searcher's expertise in navigating an interface or selecting electronic resources. If continued again after instruction is provided, the verbal data might indicate a change in knowledge or skills in identifying information to complete the task.

Disadvantages

This is a highly labor-intensive methodology. The data reported are limited to what the subject is consciously aware of; it is difficult, if not impossible, to verbalize what is done automatically. Some believe the process of requesting verbalization may affect the cognitive process, with subjects possibly using knowledge that would not be normally engaged. Issues of self-presentation arise as well through this method, as it relies on whatever the participant self-selects to disclose.

DOCUMENTATION METHODS

Another category of methodology frequently used in qualitative study of LIS topics focuses on documentation, both as a source of data for analysis and as the result of inductively drawing insights from details. Content analysis can be used to interpret recorded communications, for example. The sources of data used in such analysis may also be documentation that existed before the study. Annual or strategic reports, customer complaints, suggestion box comments, interlibrary loan requests, Web site content, and e-mail correspondence are among the types of documentation that provide information about a problem, phenomenon, or behavior that is of research interest. The case study, on the other hand, uses different sources of information to document a problem, phenomenon, or situation in a systematic way. These two research interactions with documentation are discussed below.

Content Analysis

Steve Stemler synthesizes a number of descriptions and offers a concise definition of content analysis as "a systematic, replicable technique for compressing many words of text into fewer content categories based on explicit rules of coding."[16] He highlights Ole Holst's broader definition of content analysis as "any technique for making inferences by objectively and systematically identifying specified characteristics of messages."[17] This suggests an interpretation of *text* that goes beyond written words to include oral and visual data (e.g., recordings, videotapes, photographs, and drawings). Regardless of the content, this technique provides a way for researchers to review systematically large amounts of data and, from them, to discover and describe the focus of study.

Most discussions of the techniques of content analysis begin with the assumption that the data to be analyzed have been gathered. As in other qualitative research methodologies, a study design employing content analysis is driven by a problem, a set of questions to address it, and a rational gathering of data. In such studies, the material for analysis may be assembled from a variety of text sources, which might include, for example, published articles, library Web sites, blogs, interview transcripts, written responses to open-ended items on questionnaires, diaries, annotations, or reports. Documented content may also be in the form of visual or audio records such as videotaped observations (e.g., of reference interviews), photographs (e.g., of preferred study spaces), drawings (e.g., of the organization of information sources), maps (e.g., of proximity of libraries to schools in a city), floor plans (e.g., of the arrangement of collections and workstations), or soundtracks (e.g., of the noise levels in a reading room). The more complex forms of communication that have become the object of ethnographic study in the past twenty years are hypertexts and hypermedia. Defined as "electronic documents, read on the screen of the computer,"[18] hypertexts present text on multiple screens at the same time, with the reader having a different experience depending on links selected and resulting pathways taken. Such documents are not limited to text, but may also incorporate other media such as photographic images, sound, graphics, or video.

Once material is assembled, the researcher may select among numerous procedures to follow and issues to consider, including the six questions that Klaus Krippendorff asserts every content analysis must address:

1. Which data are analyzed?

2. How are they defined?

3. What is the population from which they are drawn?

4. What is the context relative to which the data are analyzed?

5. What are the boundaries of the analysis?

6. What is the target of the inferences?[19]

The objective is to explore whether the constructs linked to the study's research question are demonstrated in the data gathered for the study. For example: "To what extent does the content of strategic planning reports include factors identified as important to the development of the digital library?"; "Do e-mail communications among library administrators reflect issues associated with different styles of leadership?"; or "Do YouTube student reports of library experiences capture activities identified with theories of intentional learning?" Megan Winget reviews three broad steps undertaken in content analysis, including identifying the content to be analyzed (the subject of study), the inductive process by which categories are developed from the content, and the application, based on research questions, of the categories to the content.[20]

The first step in identifying the content for analysis requires clarification of the unit of focus. Many studies utilize the appearance of specified words, and content analysis is a count of frequency. The underlying assumption is that most frequently used words will express concepts of greatest concern. Concepts, however, are not always reduced to single words and may be expressed through phrases or descriptions identified through interpretation of words. Studies seeking to focus on such concepts within communications require the researcher to employ a system of notation to identify the unit of analysis, such as marginal annotations or highlighting segments of the document.

The second step entails developing categories and coding to be used in the analysis. These are groups of words with similar meaning that are mutually exclusive and exhaustive when used to represent the concepts under study.[21] Categories and codes may be established prior to the analysis or emerge from the content during analysis. Selecting a priori categories should be based on theory, and they should be revised in the process of coding, ideally by agreement of the researcher and colleagues who understand the theoretical construct being examined. Several steps are involved in establishing emerging coding categories. The process begins with two or more people reviewing the content (sometimes done simultaneously while identifying units of focus); each independently forms a checklist of categories. This is followed by a comparison of notes to reconcile interpretations and create a consolidated checklist. Each person then applies the coding to a portion of the content, and a comparison of results checks the coding's reliability; the levels of agreement recommended in the literature range from 50 to 95 percent. To achieve an acceptable level of reliability, the researchers may need to repeat the process and talk through differences, adjusting category definitions. Once achieved, the coding categories are captured in a guide for coders to use.

The third step in the process is to apply the coding to the content, selecting the unit of focus identified in the study design. Typically the appearances of the codes selected for the analysis are recorded in a chart, identifying the codes (possibly grouped by concept categories) as column headings and instances of appearance as row entries. Some analysis might only seek frequency counts; others may further group the appearances. For example, a Key-Word-in-Context (KWIC) analysis may require a mechanical count of appearances of a priori word codes, whereas analysis of a categorized concept (e.g., coded to reflect different types of leadership) may further examine the context in which the topic appears and thus benefit from recording the unit of appearance (e.g., in the mission statement or the objectives of a strategic plan).

Content analysis studies address reliability and validity through concern with stability, reproducibility, and triangulation. For reliability concerns, different people should code the content to provide consistent interpretation of meaning, category definitions, or other procedures of the study. Tests of reliability aim to show that the same coder produces the same results across different attempts (stability), and that different people using the same coding scheme produce the same application of categories to the content (reproducibility or inter-coder reliability). The validity of insights drawn from content analysis is supported by triangulation, the inclusion of multiple sources of information, methods, investigators, or theories.[22]

Advantages

Content analysis reduces large amounts of data into categories that are easier to analyze and draw inferences from, is an unobtrusive method, and can be replicated relatively simply. Implementation of the process is within the full control of the researcher and does not depend on such external factors as timing, location, or availability of subjects.

Disadvantages

This method is time consuming, requiring an unpredictable amount of effort to repeatedly review the content. It may be difficult for some to inductively formulate categories for coding or to apply them to unfamiliar content. The technique is also vulnerable to faulty definitions, as well as nonmutually exclusive and exhaustive categories. The approach is subject to criticism for bias and subjectivity of coders, especially if shortcuts are taken in systematically implementing the multiple steps and checks inherent in the methodology's design.

Case Study

The objective of a case study is to provide a "thick description" of a situation, entity, or phenomenon in response to a stated problem or question(s) to be solved or answered. A case study is both a research design (see chapter 2) and a methodology. More specifically, it is a type of research that aims to create an in-depth profile of a person, a small group of people, or an organization, or a complete accounting of a situation or problem. It includes, for example, the circumstances under which the situation occurs, characteristics of the people involved, and the cultural setting. The focus is to address the how and why questions about the target of study and to do so as thoroughly and completely as possible. Though sometimes based on a single method of data collection, more typically a case study uses multiple data-gathering strategies. For example, a case study about how the library's research education program impacts learning may involve a holistic interpretation of such documented sources as faculty interviews, observations of information-seeking behaviors, student writing samples, or library Web guides. Findings are not generalizable beyond the specific setting, or case, studied. More typically, the results of the study offer explanation and then identification of new topics for further study.

The design of a case study parallels other qualitative research protocols. Key components of a good case study include identification of study objectives and questions, a theoretical perspective, subjects, units of analysis, appropriate data-gathering methods, selection of relevant data linked to the study propositions, and criteria for interpreting the findings. Researchers may analyze data holistically, drawing insights from a full reading of data or through coding. In the course of examining data, even though guided by study questions, unanticipated factors may emerge and pose new questions. The product of a case study is fundamentally a story, sometimes presented as a narrative with a plot, detailed characters, and description of the setting. It is a well-organized account of the context of the study, what was done to understand the situation and gather data, how theory drove conclusions, and the insights and explanations reached.

Issues of validity and reliability are important to address in case studies, especially due to reliance on the researcher's objectivity in conducting the study. Multiple methods of gathering data, review of data by more than one analyst, and sometimes participant review of the narrative report are ways of dealing with these issues.

Conducting a case study comes to closure with a report, but similar to other qualitative research, it may conclude with more questions for future research. Numerous publications and online guides are available with details on designing, conducting, and presenting a case study.[23]

Advantages

The case study offers researchers considerable flexibility to expand initial questions and pursue unexpected insights to form detailed *deep* descriptions. The study design does not require anticipation of all factors to pose during the exploration. It is an attractive method for practitioners, who as researchers can incorporate their experience to the benefit of testing a theory or proposition, and as consumers can easily understand the report of a well-written case study. The case study is an excellent way to increase familiarity with a problem and to gain a brief awareness of a setting or phenomenon.

Disadvantages

The major criticism of case studies is the high subjectivity inherent in their design, implementation, and presentation. Reliance on studying a very small number of people or documents and subsequent lack of generalization limit the applicability of results. This is an expensive methodology to execute, requiring the researcher to invest time in learning about the setting and then gathering data from a limited source, as well as spending considerable time reviewing and analyzing the data.

DATA ANALYSIS

Qualitative research uses both quantitative and qualitative techniques to analyze data gathered. Using statistical analysis to describe data gathered through qualitative methodologies may seem contradictory at first. The exploratory nature of qualitative research helps a researcher identify explanations or descriptions of behavior, which in turn may become the framework by which *raw* data (e.g., textual transcripts of interviews or images and notes of observations) can be categorized. When reviewing the data, the researcher may count coded occurrences in the data that *fit* a category. Such counts, particularly when applied to large volumes of data, may be summarized with descriptive statistics to begin to give applied meaning to the framework. For example, such analysis might suggest which reasons for approaching a librarian for assistance are more common or what tools are frequently brought to the library's learning environment. Generalizing and predicting behaviors are not recommended at this stage of research, but projecting the variables for use in further quantitative research may be a result of such analysis of the qualitatively gathered verbal or observational data.

Much of the data analysis in qualitative research is done manually by annotating documents and recording observations on charts. There is, however, an increasing use of software to assist in the management and analysis of qualitative data. The tedious task of transcribing interviews, for example, has become much simpler with the use of speech recognition software such as Dragon [24] and Via Voice.[25] Most software (e.g., Ethnograph, NUD*ist, HyperRESEARCH) designed for qualitative research provides the capability to group and link concepts and to retrieve various units of text such as sentences or words to help the researcher validate inferences. Some software (e.g., General Inquirer) incorporates artificial intelligence to differentiate multiple meanings of words used in different contexts.[26] Some software (e.g., EZ-text) is free, although offered in simplified versions of these commercial products.[27] Software (e.g., ATLAS.ti, NVivo, and XSight) manages multiple formats, including text, audio, video, Web, graphic, and geo-tracked data, with features to assist the researcher in annotating, coding, and organizing data for analysis and report preparation.[28] Several helpful sources assist researchers in using qualitative research software, such as A. Lewins and C. Silver's textbook,[29] conferences,[30] and Web sites such as the University of Surrey's Computer Assisted Qualitative Data AnalysiS (CAQDAS) networking project.[31]

QUALITATIVE STUDY IN LIBRARY AND INFORMATION SCIENCE

Library and information science is both a social science and an applied science. Its researchers employ a full range of methodologies, with qualitative study appropriate for many inquiries. Some categorize LIS as a "human" science, characterized by researchers "interpreting themselves rather than explaining an objective natural world,"[32] and observe that the concept of information is so intricately linked to the human experience that its study is part of the phenomena that are under investigation. A dilemma of its research methods has been the complexity, imprecision, and subjectivity of information creation and use, a common topic of inquiry.[33] Often LIS research is conducted to achieve a practical goal, such as service improvement or development of public policy regarding information access. With this diverse set of interests, LIS researchers have adopted research tools and methodologies developed for other disciplines, including cognitive science, literary criticism, marketing, and human–computer interface. As a result, there is no single LIS methodology, and no set preference for qualitative or quantitative approaches.

Brett Sutton, who discusses the history of qualitative research as found in the LIS literature, began with Charles C. Williamson's observation in the 1920s about the "virtual absence of research" and his bias for library education to promote quantitative studies, even though "not one librarian in a hundred has ever had training in quantitative methods."[34] Three decades later, a *Library Trends* issue devoted to library research included one essay that alluded to the need for multiple methodologies; Leon Carnovsky acknowledged the case study, historical analysis, and narrative descriptions as approaches used by qualitative-oriented researchers, while continuing to favor quantitative techniques.[35] Another issue of *Library Trends*, published a few years later, was again dedicated to research, but without reference to qualitative methods, except for Jessie Shera's recognition of the value of cultural anthropology and philosophy to the development of qualitative research.

Sutton notes the absence of an endorsement of qualitative research methods for LIS through another three decades, reviewing publications in the 1970s and 1980s. Mention is made of participant observation and in-depth interviewing techniques, but with arguments endorsing the "scientific model" rather than qualitative research. Sutton mentions the continuing argument that "the modern conception of the library has been grounded in a positivistic commitment to neutrality and objectivity, values that have figured significantly in the methodological writing in LIS."[36] He indirectly dates the defense of using qualitative research in LIS to writings in the mid-1980s, citing works by Robert Grover and Jack D. Glazier. Soon after, some key works associating qualitative research with LIS emerged; the authors include Constance Mellon, Glazier and Ronald R. Powell, Stephen Ackroyd and John A. Hughes, Lynn Westbrook, Jane Bradley, and Sutton.[37] Sutton, among others, foresaw the applicability of qualitative research practiced in the social sciences to LIS, while observing that it had not yet occurred. Another critique of this approach within LIS, written by Alan Sandstrom and Pamela Effrein Sandstrom in 1995, starts with the historic observation that "the number of publications in which qualitative research philosophies and methods are either championed or employed has grown dramatically over the past few years."[38] In 1994, Tom Wilson commented that since the mid-1970s, qualitative methods "have become almost the standard in information needs research in the UK."[39]

Into the twenty-first century, LIS literature has alluded to the greater use of qualitative research methods. Marilyn Domas White and Emily E. Marsh, for example, cite twenty-five selected studies using content analysis in LIS research and published between 1991 and 2005 to explore communication in the form of responses to open-ended questions, interviews, publications, obituaries, problem statements in published articles, job advertisements, messages on electronic lists, and Web pages. They also discuss the dual approaches of content analysis among these studies, as both qualitative and quantitative.[40] Scott Walters, who introduces a qualitative methodology to the study of librarians as teachers in 2008, views the approach as "a relatively recent addition to the library literature, but . . . [the methods] have quickly become popular among scholars and practitioners in library and information science."[41] Citing fifteen studies and guides, he observes the application of qualitative research methods in LIS since around 1993. Topics of inquiry include, for example, the use of electronic resources, user information-seeking behaviors, user satisfaction with library services, the evaluation of library services, perceptions of service quality, the usability of Web sites, perceptions about information literacy, and attitudes toward information literacy instruction among college students and faculty.

A concern about the acceptance of the methodology is illustrated in Andrew K. Shenton's attempt to counter criticism that studies using a qualitative approach do not describe the process adequately; he provides a detailed, step-by-step review of data analysis of young people's information-seeking behavior.[42] In a letter to the editor responding to a reviewer of his book, which promotes qualitative methodology, Richard Dougherty advocates the value of LIS teaching both qualitative and quantitative assessment techniques to analyze efficiency and productivity of libraries.[43] Powell, in his overview of evaluation research as applied to LIS, discusses qualitative evaluation. He notes the growing popularity of qualitative methods, citing Carol H. Weiss's observation that "the most striking development in evaluation in recent years is the coming of age of qualitative methods. Where once they were viewed as aberrant and probably the refuge of those who had never studied statistics, now they are recognized as valuable additions to the evaluation repertoire."[44] Book reviews by LIS professionals also include recommendations of guides to qualitative research.[45] Searches of both *Library Literature and Information Science Full-Text* and *Library, Information Science and Technology Abstracts* (LISTA) for citations published between 2000 and 2010 each produced about seventy-five hits using the phrase "qualitative research." Although the searches were not comprehensive, the results indicate that the method is now identifiable in the LIS published research.

CONCLUDING THOUGHTS

Qualitative research is often linked to exploratory research, which draws on a knowledge base that requires greater development, values the role that context plays in generating new knowledge, and uses flexible research methodologies such as those highlighted in this chapter. Furthermore, it seeks to include critical perspectives and to do so in natural settings. The purposes of such research include the ability to gain a deeper understanding of concepts and their application, engaging in theory generation, and perhaps leading to the formulation of hypotheses. Exploratory research might draw on different types of methods, including the following:

- Heuristic methods, which comprise a systematic inquiry of a phenomenon to understand inherent biases and move to a context-rich understanding.

- Ethnographic methods, which involve immersion in and participant observation of a natural setting. Such methods apply a holistic understanding of the context.

- Grounded theory, which is the discovery of theories, concepts, propositions, and hypotheses drawn directly from the data rather than from prior assumptions, research, or existing theoretical perspectives.

- Narrative methods, which are personal or self-histories of respondents (providing a sense of a lived experience).

- Discourse analysis, which is a formal and systematic study of conversations or verbal interchanges that focus on the interactive and interpretive process between individuals.

- The case study method, which is an idiographic study of a single system (e.g., an organization).

A key element in data quality is trustworthiness, the extent to which study methods maximize objectivity and minimize bias. Triangulation is important in this regard.[46]

NOTES

1. Charles H. Davis, "On Qualitative Research," *Library & Information Science Research* 12, no. 4 (1990): 327.

2. Yvonna S. Lincoln and Egon G. Guba, *Naturalistic Inquiry* (Beverly Hills, CA: Sage Publications, 1985).

3. Ibid.

4. William M. Trochim, *The Research Methods Knowledge Base,* accessed August 8, 2010, http://www.socialresearchmethods.net/kb/.

5. Renata Tesch, *Qualitative Research: Analysis Types and Software Tools* (New York: Falmer Press, 1990).

6. The topic is addressed in other chapters. See also Beryl Glitz, *Focus Groups for Libraries and Librarians* (New York: Forbes, 1998). See also Sage Publications and the book category "research, methods, statistics, and evaluation," at http://atgstg01.sagepub.com/books.nav?display=c at&catLevel1=&prodTypes=books&level1=Course1007&currTree=Courses&_requestid=241237 (accessed October 14, 2010).

7. Tracy Gabridge, Millicent Gaskell, and Amy Stout, "Information Seeking through Students' Eyes: The MIT Photo Diary Study," *College & Research Libraries*, 69, no.6 (November 2008): 510–23.

8. See, for example, the following studies: Elaine Salter, *Mystery Shopping Project: Report of the M5 Working Group on Quality* (University of Westminster), accessed August 15, 2010, http://www.m25lib.ac.uk/mystery_shopping_project_2.html; Philip Calvert, "It's a Mystery: Mystery Shopping in New Zealand's Public Libraries," *Library Review* 54, no.1 (2006): 24–35; Elizabeth Kocevar-Weidinger and Candice Benjes-Small, "Reaching Reference Service Excellence: Developing a Mystery Shopping Program to Measure Service Quality, Performance, and the Patron Experience," in *14th National Conference, March 12–15, 2009,* Association of College & Research Libraries, 181–85 (Seattle, 2009); Felicity McGregor, "Exploring the Mystery of Service Satisfaction," in *Proceedings of the 6th Northumbria International Conference on Performance Measurement in Libraries and Information Services*, preprint draft (Durham, England, August 22–25, 2005), accessed August 15, 2010, http://ro.uow.edu.au/cgi/viewcontent.cgi?article=1026&context=asdpapers; and Joy Thomas, "Mystery Shoppers at the Library: A Planning Report" (CSUAB Library, 2000), accessed August 15, 2010, http://www.csulb.edu/divisions/aa/grad_undergrad/senate/committees/assessment/dev/awards/documents/thomas_99.pdf.

9. International Organization for Standardization, *Market, Opinion and Social Research—Vocabulary and Service Requirements*, ISO 20252 (2006), accessed August 8, 2009, http://www.iso.org/iso/iso_catalogue/catalogue_ics/catalogue_detail_ics.htm?csnumber=53439.

10. American Medical Association, Council on Ethical and Judicial Affairs, *2007 Annual Meeting Report* (2008), 250, accessed August 8, 2010, http://www.ama-assn.org/ama1/pub/upload/mm/38/a08cejoreports.pdf.

11. Mystery Shopping Providers Association Web site, accessed August 8, 2010, http://www.mysteryshop.org/.

12. Nancy Fried Foster and Susan Gibbons, eds., *Studying Students: The Undergraduate Research Project at the University of Rochester* (Chicago: Association of College and Research Libraries, 2007), accessed August 15, 2010, https://urresearch.rochester.edu/institutionalPublicationPublicView.action?institutionalItemId=7044&versionNumber=1.

13. Nancy Fried Foster and Susan Gibbons, "Understanding Faculty to Improve Content Recruitment for Institutional Repositories," *D-Lib Magazine* 11, no. 1 (2005), accessed August 15, 2010, http://www.dlib.org/dlib/january05/foster/01foster.html.

14. See, for example, Lisa M. Given and Gloria J. Leckie, "'Sweeping' the Library: Mapping the Social Activity Space of the Public Library," *Library & Information Science Research* 25, no. 4 (2003): 365–85; Howard Silver, "Use of Collaborative Spaces in an Academic Library," in *GSLIS Colloquium* (Boston: Simmons College, 2007), accessed August 15, 2010, http://gslis.simmons.edu/podcasts/podcast_extras/2007/20070227-silver-slides.pdf; Cheryl A. McCarthy and Danuta A. Nitecki, "An Assessment of the Bass Library as a Learning Commons Environment" (paper presented at the Association of Research Libraries Library Assessment Conference, Baltimore, MD, October 25–27, 2010).

15. See, for example, Heather G. Morrison, "Online Catalogue Research and the Verbal Protocol Methods," *Library Hi-Tech* 17, no. 2 (1999): 197–206; Tamal Kumar Guha and Veena Saraf, "OPAC Usability, Assessment through Verbal Protocol" *Electronic Library* 23, no. 4 (2005): 463–73.

16. Steve Stemler, "An Overview of Content Analysis," *Practical Assessment, Research & Evaluation* 7, no. 17 (2001), accessed September 11, 2010, http://PAREonline.net/getvn.asp?v=7&n=17.

17. Ole R. Holsti, *Content Analysis for the Social Sciences and Humanities* (Reading, MA: Addison-Wesley, 1969), 14.

18. Jay David Bolter, W*riting Space: The Computer, Hypertext, and the History of Writing* (Hillsdale, NJ: Lawrence Erlbaum, 1993), 21, cited in Bella Dicks and Bruce Mason, "Hypermedia and Ethnography: Reflections on the Construction of a Research Approach," *Sociological Research Online* 3, no. 3 (1998), accessed August 15, 2010, http://www.socresonline.org.uk/3/3/3.html.

19. Klaus H. Krippendorff, *Content Analysis: An Introduction to Its Methodology* (Newbury Park, CA: Sage Publications, 1980).

20. Megan Winget, "Qualitative Research: The 'Ethnography of Annotation' Model" (2005), accessed August 14, 2010, http://www.unc.edu/~winget/research/Winget_Methods.pdf.

21. Stemler, "An Overview of Content Analysis."

22. Ibid.

23. See, for example, Robert K. Yin, *Case Study Research: Design and Methods* (Newbury Park, CA: Sage Publications, 2009); Bronwyn Becker, Patrick Dawson, Karen Devine, Carla Hannum, Steve Hill, Jon Leydens, Debbie Matuskevich, Carol Traver, and Mike Palmquist, *Case Studies. Writing@CSU* (Ft. Collins: Colorado State University, Department of English, 2005), accessed September 8, 2010, http://writing.colostate.edu/guides/research/casestudy/.

24. Dragon NaturallySpeaking Web site, accessed September 11, 2010, http://www.nuance.com/talk/.

25. Via Voice Web site, accessed September 11, 2010, http://www-01.ibm.com/software/pervasive/embedded_viavoice/.

26. Stemler, "An Overview of Content Analysis."

27. U.S. Center for Disease Control and Prevention, EZ-Text Web site, accessed September 11, 2010, http://www.cdc.gov/hiv/topics/surveillance/resources/software/ez-text/index.htm.

28. See ATLAS.ti Qualitative Data Analysis Software Web site, accessed September 11, 2010, http://www.atlasti.com/; NVivo 8 Web site, accessed September 11, 2010, http://www.qsrinternational.com/products_nvivo.aspx; XSight Web site, accessed September 11, 2010, http://www.qsrinternational.com/products_xsight.aspx.

29. A. Lewins and C. Silver, *Using Software in Qualitative Research: A Step by Step Guide* (London: Sage Publications, 2007).

30. See, for example, *3rd European Workshop on Computer-Aided Qualitative Research* (Lisbon, Portugal, 2010), accessed September 11, 2010, http://www.merlien.org/upcoming-events/caqre2010.html.

31. University of Surrey, *Computer Assisted Qualitative Data AnalysiS [CAQDAS] Networking Project,* accessed September 11, 2010, http://caqdas.soc.surrey.ac.uk/.

32. Brett Sutton, "Qualitative Research Methods in Library and Information Science," in *Encyclopedia of Library and Information Sciences*, 3rd ed., vol. 1, no. 1, 4380–393 (London: Taylor & Francis, 2010).

33. S. D. Neill, *Dilemmas in the Study of Information Exploring the Boundaries of Information Science* (New York: Greenwood Press, 1992), 141.

34. Charles C. Williamson, *The Williamson Reports of 1921 and 1923* (Metuchen, NJ: Scarecrow Press, 1931), 8.

35. Leon Carnovsky, "Methodology in Research and Applications," *Library Trends* 6, no. 2 (1957): 243–46.

36. Gary P. Radford, "Positivism, Foucault, and the Fantasia of the Library: Conceptions of Knowledge and the Modern Library Experience," *The Library Quarterly* 64, no. 4 (1992): 408–24.

37. See Constance Mellon, *Naturalistic Inquiry for Library Sciences* (New York: Greenwood Press, 1990); Jack D. Glazier and Ronald R. Powell, eds., *Qualitative Research in Information Management* (Englewood, CO: Libraries Unlimited, 1992); Stephen Ackroyd and John A. Hughes, *Data Collection in Context*, 2nd ed. (London: Longman, 1992), 3; Lynn Westbrook, "Qualitative Research Methods: A Review of Major Stages, Data Analysis Techniques, and Quality Controls," *Library & Information Science Research* 16, no. 3 (Summer 1994): 241–54; Jane Bradley and Brett Sutton, eds., "Symposium on Qualitative Research Theory, Methods, and Applications," *The Library Quarterly* 63, no. 4 (1993): 411–527.

38. Alan R. Sandstrom and Pamela Effrein Sandstrom, "The Use and Misuse of Anthropological Methods in Library and Information Science Research," *The Library Quarterly* 65, no. 2 (April 1995): 161–99.

39. Tom Wilson, "Information Needs and Uses: Fifty Years of Progress?" in *Fifty Years of Progress: A Journal of Documentation Review*, ed. B. C. Vickery, 15–51 (London: Aslib, 1994), cited in Andrew K. Shenton and Pat Dixon, "Debates and Paradoxes Surrounding the Use of Qualitative Methods," *Education for Information* 22, no. 22 (2004): 1–42.

40. Marilyn Domas White and Emily E. Marsh, "Content Analysis: A Flexible Methodology," *Library Trends* 55, no. 1 (Summer, 2006): 22–45.

41. Scott Walters, "Librarians as Teachers: A Qualitative Inquiry into Professional Identity," *College & Research Libraries* 69, no. 1 (January 2008): 54.

42. Andrew K. Shenton, "The Analysis of Qualitative Data in LIS Research Projects: A Possible Approach," *Education for Information* 22, nos. 3/4 (2004): 143–62.

43. Richard M. Dogherty, "Letter to the Editor," *College & Research Libraries* 70 no. 2 (March 2009): 107.

44. Carol H. Weiss, *Evaluation: Methods for Studying Programs and Policies* (Upper Saddle River, NJ: Prentice Hall, 1998), 252.

45. See, for example, *The Sage Encyclopedia of Qualitative Research Methods*, ed. Lisa M. Given (Los Angeles, CA: Sage, 2008). It was reviewed by Colleen Lougen in *Reference & User Services Quarterly* 49, no.1 (Fall 2009): 101–2.

46. This section is based on a slide set, "Exploratory Research," that Abbie K. Frost, School of Social Work, Simmons College, used in a presentation for the Simmons Managerial Leadership in the Information Professions, June 9, 2010.

A SELECTED BIBLIOGRAPHY FOR QUALITATIVE RESEARCH

Delia Neuman, Drexel University

This brief bibliography is an outgrowth of a doctoral seminar in qualitative research taught by the author at the University of Maryland and at Drexel University regularly over a period of twenty years. It includes classic works, useful texts, and examples of qualitative studies in a wide range of areas in the information professions. Among the thousands of resources available on the topic of qualitative research and evaluation, those included here are both the author's favorites and an array of pieces that illustrate the use of a range of qualitative methods in a variety of specialized areas in library and information science. As an instructional tool in a course for beginning qualitative researchers, the bibliography is eclectic rather than tightly focused—and, one hopes, informative and useful to others as well.

Agosto, Denise E., and Sandra Hughes-Hassell. "Toward a Model of the Everyday Life Information Needs of Urban Teenagers, Part 1: Theoretical Model." *Journal of the American Society for Information Science and Technology* 57, no. 10 (2006): 1394–1403.

Agosto, Denise E., and Sandra Hughes-Hassell. "Toward a Model of the Everyday Life Information Needs of Urban Teenagers, Part 2: Empirical Model." *Journal of the American Society for Information Science and Technology* 57, no. 11 (2006): 1418–426.

Bradley, Jana. "Methodological Issues and Practices in Qualitative Research." *The Library Quarterly* 63, no. 4 (1993): 431–49.

Chatman, Elfreda A. *The Information World of Retired Women*. Westport, CT: Greenwood Press, 1992.

Cooper, Linda Z. "A Case Study of Information-Seeking Behavior in 7-Year-Old Children in a Semistructured Situation." *Journal of the American Society for Information Science and Technology* 53, no. 11 (2002): 904–22.

Corbin, Juliet M., and Anselm L. Straus. *Basics of Qualitative Research*. 3rd ed. Thousand Oaks, CA: Sage Publications, 2008.

Creswell, John W. *Research Design: Qualitative, Quantitative, and Mixed Methods Approaches*. 2nd ed. Thousand Oaks, CA: Sage Publications, 2003.

Devakos, Rea. "Towards User Responsive Institutional Repositories: A Case Study." *Library Hi Tech* 24, no. 2 (2006): 173–82.

Eisenhardt, Kathleen M. "Building Theories from Case Study Research." *Academy of Management Review* 14, no. 4 (1989): 532–50.

Fidel, Raya. "Qualitative Methods in Information Retrieval Research." *Library & Information Science Research* 15, no. 3 (1993): 219–47.

Fidel, Raya, Rachel K. Davies, Mary H. Douglass, Carla J. Holder, Elisabeth J. Kushner, Bryan K. Miyagishima, and Christina D. Toney. "A Visit to the Information Mall: Web Searching Behavior of High School Students." *Journal of the American Society for Information Science and Technology* 50, no. 1 (1999): 24–37.

Finegold, Adam R. D., and Louise Cooke. "Exploring the Attitudes, Experiences, and Dynamics of Interaction in Online Groups." *Internet and Higher Education* 9, no. 3 (2006): 201–15.

Ford, Nigel, and Yazdan Mansourian. "The Invisible Web: An Empirical Study of 'Cognitive Invisibility'." *Journal of Documentation* 62, no. 5 (2006): 584–96.

Given, Lisa. "Qualitative Research in Evidence-based Practice: A Valuable Partnership." *Library Hi Tech* 24, no. 3 (2006): 376–86.

Glazier, Jack D., and Ronald R. Powell. *Qualitative Research in Information Management.* Englewood, CO: Libraries Unlimited, 1992.

Gracy, Karen F. "Documenting Communities of Practice: Making the Case for Archival Ethnography." *Archival Science* 2004, no. 4 (2006): 335–65.

Guba, Egon G. "Criteria for Assessing the Trustworthiness of Naturalistic Inquiries." *Educational Communications and Technology Journal* 29, no. 2 (1981): 75–91.

Guba, Egon G., and Yvonna S. Lincoln. "Epistemological and Methodological Bases of Naturalistic Inquiry." *Educational Communications and Technology Journal* 30, no. 4 (1982): 233–52.

Haythornthwaite, Caroline. "Social Network Analysis: An Approach and Technique for the Study of Information Exchange." *Library & Information Science Research* 18, no. 4 (1996): 323–42.

Hertzum, Morten. "Requests for Information from a Film Archive: A Case Study of Multimedia Retrieval." *Journal of Documentation* 59, no. 2 (2003): 168–86.

Klein, Heinz K., and Michael D. Myers. "A Set of Principles for Conducting and Evaluating Interpretive Field Studies in Information Systems." *MIS Quarterly* 23, no. 1 (1999): 67–94.

Kracker, Jacqueline, and Peiling Wang. "Research Anxiety and Students' Perceptions of Research: An Experiment. Part II: Content Analysis of Their Writings on Two Experiences." *Journal of the American Society for Information Science and Technology* 53, no. 4 (2002): 295–307.

Kuhlthau, Carol C. "Inside the Search Process: Information Seeking from the User's Perspective." *Journal of the American Society for Information Science* 42, no. 5 (1991): 361–71.

Lincoln, Yvonna S. "Insights into Library Services and Users from Qualitative Research." *Library & Information Science Research* 24, no. 1 (2002): 3–16.

Lincoln, Yvonna S., and Egon G. Guba. "Paradigmatic Controversies, Contradictions, and Emerging Confluences" (Chapter 6). In *Handbook of Qualitative Research,* 2nd ed., edited by Norman K. Denzin and Yvonna S. Lincoln. Thousand Oaks, CA: Sage Publications, 2000.

Maxwell, Joseph A. *Qualitative Research Design: An Interactive Approach.* 2nd ed. Thousand Oaks, CA: Sage Publications, 2005.

Mellon, Constance A. *Naturalistic Inquiry for Library Science.* New York: Greenwood Press, 1990.

Miles, Matthew B., and A. Michael Huberman. *Qualitative Data Analysis.* 2nd ed. Thousand Oaks, CA: Sage Publications, 1994.

Neuman, Delia. "Designing Databases as Tools for Higher-Level Learning: Insights from Instructional Systems Design." *Educational Technology Research & Development* 41, no. 4 (1993): 25–46.

Newman, Michael, and Daniel Robey. "A Social Process Model of User-Analyst Relationships." *MIS Quarterly* 16, no. 2 (1992): 249–66.

Patton, Michael Q. *Qualitative Research and Evaluation Methods.* 3rd ed. Thousand Oaks, CA: Sage Publications, 2004.

Prom, Christopher J. "User Interactions with Electronic Finding Aids in a Controlled Setting." *The American Archivist* 67, no. 2 (Fall–Winter 2004): 234–68.

Radford, Marie L. "Encountering Virtual Users: A Qualitative Investigation of Interpersonal Communication in Chat Reference." *Journal of the American Society for Information Science and Technology* 57, no. 8 (2006): 1046–59.

Savolainen, Reijo, and Jarkko Kari. "User Defined Relevance Criteria in Web Searching." *Journal of Documentation* 62, no. 6 (2006): 685–707.

Schwandt, Thomas A. "The Epistemological Stances for Qualitative Inquiry: Interpretivism, Hermeneutics, and Social Constructionism" (Chapter 7). In *Handbook of Qualitative Research*, 2nd ed., edited by Norman K. Denzin and Yvonna S. Lincoln. Thousand Oaks, CA: Sage Publications, 2000.

Stake, Robert E. *Standards-Based and Responsive Evaluation.* Thousand Oaks, CA: Sage Publications, 2004.

Star, Susan L. "Grounded Classification: Grounded Theory and Faceted Classification." *Library Trends* 47, no. 2 (1998): 218–32.

Tan, Jin. "Grounded Theory in Practice: Issues and Discussion for New Qualitative Researchers." *Journal of Documentation* 66, no. 1 (2010): 93–112.

Tudhope, Douglas, Ceri Binding, Dorothee Blocks, and Daniel Cunliffe. "Query Expansion via Conceptual Distance in Thesaurus-Indexed Collections." *Journal of Documentation* 62, no. 4 (2006): 509–33.

Twait, Michelle. "Undergraduate Students' Source Selection Criteria: A Qualitative Study." *The Journal of Academic Librarianship* 31, no. 6 (2005): 567–73.

Vakari, Pertti, Mikko Pennanen, and Sami Serola. "Changes of Search Terms and Tactics while Writing a Research Proposal: A Longitudinal Case Study." *Information Processing & Management* 39, no. 3 (2002): 445–63.

Walsham, G. "Interpretive Case Studies in IS Research: Nature and Method." *European Journal of Information Systems* 4, no. 2 (1995): 74–81.

White, Marilyn D., and Emily E. Marsh. "Content Analysis: A Flexible Methodology." *Library Trends* 55, no. 1 (2006): 83–101.

Wolcott, Harry F. *Writing up Qualitative Research.* 3rd ed. Thousand Oaks, CA: Sage Publications, 2009.

Yakel, Elizabeth, and Deborah A. Torres. "AI: Archival Intelligence and User Expertise." *The American Archivist* 66, no. 1 (2003): 51–58.

Yin, Robert K. *Case Study Research: Design and* Method. 4th ed. Thousand Oaks, CA: Sage Publications, 2009.

Chapter 9

Statistics

After the surveys have been returned, interviews carried out, or focus groups conducted, data analysis can begin. This process involves identifying trends or recurring themes and prioritizing them in order of importance, then drawing conclusions concerning actions to be taken in light of the results, what resources those actions will require, and what effects those actions might have. Before analysis can begin, the data or information collected should be organized. Quantitative data can be tabulated (e.g., adding up the number of ratings, producing rankings, and compiling the responses to each question), and the investigator can identify patterns, or associations, and causal relationships. An evaluation study puts the information or data collected, organized, and analyzed in perspective by comparing the results to what was expected from the original program goals (program evaluation) or by producing descriptions of the program's experiences, strengths, and weaknesses (process evaluation) or indications of accomplishing outcomes (outcomes evaluation). The results may also be compared with any available internal or external benchmarks and standards.

Qualitative information includes the respondents' verbal answers in interviews, focus groups, or written commentary on questionnaires and surveys. To organize the information, it is important to read through what has been compiled and then to organize the comments into similar categories or themes, such as concerns, suggestions, strengths, weaknesses, similar experiences, recommendations, and outcome indicators.

Perusal of data-collection services that provide libraries with products to measure service quality and satisfaction suggests a preference for displaying data in dashboards that provide at-a-glance data about performance in visual form. Dashboards may offer descriptive statistics about student outcomes (outputs that convey, for instance, graduation rate, time-to-degree rate, the extent of diversity within the institution, persistence rate, and transfer rate), outputs (the amount of service performed), and perhaps basic outcomes for academic institutions, namely passage rate for entry into a profession. There might also be cross-tabulated tables that lay out study findings for two variables. Some of these tables, however, might be too large to see trends easily and quickly, and they may not include the types of variables that the chi-square of independence can analyze. Counting

Opinions (Toronto, Canada) reports satisfaction data in quadrant charts, providing a visual correlation that reveals service priorities to managers. The advantage of such techniques is that staff do not need a strong foundation in statistical analysis. Researchers and those engaged in pre-testing and post-testing and the use of experimental designs will require knowledge of inferential statistics, that is, drawing inferences from a sample to a population.

This chapter focuses on descriptive, not inferential, statistics and complements *Assessing Service Quality*, which provides an overview of statistics, quadrant charts, and the radar charts associated with LibQUAL+®.[1] For readers wanting a more in-depth coverage of statistics, figure 9.1 identifies some introductory textbooks that are clear and easy to follow. This chapter only addresses measurement, frequency distributions and percentiles, measures of variability, and the graphic presentation of data. Chapter 10, which is complementary, covers graphical presentation of data in the form of dashboards and quadrant charts.

Norušis, Marija J. *PASW Statistics: 18 Advanced Statistical Procedures*. Upper Saddle River, NJ: Prentice-Hall, 2011.

Norušis, Marija J. *PASW Statistics: 18 Guide to Data Analysis*. Upper Saddle River, NJ: Prentice-Hall, 2011.

Norušis, Marija J. *PASW Statistics: 18 Statistical Procedures Companion*. Upper Saddle River, NJ: Prentice-Hall, 2011.

Swisher, Robert, and Charles R. McClure. *Research for Decision Making*. Chicago: American Library Association, 1984.

Utts, Jessica M. *Seeing though Statistics*. Belmont, CA: Thomson Brooks/ Cole, 2005.

Vaughan, Liwen. *Statistical Methods for the Information Professional: A Practical, Painless Approach to Understanding, Using and Interpreting Statistics*. Medford, NJ: Information Today, 2001.

Figure 9.1. Some Introductions to Statistical Analysis

MEASUREMENT

Measurement, associated with quantitative research, is a means of quantifying variables and making comparisons among them. Central to measurement is measurement level, "which reflects the ordering or distance properties inherent in the measurement scale."[2] "A knowledge of the levels of measurement and their implications is important" because specific statistical tests (descriptive and inferential) are associated with certain levels. There are four levels:

1. *Nominal*, which "simply . . . [sorts] units into unique classifications, by assigning a name or label to each one. . . . [The] aim is to sort them into categories that are similar, often with the hope that they will be similar with respect to other data values as well. For example, we might categorize people according to gender. At this level of measurement, no assumptions of ordering between the categories is made."[3]

2. *Ordinal*, in which "the measurement categories may have been ordered according to the degree to which they possess a characteristic, even though we cannot say how much of it they possess. Ordinal measures manifest all of the features of the nominal level, with the addition of an order."[4] An example is library use, with an unequal scale of 0, 1–5, 6–9, and more than 10 times.

3. *Interval*, which refers to both the order of the categories and the magnitude of the difference between them. "For example, we know that the difference between 35 and 40 degrees on a thermometer is the same as the difference between 80 and 85 degrees. The important thing to note is that the interval scale does *not* have an inherently determined zero point (zero is determined by an agreed-upon definition). By this we mean that while the difference in both cases is 5 degrees, we cannot say that 80 degrees is twice as hot or twice as cold as 40 degrees. Consequently, this scale allows us to study the differences between values but not their proportionate magnitudes."[5]

4. *Ratio*, which "has all of the properties of the interval scale plus a natural zero point. Common ratio scale measurements are weight, distance, speed, and monetary value."[6]

Whether a variable is explained by a particular measurement scale depends on the conceptual underpinnings of the variable.[7] A data collection instrument may include questions representing different measurement scales.

FREQUENCY DISTRIBUTIONS AND PERCENTILES

Arranging data from the largest to the smallest (or vice versa) in relation to some quantifiable characteristic reduces the raw data into a more manageable form—a frequency distribution that shows the frequency of occurrence and highlights patterns in the distribution of scores for individual categories. Such distributions are more meaningful when they are linked to percentiles, which are score points in a distribution and identify the relative position of one score to the others. To identify the position of a score, researchers might also calculate frequency scores, cumulative percentages, and perhaps deciles or quartiles.

AVERAGES

Averages, known as measures of central tendency, define a point around which other scores tend to cluster. They indicate the most typical or representative score in a larger group of scores or responses. There are three types of averages:

1. Mode, which is the most frequently occurring numerical value or the category that has the greatest number of units in the population belonging to it. When scores are tied or data are grouped into classes, more than one mode may emerge. The mode, the least stable of the measures of central tendency, can theoretically be used with any measurement level. It is, however, rarely used beyond nominal measurement.

2. Median, which is the midway numerical value of the values arranged in order of their size. The median can accompany ordinal, interval, or ratio measurement. It is not used with nominal measurement.

3. Mean, which is the arithmetical average, the sum of all the scores divided by the number of scores. The mean is used with interval and ratio, but not nominal or ordinal, measurement.

MEASURES OF VARIABILITY

Measures of variability, which indicate how widely the scores are dispersed around the average, include the range, variance, and standard deviation. The *range* is the difference between the highest and lowest values, and it applies to ordinal measurement. The range does not reflect variations between those two values or the nature of the spread around any measure of central tendency. The range also does not take into account the number of cases in the distribution.

Variance, sometimes called the average squared deviation, is computed from the distribution of raw scores; it is the sum of the squared deviation of each score from the mean and the division of that sum by the number of raw scores minus 1. The *standard deviation* (SD), the square root of the variance, measures the dispersion of scores around the mean. The greater the scatter of scores, the larger the standard deviation becomes. If all the scores in a distribution were identical, both the variance and standard deviation would equal zero. The standard deviation, which uses interval or ratio data, can range from zero to a small or large number.

The standard deviation is depicted in terms of a normal curve, a family of distributions that assumes the shape of a symmetrical, bell-shaped curve. The curve extends infinitely in both directions on a continuum in close proximity to the horizontal axis or baseline, but never touching it. The fact that the tails of the curve do not actually touch the baseline is not important, because the areas under the extreme ends or tails are negligible. The most important feature of the curve is that it is symmetrical about its mean; this means that if a normal curve were folded along its mean, the two halves of the curve would coincide. The fact that the areas under the curve are given in standard deviation units associated with a percentage of the population that falls within that range enables evaluators to place a random value obtained from a normal distribution in the context of the population.

It merits mention that some products present the mean and the standard deviation on a single graph that shows the margin of error.[8] These are helpful because they place the value of a mean in context.

GRAPHIC PRESENTATION OF DATA

Instead of reporting findings to their stakeholders in terms of statistics, library managers might prefer a graphic presentation. Such a pattern might also help managers to chart patterns and trends over time. Tables might contain too much data or be set up incorrectly. Dashboards such as those presented in *Viewing Library Metrics from Different Perspectives* serve as a reminder that, when organizations and institutions communicate with numerous stakeholders, they want to present data simply, without numerous footnotes and in a way that many people will understand.[9] Dashboards ensure that the organization and its institution engage in transparency and show how they accomplish their mission.

The graphic presentation might take the form of histograms, bars that represent the frequency with which different values of a variable occur. In constructing a histogram, the key is to find the intervals that reflect changes, yet group the data in meaningful ways.

Bar charts may take different forms. A clustered bar chart displays two or more variables, with the bars being either vertical or horizontal. A stacked bar chart includes the variables in one bar, with each segment of the bar representing a different value label. A frequency polygon is another type of graphing technique for frequency distributions. The coordinates of the variables are plotted and then connected with straight lines. The end points of a frequency polygon are placed on the horizontal axis. This type of graph reflects changes over time. A line graph is similar to the frequency polygon, but each line represents a different variable. An area chart takes the line graph, but shades each group in a different color. A scattergram, or scatter chart, portrays the degree with which the variables occur in association with each other.

Pie charts, another common form for graphing data, show the proportion of each variable to the whole. That proportion is expressed in percentages. When a portion of that whole is visually separated so that it stands out, this form of a pie chart is known as an exploding pie chart. It is an effective way to make a point; however, it can also influence others to see what the evaluators want them to see. A Pareto chart, named after the famous economist Vilfredo Pareto (1848–1923), is a bar graph in which the lengths of the bars are arranged with the longest bars on the left and the shortest on the right. In this way the chart visually depicts which situations are more important.

Before constructing graphs and tables, it is important to review some of the key literature on graphing and mining data, including works by Edward R. Tufte.[10] There are also numerous Web sites that provide an overview of statistics and graphs. One of the best is "Using Data and Statistics," which covers line, pie, and bar charts and measures of central tendency.[11] Because of its utilization in marketing, Google Analytics (http://

www.google.com/analytics/) might be useful in tracking and reporting use of the library's homepage.

Examples

Chapter 10 illustrates different types of graphics useful for planning and decision making. Most important, the formats are well known to various stakeholders. When they are not (e.g., quadrant charts), however, they are easy to follow and interpret.

OUTCOMES ASSESSMENT

Outcomes assessment is a broad term that applies to student outcomes and student learning outcomes (or more broadly, impact metrics). The former can easily be displayed graphically over time, perhaps in the form of dashboards or line charts. Program and service impact associated with outcomes assessment most likely is not so easily summarized. Library managers cannot represent success through simple metrics. Still, they need to find ways to show their contributions in a simple but effective manner.

CONCLUDING THOUGHTS

Numbers by themselves are meaningless. They must be placed within a context—data collection and interpretation. The word *statistics*, like the word *research*, has many different meanings. This book looks at statistics as part of the research process and a set of procedures to impose meaning, sense, and order on a dataset. In this context, the statistics discussed are useful for managerial decision making and planning. The statistics and the form in which they are reported make the data collected more understandable and direct managers and stakeholders to what the library does, its accomplishments, areas requiring attention, and how the library advances the mission of the overall institution.

Through data collection and data summarization using statistics and graphic presentations, the library documents its efficiency, effectiveness, impact, and value to the institution and its accomplishment of formal goals and objectives. The library can also use data to make forecasts and create data aggregations that are not found elsewhere. Library managers can also use the data to engage in best practices and benchmarking.[12] Still, when evaluators engage in evaluation and assessment research, the statistical procedures discussed in this chapter will be insufficient; this is when evaluators rely on the fuller array of statistical procedures discussed in the works presented in figure 9.1 (p. 172).

NOTES

1. Peter Hernon and Ellen Altman, *Assessing Service Quality: Satisfying the Expectations of Library Customers* (Chicago: American Library Association, 2010), 153–62.

2. U.S. General Accounting Office, Program Evaluation and Methodology Division, *Using Statistical Sampling*, GAO/PEMD-10.1.6 (Washington, DC: General Accounting Office, 1992), 20.

3. Ibid., 21.

4. Ibid.

5. Ibid.

6. Ibid., 22.

7. For guidance in selecting the appropriate scale, see Delbert C. Miller, *Handbook of Research Design and Social Measurement* (Newbury Park, CA: Sage Publications, 1991).

8. See "Standard Deviation Graphs," accessed March 14, 2010, http://images.google.com/images?hl=en&rls=com.microsoft:en-us:IE-SearchBox&rlz=1I7SUNA_en&q=standard+deviation+graph&um=1&ie=UTF-8&ei=jfCcS4HVPMP48Abvl_yWDg&sa=X&oi=image_result_group&ct=title&resnum=4&ved=0CBcQsAQwAw.

9. See Robert E. Dugan, Peter Hernon, and Danuta A. Nitecki, *Viewing Library Metrics from Different Perspectives: Inputs, Outputs, and Outcomes* (Santa Barbara, CA: ABC-CLIO, 2009), 223–35.

10. Edward R. Tufte, *Beautiful Evidence* (Cheshire, CT: Graphics Press, 2006), *Envisioning Information* (Cheshire, CT: Graphics Press, 1990), *Visual and Statistical Thinking: Displays of Evidence for Making Decisions* (Cheshire, CT: Graphics Press, 2003), *The Visual Display of Quantitative Information* (Cheshire, CT: Graphics Press, 1983), and *Visual Explanations: Images and Quantities, Evidence and Narrative* (Cheshire, CT: Graphics Press, 1997). See also his *The Cognitive Style of PowerPoint* (Cheshire, CT: Graphics Press, 2003).

11. "Using Data and Statistics" (Math League Press, 2006), accessed March 12, 2010, http://www.mathleague.com/help/data/data.htm.

12. See Dugan, Hernon, and Nitecki, *Viewing Library Metrics from Different Perspectives*.

Chapter 10

Presenting Findings

Once an evaluation or assessment study has been planned and implemented, and the data have been collected and analyzed, those conducting the study need to prepare a report that presents the proposal (see chapter 3), data collection efforts, the findings and the analysis of the data, a set of recommendations, and a conclusion. This chapter focuses on presenting the findings, a critical step in building support for a library program and services.

Communicating and disseminating the findings should be carefully planned. The reporting process should build opportunities to share findings with stakeholders, especially those that approved, funded, and used the program. It is best to realize that the findings can be used for various purposes (e.g., to communicate the value of the library, promote and advocate for the library, maintain or request additional funding, demonstrate accountability, and improve library services and programs).

GENERAL TYPES OF REPORTS AND DATA TO PRESENT

How the findings are presented varies with the objective or intent of the report. The use of the report to communicate value, advocate, seek funding, or improve service defines its intended audience and the venue in which it will best be received and understood. Decisions about how to present the findings should be guided by an understanding of the audience and conditions influencing its receptivity to the results. As a result, there may be several versions of the findings, each geared to meet the needs of specific and diverse stakeholders and delivered in oral or written form, or both. Presentations may be formal or informal. Sharing the findings informally during a library staff meeting as an oral presentation or with the library's community through a Web site may generate ideas and engage the community and stakeholders to offer important feedback. An example of a more formal oral presentation is a briefing for stakeholders outside the program who do not have time to read a written report. A formal presentation may consist of a keynote address in which the speaker highlights findings from a more detailed written study report. The presentation may be supplemented with visuals of related data or text.

Libraries have reported findings in written form for years, typically for accountability related to funding, in monthly or annual reports concerning library operations. The data may include input and output metrics in such areas as collection development, expenditures, staffing, usage and circulation, and program/event attendance. These reports may be text-based, graphical, or both. The written text may include concept maps that show interrelationships within a topic and Venn diagrams to show broad relationships between concepts.[1] Column-based text and numerical tables may also be included and used to organize and illustrate results and relationships of data elements.

In addition to monthly or annual reports, libraries provide written findings for advocacy in executive summaries and in promotional materials such as library newsletters and press releases for local media. The findings also may be distributed electronically through e-mail announcements or on the library's public Web site.

Evaluation and assessment studies apply either quantitative or qualitative methods, or a combination of the two. The data derived from qualitative data collection are text-based, whereas those from quantitative data collection are numeric. The reader is reminded that the resulting findings require different consideration when one or the other approach is taken. Qualitative data have no discrete units of measurement, rendering arithmetical computations, such as averages, meaningless. For example, qualitative findings may be drawn from meetings minutes, open-ended text-based responses to questions, reflective writings, and notes from focus group interviews.[2] Qualitative data may be analyzed and interpreted by themes, with repeated responses tallied and percentages derived producing quantitative data. For example, from a survey questionnaire, comments on why library customers want the hours increased on weekends may identify suggested reasons that, in turn, may be counted, and the most frequently occurring ones may be reported as initial insight into customer preferences. Qualitative results may also be categorized based on previously identified factors. For example, from a focus group discussion, comments may be read to identify the frequency of stated preferences for using library-provided e-books rather than print copies for popular reading. Categories might have reflected early observations about use of the collection, so counts are generated from interpreting comments to identify, for example, acceptable time to wait for availability of a copy, with general categories such as "soon after reviewed in the *New York Times*" or "when finished with my readings." A statistical average cannot be meaningfully calculated from counts of such qualitative data. One cannot state that, on average, acceptable time for expecting a new title to be available is 3.6 days.

Presenting categorical results should follow the appropriate qualitative or quantitative reasoning. One might report that "most readers will wait a day or two to download an e-mail version" or "55 percent (n = 250) indicated that a 'one- to two-day' delay is acceptable." Unless the question posed in the study is structured to solicit quantitative data with appropriate metrics, such results cannot report insights using means or other descriptive statistics.

Quantitative data, on the other hand, are numeric and are analyzed and reported differently. Units of measurement are available, and arithmetic computations (e.g., averages) are often possible to present results. Numeric results can be aggregated and summarized by an overall score. For example, scores from the components of a test can be aggregated into one overall score. If the results can be characterized with the use of ordinal, interval, or ratio scales, they can be put into a meaningful order. Depending on the scale used, the median or mean scores can be calculated and the results analyzed statistically. Interval- or ratio-scaled numeric results are further characterized by having equal intervals between units of measurement (e.g., the difference between a 1 and a 2 are the same as between a 4 and a 5). Examples of numeric scaled results are grade-point averages, retention and graduation rates, and job placement rates and salaries. Mean scores can be calculated, and the results can be analyzed using a variety of statistical techniques. An effective way to present such data, particularly when much information is gathered, is to take into account the audience and the purpose of the report. The informal communication for readers with little time or interest in details should highlight key insights in a narrative or bullets, while a detailed argument for funding directed at readers expecting data may include a table concisely presenting data, but organized to summarize key points that can be emphasized in descriptive text.

CONTENT AND FORMAT OF AN ASSESSMENT OR EVALUATION REPORT

The product of most formal evaluations and assessments is a written final report, which often consists of ten parts:

1. A title page, which includes the name of the organization and the date of the report.

2. A table of contents, which offers a quick visual summary of what the reader may expect in the report.

3. An abstract, which, in one page or less of text, summarizes the study, its value, and the findings.

4. An executive summary, which is a brief (one- to two-page) summary that provides an overview of the study, its focus, its value, the findings, and its implications. The executive summary may be a substitute for an abstract with some audiences. Sometimes the executive summary also serves as a nontechnical digest of the evaluation report.

5. A background section, which provides context for the next section and addresses particular stakeholders and their information needs.

6. A study proposal, which encompasses the activities covered in chapter 3 and includes any notable constraints to data collection, what decisions are being aided by the findings of the study, and who is making these decisions.

7. A data analysis section, which describes the techniques used to analyze the data collected. (A summary matrix is a very useful illustrative tool.)

8. A findings section, which presents the results of the analyses described previously. The findings are usually organized in terms of the study questions presented earlier in the report. Each question is addressed, regardless of whether or not a satisfactory answer can be provided. It is just as important to point out where the data are inconclusive as where they provide a positive or negative answer to an evaluation question. Visuals such as tables and graphical displays are an appropriate complement to the narrative discussion. At the end of the findings section, it is helpful to have a summary that presents the major conclusions. Here, "major" is defined in terms of both the priority of the question in the evaluation and the strength of the finding from the study.

9. A recommendations section, which reports the findings with more broad-based and summative statements.

10. A conclusion section, which emphasizes the study's value. If the study was conducted to seek funding, then conclusions supporting the reasons the library should receive resources should be highlighted, or if it was to improve services, then recommendations evolving from the results should be provided to advance the improvement process.

VISUAL PRESENTATIONS

Many written reports include charts, tables, graphs, and other visuals that are intended to convey information to make it easier for readers to understand relationships between data points. As a result of the emergence and availability of charting and graphing applications embedded into software programs and productivity suites or available through the Web, almost anyone can create a visualization in minutes. As a result, there is a noticeable growth in the use of graphics and visualizations in reports and in accessible media such as Web pages to help display data visually.

Examples of visualization tools are numerous. Microsoft Excel is a frequently used productivity program capable of creating a multiplicity of charts and graphs. Users unfamiliar with this application can seek and find help from numerous resources, including instructional books, online print and animated tutorials, and Web-based user forums. Graphviz (http://www.graphviz.org/) is a downloaded, open source visualization software enabling users to build a variety of graphs. Web-based applications include ManyEyes (http://www.958.ibm.com/software/data/cognos/manyeyes/) from IBM Research and the IBM Cognos software group. They provide the user with the option to upload or enter data to create a visualization from dozens of options, including charts and graphs. Google provides Google Chart Tools/Image Charts via its Chart API; this is an online tool that enables users to create a chart from input data and then embed it into a Web page (http://code.google.com/apis/chart/docs/chart_wizard.html).

"Mostly" Text

Text, which dominates most library presentations and reports, is the most common presentation of library findings in annual reports. Annual reports are highly individualized and have no universally accepted format; they take as many forms and differences in content as there are libraries. A library annual report discusses what occurred during the year and includes statistical information in such areas as collection development, expenditures, fund-raising, public services, programs and events, staffing, and infrastructure usage.

The text of the report may be supplemented with tables, charts, and graphs. Tables (charts and graphs are discussed below) are used to present numerical information more efficiently than can be expressed in text. Gary M. Klass, an associate professor in the Department of Politics and Government at Illinois State University, states that if a paragraph has more than five numbers, a table should be considered.[3] Tables in annual reports should present numerical evidence relevant to support study objectives and the conclusions contained in the text. The presentation of the table should convey the most important ideas about the data through the table's title and the labeling of the rows and columns. The table's data must be clear and precise to be effective in communicating to stakeholders.

Understanding their differing audiences and stakeholders, libraries may prepare a variety of focused findings. For example, the "for the record" annual report may be dozens of pages long, with several charts, tables, and graphs. This report will be available in the library and often at its Web site, and may also be the version sent to the parent institution as well as governing bodies, such as trustees. Although this report is the most complete, it is also likely to be the least read. Many libraries therefore create a *public* version, which is available in different formats. This may include an annual *fact sheet*, which highlights inputs and outputs concerning physical and digital collections, library use, technologies deployed, the facility, and benefits to the users. Another popular one-page summary may include little-known facts about the library such as the number of volumes shelved, public computer workstations, user seats, miles of shelving, reference questions answered, users engaged with the library in a week, logins to databases, Web pages viewed, and even replaced lightbulbs or the number of doors. This version may be handed out to visitors to the library or may appear as an "About the Library" page on the library's Web site. Another version is a one-sheet, back-to-back summary of selected activities (notable popular library events) with some numbers, graphs, and photos of the library or some other graphic representation (the cover of the most checked-out book the past year, for example). This one pager may be folded into thirds and be included as a mailer or handout for tours of prospective students and their parents, or be shelved in a brochure stand with other library handouts.

An increasingly popular purpose of a report focuses on the value of the library. This may, again, take several forms, such as a student return on investment, as well as an institutional return (see chapter 6). Other valuation presentations found via a library's Web site include those that calculate the value of several user services and then a summed valuation of all the services. For example, users borrowed 10,000 books, and each book was valued at $25.00. Therefore, the value of this service is $250,000. In addition, users asked 10,000 reference questions, and each question is valued at $10.00. The value of this service is therefore $100,000. These two services add up to $350,000. More services are added, and the aggregate value may grow to $50,000,000 very quickly for a medium-sized academic library. The library then finds that if customers had to purchase these resources and services, they would have had to pay $50,000,000, which far exceeds the library's annual allocation for the services provided.

Another library valuation presentation compares *equal value*. For example, a person may spend $2,000 on a fifty-inch flat-panel HDTV or the same amount for a one-year subscription to a scholarly journal. A new $20,000, four-door sedan may be compared to the cost of a one-year subscription to a database inclusive of full-text articles. This type of presentation may include an icon or photograph representing the television or the car and an image of the cover of a journal issue representing the subscription, and may appear in the library's newsletter or in a flyer.

Findings from user surveys conducted by the library may also be reported. The full report may be available to selected stakeholders, while a summary is made available through the library's Web site. The summary highlights important findings ("users are satisfied with the library's hours open on weekdays, but are dissatisfied with weekend open hours") and may include a statement from library administration on how the dissatisfaction with hours open will be addressed.

Charts and Graphs

Data in raw form tell no story; visual representation of data communicates something. A graphical chart can provide a visual display of numeric information that otherwise would be presented in a table or as text. A chart should convey ideas about the data that would not be readily apparent if they were displayed in a table or as text. In *The Visual Display of Quantitative Information*, Edward Tufte states that graphical displays should show the data; induce the viewer to think about the information's substance rather than about the methodology, graphic design, technology of graphic production, or other preparatory factors; avoid distorting what the data have to say; present many numbers in a small space; encourage people to compare different pieces of data; reveal the data at several levels of detail, from a broad overview to fine structure; serve a reasonably clear purpose of description, exploration, tabulation, or decoration; and be closely integrated with the statistical and verbal descriptions of a dataset.[4] It is harder to create good charts than tables, because not only does one have to understand the data as portrayed in a table, "but you also need a good sense of how the reader will visualize the chart's graphical elements."[5]

There are three basic components to most charts: the text, the axes, and the graphical elements. The text includes the chart's title, axes titles, axis labels, legends, and notes that are used to define the numbers. The chart's graphical elements are the bars, the pie slices, and the lines that visually represent the magnitude of the numbers. The X and Y axes define the scale of the numbers represented in the chart. A critical standard for good charting is that the chart should be self-explanatory. Tufte's principles of efficient data graphics state that the "ink" of the chart should be focused on the data and that ink used for nondata elements such as the chart area, borders, and shading, as well as ink used for redundant data, should be eliminated.[6]

From a perusal of dozens of library findings and presentations, there are four types of charts most frequently used: pie, bar, time series, and scatterplots.

Pie Charts

Pie charts are a popular way of showing proportions, often using percentages encoded as slices of the pie. The proportional pieces must combine for the 100 percent of the graphic.

Figure 10.1 is an example of a simple pie chart showing the percentages of expenditures for staffing, information resources, and other direct expenses (e.g., supplies and equipment). The amount expended is unimportant for this chart; it is the ratio of the three expenses that is being emphasized. In this instance, the library expended more on its collections than it did on staffing.

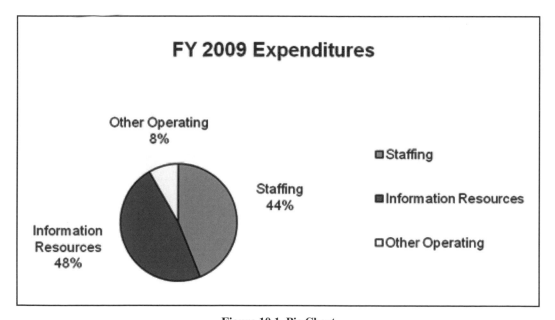

Figure 10.1. Pie Chart

Klass advises against the use of pie charts and argues that a simple bar chart conveys all the information in a pie chart more precisely and with less ink. If one should decide to include a pie chart, as is frequently done in library reports, he urges managers not to include a three-dimensional pie chart and not to display two pie charts side-by-side for comparison.[7] Some data users, however, disagree and state that a pie chart is easier to understand than a bar chart.[8]

Bar Charts

Bar charts display the relationship between one or more categorical variables, with one or more quantitative variables, usually frequency, represented by the length and height of the bars. The categorical variables are usually defined by the categories displayed on the X-axis and, if there is more than one data series, by the legend. Figure 10.2 charts the number of instructional sessions by fiscal year. The Y-axis starts at 60; there was no need to start the chart at "0", which would have just compressed the Y-axis.

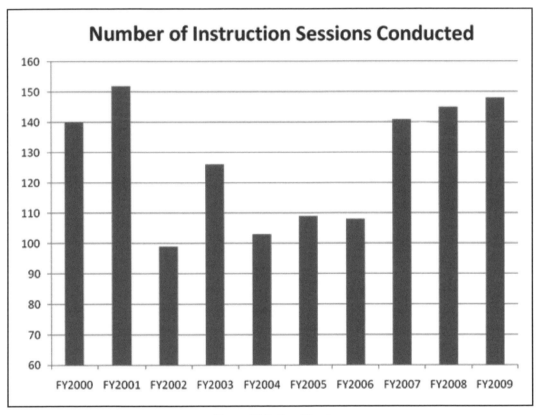

Figure 10.2. Bar Chart

A variation of the bar chart is the stacked bar chart, which is a method for visualizing change in a set of items, where the sum of the values is as important as the individual items. Figure 10.3 accomplishes two things. First, by looking at the height of each bar by fiscal year one can learn that the total number of desktops and laptops has increased from FY2000 through FY2009. Second, the number of available laptop workstations has increased in proportion to the number of available desktop workstations. This stacked bar chart suggests that this library had adopted a technology direction of providing more laptops than desktop workstations for use.

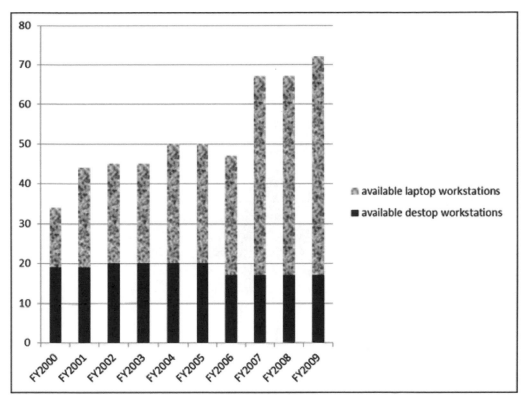

Figure 10.3. Stacked Bar Chart

A third type of bar chart is the histogram, which is used to display a frequency distribution of a continuous variable along a set of defined categorical ranges. A histogram displays the distribution of numeric values in a data set. The X-axis is divided into "bins" that correspond to value ranges. Each item in the data set is drawn as a rectangular block, and the blocks are piled into the bins to show how many values exist in each range. Figure 10.4 shows the number of volumes in an academic library in the Library of Congress Classification Outline in the Ds: World History and History of Europe, Asia, Africa, Australia, and New Zealand, for example. The majority of the books in this library are on European history.

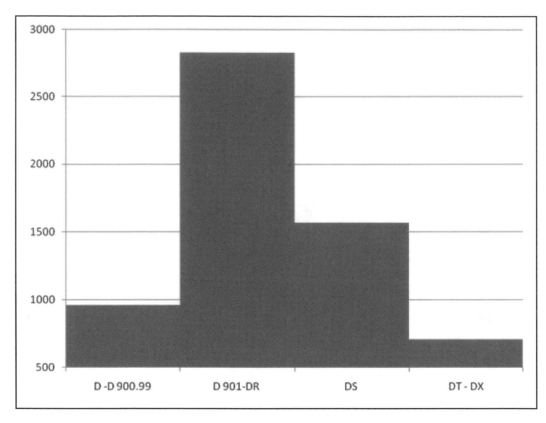

Figure 10.4. Histogram

In bar charts, each column represents a group defined by a categorical variable; in histograms, each column represents a group defined by a quantitative variable. Klass also finds fault with bar charts. Bar charts use a lot of ink to display little data and rarely exceed the efficiency of using a table to display the data. To be effective, the data must be sorted on their most significant variable. Klass recommends reversing the X- and Y-axes if there are more than seven categories, resulting in displaying horizontal bars rather than vertical ones.[9]

Time Series Line Charts

The time series chart is an efficient method for displaying large amounts of data to visualize continuous change. Usually time is displayed on the X-axis from left to right; because of the use of a line rather than a bar, this chart uses less ink, and multiple lines can be displayed on a single time series chart.

Figure 10.5 includes three time series lines of expenditures from FY2000 through FY2009. This chart leads one to several conclusions. First, it shows how the expenditures change over time and their relative positioning to each other; for example, "other operating" always has been the lowest expenditure. Second, the "staffing" expenditures have been decreasing in relationship to the other two expenditure lines, while the expenditures for "information resources" have been increasing. Third, during FY2007 the descending trend line for expenditures on "staffing" and the ascending trend line for the expenditures on "information resources" crossed as this library expended more for "information resources" than for "staffing."

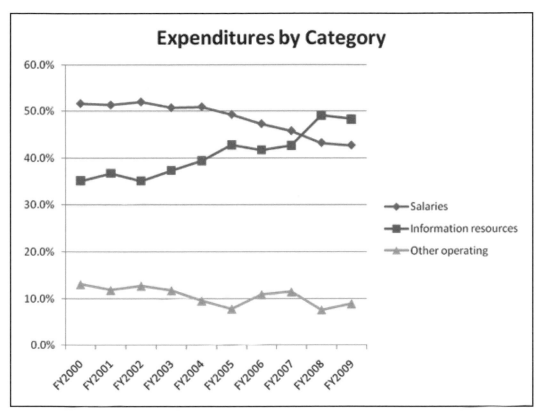

Figure 10.5. Time Series Chart

Scatterplots

Another efficient visual display chart is the two-dimensional scatterplot. A simple scatterplot can show relationships between two continuous or interval-level variables more simply than any other method of presenting data.

Figure 10.6 plots two variables: the number of loans of laptops and the number of loans of reserve books over fiscal years 2000 through 2009, resulting in twenty data points. One can see that the number of reserve loans is more or less clustered together, while the number of laptop loans ranges from less than 5,000 to more than 40,000. The data points in this scatterplot are unlabeled; data points might be labeled, providing the reader with additional information.

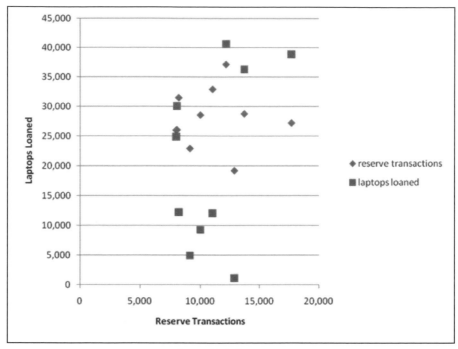

Figure 10.6. Scatterplot

Figure 10.7 is the same chart as the previous figure, but a line of best fit has been added. With the inclusion of this line, the viewer can easily see that reserve transactions are virtually flat, while there is an increased trend for laptop loans.

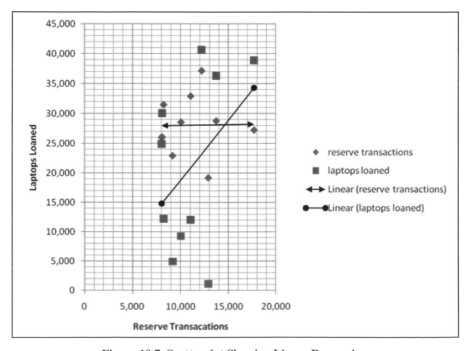

Figure 10.7. Scatterplot Showing Linear Regression

Another type of scatterplot is a quadrant, which is a useful tool for librarians in three ways: visual analysis and presentation, decision making, and impact analysis. In its most basic form, the quadrant has one or more points of a combined representation of a user's perception of the importance of a service, activity, or program, and of the satisfaction or effectiveness of its performance. The quadrant can therefore be used as a visual presentation of user perceptions of the importance and satisfaction of library services, programs, or other activities as framed by the question asked of the user as a respondent. All of the points will fall into one of the four sectors of the quadrant, and quadrant viewers can visually see the user perceptions as measured. Viewers will be able to see, for example, what services or programs users find important or unimportant, and whether they are satisfied or unsatisfied with their performance.

Though there are many possibilities for the vertical and horizontal axes, figure 10.8 uses perceived importance for the vertical axis, arranged with low satisfaction on the bottom and high satisfaction on the top of the axis. Perceived satisfaction is mapped on the horizontal axis, with low satisfaction to the left and high satisfaction to the right. Therefore, looking at the quadrant clockwise from the top left sector, the groupings communicate which services fall into the four categories:

- upper left: high importance, low satisfaction

- upper right: high importance, high satisfaction

- lower right: low importance, high satisfaction

- lower left: low importance, low satisfaction

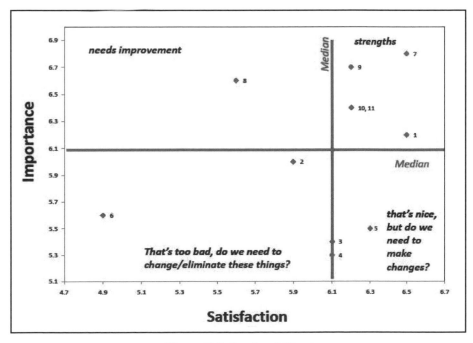

Figure 10.8. Quadrant Chart

The numbered data points in figure 10.8 correspond with the responses to the importance and satisfaction questions in a user survey conducted via the Web at Drexel University (see table 10.1).

Table 10.1. Survey Responses

Question No.	Satisfaction	Importance	
1	6.5	6.2	Attending instruction sessions
2	5.9	6.0	Borrowing materials
3	6.1	5.4	Using materials in library
4	6.1	5.3	Using library equipment
5	6.3	5.5	Attending events at library
6	4.9	5.6	Using library facilities
7	6.5	6.8	Accessing library remotely
8	5.6	6.6	Accessing Internet in library
9	6.2	6.7	Accessing library databases
10	6.2	6.4	Accessing online catalog
11	6.2	6.4	Accessing library Web site
Mean	**6.0**	**6.1**	

Control over the value point for the placement of the quadrant lines resets with the presenter. If a library's ambitions for service quality are high, for example, where satisfaction should exceed perceived importance, then the presentation of data points to measure the service quality might draw the quadrant lines higher on the Y-axis and further to the right on the X-axis. The relative position of the data points will not change, but the breakout of which service falls into which quadrant will change.

A quadrant chart might be used, for example, to visualize current user perceptions, identify and visualize a gap between user and staff perceptions, aid decision making regarding resource allocation, identify actionable strategic options that are framed by research results (the survey and resultant user perceptions as plotted on the quadrant), and visualize positive and negative impacts to better understand related benefits as libraries apply resources to affect outcomes in a continuous effort to improve services for users.

CHOOSING AN EFFECTIVE CHART

The key to the visual display of information includes choosing the appropriate chart to support the text. The following two charts were created using identical information: circulation of three variables of circulated items (laptops loaned, reserve transactions, and circulation from the general collection) by student FTE. Figure 10.9 is a stacked bar chart showing the three variables of circulated items. A reviewer can see that the proportion of laptops loaned to the circulation of reserve materials and the general collection has increased.

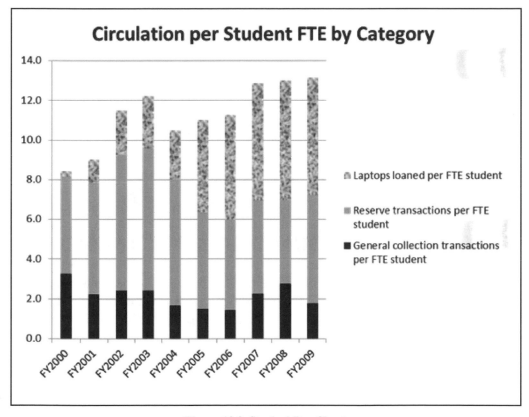

Figure 10.9. Stacked Bar Chart

Figure 10.10 is a time series chart. If the reviewer is looking for trends, the time series chart may be suitable. It does not, however, display the relative ratio of the three variables to each other as well as the stacked bar chart does. Those preparing the report will have to decide which of the two charts to use.

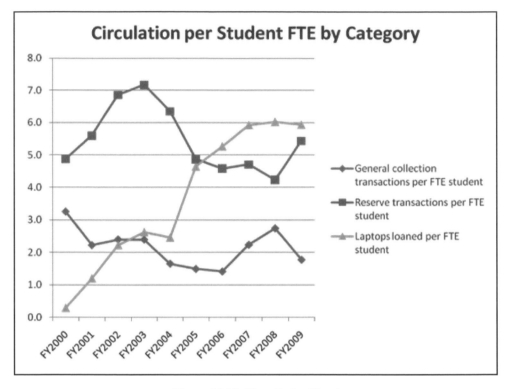

Figure 10.10. Time Series Chart

OTHER TYPES OF VISUAL DISPLAYS FOR NUMBERS

In addition to the traditional charts, several other types of visual displays are used to represent numbers. One is the use of pictographs in place of the numbers themselves. Two common examples are the use of a silhouette human figure as a replacement for a number of people (see figure 10.11) and an icon of a dollar bill or dollar sign to represent funds appropriated or expended (see figure 10.12).

Figure 10.11. Pictograph: Human Silhouette Represents Users

Figure 10.12. Pictograph: Dollar Bill for Budget or Expenditure

Another type of visual display is an icon or pictograph used as a ranking system. One of the most recent is the *LJ* Index of Public Library Service's "American Star Libraries," which displays a maximum of five gold stars for the highest-ranked libraries in ranges.[10] *LJ* Index scores are based on per capita service output statistics of library visits, circulation, program attendance, and public Internet computer use. As libraries descend in rankings, fewer stars are displayed.

An increasingly popular visual display is dashboards, which are visual representations of key performance indicators that give the viewer a snapshot of how a selected objective is performing against a standard or benchmark. Figure 10.13 is an example of a dashboard from the University of Minnesota's Office of Information Technology. It is an expenditure dashboard, and the performance indicator is that information technology expenditure is 6.90 percent of total University of Minnesota expenditures. Interpreting the scale on the dashboard, the goal is for information technology expenses to reach 10 percent of total institutional expenditures.[11]

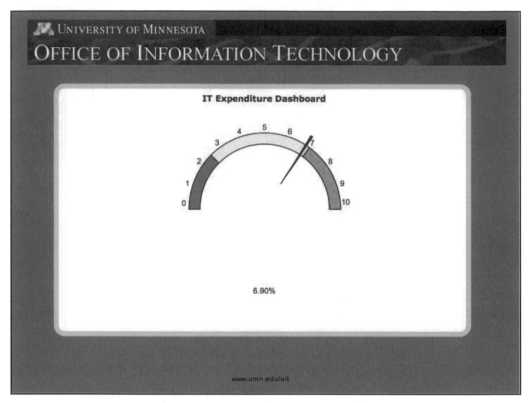

Figure 10.13. Dashboard: University of Minnesota. See University of Minnesota, Office of Information Technology, "Scorecard & Dashboard Development," accessed November 28, 2010, http://www.tc.umn.edu/~bernard/oit/Scorecard/.

VISUAL DISPLAY FOR TEXT

A word cloud is a visualization of the frequency of a word in a text. The size of a word in the cloud is proportional to the quantity associated with that word, which, in the case of free text, is the word count. For instance, if your text consists of the words "access access access open open free," "open" will appear in a font size twice that of "free," and "access" will appear in a font size 1.5 times (3/2) as large as "open."

Figure 10.14, created by TagCrowd (http://tagcrowd.com/), is an example of text as a visual representation. A word cloud can be useful when reviewing the relative frequency of word occurrences in a text. It may be that, based on the visual frequency, the words that are emphasized (appear larger than others) are, or are not, the words the writer wants to emphasize. When used with recorded feedback from library users, the cloud might be helpful to raise awareness of what is most frequently associated with the library.

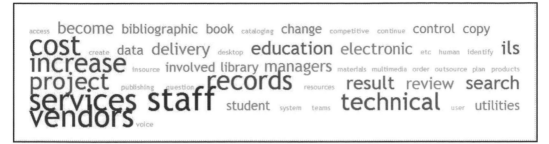

Figure 10.14. Word Cloud

BEST PRACTICES

Before releasing the final report, a best practice is to include some of the stakeholders in a review of the findings and preliminary conclusions. Circulating an interim or draft report and meeting to discuss it provides a means of obtaining feedback. Discussions with program committees responsible for managing the service or program, staff, and users can provide new perspectives on the meaning and interpretation of the findings. These perspectives can then be included in the final report. The study writers should also consider asking colleagues, external reviewers, or experts to edit or review the report for readability and content prior to releasing the report.[12]

The level and scope of the final report should have the intended audience in mind. These stakeholders include institutional administrators such as senior managers and the board of trustees, in order to inform planning and budgeting. Internal and external funders have a stake in library services, as do the users, of course. Regional and program accreditation organizations seek to discover what was learned from evaluative and assessment studies and, more specifically, how the results were applied to support the continuous improvement cycle.

CONCLUDING THOUGHTS

The content of the report should tell an important, interesting part of the library's story. It should be structured with a meaningful title and easy-to-navigate section headings. Sections should begin with an overall descriptive summary of the major points before providing the detail, creating a sectional context for the discussion and results. A one- or two-page executive summary should include a brief description of the library and the program under evaluation; explanation of the evaluation or assessment study goals, methods, and analysis procedures; and a listing of conclusions and recommendations. The text should explain how the results answer the question that formed the purpose of the assessment, make clear the implications of the results, ensure that the recommendations are explicit, and offer strategies for how the recommendations can be implemented.

If possible, the report should avoid lengthy and detailed descriptions of data in paragraph form by using high-quality graphics, tables, and summary charts. The tables should supplement the text, making it easier to read. The appropriate type of chart should be used so that it could stand alone, leading the reader to understand the context with its title and axis titles and data points. Commonly found charts include pie, bar, time series lines, and scatterplots. Tufte strongly encourages the use of as little ink as possible to convey the data. Pie and bar charts use the most ink; time series lines and scatterplots use less. In *Beautiful Evidence,* he suggests using sparklines, a small, high-resolution, intense, simple, word-sized graphic that can be embedded in a context of words, numbers, and images.[13]

Figure 10.15 displays two sparklines as envisioned by Tufte for presenting library expenditure data based on two of the time series lines in figure 10.5. An ideal sparkline is fourteen letter spaces, with no gridlines or borders, placed next to a noun in a sentence, and primarily used to graphically present trends. Most editions of Microsoft's Excel can produce usable pie, bar, time series, and scatterplots. Microsoft Excel 2010 includes sparklines as one of its packaged charts.

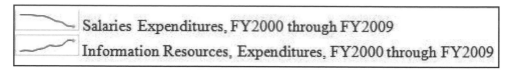

Salaries Expenditures, FY2000 through FY2009

Information Resources, Expenditures, FY2000 through FY2009

Figure 10.15. Sparklines

The report should be short, concise, and to the point. Any relevant attachments, such as evaluation questionnaires and interview guides, should be located in appendices. An effective report will be characterized by clarity; effective format and graphics; timeliness; candor about strengths and weaknesses of the study; and the adequate use of sources and documentation and appropriate data analysis, interpretation, and conclusions.

Face-to-face presentations should be short and convey the content of the written report. It is important for the presenters to know and rehearse the message by focusing on study benefits. If a particular result does not make a meaningful contribution and will not help decision makers, leave it out. It is also important to avoid the use of jargon and to mention numbers sparingly. The purpose is to report, educate, and engage the audience and not to bore them.

NOTES

1. See Mary Kane and William M. K. Trochim, *Concept Mapping for Planning and Evaluation* (Thousand Oaks, CA: Sage, 2007).

2. See also Leonard Webster and Patrice Mertova, *Using Narrative Inquiry as a Research Method: An Introduction to Using Critical Event Narrative Analysis in Research on Learning and Teaching* (New York: Routledge, 2007); and Karin Klenke, *Qualitative Research in the Study of Leadership* (Bingley, UK: Emerald Group Publishing Ltd., 2008).

3. Gary M. Klass, *Just Plain Data Analysis: Finding, Presenting, and Interpreting Social Science Data* (Lanham, MD: Rowman & Littlefield Publishers, Inc., 2008), 33–35, 45.

4. Edward R. Tufte, *The Visual Display of Quantitative Information*, 2nd ed. (Cheshire, CT: Graphics Press, 2001), 13.

5. Klass, *Just Plain Data Analysis*, 49.

6. Tufte, *The Visual Display of Quantitative Information*, 105.

7. Klass, *Just Plain Data Analysis*, 57–58.

8. William Greene, "Statistics and Data Analysis" (Stern School of Business, New York University), slides 21–22, accessed March 27, 2010, http://pages.stern.nyu.edu/~wgreene/ Statistics/Statistics-1-DataPresentation.ppt.

9. Klass, *Just Plain Data Analysis*, 61.

10. LibraryJournal.com, "The LJ Index of Public Library Service 2010: America's Star Libraries," accessed November 28, 2010, http://www.libraryjournal.com/lj/ articlereview/886935-457/americas_star_libraries_2010_top-rated.html.csp.

11. University of Minnesota, Office of Information Technology, "Productivity & Efficiency DB," accessed November 28, 2010, http://www.tc.umn.edu/~bernard/oit/Scorecard/ ProductivityEfficiency/index.html.

12. Charles R. McClure, "Strategies for Collecting Networked Statistics: Practical Suggestions," *VINE: The Journal of Information and Knowledge Management Systems* 34, no. 4 (June 2004): 170.

13. Edward R. Tufte, *Beautiful Evidence* (Cheshire, CT: Graphics Press, 2006), 7–8, 18.

Chapter 11

Creating a Culture of Evidence Gathering and Managerial Use

A common practice among librarians is to discuss the need to foster or otherwise create a culture of assessment, one in which librarians conduct assessments in an effort to learn something that will, in turn, be used as well as be useful in the process of continuous quality improvement. Because this culture actually relates to both assessment and evaluation (as covered in chapter 1), quantitative and qualitative data collection, and gathering and using relevant metrics (both outputs and outcomes), the authors refer to the culture of assessment as the culture of evidence gathering and managerial use. (Perhaps a better term is a culture of evidence based management.)

Such a culture comprises a set of beliefs, behaviors, and assumptions that drive an ongoing cycle of data gathering, analysis, interpretation, organization, presentation, and use to achieve planned objectives. Amos Lakos, among others, finds that libraries need to embrace a culture in which a basic value is to be customer focused; library services are planned and delivered to maximize outputs, outcomes, and impacts for its customers and other stakeholders. Managerial decisions are based on evidence, research, and analysis, and those decisions are linked to the planning process.[1] In addition, there should be a feedback loop from the analysis and interpretation of results to planning, and the process repeats itself.[2]

Collaboration with others is another trait of the desired culture. It should be noted that there is a fundamental difference between a culture of assessment and what others refer to as a culture of evidence. For them, a culture of evidence requires valid and reliable evidence, but not always collaboration. For us, however, the effectiveness of the type of culture we propose depends on collaboration, and often with various stakeholders. Without such collaboration, the library does not become an integral support service to the entire institution or local government.

It is important to create a positive environment for assessment and evaluation to occur and to use the evidence gathered to produce a learning organization and improve products, programs, and services. Through reporting (presenting what was found and how the evidence is used), the library addresses the information needs and expectations of customers and the multiplicity of perspectives held by the various stakeholders interested (or directly invested) in reviewing the evidence that shows the impact that the library has on its, customers, communities served, and stakeholders. In late 2009 in an interview, George Kuh, who directs the National Institute for Learning Outcomes Assessment, stated that the most common use of institutional assessment data is to prepare for accreditation.[3] Alexander C. McCormick finds that the more common application of accountability is in meeting the information demands of external stakeholders of higher education on which the institution has differing degrees of dependency. Those demands mostly relate to access to resources. Externally driven accountability from whatever source is viewed as coercive and results in resistance by those being held accountable.[4]

In addition, the assessment data collected and compiled may only be applied for accreditation purposes; they may not be used to inform decision making in order to make improvements. In a study reported in 2010, three-quarters of the faculty members surveyed stated that their institutions are, to a large extent, involved in assessment projects. Just one-third of the respondents, however, find the assessment results useful. The compilation of assessment statistics might be compared to a telephone book; campus administrators review the data and look for something meaningful to "pop out at them. If a college has collected data for general reporting purposes, assessment researchers and consultants say, unless a particular finding seems devastating, results typically don't spur action."[5] The point is that a culture of accountability to meet accreditation needs and other stakeholder demands for information is frequently practiced rather than the type of culture highlighted in this chapter—working to improve something (e.g., the educational experience).

As a result of the current economic environment, governments at all levels have reduced funding to many public institutions. Stakeholder expectations of quality performance, however, have increased. Although the number of resources allocated has decreased, stakeholders expect and demand that public institutions contribute to the economic well-being of the locality and region, and that they prove their contribution. Lakos states that, for libraries, the "pressure to be accountable to stakeholders, funding agencies, governments, accreditation bodies is increasing. In order to succeed in this pressurized environment, libraries have to incorporate assessment into their everyday activities and use the results to create environments that are effective and truly client-oriented."[6] This reinforces the point that accountability is coercive. As McCormick argues, assessment should be reflective, and educators and institutional leaders have a professional responsibility to assess continuously the achievement of the core purposes identified in the institutional mission and to do so on a continuous basis to improve on that achievement.[7]

Lakos and Shelley Phipps list the following reasons for libraries to create the type of culture discussed in this chapter: to

- be accountable;

- be competitive in the information-rich environment (library versus Internet);

- comply with accreditation standards;

- be competitive for budget at the institution;

- inform the institution about what libraries are doing (organizational survival);

- help the library to frame the measures of success by using assessment as both an expectation and a result;

- create a culture of evidence in which stakeholders see what the library does;

- learn that what librarians are doing is the right thing; librarians need data to undertake a systematic assessment process; and

- help librarians to plan better.[8]

Despite these reasons, libraries continue to gather traditional input and output metrics to show their potential to provide service and how much actual service they provide. These metrics convey meaningful data and insights, but more powerful metrics are outcomes and performance metrics that show what libraries do and, given the available resources, how well they perform. Metrics of efficiency, effectiveness, quality, and usability that demonstrate the difference that libraries make in the lives of their customers are needed. Such metrics can be persuasive in an era in which stakeholders pressure libraries and other organizations for accountability.[9] What may be missing in the current and ongoing debate, to borrow an old telecommunications term, is the "last mile," which means using the results to inform decision making, to improve, and to demonstrate the value of libraries by communicating impact and outcomes in an understandable manner to the stakeholders. Herein is the essence of the culture of evidence gathering and managerial use.

BARRIERS

In answer to the question, "Why are assessment and evaluation not a more common practice?," two major sets of barriers emerge. One involves the resources available to conduct assessment and evaluation and to apply the results of the study. The other involves organizational culture.

Resources to support assessment and evaluation may be insufficient to elevate evaluation and assessment research to being important or central to libraries. The library's staff may not have the skills to develop a research design relevant to the assessment or evaluation (see chapter 3), collect complex data (e.g., those generated by the use of pre-tests and post-tests and those involving hypothesis testing), analyze the data, interpret and report the results, and apply the findings to inform decision making. Librarians may also have difficulty designing and writing objectives and research questions that measure performance and expectations on an ongoing basis.

We all know that a lot of data exist, some of which libraries use, but for what purposes? Do libraries apply the data in such a way that they can change and improve current practices and services? Kuh maintains that few institutions of higher education spend much time or money on conducting assessment research, in analyzing the data, and having personnel give a synthesized and aggregated summary of what is occurring at an institution.[10] Providing staff with these skills through training and development, or outsourcing assessment and evaluation research to experienced third-parties, might reduce this barrier if the resources are available.

Another resource barrier may be the data-collection instrument and not the data generated. If the data are not used, it may be because they are not useful. For example, Stephen R. Porter, an associate professor in Iowa State University's educational leadership and policy studies department, among others, states that the National Survey of Student Engagement (NSSE) "is seriously flawed, lacking validity for its conclusions and asking questions of students in ways that are sure to doom the value of the data collected." He finds that students do not necessarily know what it means when they are asked if they engage in certain practices or experiences frequently or rarely, even though such measurement scales are critical to NSSE questions. Second, students may not be entirely honest when asked about their academic performance and tend to answer questions in ways that will result in making themselves look like better students than they really are.[11]

Engaging in assessment and evaluation research and using the evidence gathered help libraries to transform themselves. For example, some research libraries are investing in digital publishing and in preserving data sets that faculty generate as part of their funded research. Such libraries are becoming change agents, are engaged in new campus partnerships, and are transforming the internal organization to assume new roles and responsibilities (see appendix A).

Implementing significant changes can be difficult because of the second barrier, organizational culture. As defined by Lakos and Phipps, organizational culture focuses on the beliefs, values, and meanings used by members of an organization and on the practices and behaviors that exemplify and reinforce them. The manner in which workers greet each other, such as by first name or by title; whether or not staff wear name tags while at public service desks; and if meetings begin on time or always start late are simple examples of organizational culture. Culture matters, because it is a powerful, latent, and often invisible set of forces that determine both individual and collective behavior, ways of perceiving beliefs, principles, and values. Understanding organizational culture is important because libraries might undertake many initiatives and changes without considering that they might lead to a change in the culture and that unforeseen and potentially negative consequences may arise.[12] A common characteristic of organizational culture is that evaluation and assessment findings may be rejected, and studies abandoned, because they challenge the assumptions and preferences of librarians or because the librarians did not understand the research process. Another characteristic is that libraries often gather data without a clear purpose or there is no follow-through to relate the data collected to strategic goals. This may be the result of a third characteristic concerning professional values. Although wanting to be accountable and transparent, many in the library profession believe that libraries are a public good and that there is no need to demonstrate outcomes and articulate the impact of library programs and services to those served. The assumption that the public good is widely recognized and that the value of library service is universally appreciated may in fact result in resistance to change and continuous assessment.

The status quo cannot be maintained when stakeholders increasingly expect libraries to demonstrate their value and to apply what was learned from assessments or evaluations to improve their programs and services. Lakos and Phipps find that the key to successful organizational change is to change the organizational culture.[13] When organizational culture is stable and deeply seated, it is difficult to change. Libraries, according to Covey, allow a gap to exist between their current culture and their desire to create the type of culture discussed in this chapter. When a gap exists, the current culture always wins.[14]

ATTRIBUTES OF A CULTURE OF EVIDENCE GATHERING AND MANAGERIAL USE

Proposing something similar to plan-do-study-act (PDSA),[15] Joseph R, Matthews has identified an ongoing cycle of activities that represents a culture of evidence gathering and managerial use:

> Planning → Implementation → Evaluation → Improvement → Planning

During the planning process, a library ensures that its mission aligns with the campus's mission and goals. It also uses the campus assessment plan as a foundation to create its own assessment plan. The library implements its assessment plan by selecting appropriate assessment metrics and gathering data that address the library's impact on learning, teaching, and research. Using the evidence gathered, the library communicates the results to stakeholders (including the institutional administration and library staff), uses the data to inform decision making about needed improvements, and then revisits the planning process.[16]

Although these steps are helpful for visualizing an assessment or evaluation cycle, what are the attributes of a library possessing the culture discussed in this chapter? Lakos and Phipps provide an answer with their useful list of characteristics that describe a library that has attained the desired culture.[17] Part of the list is grouped into a framework for the following discussion.

Sarah M. Pritchard states that a culture of evidence gathering and managerial use requires an ongoing, organization-wide approach to continuous planning, measuring, and evaluating services within the context of meeting the goals and needs of stakeholders.[18] The library's mission, planning, and policies focus on supporting customer expectations and need for access to information. In addition, performance metrics are included in library planning documents (e.g., as strategic plans and unit goals). Individual units are empowered to take responsibility for determining their measures of success and to build processes that allow them to try to achieve standards. The standards and the derived processes are tied to the library's articulated mission and the library's strategic plan. In addition, after setting standards for each library process and service component, in accord with the strategic priorities of the library, the staff commits to S*M*A*R*T* (Specific, Measurable, Attainable, Results-Oriented, and Timely) performance goals.[19]

Following the implementation phase, library services, programs, and products are evaluated for quality, impact, effectiveness, and efficiency. Services should be evaluated from various perspectives, one of which relates to customer expectations, and rely on a variety of assessment and evaluation methodologies and tools to discover, for example, whether customers value these services and programs and whether or not desired qualities or expectations are fulfilled.[20] Relevant data and customer feedback are collected and analyzed. Because of the complexity of the data collected, libraries should have a management information system (MIS) or decision support system (DSS). In both systems librarians routinely input, harvest, and update meaningful data. There is little point in having an assessment or evaluation program unless the results are used to improve services.[21] Once relevant data and user feedback are collected and analyzed, they should be used to set priorities, allocate resources, and make decisions.

Academic and public libraries need not create their own MIS or DSS; rather, they might rely on for-profit firms. For instance, Counting Opinions offers LibPAS (Library Performance Assessment System), which in essence is a management information system that enables academic and public libraries to merge assorted data elements beyond customer responses to a satisfaction survey. Academic libraries might add, among other things, IPEDS (Integrated Postsecondary Education Data System) data about the library and institution, or complete the annual survey for the National Center for Education Statistics (NCES). IPEDS gathers information from every college, university, and technical and vocational institution that participates in the federal student financial aid programs. The Higher Education Act of 1965, as amended, requires that institutions that participate in federal student aid programs report data on enrollments, program completions, graduation rates, faculty and staff, finances, institutional prices, and student financial aid. In contrast, the Institute of Museum and Library Services offers data on more than 9,000 public libraries (http://harvester.census.gov/imls/publib.asp), which likewise could be added as part of a public library MIS.

In a library displaying the type of culture discussed in this chapter, assessment and evaluation research and evidence gathering for relevant metrics become ordinary, in that they are integrated into the regular assignments of staff and library managers.[22] Employee job descriptions address individual and organizational responsibility for assessment and evaluation and for engaging in these activities as part of the everyday work process. The library plans and designs each job to include enough time and opportunity for the staff to build new knowledge, abilities, and skills. The staff is supported in the improvement of its capability to serve customers. There is continuous staff development in measurement and evaluation and assessment research. The staff is rewarded for the application of new learning that leads to improved program and service quality and for its commitment to the provision of outstanding customer service. In essence, the library becomes a learning organization and continually increases its capacity for improved performance.

Managerial leadership is critical to a library trying to form the type of culture discussed in this chapter. The assigned leader of the library—the director—and that person's senior management team must commit to, and financially support, assessment and evaluation activities. For an assessment or evaluation agenda to work, it needs to become an organizational priority, extended over time, and directed at facilitating improvement rather than passively documenting performance. The assigned leader and the senior management team are responsible for demonstrating purpose, consistency, and determination in using assessment- and evaluation-generated data to make changes that improve products, programs, and services. In addition, managerial leaders need to develop channels of communication whereby they share interpretations of results and incorporate recommended changes into budgeting, decision making, and strategic planning, as these processes will likely need to respond to and support proposed changes. If managerial leaders are truly and actively committed to assessment and evaluation and the staff understands the value of assessment and evaluation, assessment and evaluation get done, and done well.

FOSTERING A CULTURE OF EVIDENCE GATHERING AND MANAGERIAL USE

Results from a 2002 Digital Library Federation study found that, in many cases, libraries collect data without really having the will, organizational capacity, or interest to interpret and use the data effectively in their planning.[23] Fostering a culture of evidence gathering and managerial use addresses this issue. A framework that creates this culture includes the application of leadership, cooperation and collaboration, and systems thinking.

Managerial leaders who articulate a purpose and vision and communicate them clearly and throughout the organization will try to foster the type of culture discussed in this chapter and to achieve organizational effectiveness.[24] In addition, they must facilitate change by guiding and teaching staff and by stewarding resources for the accomplishment of the mission and goals. They must also be committed to the continuous improvement of programs and services for the benefit of customers and to the demonstration of accountability to stakeholders to guide the transformation of the organizational culture.

Managerial leaders must recognize and honor assessment and evaluation efforts in tangible ways, specifically by supporting staff with appropriate resources, tools, and incentives. Leaders must value inclusiveness as they create an environment of open, honest, and effective communication—establishing communication channels with those working on assessment and evaluation studies. The leaders must design and implement organizational systems that support customer-focused services and gain the support and involvement of library staff members in learning about customer information needs and expectations and setting priorities through the planning process. It is critical that staff feel empowered to meet the information needs and expectations of customers and that staff members transcend a role as followers and become team and project leaders.

Staff members must recognize and embrace the value of assessment and evaluation. They must commit themselves to participating meaningfully in the assessment and evaluation process. For those staff members lacking the skills needed to carry out assessment and evaluation projects, managerial leaders must support their professional development through workshops and training. Library staff needs to continue to develop new skills (e.g., such as those related to research [see chapter 3] and basic statistical analysis) and to insist on having adequate resources to do their best work.

Staff members care about results; they want to know that their work has positive benefits for the organization and the communities served. Managerial leaders need to communicate to staff how and when assessment and evaluation works so that the staff can understand how the efforts of everyone contribute to successful customer experiences. The goal is to advance the organization in meeting its mission and that of the institution, contribute to job satisfaction, and motivate additional staff to participate. Furthermore, managerial leaders should recognize and reward staff members who contribute to the library's success.

Another means to foster a culture of evidence gathering and managerial use is to adopt systems thinking, which is a framework for analyzing how organizations work. This means that everyone needs to be involved in identifying and understanding inputs, processes, throughputs, and outputs; the external environments affecting inputs (e.g., suppliers); and the outputs or outcomes that library customers and stakeholders value. In the system model, the results and information culled from assessment or evaluation studies should serve as feedback that informs those working within the library about how well the organization and its various parts function and how successfully each unit of the library meets stated goals and objectives. A MIS or DSS facilitates and organizes systems thinking.

Fostering a culture of evidence gathering and managerial use is only possible in an environment in which all opinions and points of view are respected and where a diversity of views is appreciated and encouraged. In addition, assessment and evaluation research is not about systems and tools; it is about people working together toward a common goal. Academic libraries must develop cooperative and effective partnerships with other academic departments and institutional organizations to share responsibility for campus assessment and to demonstrate the library's contribution to the institutional mission by incorporating assessment in its everyday operations. For public libraries the focus is on a partnership with other city departments and meeting the expectations of the mayor, city manager, and city council as well as voters.

Research on organizational change indicates that if there is a discrepancy between the existing culture and the objectives of a proposed change, the existing culture prevails. The options are to

- modify the need to assess or evaluate and thereby to decrease accountability,

- modify the existing culture to align it with a culture of evidence gathering and managerial use, or

- fail to make any changes and thereby have a negative impact on the perceptions of stakeholders.

Creating the desired culture is not simply a matter of developing and deploying new metrics or acquiring new skills. It means changing the mindset and daily activities of library staff and paying attention to shifts in the librarians' mental model that Lakos laid out for an organization wanting to create the desired new culture. That model highlights the shift from the "status quo" to "change," "management" to "leadership," "authority" to "collegiality", "distrust" to "trust" and "integrity," "rigidity" to "flexibility," "inward focus" to a "customer focus," and so on.[25]

CONCLUDING THOUGHTS

Libraries tend to exhibit cultures of accountability or evidence rather than of evidence gathering and use. Data are collected to report to a multiplicity of stakeholders, often as requirements to comply with regional and program accreditations and in annual organizational reports. The library may not routinely engage in data collection to inform decision making in a continuous effort to improve. This may be a result of the multitude of data compiled from the integrated library system and other transaction logs, reports through the IPEDS and IMLS, and other surveys. In addition, the data collected for input and output metrics may be suitable only when describing past activities and the status quo, not for informing decisions. This description is more characteristic of summative evaluation and for using the data when making organizational and peer comparisons. There is often little application of the feedback loop to the organization's planning process.

A culture of evidence gathering and managerial use is a means of organizational and institutional improvement, and not just to demonstrate accountability to stakeholders. Fostering that culture is not an overnight process. It requires patience, clear and effective communication, and a desire to change the organization and its role in the community.

Fostering the new culture should be a library goal. The engagement in assessment and evaluation should be reflective rather than viewed as coercive, and whatever data are collected, analyzed, interpreted, and reported, they should be applied to the library's ongoing effort to improve programs, services, and processes that positively affect customers. The type of culture discussed in this chapter involves the development of effective managerial leaders, articulation of a purpose and external focus, time for group learning, and the creation of supportive organizational systems. Furthermore, it requires acceptance and recognition throughout the organization, from library administration to all levels of the staff. The goal is to change the organizational culture in a positive way and to move assessment and evaluation into day-to-day operations so that both become routine. At the same time, some routines may have to be abandoned as more time is devoted to conducting assessment and evaluation research and as libraries revisit and revise job duties and functions; perhaps the revision of job duties and responsibilities results in a dramatic overall improvement in the effectiveness of staff work and acceptance of new responsibilities.[26] Realization of the new culture will not emerge in a day; it is an ongoing, never-ending process.

NOTES

1. Amos Lakos, "Evidence-Based Library Management: The Leadership Challenge," *portal: Libraries and the Academy* 7, no. 4 (2007): 432.

2. See Peggy I. Maki, *Assessing for Learning: Building a Sustainable Commitment across the* Institution (Sterling, VA: Stylus, 2004).

3. Eric Hoover, "An Expert Surveys the Assessment Landscape," *The Chronicle of Higher Education* (October 27, 2009), accessed March 28, 2010, http://chronicle.com/article/An-Expert-Surveys-the/48945/.

4. Alexander C. McCormick, "Toward Reflective Accountability: Using NSSE for Accountability and Transparency," in *Using NSSE in Institutional Research*, ed. Robert M. Gonyea and George D. Kuh, 99, New Directions for Institutional Research 141 (Spring 2009).

5. Sara Lipka, "It's Not How Much Student Data You Have, but How You Use It," *The Chronicle of Higher Education* (November 4, 2010), accessed November 12, 2010, http://chronicle.com/article/Its-Not-How-Much-Student-Data/125255/.

6. Amos Lakos, "The Missing Ingredient—Culture of Assessment in Libraries: Opinion Piece," *Performance Measurement & Metrics* 1, no. 1 (1999): 5.

7. McCormick, "Toward Reflective Accountability."

8. Amos Lakos and Shelley Phipps, "Building a Culture of Assessment in Libraries: The New Imperative" (presented at the ACRL Pre-Conference, sponsored by the Association of Research Libraries, Office of Leadership and Management Services, Denver, CO, March 15, 2001).

9. Denise Troll Covey, "Using Data to Persuade: State Your Case and Prove It," *Library Administration & Management* 19, no. 2 (Spring 2005): 84.

10. Hoover, "An Expert Surveys the Assessment Landscape."

11. Scott Jaschik, "Engaged or Confused," *Inside Higher Ed* (November 9, 2009), accessed March 28, 2010, http://www.insidehighered.com/layout/set/print/news/2009/11/09/porter.

12. Amos Lakos and Shelley Phipps, "Creating a Culture of Assessment: A Catalyst for Organizational Change," *portal: Libraries and the Academy* 4, no. 3 (July 2004): 348.

13. Lakos and Phipps, "Building a Culture of Assessment in Libraries."

14. Covey, "Using Data to Persuade," 83.

15. See Institute for Healthcare Improvement, "Testing Changes," accessed February 2, 2011, http://www.ihi.org/IHI/Topics/Improvement/ImprovementMethods/HowToImprove/testingchanges.htm.

16. Joseph R. Matthews, *Library Assessment in Higher Education* (Westport, CT: Libraries Unlimited, 2007), 121.

17. Lakos and Phipps, "Building a Culture of Assessment in Libraries;" Lakos and Phipps, "Creating a Culture of Assessment."

18. Sarah M. Pritchard, " 'No Library Is an Island': Finding Ground in the Culture of Assessment," slide 2, accessed January 21, 2010, http://www.sla.org/Presentations/sldc/sarah_LAB2002pp.ppt.

19. Lakos and Phipps, "Creating a Culture of Assessment," 352, 356.

20. Peter Hernon and Joseph R. Matthews, *Listening to the Customer* (Santa Barbara, CA: ABC-CLIO, 2011).

21. Stephanie Wright and Lynda S. White, *Library Assessment*, SPEC Kit 303 (Washington, DC: Association of Research Libraries, 2007), 13.

22. Denise Troll Covey, "Academic Library Assessment: New Duties and Dilemmas," *New Library World* 103, nos. 1175/1176 (2002): 162.

23. Steve Hiller and James Self, "From Measurement to Management: Using Data Wisely for Planning and Decision-Making," *Library Trends* 53, no. 1 (Summer 2004): 138.

24. See John P. Kotter, *Leading Change* (Boston: Harvard Business School Press, 1996).

25. Lakos, "The Missing Ingredient—Culture of Assessment in Libraries," 5–6.

26. See Elizabeth J. Wood, Rush Miller, and Amy Knapp, *Beyond Survival: Managing Academic Libraries in Transition* (Westport, CT: Libraries Unlimited, 2007).

Chapter 12

Reality Evaluation and Assessment

This chapter encourages reader participation in evaluation and assessment research. Novice researchers should develop familiarity with the research process, the role of research design, and different methodologics. This chapter offers a checklist of encouragements to undertake an evaluation or assessment. Perhaps readers who find such research a mystery will want to know the punch line first and will have started their engagement with this book with this chapter. *Engaging in Evaluation and Assessment Research* provides an overview from a practical perspective of what is important to conducting an evaluation or assessment. We identified these tips by reviewing our experiences and those of others who enjoy and value such research. We seek to distill the theories and technical knowledge about evaluation and assessment, all very important to successful evidence-based management and improvements in libraries, and provide a glimpse at the reality of evaluation and assessment. The insights offered aim to discourage myths and leave readers with some confidence that conducting an evaluation or assessment is important and helpful to improving library performance and services to its customers, is doable, is achievable without a detailed knowledge of research methods, and can be fun and personally rewarding.

To make it easier for the impatient reader, this chapter's tidbits are organized around ideas that can be quickly scanned. Those that seem irrelevant may be skipped. Those that are intriguing may be further explored elsewhere in the book and beyond. In short, these few pages may be read either as the introduction or the summary to your journey into evaluations of library and other information services.

TIDBIT ONE: IT IS A LIBRARY, NOT BRAIN SURGERY

There is a fair amount of evidence from modern management theory and practice that understanding how well workflows function and what customers expect and think about how they are treated are critical to managing a successful service-providing organization. Libraries seeking to survive among competitive suppliers of information, serving as places to reflect and learn and keepers of cultural artifacts, are keen to employ the skills needed to develop such understanding. Conducting evaluations of operational performance and customer satisfaction has become a signature of well-run libraries. Librarians and other information professionals see the words *assessment* and *evaluation* frequently in their conference programs and publication advertisements. Special courses on evaluations or lectures on needs assessment are taught in schools of library and information science. Knowledgeable reference to statistics is becoming unavoidable, as is awareness of ways that anthropologists make observations. Interest in creating a culture of evidence gathering and use for planning and decision making is evolving and is nurtured by such demonstrated commitments to the momentum as reports of how many attendees at an assessment conference are repeat participants and how many researchers are exploring new topics that have relevance to planning and decision making. Evaluation has arrived in the library management toolkit, but still carries a certain enigmatic and mysterious aura to those less familiar with it.

The good news is that techniques to conduct useful evaluations are learnable, and that more and more colleagues are experienced and willing to share their understanding of how to design and conduct evaluations and assessments. In most institutions, administrators do not expect a library to manage with evidence obtained through systematic evaluations, so those that try, however small in scope, are respected as responsible players seeking to be accountable. Unlike brain surgery, in which a small mistake could be fatal, libraries have room for experimentation. Lighten up and do not be intimidated by data, whether reflected in lots of numbers and statistical reports or in comments categorized into seemingly obvious insights. Get over the fear of research—evaluation need not be as precise, and "good enough" results are far better than the absence of perfect findings. Learn the basics of what it takes to conceive an evaluation, design it, conduct it, and apply its results. The important point is to get into the operating room even if you have not spent many years studying about it.

TIDBIT TWO: IF YOU DO NOT NEED TO KNOW, DO NOT ASK

The starting point of a good evaluation is not simply a questionnaire or a list of invitees for a focus group. It starts with a problem. An evaluation is a focused approach to seeking information that has application to addressing a problem. Library problems may include reduced budgets, deteriorating collections, disgruntled employees, changing roles in educating learners, or not connecting with potential users. Articulating a problem in terms of information needed to address it becomes the basis for conceiving an evaluation. For example, budget reductions may highlight the need for efficiencies that can be improved through identifying bottlenecks and measuring productivity in workflows, or they may reflect the political process of allocating funds, which benefits from comparisons with identified benchmarks. Preserving collections may be viewed by measuring the extent of damage and effects of destructive environmental factors or the need for different space arrangements. Improving workplace satisfaction begins with gauging and acknowledging employee perceptions of recognition or opportunities to grow. Strengthening contributions to lifelong learning is a tall order that holds meaning with evidence of the impact information literacy has on solving problems or with tracking student recruitment and retention. Reaching library users may be more effective when their information-seeking behaviors are understood and especially as these change with evolving information delivery methods. Different evaluations are appropriate depending on the nature of the problem and the identified information sought to address it. One evaluation template does not fit all situations.

A starting point for organizing thinking about an evaluation involves making choices from among the many options that surround a problem. Applying a logical structure, as explained in chapter 3, is useful to systematically consider what is important to study and why certain relationships between factors under review are relevant to the examination. Let go of those interesting side points of information that take effort to collect but do not contribute to the issues being evaluated. If you do not need to know, do not ask, at least not this time around. Planning an evaluation also requires thinking who should be involved, when to conduct it, and how to gather the needed information. Often librarians and other staff equate conducting an evaluation with a method of gathering data. In doing so, they clearly reveal their unawareness that an evaluation involves an articulation of the problem to address in measurable terms. Selecting the methods to gather data follows the choices about what will be evaluated. Appendix C reviews some data-gathering methods used in library evaluations, suggesting advantages and disadvantages to employing them; detailed discussions about procedures and required resources may be found elsewhere.

Resources available to conduct an evaluation may be a deciding factor in how extensive or thorough it can be. Consider the amount of staff time, expertise, and system support available as well as the effort required of those invited to participate (e.g., students, faculty, community leaders, and employees) in the evaluation. Balancing what information is beneficial with what resources are needed to gather it is a critical reality factor to designing a good evaluation. Keep it simple (and within available resources), systematic (and replicable), and structured (and following established and reliable protocols).

TIDBIT THREE: THE CUSTOMER IS ALWAYS RIGHT . . . OR DOES IT MATTER?

Evaluations of services are not predicated on the notion that "the customer is always right." Of course when people are involved, there may be misunderstandings and unmet expectations that can lead to dissatisfaction with services. This slogan, which dates back to the turn of the twentieth century, was associated with Chicago's once leading department store, Marshall Field's, where it was used to instill an attitude among staff that the customer is special and comes first. The phrase was promoted in the United Kingdom by Wisconsin-born Harry Gordon Selfridge, who had worked with Fields for over two decades and founded London's Selfridges store. Either of these dynamic entrepreneurs may have coined the phrase, which became adapted by other leading businessmen, including the French hotelier Cesar Ritz, who coined the phrase "*le client n'a jamais tort*" (the customer is never wrong).[1] Not intended to be taken literally, the phrase brings attention to the distinction, important in evaluations, between perceptions and occurrences. Whether a customer is right or wrong is not the problem to address. Rather, what has persisted from this phrase over the century into our thinking about evaluation is that the customer's perceptions and opinions are important and need to be measured.

The distinction between fact and perception reflects paradigms of reality that can be reviewed in detail elsewhere. What is important for thinking about an evaluation is not to confuse perceptions with fact, but to use data gathered to measure either within problem-appropriate situations. For instance, library customers may perceive that interlibrary loan services are slow or that the library is too crowded or that online resources are not available. Data gathered to identify these perceptions are quite real and are important to factor into designing service and marketing improvements. However, they come with assumptions about quality expectations and judgments of levels of performance. These may differ from person to person who engages with the library. The Service Quality Gaps Model offers managers a framework to use such data in identifying gaps, for example, between what customers expect and what managers think they expect, between managers' understanding of customers and service standards designed to satisfy them, between the standards and actual delivery of services, and between the delivery of a service and the public pronouncement of what to expect of it (see figure 4.1, p. 63). Measuring gaps of the model require both data on customer perceptions (of expectations and delivery of services) as well as actual fact (levels of achieving standards over time, such as the number of days to deliver loans, the number of empty library seats, or the number of times an e-resource is not available to a library user). When designing an evaluation, consider whether you are trying to identify the customer's viewpoint or library performance. As the Gaps Model suggests, both types of data are important to managing an outstanding library, but different segments of what contributes to improving service quality are not addressed by the same data.

TIDBIT FOUR: LISTEN TO YOUR ELDERS

Evaluations and assessments, like other forms of systematic inquiry, benefit from building on what has been previously gathered. Our evaluation and assessment "elders," regardless of their age, have conducted evaluations and assessments, and they have created knowledge that helps frame our problems and identify methods useful to identify data to address them. As recognized in *Value of Academic Libraries*,

Academic librarians can learn a great deal about assessing library value from their colleagues in school, public, and special libraries. In particular, school libraries and academic libraries share a mandate to help students learn and teachers teach; they have similar missions and, consequently, similar assessment challenges.[2]

School librarians for example, engage extensively in evidence-based practice, described as the "collection, interpretation, and evaluation of the research on a particular issue and using that evaluation to make a decision concerning the issue."[3] Numerous assessment tools are found in the school library literature that may offer academic librarians methods to assess student learning related to academic library activities.

To be able to listen to those who have something to say about evaluation, you need to engage in conversations about the topic. Numerous conferences regularly focus on library evaluations. The Northumbria International Conference on Performance Measurement in Libraries and Information Services, originally sponsored by UK academics, has generated extensive in-person conversations every other year, with its ninth gathering in 2011. Since 2006, a partnership among the Association of Research Libraries, the University of Virginia Library, and the University of Washington Libraries has organized an American-based, but also international, Library Assessment Conference, during alternate years. Both of these venues encourage formal presentations and informal discussions at which young and old, new and seasoned professionals and students focus on assorted topics, measurement techniques, and practical applications of data to improving library and information services and performance. Published proceedings follow these conferences, as do ongoing blogs and numerous untracked relationships that generate other presentations, workshops, and publications. Other specialized conferences are emerging among local and regional groups, as well as through international funders (e.g., one funded by the European Community Social Funds being held annually in Greece is attracting librarians from Third World countries as well as many of the "elders" from Europe, Asia, and the United States). Focused tracks and individualized sessions on library evaluations can also be identified in conferences such as the annual American Library Association, regional conferences such as those of the Association of College and Research Libraries, and programs sponsored by organizations in other fields such as EDUCAUSE or the Coalition for Networked Information (CNI). There is no shortage of places to find people to discuss library evaluation topics and to float ideas about local problems, challenges to gathering data, or strategies for utilizing results in advocating and implementing improvements to library services. For those who have difficulty traveling or are less inclined to discuss evaluation needs in person, the literature and Web sources also address practical topics of design, execution, and application of evaluations for libraries.

TIDBIT FIVE: THE HARDEST THING IS TO START . . . "JUST DO IT"

Conducting evaluations and assessments does not rank high among the activities that librarians are eager to do, so it is easy to make excuses to avoid them. It is not uncommon to hear library managers voice concerns like, "it might be risky," "it might get us in trouble," or, on the other hand, "data about the library will not make any difference to administration," and "besides, we do not have resources to do it." Librarians and staff may believe that "you cannot possibly reduce to numbers what I do," or "users should not judge us since they do not know what we do or what they need." Others honestly are stuck at "I do not know where to start" or "I do not know how."

In large part, such comments are indicators of skepticism and fear of the unknown. Leadership at different levels of the library's organization can help overcome these and evolve an alternative *can do* attitude. The discipline of conducting an evaluation and assessment offers ways to develop an understanding of the library as a workplace, its activities as efficient workflows, its customers as people having expectations for excellence, its generated impressions as contributors to judgments about its worth, and the library as an important benefit to the community. The risks of failure are low if there is willingness to learn, in incremental steps and through exploration, not only about the library but also how to gain evidence-based insights. Some libraries have designated an individual to be responsible for managing evaluations and assessments and to have the necessary expertise. The skill needed to succeed in coupling a "can do" approach with an evidence-based culture and having it emerge throughout the library involves providing clear and sometimes simplified communications, engaging staff at all levels, and guiding small efforts to address identified problems. The goal is to create an environment of inquiry in which mistakes are opportunities to learn rather than being treated as failures, and a need to have data about problems is necessary to make decisions. Tolerance of imperfection and learning through doing are well accepted. Procrastination and avoidance are not. The more time is lost to not taking action, the longer the library is at risk of heading down a path of being unresponsive to its clients, inefficient in its operations, and ineffective in being a valued part of its institution.

"Just do it" is the substance of a strategy toward shifting in this direction. This motto was the clever basis of an advertising campaign that helped the leading sneaker manufacturer gain market share and raise profits over twenty years ago. A case study of Nike's success can apply to the successful transformation of a library getting started with using evaluations: the " 'Just do it' campaign was able to turn sweaty, pain-ridden, time-consuming exercise . . . into something sexy and exciting."[4] Get started and enjoy the process of learning about what you do and the effect it has on those you serve. Assessment is becoming an expected piece of a successful professional's toolkit, and using evaluation data to make decisions is becoming "cool" among librarians.

TIDBIT SIX: MAKE EVALUATION PART OF YOUR WORK

The corollary to getting started is to make evaluation part of your work. Not only does upper management need to adapt the practice of gathering and using data about problems in the library's performance or relationships with its clients. Much of what practitioners among library and information professionals do relates to problem solving. Conceiving library work as problem solving (rather than working with books or helping people, which many candidates state is what drew them to the profession) requires the activities core to evaluations: clarifying the problem, identifying the information needed to address it, applying appropriate methods of data gathering, and analyzing and using the resulting information to make decisions. Reference librarians would not think of letting someone else explore and identify what resources are relevant to guide their customers to consult, nor would a cataloger solely rely on another's interpretation of a book's content to create an original record for it. So in our capacity as managers of information and its utilization, whether in these specialized service roles or being responsible for the library organization, evaluation activities have an important place in our work. Within the library there may be individual guides to help execute any of the steps, from defining the problem in measurable terms to interpreting data reports, but an evaluator cannot be effective without the integration of data with problem solving and associated decision making. Engaging in evaluation as part of the job will collectively strengthen the library's functions, but also will diminish the perception for individuals that it is an add-on and irrelevant to core job responsibilities. It makes sense to incorporate basic awareness and use of evaluations in most if not all library jobs. The increasingly frequent appearance of "assessment" or "evaluation" in job postings attests to this trend in modern libraries.

TIDBIT SEVEN: PLAY WITH IDEAS

Evaluations are specific to a problem. Problems are different in different libraries. Some questions, however, appear about many libraries, such as the following:

- How much does it cost?

- Who uses it?

- What value does it offer?

Some of the same data are collected by many libraries, as illustrated by input and output data submitted by members of the Association of Research Libraries (ARL) to produce the annual ARL Statistics Reports (http://www.arl.org/stats/annualsurveys/arlstats/preveds.shtml). The data may be viewed through comparisons and over time, but results are used in different ways depending on the local problems addressed by them. Position in annual rankings among this group may be an important factor of evaluating reputation and implied worth by administrators on some campuses. Library managers at other institutions may focus on changes in the number of acquisitions over the past year to argue for funds to maintain capacity to meet research needs for information. New questions for which evaluations are undertaken challenge the librarian to be creative and play with ideas about how data can help develop understanding of the library. For example, consider the following real questions posed by provosts or trustees:

- How does the library contribute to student engagement and retention?

- How does it contribute to faculty recruitment?

- What evidence is there that we need a library any more?

Such problems trigger discussions, often with others beyond the library, about factors that influence student and faculty behavior, that matter to students and their parents who are debating about the return on their investment in higher education, or that weigh the allocations of limited institutional resources among competitive and often well-established programs. Student enrollment and academic life professionals are studying what affects the choices of university customers. Greater personal contacts and a sense of belonging are identified by some as critical for a student to remain enrolled. Applying this idea to positioning the library within the university, librarians might explore which services contribute to building relationships with students, and they might play with evaluating the impact of these activities on engagement and retention. College students face major differences in the use of a library compared to their parents' behavior, due in part to changes in the way they learn, interact with electronic as well as print information resources, and use their time. Evaluations of behavior, expectations, and perceptions become important to librarians to evolve services and operations and then to gather data to respond to such new concerns.

TIDBIT EIGHT: BE TRUE TO YOURSELF

Nervousness about evaluations stems in part from the concern that gathered data might contradict popularly accepted assumptions or could be interpreted as critical of existing operations or service deliveries. There is some risk, especially for staff with less clout in the organization, of gathering seemingly condemning data and reporting unexpected, and worse, "negative" findings. The responsibility of leadership is to set the evaluation process as a true inquiry, entered into without bias toward results. In turn, the responsibility of the evaluator, or group of staff involved in reviewing data and interpreting results, is to be true to themselves.

This tidbit does not come with a license to be irresponsible in passing judgment about a library problem under evaluation, nor to push a personal agenda. Several ethical principles should govern the conduct of those involved with an evaluation and can be reviewed in detail elsewhere. For the practice of any research project, an obvious but not always followed principle is to be honest in gathering and handling data; for example, responses to questions on survey instruments cannot be filtered to record only the favorable ones, observations cannot be manufactured, interview participants cannot be influenced to respond other than with their own thoughts, and conclusions cannot be drawn from evaluations designed for differing purposes; for example, self-reported opinions on a Web-based questionnaire cannot generate conclusive impressions of a university's student body. When working with human subjects, most universities and other institutions receiving federal funds are required by law to establish a review process with protocols aimed to protect the welfare and rights of participants, including to protect their privacy. If there is any thought to publish or otherwise publicly share results of an evaluation, then the effort is subject to a review, typically handled by an institutional review board (IRB). Sometimes an IRB refers administrative evaluations to someone in an academic department or administration with responsibility for protecting university interests in conducting research. Evaluations that librarians conduct are not psychological experiments or trials using drugs or otherwise changing people, but nonetheless, conducting interviews, soliciting survey responses, or observing behavior involves human beings. Submitting a proposal for an evaluation involving people to an IRB for review is recommended, not only to avoid debate over whether an evaluation is research or administrative work, but also for what usually is helpful feedback to design an effective and ethically conducted evaluation. Another basic principle that may be abused, intentionally or not, involves literature reviews. Providing proper recognition, through citations, of the work of others, and not plagiarizing the reports of others are practices librarians repeatedly stress in instructional sessions, and they should follow their own advice religiously when designing evaluations and producing data for original interpretation and application to decision making.

TIDBIT NINE: STRIVE FOR THE PRACTICAL

Conducting an evaluation or an assessment is a managed set of activities that should be well planned. Steps to design and implement a good evaluation or assessment are discussed throughout this book. These steps take people's time to undertake and may be influenced by when the time is sought. Equipment, space, and possibly incentives or supplies may be needed, each of which could incur costs. Commanding such resource requirements with the intent to accomplish the gathering of data for a specified purpose is the element of project management. Organizing who does what when and where requires preparing and executing a plan for effectively using such resources. Experience suggests that library evaluations and assessments underestimate the amount of time needed to analyze data, which sometimes calls for iterative reviews. Another vulnerability witnessed in library evaluations is missed launches, which end up gathering data on participation or activities when they are not representatively undertaken; for example, expecting students to respond to a survey or observing library use during exams may not be representative of the rest of the term. Librarians are savvy to factoring incentives for evaluation participations, though sometimes we question how much needs to be expended to ensure high response; candy or coffee cards may be sufficient, whereas drawings to receive equipment such as an iPad or Kindle Reader seem excessive for most studies. Some evaluations warrant external assistance, but then the library should be sure to clarify scope, ownership, and use of data gathered, and resources required; for example, beware of an offer to conduct an evaluation of workplace climate from a consultant who is a graduate student and may have a particular framework to test or additional data to gather for personal research. In short, evaluations (and assessments) should be undertaken with clear awareness of objectives and availability of means to address them. Be practical and do what you can rather than start what you cannot finish.

TIDBIT TEN: SHARE RESULTS

Evaluations and assessments produce information that may be of interest and use to a number of people. Part of any evaluation or assessment plan should be identification of who should receive its findings. Obviously the decision makers for whom the data are gathered should be among the first to learn the results. Serious thought to the ways the findings are presented, the extent of interpretation, and recommendations for action should be influenced by the stakeholders' interest, degree of involvement with details, and manner of receiving information. Suggestions for planning the presentation of results are covered elsewhere and should not be passed over lightly. All the work undertaken to gather data will be wasted if at the end of the day, the results are not useful for making decisions and improving the library and its services.

People other than the decision makers may also welcome seeing the results of an evaluation. The library's staff members may not always express interest in an evaluation, but seldom are blasé about feedback related to what they do and how it is perceived. Good practice in conducting an evaluation is to keep staff informed of what is happening and to share the results. More and more, libraries are engaging staff in gathering and interpreting data, both to benefit from frontline perspectives and to build trust, participation, and a valued workplace. Those participating in evaluations—students, faculty, employees— are always identified as interested in receiving the results, and in some data-gathering protocols (e.g., surveys and focus group interviews) they are promised the findings as an incentive to respond. Experience suggests that expressions of interest in seeing results among participants are infrequent, but since there is relatively little effort to provide them, the occasional strengthening of loyalty and relationships built are a great return on the investment. We have experienced, for example, a faculty member sending the library a gift in response to reading the results of a survey and a student leader articulating the importance of the library to trustees with data received from an evaluation.

CONCLUDING THOUGHTS

The ten tidbits underscore that evaluation and assessment research have practical implications related to planning and decision making. Furthermore, unlike basic research, the goal is not to generate new theory devoid of practical applications, and unlike policy research, the goal is not to investigate particular government and corporate information policies and their applications; in other words, do policymakers need to rethink or revise those policies? As service organizations, libraries often partner with other stakeholders as they explore how effectively and efficiently they meet the mission of the broader organizations and, in the case of academic institutions, their learning goals. In this regard, assessment will increase in importance.

Finally, some readers might envision other tidbits. For example, conducting research gets easier and better with practice and repetition. When librarians engage in benchmarking and making comparisons over time, this tidbit applies. Furthermore, researchers might continue to pursue the same topical area and same methodology. As librarians pursue more complex research designs and explore the methodological tool chest, research is not likely to become easier. Researchers, however, become more versatile and expand their knowledge, skill set, and ability to address different problems, especially those related to assessment and the use of experimental designs and inferential statistics.

NOTES

1. Gary Martin, "The Phrase Finder," accessed January 17, 2011, http://www.phrases.org.uk/meanings/106700.html.

2. Association of College and Research Libraries, *Value of Academic Libraries: A Comprehensive Research Review and Report*, by Megan Oakleaf (Chicago: Association of College and Research Libraries, 2010), 58.

3. Gayle Bogel, "Facets of Practice," *Knowledge Quest* 37, no. 2 (2008): 10–15, as cited in *Value of Academic Libraries*, 59.

4. Center for Applied Research, "Mini-case Study: Nike's "Just Do It" Advertising Campaign," accessed January 16, 2011, http://www.cfar.com/Documents/nikecmp.pdf.

Bibliography

ARTICLES

Beutter-Manus, Sara J. "Librarian in the Classroom: An Embedded Approach to Music Information Literacy for First-Year Undergraduates." *Notes* 66, no. 2 (December 2009): 249–61.

Bogel, Gayle. "Facets of Practice." *Knowledge Quest* 37, no. 2 (2008): 10–15.

Bradley, Jane, and Brett Sutton, eds. "Symposium on Qualitative Research Theory, Methods, and Applications." *The Library Quarterly* 63, no. 4 (1993): 411–527.

Burkamp, Marlu, and Diane E. Virbick. "Through the Eyes of a Secret Shopper." *American Libraries* 33, no. 10 (November 2002): 56–57.

Cahoy, Ellysa Stern, and Loanne Snavely. "Maximizing Local and National Assessment for Evidence-Based Librarianship." *Reference and User Services Quarterly* 48, no. 3 (spring 2009): 216–23.

Calvert, Philip C. "It's a Mystery: Mystery Shopping in New Zealand's Public Libraries." *Library Review* 54, no. 1 (2006): 24–35.

Campbell, Jerry D. "Changing a Cultural Icon: The Academic Library as a Virtual Destination." *EDUCAUSE Review* 41, no. 1 (January 2008): 16–31.

Carlson, Scott. "A Place to See and Be Seen (and Learn a Little, Too)." *The Chronicle of Higher Education* LVI, no. 27 (June 4, 2010): A16–17.

Carnovsky, Leon. "Methodology in Research and Applications." *Library Trends* 6, no. 2 (1957): 243–46.

Chatman, Elfrada. "A Theory of Life in the Round." *Journal of the American Society for Information Science* 50, no. 3 (1999): 207–17.

Chen, T. "An Evaluation of the Relative Performance of University Libraries in Taipei." *Library Review* 3 (1997): 190–200.

Childers, Thomas A., and Nancy A. Van House. "Dimensions of Public Library Effectiveness." *Library & Information Science Research* 11, no. 3 (1989): 273–301.

Choban, Michael C., Gary M. Choban, and David Choban. "Strategic Planning and Decision Making in Higher Education: What Gets Attention and What Doesn't." *Assessment Update* 20, no. 2 (March-April 2008): 1–2, 13–14.

Covey, Denise Troll. "Academic Library Assessment: New Duties and Dilemmas." *New Library World*, 103, nos. 1175/1176 (2002): 156–64.

Covey, Denise Troll. "Using Data to Persuade: State Your Case and Prove It." *Library Administration & Management* 19, no. 2 (spring 2005): 82–89.

Cullan, Rowena. "Perspectives on User Satisfaction Surveys." *Library Trends* 49, no. 4 (spring 2001): 662–86.

Cunningham, Avril. "Using "Ready-to-Go" Assessment Tools to Create a Year Long Assessment Portfolio and Improve Instruction." *College & Undergraduate Libraries* 13, no. 2 (2006): 75–90.

Czopek, Vanessa. "Using Mystery Shoppers to Evaluate Customer Service in the Public Library." *Public Libraries* 37, no. 6 (November/December 1998): 370–71.

Davis, Charles H. "On Qualitative Research." *Library & Information Science Research* 12, no. 4 (1990): 327–28.

Dervin, Brenda. "Sense-Making Theory and Practice: An Overview of User Interests in Knowledge Seeking and Use." *Journal of Knowledge Management* 2, no. 2 (December 1998): 36–46.

Dogherty, Richard M. "Letter to the Editor." *College & Research Libraries* 70, no. 2 (March 2009): 107.

Dugan, Robert E., and Peter Hernon. "Outcomes Assessment: Not Synonymous with Inputs and Outputs." *The Journal of Academic Librarianship* 28, no. 6 (November 2002): 376–80.

DuMont, Rosemary R. "A Conceptual Basis for Library Effectiveness." *College & Research Libraries* 41, no. 2 (March 1980): 103–11.

Dunn, Kathleen. "Assessing Information Literacy Skills in the California State University: A Progress Report." *The Journal of Academic Librarianship* 28, nos. 1–2 (January–March 2002): 26–35.

Edwards, Susan, and Mairead Browne. "Quality in Information Services: Do Users and Librarians Differ in Their Expectations?" *Library & Information Science Research* 17, no. 2 (1995): 163–82.

Evans, Edward, Harold Borko, and Patricia Ferguson. "Review of Criteria Used to Measure Library Effectiveness." *Bulletin of Medical Library Association* 60, no. 1 (January 1972): 102–10.

Farmer, Lesley S. J. "Using Technology to Facilitate Assessment of Library Education." *Teacher Librarian* 32, no. 3 (February 2005): 12–15.

Finn, Adam, and Ujwal Kayandé. "Scale Modification: Alternative Approaches and Their Consequences." *Journal of Retailing* 80, no. 1 (January 2004): 37–52.

Finn, Adam, and Ujwal Kayandé. "Unmasking a Phantom: A Psychometric Assessment of Mystery Shopping." *Journal of Retailing* 75, no. 2 (1999): 195–217.

Gabridge Tracy, Millicent Gaskell, and Amy Stout. "Information Seeking through Students' Eyes: The MIT Photo Diary Study." *College & Research Libraries* 69, no.6 (November 2008): 510–23.

Given, Lisa M., and Gloria J. Leckie. "'Sweeping' the Library: Mapping the Social Activity Space of the Public Library." *Library & Information Science Research* 25, no. 4 (2003): 365–85.

Greenstein, Daniel. "Strategies for Sustaining the University Library." *portal: Libraries and the Academy* 10, no. 2 (April 2010): 121–25.

Guha, Tamal Kumar, and Veena Saraf. "OPAC Usability, Assessment through Verbal Protocol." *Electronic Library* 23, no. 4 (2005): 463–73.

Hannabuss, Stuart. "Scenario Planning for Libraries." *Library Management* 22, nos. 4/5 (2001): 168–76.

Hardesty, Larry. "Future of Academic/Research Librarians: A Period of Transition—to What?" *portal: Libraries and the Academy* 2, no. 1 (January 2002): 79–97.

Hébert, Francoise. "Service Quality: An Unobtrusive Investigation of Interlibrary Loan in Large Public Libraries in Canada." *Library & Information Science Research* 16, no. 1 (1994): 3–21.

Henry, Elizabeth, Rachel Longstaff, and Doris Van Kampen. "Collection Analysis Outcomes in an Academic Library." *Collection Building* 27, no. 3 (2008): 113–17.

Hernon, Peter, and Robert E. Dugan. "Assessment and Evaluation: What Do the Terms Really Mean?" *College & Research Libraries News*, 70, no. 3 (March 2009): 146–49.

Hernon, Peter, and Danuta A. Nitecki. "Service Quality: A Concept Not Fully Explored." Library *Trends* 49, no. 4 (spring 2001): 687–708.

Hernon, Peter, and Laura Saunders. "The Federal Depository Library Program in 2023: One Perspective on the Transition to the Future." *College & Research Libraries* 70, no. 4 (July 2009): 351–70.

Hernon, Peter, Allen Smith, and Mary B. Coxen. "Publication in *College & Research Libraries*: Accepted, Rejected, and Published Papers, 1980–1991." *College & Research Libraries* 54, no. 4 (July 1993): 303–21.

Hiller, Steve, and James Self. "From Measurement to Management: Using Data Wisely for Planning and Decision-Making." *Library Trends* 53, no. 1 (summer 2004): 128–55.

Jackson, Shaun, Carol Hansen, and Lauren Fowler. "Using Selected Assessment Data to Inform Information Literacy Program Planning with Campus Partners." *Research Strategies* 20, nos. 1–2 (2004): 44–56.

Jankowska, Maria Anna, and James W. Marcum. "Sustainable Challenge for Academic Libraries: Planning for the Future." *College & Research Libraries* 71, no. 2 (March 2010): 160–70.

Jordan, Mary Wilkins. "What Is Your Library's Friendliness Factor?" *Public Library Quarterly* 24, no. 4 (August 2007): 81–99.

Kano, N., N. Seraku, F. Takahashi, and S. Tsuji. "Attractive Quality and Must-Be Quality." *Hinshitsu Quality: The Journal of Japanese Society for Quality Control* 14 (1984): 39–48.

Kao, C., and Y. Lin. "Comparing University Libraries of Different University Size." *Libri* 49 (1999): 150–58.

Kaplan, Robert S., and David P. Norton. "The Balanced Scorecard—Measures That Drive Performance." *The Harvard Business Review* 70, no. 1 (January–February 1992): 71–79.

Kaufman, Paula T. "The Library as Strategic Investment: Results of the Illinois Return on Investment Study." *LIBER Quarterly* 18, nos. 3/4 (December 2008): 424–36.

Kocevar-Weidinger, Elizabeth, Candice Benjes-Small, Eric Ackerman, and Virginia R. Kinman. "Why and How to Mystery Shop Your Reference Desk." *Reference Services Review* 38, no. 1 (2010): 28–43.

Kuhlthau, Carol C. "Accommodating the User's Information Search Process: Challenges for Information Retrieval System Designers." *Bulletin of the American Society for Information Science and Technology* 25, no. 3 (February/March 1999): 12–16.

Lakos, Amos. "Evidence-Based Library Management: The Leadership Challenge." *portal: Libraries and the Academy* 7, no. 4 (2007): 431–50.

Lakos, Amos. "The Missing Ingredient—Culture of Assessment in Libraries: Opinion Piece." *Performance Measurement & Metrics* 1, no. 1 (1999): 3–7.

Lakos, Amos, and Shelley Phipps. "Creating a Culture of Assessment: A Catalyst for Organizational Change." *portal: Libraries and the Academy* 4, no. 3 (July 2004): 345–61.

Lewis, David W. "A Strategy for Academic Libraries in the First Quarter of the 21st Century." *College & Research Libraries* 68, no. 5 (September 2007): 418–34.

Lindauer, Bonnie Gratch. "Comparing the Regional Accreditation Standards: Outcomes Assessment and Other Trends." *The Journal of Academic Librarianship* 28, nos. 1–2 (January–March 2002): 14–25.

Lindauer, Bonnie Gratch. "Defining and Measuring the Library's Impact on Campuswide Outcomes." *College & Research Libraries* 59, no. 6 (November 1998): 546–70.

Lopéz, Cecilia L. "Assessment of Student Learning: Challenges and Strategies." *The Journal of Academic Librarianship* 28, no. 6 (November 2002): 356–67.

Lougen, Colleen. "Review." *Reference & User Services Quarterly* 49, no.1 (Fall 2009): 101–2.

Maki, Peggy L. "Developing an Assessment Plan to Learn about Student Learning." *The Journal of Academic Librarianship* 28, nos.1–2 (January–March 2002): 8–13.

Markless, Sharon, and David Streatfield. "Developing Performance and Impact Indicators and Targets in Public and Education Libraries." *International Journal of Information Management* 21, no. 2 (April 2001): 167–79.

Martino, Joseph P. "The Precision of Delphi Estimates." *Technological Forecasting* 1, no. 3 (1970): 293–99.

Matheson, Nina W. "Perspectives on Academic Health Sciences Libraries in the 1980s: Indicators from a Delphi Study." *Bulletin of the Medical Library Association* 70, no. 1 (January 1982): 28–49.

McClamroch, Jo, Jacqueline J. Byrd, and Steven L. Sowell. "Strategic Planning: Politics, Leadership, and Learning." *The Journal of Academic Librarianship* 27, no. 5 (September 2001): 372–78.

McClure, Charles R. "Strategies for Collecting Networked Statistics: Practical Suggestions." *VINE: The Journal of Information and Knowledge Management Systems* 34, no. 4 (June 2004): 166–71.

McCormick, Alexander C. "Toward Reflective Accountability: Using NSSE for Accountability and Transparency." In Robert M. Gonyea and George D. Kuh, "Using NSSE in Institutional Research," *New Directions for Institutional Research* 141 (Spring 2009), 97–106.

Morrison, Heather G. "Online Catalogue Research and the Verbal Protocol Methods." *Library Hi-Tech* 17, no. 2 (1999): 197–206.

Mullins, James L. "Bringing Librarianship to E-Science." *College & Research Libraries* 70, no. 3 (May 2009): 212–13.

Mullins, James L., Frank R. Allen, and Jon R. Hufford. "Top Ten Assumptions for the Future of Academic Libraries and Librarians: A Report from the ACRL Research Committee." *College & Research Libraries News* 68, no. 4 (April 2007): 240–241, 246.

Nicholas, David, D. Clark, Ian Rowlands, and Hamid R. Jamali. "Online Use and Information Seeking Behaviour: Institutional and Subject Comparisons of UK Researchers." *Journal of Information Science* 35, no. 6 (2009): 660–76.

Nicholas, David, Paul Huntington, and Hamid R. Jamali. "Diversity in the Information Seeking Behaviour of the Virtual Scholar: Institutional Comparisons." *The Journal of Academic Librarianship* 33, no. 6 (2007): 629–38.

Nicholas, David, Paul Huntington, Hamid R. Jamali, Ian Rowlands, Tom Dobrowolski, and Carol Tenopir. "Viewing and Reading Behaviour in a Virtual Environment: The Full-Text Download and What Can Be Read into It." *Aslib Proceedings: New Information Perspectives* 60, no. 3 (2008): 185–98.

Nicholas, David, Ian Rowlands, Paul Huntington, Hamid R. Jamali, and Patricia H. Salazar. "Diversity in the E-journal Use and Information-Seeking Behaviour of UK Researchers." *Journal of Documentation* 66, no. 3 (2010): 409–33.

Nicholas, David, Peter Williams, Ian Rowlands, Hamid R. Jamali. "Researchers' E-journal Use and Information Seeking Behaviour." Journal *of Information Science* 36, no. 4 (August 2010): 494–516.

Nitecki, Danuta A. "Changing the Concept and Measure or Service Quality in Academic Libraries." *The Journal of Academic Librarianship* 22, no. 3 (May 1996): 181–90.

Nitecki, Danuta A. "Program Evaluation in Libraries: Relating Operations and Clients." *Archival Science* 4, no. 1 (March 2004): 17–44.

Nitecki, Danuta A., and Peter Hernon. "Measuring Service Quality at Yale University's Libraries." *The Journal of Academic Librarianship* 26, no.4 (July 2000): 259–73.

Oakleaf, Megan. "Dangers and Opportunities: A Conceptual Map of Information Literacy Assessment Approaches." *portal: Libraries and the Academy* 8, no. 3 (July 2008): 233–53.

Oakleaf, Megan, and Neal Kaske. "Guiding Questions for Assessing Information Literacy in Higher Education." *portal: Libraries and the Academy* 9, no. 2 (April 2009): 276–83.

Orr, Richard M. "Measuring the Goodness of Library Services: A General Framework for Considering Quantitative Measures." *Journal of Documentation* 29, no. 3 (September 1973): 315–32.

Parasuraman, A., Valarie A. Zeithmal, and Leonard L. Berry. "A Conceptual Model of Service Quality and Its Implications for Future Research." *Journal of Marketing* 49, no. 4 (fall 1985): 41–50.

Peters, Thomas A. "The History and Development of Transactional Log Analysis." *Library Hi Tech* 11, no. 2 (1993): 41–66.

Portmann, Chris A., and Adrienne J.Roush. "Assessing the Effects of Library Instruction." *The Journal of Academic Librarianship* 30, no. 6 (November 2004): 461–65.

Powell, Ronald R. "Evaluation Research: An Overview." *Library Trends* 55, no. 1 (summer 2006): 102–20.

Radford, Gary P. "Positivism, Foucault, and the Fantasia of the Library: Conceptions of Knowledge and the Modern Library Experience." *The Library Quarterly* 64, no. 4 (1992): 408–24.

Reichmann, Gerhard. "Measuring University Library Efficiency Using Data Envelopment Analysis." *Libri* 54, no. 2 (2004): 136–46.

Rockman, Irene F. "Strengthening Connections between Information Literacy, General Education, and Assessment Efforts." *Library Trends* 51, no. 2 (fall 2002): 185–98.

"The Sage Encyclopedia of Qualitative Research Methods." *Reference & User Services Quarterly* 49 no.1 (Fall 2009): 101–2.

Sandstrom, Alan, and Pamela Effrein Sandstrom. "The Use and Misuse of Anthropological Methods in Library and Information Science Research." *The Library Quarterly* 65, no. 2 (April 1995): 161–99.

Saunders, Laura. "The Future of Information Literacy in Academic Libraries: A Delphi Study." *portal: Libraries and the Academy* 9, no. 1 (January 2009): 99–114.

Sennyey, P., Lyman Ross, and Caroline Mills. "Exploring the Future of Academic Libraries: A Definitional Approach." *The Journal of Academic Librarianship* 35, no. 3 (May 2009): 252–59.

Shenton Andrew K. "The Analysis of Qualitative Data in LIS Research Projects: A Possible Approach." *Education for Information* 22. nos. 3/4 (2004): 143–62.

Shenton, Andrew K., and Pat Dixon. "Debates and Paradoxes Surrounding the Use of Qualitative Methods." *Education for Information* 22, no. 22 (2004): 1–42.

Shim, Wonsik. "Assessing Technical Efficiency of Research Libraries." *Advances in Library Administration and Organisation* 17 (2000): 243–339.

Shipman, Amanda S., Cristina L. Byrne, and Michael D. Mumford. "Leader Vision Formation and Forecasting: The Effects of Forecasting Extent, Resources, and Timeframe." *The Leadership Quarterly* 21, no. 3 (June 2010): 439–56.

Smith, Kenneth R. "New Roles and Responsibilities for the University Library Advancing Student Learning Through Outcomes Assessment." *Journal of Library Administration* 35, no. 4 (2002): 29–36.

Smith, P. M. "Cataloging Production Standards in Academic Libraries." *Technical Services Quarterly* 6, no. 1 (1988): 3–14

Somerville, Mary M., Gordon W. Smith, and Alexius Smith Macklin. "The ETS iSkillsTM Assessment: A Digital Age Tool." *The Electronic Library* 26, no. 2 (2008: 158–71.

St. Clair, Gloriana. "Editorial: Improving Quality: An Editor's Advice to Authors." *College & Research Libraries* 54, no. 3 (May 1993): 195–97.

Stein, Merrill. Teresa Edge, John M. Kelley, Dane Hewlett, and James F. Trainer. "Using Continuous Quality Improvement Methods to Evaluate Library Service Points." *Reference and User Services Quarterly* 48, no. 1 (fall 2008): 78–85.

VandeCreek, Leanne M. "E-Mail Reference Evaluation: Using the Results of a Satisfaction Survey." *The Reference Librarian* 45, no. 93 (2006): 99–108.

Walters, Scott. "Librarians as Teachers: A Qualitative Inquiry into Professional Identity." *College & Research Libraries* 69, no. 1 (January 2008): 51–71.

Wells, Andrew. "A Prototype Twenty-First Century University Library: A Case Study of Change at the University of New South Wales Library." *Library Management* 28, nos. 8/9 (2007): 450–59.

Westbrook, Lynn. "Qualitative Research Methods: A Review of Major Stages, Data Analysis Techniques, and Quality Controls." *Library & Information Science Research* 16, no. 3 (summer 1994): 241–54.

White, Marilyn Domas, and Emily E. Marsh. "Content Analysis: A Flexible Methodology." *Library Trends* 55, no. 1 (summer, 2006): 22–45.

Wonsik, Shim. "Applying DEA Technique to Library Evaluation in Academic Research Libraries." *Library Trends* 51, no. 3 (winter 2003): 312–33.

BOOKS

Ackroyd, Stephen, and John A. Hughes. *Data Collection in Context.* 2nd ed. London: Longman, 1992.

Alire, Camila A., and G. Edward Evans. *Academic Librarianship.* New York: Neal-Schuman, 2010.

Allen, Mary J. *Assessing General Education Programs.* Bolton, MA: Anker Publishing Company, 2006.

Anfana, Vincent A., Jr., and Norman T. Metz, eds. *Theoretical Frameworks in Qualitative Research.* Thousand Oaks, CA: Sage, 2006.

Bennis, Warren, and Patricia W. Biederman. *Still Surprised: A Memoir of a Life in Leadership.* San Francisco: Jossey-Bass, 2010.

Bolter, Jay David. W*riting Space: The Computer, Hypertext, and the History of Writing.* Hillsdale, NJ: Lawrence Erlbaum, 1993.

Case, Donald O. *Looking for Information: A Survey of Research on Information Seeking, Needs, and Behavior.* New York: Academic Press, 2002, 2007.

Childers, Thomas A., and Nancy A. Van House. *What's Good? Describing Your Public Library's Effectiveness.* Chicago: American Library Association, 1993.

Connaway, Lynn S., and Ronald R. Powell. *Basic Research Methods for Librarians.* 5th ed. Santa Barbara, CA: ABC-CLIO, 2010.

Cronin, Blaise. *The Citation Process: The Role and Significance of Citations in Scientific Communication*. London: Taylor Graham, 1984.

Dugan, Robert E., Peter Hernon, and Danuta A. Nitecki. *Viewing Library Metrics from Different Perspectives: Inputs, Outputs, and Outcomes*. Santa Barbara, CA: ABC-CLIO, 2009.

Durrance, Joan C., and Karen E. Fisher. *How Libraries and Librarians Help: A Guide to Identifying User-Centered Outcome*s. Chicago: American Library Association, 2005.

Elliott, Donald S., Glen E. Holt, Sterling W. Hayden, and Leslie E. Holt. *Measuring Your Library's Value: How to Do a Cost-Benefit Analysis for Your Public Library*. Chicago: American Library Association, 2007.

Evaluating Bibliographic Instruction: A Handbook. Chicago: American Library Association, Association of College and Research Libraries, Bibliographic Instruction Section, 1983.

Foster, Nancy Fried, and Susan Gibbons, eds. *Studying Students: The Undergraduate Research Project at the University of Rochester*. Chicago: Association of College and Research Libraries, 2007.

Glazier, Jack D., and Ronald R. Powell, ed. *Qualitative Research in Information Management*. Englewood, CO: Libraries Unlimited, 1992.

Glitz, Beryl. *Focus Groups for Libraries and Librarians*. New York: Forbes, 1998.

Harada, Violet H., and Joan M. Yoshina. *Assessing for Learning: Librarians and Teachers as Partners*. Westport, CT: Libraries Unlimited, 2005; 2nd ed. Santa Barbara, CA: ABC-CLIO, 2010.

Heifetz, Ronald A., Marty Linsky, and Alexander Grashow. *The Practice of Adaptive Leadership: Tools and Tactics for Changing Your Organization and the World*. Boston: Harvard Business Press, 2009.

Hernon, Peter. *Shaping the Future: Advancing the Understanding of the Future*. Santa Barbara, CA: ABC-CLIO, 2010.

Hernon, Peter, and Ellen Altman. *Assessing Service Quality: Satisfying the Expectations of Library Customers*. Chicago: American Library Association, 1998, 2010.

Hernon, Peter, and Philip Calvert. *Improving the Quality of Library Services for Students with Disabilities*. Santa Barbara, CA: ABC-CLIO, 2006.

Hernon, Peter, and Robert E. Dugan. *An Action Plan for Outcomes Assessment in Your Library*. Chicago: American Library Association, 2002.

Hernon, Peter, and Robert E. Dugan. *Outcomes Assessment in Higher Education: Views and Perspectives*. Westport, CT: Libraries Unlimited, 2004.

Hernon, Peter, Robert E. Dugan, and Candy Schwartz. *Revisiting Outcomes Assessment in Higher Education*. Westport, CT: Libraries Unlimited, 2006.

Hernon, Peter, and Joseph R. Matthews. *Listening to the Customer*. Santa Barbara, CA: ABC-CLIO, 2011.

Hernon, Peter, and Charles R. McClure. *Evaluation and Library Decision Making*. Norwood, NJ: Ablex, 1990.

Hernon, Peter, and Charles R. McClure. *Unobtrusive Testing and Library Reference Services*. Norwood, NJ: Ablex, 1987.

Hernon, Peter, and Ronald R. Powell. *Convergence and Collaboration of Campus Information Services*. Westport, CT: Libraries Unlimited, 2008.

Hernon, Peter, and John R. Whitman. *Delivering Satisfaction and Service Quality: A Customer-Based Approach for Libraries*. Chicago: American Library Association, 2001.

Holsti, Ole R. *Content Analysis for the Social Sciences and Humanities*. Reading, MA: Addison-Wesley, 1969.

Kane, Mary, and William M. K. Trochim. *Concept Mapping for Planning and Evaluation*. Thousand Oaks, CA: Sage, 2007.

Kaplan, Robert S., and David P. Norton. *The Balanced Scorecard: Translating Strategy into Action*. Boston: Harvard Business School Press, 1996.

Kent, Allen. *Use of Library Materials: The University of Pittsburgh Study*. New York: M. Dekker, 1979.

Klass, Gary M. *Just Plain Data Analysis: Finding, Presenting, and Interpreting Social Science Data*. Lanham, MD: Rowman & Littlefield Publishers, 2008.

Klenke, Karin. *Qualitative Research in the Study of Leadership*. Bingley, UK: Emerald Group Publishing Ltd., 2008.

Kotter, John P. *Leading Change*. Boston: Harvard Business School Press, 1996.

Krathwohl, David R. *Social and Behavioral Science Research: A New Framework for Conceptualizing, Implementing, and Evaluating Research Studies*. San Francisco: Jossey-Bass, 1985.

Krippendorff, Klaus H. *Content Analysis: An Introduction to Its Methodology*. Newbury Park, CA: Sage, 1980.

Kuhlthau, Carol C. *Seeking Meaning: A Process Approach to Library and Information Services*. Norwood, NJ: Ablex Publishing Corp., 1993; 2nd ed. Westport, CT: Libraries Unlimited, 2004.

Lancaster, F. W. *If You Want to Evaluate Your Library . . . .* Champaign: University of Illinois, Graduate School of Library and Information Science, 1988, 1993.

Lancaster, F. W. *The Measurement and Evaluation of Library Services*. Washington, DC: Information Resources Press, 1977.

Lancaster, F. W., and Sharon L. Baker. *The Measurement and Evaluation of Library Services*. Arlington, VA: Information Resources Press, 1991.

Leckie, Gloria J., Lisa M. Given, and John E. Bushman. *Critical Theory for Library and Information Science: Exploring the Social from Across the Disciplines*. Santa Barbara, CA: ABC-CLIO, 2011.

Lewins, A., and Silver, C. *Using Software in Qualitative Research: A Step by Step Guide*. London: Sage Publications, 2007.

Lincoln, Yvonna S., and Egon G. Guba. *Naturalistic Inquiry*. Beverly Hills, CA: Sage Publications, 1985.

Maki, Peggy L. *Assessing for Learning: Building a Sustainable Commitment across the Institution*. Sterling, VA: Stylus, 2004.

Marshall, Joanne G. *An Introduction to Research Methods for Health Sciences Librarians*. Chicago: Medical Library Association, Courses for Continuing Education, 1989.

Matthews, Joseph R. *The Evaluation and Measurement of Library Services*. Westport, CT: Libraries Unlimited, 2007.

Matthews, Joseph R. *Library Assessment in Higher Education*. Westport, CT: Libraries Unlimited, 2007.

Matthews, Joseph R. *Scorecard for Results: A Guide for Developing a Library Balanced Scorecard*. Westport, CT: Libraries Unlimited, 2008.

McClure, Charles R., and Peter Hernon. *Improving the Quality of Reference Service for Government Publications*. Chicago: American Library Association, 1983.

McDavid, James C., and Laura L. Hawthorn. *Program Evaluation and Performance Measurement: An Introduction to Practice*. Thousand Oaks, CA: Sage, 2006.

McGiverin, Rolland H. *Educational and Psychological Tests in the Academic Library*. New York: Haworth Press, 1990.

McKnight, Sue. *Envisioning Future Academic Library Services: Initiatives, Ideas, and Challenges*. New York: Neal-Schuman Publishers, 2010.

Mellon, Constance. *Naturalistic Inquiry for Library Sciences*. New York: Greenwood Press, 1990.

Metoyer-Duran, Cheryl. *Gatekeepers in Ethnolinguistic Communities*. Norwood, NJ: Ablex, 1993.

Middle States Commission on Higher Education. *Student Learning Assessment: Options and Resources*. 2nd ed. Philadelphia, PA: Middle States Commission on Higher Education, 2007.

Miller, Delbert C. *Handbook of Research Design and Social Measurement*. Newbury Park, CA: Sage, 1991.

Neill, S. D. *Dilemmas in the Study of Information: Exploring the Boundaries of Information Science*. New York: Greenwood Press, 1992.

Nelson, William Neal, and Robert W. Fernekes. *Standards and Assessment for Academic Libraries: A Workbook*. Chicago: Association of College and Research Libraries, 2002.

No Brief Candle: Reconceiving Research Libraries for the 21st Century. Washington, DC: Council on Library and Information Resources, 2008.

Preskill, Hallie, and Tessie T. Catsambas. *Reframing Evaluation through Appreciative Inquiry*. Thousand Oaks, CA: Sage, 2006.

Radcliff, Carolyn J., Mary Lee Jansen, Joseph A. Salem Jr., Kenneth J. Burhanna, and Julie A. Gedeon. *A Practical Guide to Information Literacy Assessment for Academic Librarians*. Westport, CT: Libraries Unlimited, 2007.

Rossi, Peter H., Howard E. Freeman, and Sonia R. Wright. *Evaluation: A Systematic Approach*. Beverly Hills, CA: Sage, Publications, 1979.

Rossi, Peter H., Mark W. Lipsey, and Howard E. Freeman. *Evaluation: A Systematic Approach*. 7th ed. Thousand Oaks, CA: Sage Publications, 2004.

Rothstein, Samuel. *The Development of Reference Services through Academic Traditions, Public Library Practice and Special Librarianship*. Chicago: Association of College and Reference Libraries, 1955.

Rubin, Rhea Joyce. *Demonstrating Results: Using Outcome Measurement in Your Library*. Chicago: American Library Association, 2006.

The Sage Encyclopedia of Qualitative Research Methods. Edited by Lisa M. Given. Los Angeles, CA: Sage, 2008.

Schneider, Benjamin, and Susan S. White. *Service Quality Research Perspectives*. Thousand Oaks, CA: Sage Publications, 2004.

Smith, G. Stevenson. *Managerial Accounting for Libraries and Other Not-for-Profit Organizations*. 2nd ed. Chicago: American Library Association, 2002.

Suskie, Linda. *Assessing Student Learning: A Common Sense Guide*. Bolton, MA: Anker, 2004; 2nd ed. San Francisco: Wiley, 2009.

Swisher, Robert, and Charles R. McClure. *Research for Decision Making Methods for Librarians*. Chicago: American Library Association, 1984.

Tesch, Renata. *Qualitative Research: Analysis Types and Software Tools*. New York: Falmer Press, 1990.

Tichy, Noel, and Warren Bennis. *Judgment: How Winning Leaders Make Great Calls*. New York: Portfolio, 2007.

Tufte, Edward R. *Beautiful Evidence*. Cheshire, CT: Graphics Press, 2006.

Tufte, Edward R. *The Cognitive Style of PowerPoint*. Cheshire, CT: Graphics Press, 2003.

Tufte, Edward R. *Envisioning Information*. Cheshire, CT: Graphics Press, 1990.

Tufte, Edward R. *Visual and Statistical Thinking: Displays of Evidence for Making Decisions*. Cheshire, CT: Graphics Press, 2003.

Tufte, Edward R. *The Visual Display of Quantitative Information*. Cheshire, CT: Graphics Press, 1983, 2001.

Tufte, Edward R. *Visual Explanations: Images and Quantities, Evidence and Narrative*. Cheshire, CT: Graphics Press, 1997.

Van House, Nancy A., and Thomas A. Childers. *The Public Library Effectiveness Study: The Complete Report*. Chicago: American Library Association, 1993.

Van House, Nancy A., Beth T. Weil, and Charles R. McClure. *Measuring Academic Library Performance: A Practical Approach*. Chicago: American Library Association 1990.

Walvoord, Barbara E. *Assessment Clear and Simple: A Practical Guide for Institutions, Departments, and General Education*. San Francisco: Jossey-Bass, 2004.

Walter, Scott, and Karen Williams, eds. *The Expert Library: Staffing, Sustaining, and Advancing the Academic Library in the 21st Century*. Chicago: American Library Association, 2010.

Webster, Leonard, and Patrice Mertova. *Using Narrative Inquiry as a Research Method: An Introduction to Using Critical Event Narrative Analysis in Research on Learning and Teaching*. New York: Routledge, 2007.

Weiss, Carol H. *Evaluation: Methods for Studying Programs and Policies*. Upper Saddle River, NJ: Prentice Hall, 1998.

Weiss, Carol H. *Evaluation Research: Methods for Assessing Program Effectiveness*. Englewood Cliffs, NJ: Prentice-Hall, 1972; 2nd ed. Upper Saddle River, NJ: Prentice Hall, 1998.

Williamson, Charles C. *The Williamson Reports of 1921 and 1923*. Metuchen, NJ: Scarecrow Press, 1931.

Wood, Elizabeth J., Rush Miller, and Amy Knapp. *Beyond Survival: Managing Academic Libraries in Transition*. Westport, CT: Libraries Unlimited, 2007.

Yin, Robert K. *Case Study Research*. 4th ed. Newbury Park, CA: Sage, 2009.

Zeithaml, Valarie, A. Parasuraman, and Leonard L. Berry. *Delivering Quality Service: Balancing Customer Perceptions and Expectations*. New York: The Free Press, 1990.

BOOK CHAPTERS

Cronback, Lee J. "Test Validation." In *Educational Measurement*, edited by Robert L. Thorndike. Washington, DC: American Council for Education, 1971.

Nitecki, Danuta A. "User Expectations for Quality Library Services Identified through Application of the SERVQUAL Scale in an Academic Library." In *Continuity and Transformation: The Promise of Confluence. Proceedings of the 7th Association of College and Research Libraries National Conference*, edited by Richard AmRhein, 53–66. Chicago: Association of College and Research Libraries, 1995.

Sutton, Brett. "Qualitative Research Methods in Library and Information Science." [ELIS Classic]. In *Encyclopedia of Library and Information Sciences*. 3rd ed., 1 no. 1. London: Taylor & Francis, 2010.

Wilson, Tom. "Information Needs and Uses: Fifty Years of Progress?" In *Fifty Years of Progress: A Journal of Documentation Review*, edited by B. C. Vickery. London: Aslib, 1994.

DISSERTATIONS AND THESES

Kyrillidou, Martha. "Item Sampling in Service Quality Assessment Surveys to Improve Response Rates and Reduce Respondent Burden: The LibQUAL+® Lite Randomized Control Trial (RCT)." PhD diss., University of Illinois, Graduate School of Library and Information, 2009.

Saunders, Laura. "Information Literacy as a Student Learning Outcome: As Viewed from the Perspective of Institutional Accreditation." PhD diss., Simmons College, 2010.

GOVERNMENT PUBLICATIONS

Florida Department of State, Division of Library and Information Services. *Return on Investment Study.* Accessed October 16, 2010. http://dlis.dos.state.fl.us/bld/roi/2004–ROI.cfm.

Florida Department of State, Division of Library and Information Services. *Workbook: Outcome Measurement of Library Programs*. Tallahassee, FL: Division of Library and Information Services, 2000. Accessed March 6, 2010. http://dlis.dos.state.fl.us/bld/Research_Office/OutcomeEvalWkbk.doc.

Rudd, Peggy D. *Perspectives on Outcome Based Evaluation for Libraries and Museums: Documenting the Difference: Demonstrating the Value of Libraries through Outcome Measurement*. Washington, DC: The Institute of Museum and Library Services, n.d.

Texas State Library and Archives Commission. "Outcome Measures." Accessed March 6, 2010. http://www.tsl.state.tx.us/outcomes/.

Texas State Libraries and Archives Commission. "Resources." Accessed February 18, 2010. http://dev.texshare.edu/outcomes/resources.html.

University of West Florida, Haas Center for Business Research and Economic Development. *Taxpayer Return on Investment in Florida Public Libraries.* Tallahassee: Florida Department of State, Division of Library and Information Services, May 2010.

University of West Florida, Haas Center for Business Research and Economic Development. *Taxpayers Return on Investment in Florida Public Libraries: Survey Results Site Navigation [by County]*. Accessed October 16, 2010. http://haas.uwf.edu/library/county_data/escambia.htm.

U.S. Bureau of Justice Assistance, Center for Program Evaluation. *Guide to Program Evaluation.* Accessed January 2, 2010. http://www.ojp.usdoj.gov/BJA/evaluation/guide/bja-guide-program-evaluation.pdf.

U.S. Center for Disease Control and Prevention. EZ-Text Web site. Accessed September 11, 2010. http://www.cdc.gov/hiv/topics/surveillance/resources/software/ez-text/index.htm.

U.S. General Accounting Office, Program Evaluation and Methodology Division. *Case Study Evaluations.* Transfer Paper 10.1.9. Washington, DC: General Accounting Office, 1990.

U.S. Government Accounting Office, Program Evaluation and Methodology Division. *Designing Evaluations.* GAO/PEMD-10.1.4. Washington, DC: Government Accounting Office, 1991.

U.S. General Accounting Office, Program Evaluation and Methodology Division. *Using Statistical Sampling.* GAO/PEMD-10.1.6. Washington, DC: General Accounting Office, 1992.

U.S. Government Accountability Office. *Program Evaluation: A Variety of Rigorous Methods Can Help Identify Effective Interventions.* GAO-10–30. Washington, DC: Government Accountability Office, 2009. Accessed January 11, 2010. http://www.gao.gov.

U.S. Institute of Museum and Library Services. *Perspective on Outcome Based Evaluation for Museums and Library Services.* Washington, DC: Institute of Museum and Library Services, n.d. Accessed February 18, 2010. http://www.imls.gov/pdf/pubobe.pdf.

REPORTS

Association of College and Research Libraries. *Value of Academic Libraries: A Comprehensive Research Review and Report.* By Megan Oakleaf. Chicago: Association of College and Research Libraries, 2010.

Association of Research Libraries. *The ARL 2030 Scenarios: A User's Guide for Research Libraries.* Washington, DC: Association of Research Libraries, 2010.

Kocevar-Weidinger, Elizabeth, and Candice Benjes-Small. "Reaching Reference Service Excellence: Developing a Mystery Shopping Program to Measure Service Quality, Performance, and the Patron Experience." Paper presented at Association of College & Research Libraries 14th National Conference, Seattle, WA, 2009.

Koltay, Zsuzsa, and Xin Li. *Impact Measures in Research Libraries.* SPEC Kit 318. Washington, DC: Association of Research Libraries, 2010.

Wright, Stephanie, and Lynda S. White. *Library Assessment.* SPEC Kit 303. Washington, DC: Association of Research Libraries, 2007.

WEB RESOURCES (NONGOVERNMENT)

American Evaluation Association. "About Us." Accessed February 18, 2010. http://www.eval.org/aboutus/organization/aboutus.asp.

American Library Association, Public Library Association. *Public Library Data Service Statistical Report.* Chicago: Public Library Association, 2009. Accessed December 30, 2009. http://www.ala.org/ala/mgrps/divs/pla/plapublications/pldsstatreport/index.cfm.

American Medical Association, Council on Ethical and Judicial Affairs. *2007 Annual Meeting Report.* 2008. Accessed August 8, 2010. http://www.ama-assn.org/ama1/pub/upload/mm/38/a08cejoreports.pdf.

Association of Research Libraries. "Major Initiatives: LibQual+." Accessed December 28, 2010. http://www.arl.org/major-initiatives/lq/index.shtml.

ATLAS.ti Qualitative Data Analysis Software Web site. Accessed September 11, 2010. http://www.atlasti.com/.

Authenticity Consulting, LLC. "How to Design Successful Evaluation and Assessment Plan." Accessed January 23, 2010. http://managementhelp.org/misc/designing-eval-assess.pdf.

Barnes, Susan, and Maryanne Blake. *Measuring Your Impact: Using Evaluation for Library Advocacy.* Chicago: Medical Library Association, 2008. Accessed January 3, 2010. http://nnlm.gov/evaluation/workshops/measuring_your_impact/myi_slides.pdf.

Becker, Bronwyn, Patrick Dawson, Karen Devine, Carla Hannum, Steve Hill, Jon Leydens, Debbie Matuskevich, Carol Traver, and Mike Palmquist. *Case Studies. Writing@CSU*. Ft. Collins, CO: Colorado State University, Department of English, 2005. Accessed September 8, 2010. http://writing.colostate.edu/guides/research/casestudy/.

Becker, Samantha, Michael D. Crandall, Karen E. Fisher, Bo Kinney, Carol Landry, and Anita Rocha. *Opportunity for All: How the American Public Benefits from Internet Access at U.S. Libraries*. Washington, DC: Institute of Museum and Library Services, 2010. Accessed October 29, 2010. http://www.gatesfoundation.org/learning/Documents/OpportunityForAll.pdf.

Branin, Joseph, Frances Groen, and Suzanne Thorin. *The Changing Nature of Collection Management in Research Libraries*. Washington, DC: Association of Research Libraries, 2002. Accessed October 30, 2010. http://www.arl.org/bm~doc/changing-nature-coll-mgmt.pdf.

British Library. "Measuring Our Value." Accessed December 31, 2010. http://www.bl.uk/pdf/measuring.pdf; http://www.bl.uk/about/annual/pdf/ar0304mcas.pdf.

Carnegie Library of Pittsburgh. *Community Impact and Benefits*. April 2006. Accessed December 31, 2000. http://www.clpgh.org/about/economicimpact/CLPCommunityImpactFinalReport.pdf.

Center for Applied Research. "Mini-case Study: Nike's 'Just Do It' Advertising Campaign." Accessed January 16, 2011. http://www.cfar.com/Documents/nikecmp.pdf.

Chakraborty, Debapriya. "Kano Model: Tool for Measuring Consumer Satisfaction." Accessed December 28, 2010. http://ayushveda.com/blogs/business/kano-model-tool-for-measuring-consumer-satisfaction/.

Columbia University Libraries, CUL Assessment Team. *Assessment Plan, Columbia University Libraries: 2007 through 2009*. February 1, 2007. Accessed January 23, 2010. https://www1.columbia.edu/sec/cu/libraries/bookmarks/img/assets/9436/CUL_Assessment_Plan.pdf.

Counting Opinions. Accessed December 21, 2009. http://www.countingopinions.com/.

Creative Research Systems. "The Survey System: Survey Design." 2010. Accessed January 6, 2010. http://www.surveysystem.com/sdesign.htm.

Daniel Cline's Website for Graduate Students in Educational Leadership. Accessed December 26, 2010. http://education.astate.edu/dcline/guide/framework.html.

Denmark's Electronic Research Library. *The Future of Research and the Research Library*. 2009. Accessed June 1, 2010. http://www.resourceshelf.com/2010/02/26/report-the-future-of-research-and-the-research-library/.

Dervin, Brenda. "Welcome to the Sense-Making Methodologies Site." Accessed December 29, 2010. http://communication.sbs.ohio-state.edu/sense-making/.

Dicks, Bella, and Bruce Mason. "Hypermedia and Ethnography: Reflections on the Construction of a Research Approach." *Sociological Research Online* 3, no. 3 (1998). Accessed August 15, 2010. http://www.socresonline.org.uk/3/3/3.html.

Dragon NaturallySpeaking Web Site. Accessed September 11, 2010. http://www.nuance.com/talk/.

Dupuis, John. "Confessions of a Science Librarian: Twenty-nine Report about the Future of Academic Libraries." Accessed May 1, 2010. http://jdupuis.blogspot.com/2009/02/twenty-nine-reports-about-future-of.html.

"The Executive Fast Track: Customer Satisfaction Model (Kano)." *12 Manage* Accessed December 30, 2010. http://www.12manage.com/methods_kano_customer_satisfaction_model.html.

Family Health International. *Qualitative Research Methods: A Data Collector's Field Guide, Module 2: Participant Observation.* Accessed February 12, 2010. http://www.fhi.org/NR/rdonlyres/d2ruznpftevg34lxuftzjiho65asz7betpqigbbyorggs6tetjic367v44baysyomnbdjkdtbsium/participantobservation1.pdf.

Fister, Barbara. "Leaders of Academic Institutions Reflect on the Value and Role of the Library." *Library Journal* (May 1, 2010). Accessed May 11, 2010. http://www.libraryjournal.com/article/CA6726948.html.

Foster, Nancy Fried, and Susan Gibbons, eds. *Studying Students: The Undergraduate Research Project at the University of Rochester.* Accessed August 15, 2010. https://urresearch.rochester.edu/institutionalPublicationPublicView.action?institutionalItemId=7044&versionNumber=1.

Foster, Nancy Fried, and Susan Gibbons. "Understanding Faculty to Improve Content Recruitment for Institutional Repositories." *D-Lib Magazine* 11, no. 1 (2005). Accessed August 15, 2010. http://www.dlib.org/dlib/january05/foster/01foster.html.

Frechtling, Joy. *The 2002 User Friendly Handbook for Project Evaluation.* Washington, DC: National Science Foundation, 2002. Accessed March 7, 2010. http://www.nsf.gov/pubs/2002/nsf02057/nsf02057.pdf.

Georgetown College Library. "Assessment of the Library: Library Evaluation Plan, 1." Accessed March 5, 2010. http://library.georgetowncollege.edu/Assessment.htm.

Greene, William. "Statistics and Data Analysis." Stern School of Business, New York University. Accessed March 27, 2010. http://pages.stern.nyu.edu/~wgreene/Statistics/Statistics-1–DataPresentation.ppt.

Hoover, Eric. "An Expert Surveys the Assessment Landscape." *The Chronicle of Higher Education* (October 27, 2009). Accessed March 28, 2010. http://chronicle.com/article/An-Expert-Surveys-the/48945/.

Huitt, William, John Hummel, and Dan Kaeck. "Assessment, Measurement, Evaluation, and Research." In *Educational Psychology Interactive*. Valdosta, GA: Valdosta State University. Accessed January 21, 2010. http://www. edpsycinteractive.org/topics/intro/sciknow.html.

Humboldt State University Library. "Kuhlthau's Model of the Stages of the Information Process." Accessed December 28, 2010. http://library.humboldt. edu/~ccm/fingertips/kuhlthau.html.

Institute for Healthcare Improvement. "Testing Changes." Accessed February 2, 2011. http://www.ihi.org/IHI/Topics/Improvement/ImprovementMethods/How ToImprove/testingchanges.htm.

International Organization for Standardization. *Market, Opinion and Social Research—Vocabulary and Service Requirements.* ISO 20252 (2006). Accessed August 8, 2009. http://www.iso.org/iso/iso_catalogue/catalogue_ics/catalogue_ detail_ics.htm?csnumber=53439.

Jansen, Bernard J., and Isak Taksa. "Research and Methodological Foundations of Transaction Log Analysis." Accessed December 31, 2009. http://www.igi-global.com/downloads/excerpts/8282.pdf.

Jaschik, Scott. "Engaged or Confused." *Inside Higher Ed* (November 9, 2009). Accessed March 28, 2010. http://www.insidehighered.com/layout/set/print/ news/2009/11/09/porter.

Kupersmith, John. "Library Terms Evaluated in Usability Tests and Other Studies." 2009. Accessed January 5, 2010. http://www.jkup.net/terms-studies.html.

"Lib Value." Accessed February 1, 2011. http://libvalue.cci.utk.edu/.

LibQUAL+®: Charting Library Service Quality. Washington, DC: Association of Research Libraries, 2009. Accessed December 21, 2009. http://www.libqual. org/home.

"Libraries of the Future." *Inside Higher ED* (September 24, 2009). Accessed May 1, 2010. http://www.insidehighered.com/layout/set/print/news/2009/09/24/libraries.

LibraryJournal.com. "The LJ Index of Public Library Service 2010: America's Star Libraries." Accessed November 28, 2010. http://www.libraryjournal.com/lj/ articlereview/886935–457/americas_star_libraries_2010_top-rated.html.csp.

Lipka, Sara. "It's Not How Much Student Data You Have, but How You Use It." *The Chronicle of Higher Education* (November 4, 2010). Accessed November 12, 2010. http://chronicle.com/article/Its-Not-How-Much-Student-Data/125255/.

Marcum, James W. "Visions: The Academic Library in 2012." *D-Lib Magazine* 9, no. 5 (May 2003). Accessed May 1, 2010. http://www.dlib.org/dlib/may03/ marcum/05marcum.html.

Martin, Gary. "The Phrase Finder." Accessed January 17, 2011. http://www.phrases. org.uk/meanings/106700.html.

Massachusetts Library Association. "Value of Library Service Calculator." Accessed October 16, 2010. http://69.36.174.204/value-new/calculator.html.

The Mathematical Association of America. "Frequently Asked Questions." Accessed January 21, 2010. http://www.maa.org/SAUM/faq.html#diffeval.

McGregor, Felicity. "Exploring the Mystery of Service Satisfaction." Wollongong, Australia: University of Wollongong, Academic Services Division, 2005. Accessed February 11, 2010. http://ro.uow.edu.au/cgi/viewcontent.cgi?article= 1026&context=asdpapers.

McNamara, Carter. "Basic Guide to Program Evaluation." Authenticity Consulting, LLC, 2008. Accessed January 2, 2010. http://www.managementhelp.org/ evaluatn/fnl_eval.htm.

Mietzner, Dana, and Guido Reger. "Advantages and Disadvantages of Scenario Approaches for Strategic Foresight." *International Journal of Technology Intelligence and Planning* 1, no. 2 (2005). Accessed April 30, 2010. http://www. lampsacus.com/documents/StragegicForesight.pdf.

Mystery Shopping Providers Association Web Site. Accessed August 8, 2010. http:// www.mysteryshop.org/.

Neal, James G. "Information Anarchy or Information Utopia?" *The Chronicle of Higher Education* (December 9, 2005). Accessed April 29, 2010. http:// chronicle.com/article/Information-Anarchy-or/2773.

Nevena, Stancheva, and Vyara Angelova. "Measuring the Efficiency of University Libraries Using Data Envelopment Analysis." *Proceedings from INFORUM 2004* (May 25–27, 2004). Accessed October 16, 2010. http://www.inforum.cz/ pdf/2004/Stancheva_Nevena.pdf.

NVivo 8 Web Site. Accessed September 11, 2010. http://www.qsrinternational.com/ products_nvivo.aspx.

Pritchard, Sarah M. "No Library Is an Island: Finding Ground in the Culture of Assessment." Accessed January 21, 2010. http://www.sla.org/Presentations/ sldc/sarah_LAB2002pp.ppt.

Proceedings of the 6th Northumbria International Conference on Performance Measurement in Libraries and Information Services. Preprint draft. Durham, England, August 22–25, 2005. Accessed August 15, 2010. http://ro.uow.edu.au/ cgi/viewcontent.cgi?article=1026&context=asdpapers.

Quinn, Brian A. "Adapting Service Quality Concepts to Academic Libraries." Libraries Faculty Research Texas Tech University, 2007. Accessed December 28, 2010. http://thinktech.lib.ttu.edu/bitstream/handle/2346/503/fulltext.pdf?sequence=1.

Salter, Elaine. *Mystery Shopping Project: Report of the M5 Working Group on Quality.* University of Westminster. Accessed August 15, 2010. http://www. m25lib.ac.uk/mystery_shopping_project_2.html.

Schonfeld, Roger C., and Ross Housewright. *Ithaka S+R Faculty Survey 2009: Key Strategic Insights for Libraries, Publishers, and Societies*. New York: Ithaka S+R. 2010. Accessed May 25, 2010. http://www.ithaka.org/ithaka-s-r/research/faculty-surveys-2000–2009/Faculty%20Study%202009.pdf.

Silver, Howard. "Use of Collaborative Spaces in an Academic Library." In *GSLIS Colloquium*. Boston: Simmons College, 2007. Accessed August 15, 2010. http://gslis.simmons.edu/podcasts/podcast_extras/2007/20070227–silver-slides.pdf.

Staley, David J., and Kara J. Malenfant. *Futures Thinking for Academic Librarians: Higher Education in 2025*. Chicago: Association of Research Libraries, 2010. Accessed June 23, 2010. http://www.ala.org/ala/mgrps/divs/acrl/issues/value/futures2025.pdf .

"Standard Deviation Graphs." Accessed March 14, 2010. http://images.google.com/images?hl=en&rls=com.microsoft:en-us:IE-SearchBox&rlz=1I7SUNA_en&q=standard+deviation+graph&um=1&ie=UTF-8&ei=jfCcS4HVPMP48Abvl_yWDg&sa=X&oi=image_result_group&ct=title&resnum=4&ved=0CBcQsAQwAw.

Stemler, Steve. "An Overview of Content Analysis." *Practical Assessment, Research & Evaluation* 7, no. 17 (2001). Accessed September 11, 2010. http://PAREonline.net/getvn.asp?v=7&n=17.

Suffolk University, Mildred F. Sawyer Library. "FAQ: Has the Library Calculated Its Return on Investment (ROI)?" Accessed October 17, 2010. http://www.suffolk.edu/sawlib/faq.htm#anchor40210.

Suffolk University, Mildred F. Sawyer Library. "FAQ: How Can I Get My Tuition Money's Worth from the Library?" Accessed October 17, 2010. http://www.suffolk.edu/sawlib/faq.htm#anchor13268.

Suffolk University, Mildred F. Sawyer Library. "Value of Services at the Mildred F. Sawyer Library: Academic Year 2009–2010 Based upon FY 2010 Expenditure Information." Accessed October 17, 2010. http://www.suffolk.edu/files/SawLib/value_of_library_services__2010.pdf.

3rd European Workshop on Computer-Aided Qualitative Research. Lisbon, Portugal, 2010. Accessed September 11, 2010. http://www.merlien.org/upcoming-events/caqre2010.html.

Thomas, Joy. "Mystery Shoppers at the Library: A Planning Report." 2000. Accessed February 11, 2010. http://www.csulb.edu/divisions/aa/grad_undergrad/senate/committees/assessment/dev/awards/documents/thomas_99.pdf.

Thomson Reuters. *Journal Citation Reports®*. Accessed November 23, 2010. http://thomsonreuters.com/products_services/science/science_products/a-z/journal_citation_reports/.

Trochim, William M. "Introduction to Evaluation." *The Research Methods: Knowledge Base* (October 20, 2006). Accessed September 7, 2010. http://www.socialresearchmethods.net/kb/intreval.htm; accessed August 8, 2010. http://www.socialresearchmethods.net/kb/.

University of Massachusetts, Amherst, W.E.B. Du Bois Library. "UMass Amherst Learning Commons." Accessed January 19, 2010. http://www.umass.edu/learningcommons/.

University of Minnesota, Office of Information Technology. "Productivity & Efficiency DB." Accessed November 28, 2010. http://www.tc.umn.edu/~bernard/oit/Scorecard/ProductivityEfficiency/index.html.

University of Minnesota, Office of Information Technology. "Scorecard & Dashboard Development." Accessed November 28, 2010. http://www.tc.umn.edu/~bernard/oit/Scorecard/.

University of Pennsylvania, Fels Institute of Government, Fels Research and Consulting. *The Economic Value of the Free Library in Philadelphia.* October 21, 2010. Accessed January 22, 2011. http://www.freelibrary.org/about/Fels_Report.pdf.

University of Surrey. *Computer Assisted Qualitative Data AnalysiS [CAQDAS] Networking Project.* Accessed September 11, 2010. http://caqdas.soc.surrey.ac.uk/.

University of Texas at Austin. *LibQUAL 2008 Survey.* Austin, TX: University of Texas at Austin, 2008. Accessed January 9, 2010. http://www.lib.utexas.edu/sites/default/files/vprovost/2008_LibQUAL_Institution-Results.pdf.

University of Washington, University Libraries. "Ask Us! Usability How-to Guides, Web Links, and Books." Seattle, WA: University Libraries, 2008. Accessed January 5, 2010. http://www.lib.washington.edu/usability/howto.html.

"Using Data and Statistics." Math League Press, 2006. Accessed March 12, 2010. http://www.mathleague.com/help/data/data.htm.

"Using Library Assessment Data against the Customer." *Lib[rary] Performance* (blog), April 7, 2009, http://libperformance.com/2009/04/07/using-library-assessment-data-against-the-customer/.

Via Voice Web Site. Accessed September 11, 2010. http://www-01.ibm.com/software/pervasive/embedded_viavoice/.

Welsh Library Service Mystery Shopper. *Mystery Shop Report.* Produced for the Wrexham County Borough Council. Twelfth Man Ltd., 2009. Accessed November 3, 2010. http://wales.gov.uk/docs/drah/research/091101MysteryShopperReporten.pdf.

Winget, Megan. "Qualitative Research: The 'Ethnography of Annotation' Model." 2005. Accessed August 14, 2010. http://www.unc.edu/~winget/research/Winget_Methods.pdf.

Wright, Stephanie, and Lynda S. White. "Library Assessment in North America." January 11, 2008. Accessed February 16, 2010. http://www.libqual.org/documents/admin/WrightWhite.ppt.

XSight Web Site. Accessed September 11, 2010. http://www.qsrinternational.com/products_xsight.aspx.

Zelna, Carrie L. "Basic Assessment Plan Development." n.d. Accessed January 27, 2010. http://www.ncsu.edu/assessment/presentations/assess_process/basic_plan_devt.pdf.

UNPUBLISHED MATERIAL

Cawthorne, Jon. "The Academic Library of the Future: The Vision of 2007 Senior Fellows." Unpublished manuscript, Simmons College, 2009.

Frost, Abbie. "Exploratory Research." Unpublished manuscript Simmons College, Graduate School of Library and Information Science, Managerial Leadership in the Information Professions, June 9, 2010.

Lakos, Amos, and Shelley Phipps. "Building a Culture of Assessment in Libraries: The New Imperative." Presented at the ACRL Pre-Conference, Denver, CO, sponsored by the Association of Research Libraries, Office of Leadership and Management Services, March 15, 2001.

McCarthy, Cheryl A., and Danuta A. Nitecki. "An Assessment of the Bass Library as a Learning Commons Environment." Unpublished manuscript from the proceedings of the Library Assessment Conference, Baltimore, MD, October 25–27, 2010.

Miller, Rush G. "Beyond Survival: How Can Libraries Maintain Relevance in the Digital Age." Paper presented at the ALAO conference, October 30, 2009.

Webster, Duane E. "Organizational Projections for Envisioning Research Library Futures." Unpublished manuscript, Simmons College, 2010.

Webster, Duane E. "Scenarios for Contemplating Research Library Futures." Unpublished manuscript, Simmons College, 2009.

White, Marilyn D. "Measuring Customer Satisfaction and Quality of Service in Special Libraries." Unpublished Final Report to Special Libraries Association, September 1994.

Appendix A—Academic Libraries in the Future: Looking into the Crystal Ball

As librarians engage in evaluation and assessment activities and link them to the planning process, they should be doing so in the context of a leadership vision that points the library in new directions. Those directions help the library transform and better meet the institutional mission and goals. The purpose of this appendix is to assist librarians in seeing the bigger picture and helping move the organization in that direction.

Academic research libraries have evolved from warehouses of rare and valuable collections to service organizations focused on meeting assorted information needs while addressing faculty and student expectations. The evolution is not complete and never will be. Other academic libraries have likewise changed and have begun to place higher priority on meeting the educational mission of their institutions and expressing greater interest in customer expectations. Regardless of the type of academic library, there remains a fascination about what the future will bring, but there is also a realization that the economic recession of 2008–2009 and its aftermath have had a profound impact on what future may materialize. The fascination is accompanied by, for instance, "anxiety about . . . [the] role [of academic libraries] in scholarly communication," "disruption in work-force development," rethinking the preparation required of the new and existing workforce, and the continual retraining of staff and the reengineering of positions.[1] More succinctly, what is the future of the academic library, and what is its relevance to and impact on higher education? As James G. Neal argues, the "pattern of heightened anxiety, disruption, and chaos [in higher education] will change academic libraries momentously, yet it will also offer extraordinary opportunities,"[2] but there are challenges, too.

PROBLEM STATEMENT

The challenges that academic libraries face are associated with financial, technological, political, social, and demographic changes already underway, as well as with changing patterns of information seeking and information use. Facing these challenges, institutions of higher education and a broad array of their stakeholders demand greater accountability and the gathering and use of evidence to make decisions; improve services; and demonstrate the relevance, effectiveness, and efficiency of library services and operations. In such a climate, there is a need to continue visualizing and planning for the academic library of the future, with such visualizations more fully focusing on services than past discussions and research have done. Although other studies have proposed a set of scenarios for the future, none has included the perspective of accreditation organizations and recent trends. The purpose of this study is to fill that void by advancing a new set of scenarios, gather the input of library directors in shaping the content of these scenarios, and extend thinking about services and how changing information-seeking behavior and campus environments shape them.

Today numerous conferences, institutes, and other discussion fora in library and information science (LIS) focus on leadership and the development of a vision, presumably one that is service oriented. In such settings, it is advantageous to discuss scenarios and the leadership that is necessary to make them a reality. They also provide senior managers with an opportunity to review the choices and create a favorable scenario that they can use for strategic planning and to make the organization and institution more receptive to change. That scenario, which most likely addresses the impact of the Internet and digital resources on information seeking and use, copes with the erosion of the library's place and value in users' hearts and minds, while addressing the concerns of some stakeholders that the Internet replaces library collections.

LITERATURE REVIEW

Scenarios comprise stories with critical components to challenge readers to think about the future but not to identify every trend. The goal is not to look back later to see how much of a scenario actually occurred. In essence, scenarios comprise short narratives that explore the future and lay out various possibilities, one of which might be the status quo. On a local level, senior managers can take the set of scenarios; imagine multiple futures; apply formal scenario planning, a technique that describes possible futures so that they can think about how to examine surprises and discontinuities in the planning process; and design plans to respond to changes depending on how the future actually develops.[3] Scenarios, in essence, can help organizations to answer the following question: "Are we headed in the right direction?"

In LIS, Nina W. Matheson used scenarios to illustrate the perceptions of directors of health science libraries about changes in the roles and functions of these libraries in the coming decade. Her scenarios (one highly desirable and the other highly probable),[4] however, are not stories of the future, as commonly associated with scenario planning. Since then, Duane E. Webster has developed and refined a set of scenarios applicable to research libraries,[5] and Jon Cawthorne has defined his scenarios and applied them to the libraries in which his cohort in the Senior Fellows Program, University of California–Los Angeles, work.[6] Peter Hernon and Laura Saunders developed a set of scenarios applicable to research libraries and their participation in the federal depository library program.[7]

Envisioning the future is not confined to research centered on the development and testing of scenarios using either the Delphi technique or telephone or in-person interviews. Perhaps two examples are best known: Jerry D. Campbell's discussion of the academic library as "losing its supremacy" as the conveyor of "trustworthy, authoritative knowledge" due to "the impact of digital technology";[8] and *No Brief Candle*, published by the Council on Library and Information Resources, which, among other things, identifies core functions and roles, challenges, and constraints for the academic library of the twenty-first century and offers a set of recommendations.[9] David W. Lewis sees the immediate challenge for research libraries as completing "the migration from print to electronic collections"; retiring "legacy print collections"; reconceptualizing the use of library space; repositioning "library, and information tools, resources, and expertise"; and "migrating the focus of collections from purchasing materials to curating content."[10] Larry Hardesty sees a challenge in attracting qualified professional staff to academic libraries,[11] and Laura Saunders explores the future role of information literacy in academic institutions.[12]

Ithaka S+R (http://www.ithaka.org/ithaka-s-r), part of ITHAKA, a not-for-profit organization dedicated to helping the academic community use digital technologies, examines issues relevant to academic libraries, publishers, and scholarly societies, among others, to help them serve the changing information needs of faculty. Their reports, which indicate a perceived decrease in the value of the university library by its constituent groups, contain elements useful in conceptualizing futures and should be linked to strategic planning initiatives. In one report, the authors identify a paradox, namely:

> [I]f the library shapes its roles and activities based on what is currently most highly appreciated by faculty, it may lose a valuable opportunity to innovate and position itself as relevant in the future. On the other hand, if the library develops new and innovative roles and services that address unmet needs, becoming newly relevant and even essential to those scholars who have moved farthest away from it, in the near term it may lose the support of its most ardent supporters.

Continuing, the authors ask:

> Can the academic library reengage with scientists? If not, is it realistic to expect humanists to remain wedded to it, given that humanists' declining support for the library's gateway role indicates they may be following in the footsteps of their peers in other disciplines, a trend which may only accelerate as a broader range of humanistic scholarly materials is made available in digital form? Addressing this dilemma is perhaps the most urgent strategic challenge facing academic library leaders.[13]

Drawing together a number of studies, James W. Marcum sees the driving forces for determining change in the academic library of 2012 as technological developments, library services, and librarians' roles.[14] A report from Denmark maintains that the future library will have to cope with changing information-seeking behavior of faculty and students; face a financial landscape that continues to be limited, especially with the vast array of digital resources available; have a smaller workforce with different skill sets; and confront those questions about the role of libraries in information provision and access.[15]

Daniel Greenstein, Vice Provost for Academic Planning and Programs at the University of California, views the university library of the future as sparsely staffed, highly decentralized, and having a physical plant consisting largely of special collections and study areas. He sees outsourcing some library functions as the answer for institutions in which budgets have been decimated by the economic downturn.[16] Additional insights for the development of scenarios come from Barbara Fister's interviews with more than 130 chief academic officers;[17] John Dupuis's blog, which identifies twenty-nine reports on the future of academic libraries;[18] and ARL, which has developed four scenarios that illustrate what lies ahead for research libraries and suggests that librarians will need to be "fully engaged" in campus research and what is occurring globally, especially in Asia and the Middle East. Librarians in one of those scenarios will have "responsibility to create, describe, curate, control access, and authenticate information." Future professionals will also need "knowledge and project management skills."[19]

David J. Staley and Kara J. Malenfant, in a project for the Association of College and Research Libraries, developed twenty-six scenarios that deal with "academic culture, demographics, distance education, funding, globalization, infrastructure/facilities, libraries, political climate, publishing industry, societal values, student/learning, and technology."[20] Before any library settles on any scenario such as the ones presented here and in that document, its managerial staff should review the four questions they raise:

1. If this scenario were to exist today, would we be able to leverage it to our advantage? Do we have the resources, staffing, organizational processes, and strategy right now to take advantage of this scenario?

2. If this scenario were to exist today, in what ways are we currently vulnerable to the change it represents? In what ways are we unprepared, lacking in resources and staffing, or to what degree are our strategies and underlying values unable to respond effectively to the conditions this scenario represents?

3. Assuming we had all the staffing and resources we need (a very big assumption, we concede), what could we be doing to leverage this trend to our advantage?

4. What would need to happen—internally and in the external environment—for this vision to become a reality?[21]

PROCEDURES

Dana Mietzner and Guido Reger recommend that the number of proposed scenarios not exceed four, and that each scenario should meet criteria such as plausibility (is capable of happening), differentiation (differs from the others, and together they offer multiple futures), decision-making utility (offers insights into the future that help in planning and decision making), and challenging (challenges conventional wisdom about the future).[22]

The following assumptions were made in the construction of our scenarios. First, the aftermath of the 2008–2009 economic recession will persist for several more years and will likely retard the expansive nature of any set of scenarios and the reaction of library directors to them. Library funding as a percentage of the institutional budget has also dropped in recent years. Second, many libraries are likely to have a smaller workforce and to engage in staffing and operations reengineering. As the critical knowledge, abilities, and skill set that library directors expect of their workforce change, perhaps a smaller percentage of librarians will have the master's degree from a program accredited by the American Library Association. Third, the service expectations of faculty and students will increase. Fourth, the pace of technological innovations in libraries will not diminish; in fact, it may accelerate. Fifth, any set of scenarios needs to explore new service roles; the changing role of, and access to, collections in meeting information needs; staff transformation and the redesign of positions; repurposing facilities to expand collaborate space; and recognizing the transformational role of technology. Sixth, the assumptions that James L. Mullins, Frank R. Allen, and Jon R. Hufford offer seem plausible as libraries seek to retain a central role in the life of their communities and the educational and research processes.[23] Data creation and preservation are associated with e-research and its subset, e-science,[24] while regional accreditation organizations call for another type of embedded or liaison librarians, associated with information literacy at the program and the institutional levels. Libraries that are engaged in redefining their institutional role "will need a staff with a different mix of skills and a willingness to explore new approaches and to break out of established ways of doing things."[25] Librarians therefore should relate scenario development to planning, including succession planning. In essence, implementation of a scenario (e.g., one of those presented here and any that includes elements from different scenarios) expands "the boundaries of the library" while simultaneously the library moves "away from conventional administrative hierarchies and academic bureaucracies to a combination of centralized planning and resource allocation systems, loosely coupled academic structures, and maverick units and entrepreneurial enterprises."[26]

Seventh, the content of the scenarios should build on current trends and not represent a total departure from what some libraries are doing. Seventh, instead of making each scenario completely different, some might logically build from previous ones. And finally, the set of scenarios should project no more than the next fifteen years, as suggested by forecaster Joseph P. Marino, who notes that the accuracy in predicting what will likely occur declines dramatically with a longer time frame.[27] Still, the goal is not to predict the future, but rather to provide a foundation for organizations to engage in meaningful scenario planning.

The sidebar on the following pages reprints the original scenarios revised after one library director commented on them. The first is a variation of the status quo; the second views institutions as deciding to do without a library; the third sees the library as an integral part of the educational system while outsourcing technical services; and the fourth, which builds from the previous scenario, expands the role of the library in scholarly communication.

Through in-person and telephone interviews with six library directors at doctoral-granting institutions (four that are ARL members), the investigators further refined the content of the four scenarios.[28] Participants, however, had the opportunity to offer an alternative vision.

An Initial Set of Scenarios

Service Scenario One

Although there has been no increase in the library's budget for a number of years or in the size of the professional workforce, the library retains a traditional commitment to supporting the library's print and digital collections, but tips the balance in favor of the latter. The staff recognizes that students rely heavily on databases, read e-books and other digital content, and seldom use the library's OPAC. The library retains its traditional services (circulation, reference, and interlibrary loan [ILL]) but adds digital components to them, namely the ability of remote and on-site library users to ask questions via text messaging and the library's homepage and receive prompt responses, engage in self-checkout, and place ILL requests online. The library largely outsources technical services and defines accountability in terms of the amount and quality of service it provides to students and faculty, its support of classroom instruction, and customer satisfaction. The library manages the institutional repository.

The primary motivation for this scenario is comfort with the present and a desire to avoid uncertainty, but also a willingness to expand digital services. Undoubtedly the library is wireless, and there might be an information or learning commons; however, these do not affect the service role the library director envisions.

Service Scenario Two

With the increased digital availability of information resources from an increasing array of service providers, the library sees its primary role as being a mediator of content licenses that are not available for licensing directly from academic departments. To support the educational programs, it maintains contracts with vendors or other libraries to provide support service (e.g., digital reference service or full-text, online journals). The library manages the institutional repository.

The primary motivation for this scenario is to acknowledge the need for remote students and faculty to have online access to many materials available in the library. In addition, there is a desire to convert precious campus (library) space to more directly supporting classroom learning and to relieving space congestion on campus. The institution is greatly expanding distance education, defined in terms of Web delivery of content. A major drawback of this scenario might be opposition from program and institutional accreditation organizations that might have a traditional view of a library.

Service Scenario Three

Embracing an institutional service role, the library has greatly downsized its physical collections and traditional services. The physical space emphasizes group study space and sharing space with selected campus support units (e.g., the writing center). There are four types of service roles for librarians:

1. Embedded specialists supporting faculty research teams and projects, and developing the collection and/or providing access to the it.

2. Embedded instructional design librarians working closely with academic programs to support mutually agreed-on student learning outcomes that contribute to student learning and faculty teaching, especially in the online delivery of courses and programs. These librarians include visual literacy in their program-level instruction and contribute to the institution's successful methodology for addressing general education learning outcomes.

3. Librarians engaged in special projects, such as working with the specialists and instructional design librarians to develop digital guides as finding aids and help guides. These librarians do not have a content role.

4. Librarians working in the center for digital initiatives, which produces digital content for use in campus scholarship and teaching, digitizes signature collections from the library's special collections, and offers consultative services to academic units undertaking digital projects.

The same librarians might perform all of these roles or a subset of them, as the library lacks unlimited resources. With this scenario the library assumes an active, nurturing role of information discovery, supporting and advancing teaching and learning pedagogy, and knowledge production for the institution.

To accommodate the service roles, the library further outsources technical services and no longer offers assistance at a traditionally regularly staffed reference desk. Students and others needing assistance in doing research either make appointments with knowledgeable staff members or convey their questions via the library's homepage or text messaging (librarians in type 3 above fulfill this role). The library might also manage the institutional repository.

The primary motivations for pursuing this scenario are (1) the changing information needs and information-seeking behaviors of faculty and students and (2) the critical role that the library actively plays in student learning. The library has not gained a larger percentage of the institutional budget and is engaged in reengineering operations and staff positions. Given the expectations of accreditation organizations, the library has dramatically shifted its attention to program-level assessment for all students, wherever and however they participate. The library advances the institutional mission and how it demonstrates campus-wide support, while still coping with the shift in student use of databases over the library's OPAC. Depending on the extent to which a library assumes the four service roles without having staff engaged in more than one service role, there is likely a need to expand the number of professional staff members, not necessarily librarians who hold the master's degree from a program accredited by the American Library Association.

Service Scenario Four

Building from either the first or third scenario, the library actively engages in electronic publishing for academic departments; the library has acquired the espresso book machine to print books and other resources on demand. The purpose is to expand the library's role as an online publisher engaged in knowledge creation, scholarly access, and preservation. To accomplish this role, the library invests in the technology necessary to engage in self-publishing, preferring to take a more independent role. The library has an office for digital rights, which advises academic units about choices for placement of their scholarly, research, and classroom teaching materials. The library extends this service to graduate students as well. In some instances, the library might forego such services as content suppliers and institutional networks handle vendor licensing arrangements to realize shared collection goals.

The primary motivations for pursuing this scenario are to make the library (1) a more visible partner in scholarly communication and the changing publishing model, and (2) a central campus player in knowledge preservation and production. The goal is to make the library more central to the dissemination and preservation of campus scholarship and research. A concern is the institution's tenure and review process as the faculty move into nontraditional scholarly publishing. To achieve this scenario, the library director may have to assume a broader institutional role, namely managing the information infrastructure (including information technologies) and peer-review processes, and supporting revenue generation or specific public service goals.

FINDINGS

The second sidebar provides the revised scenarios. The scenarios are no longer called "service scenarios." One participant objected to the inclusion of *service*, as he thought the word might be approached too much from the present and thereby inhibit other directors from considering a wide range of future possibilities. In this instance, he was thinking of general reference service. Most of the participants focused on the refinement of the third and fourth scenarios. One director of a non-ARL library, however, did not see any of the four as possibilities; instead, she sketched the fifth one.

The Revised Set of Scenarios

Scenario One

Although there has been no increase in the library's budget or in the size of the professional workforce for a number of years, the library retains a traditional commitment to supporting its print and digital collections, but tips the balance in favor of the latter. The staff recognizes that students rely heavily on databases, read e-books and other digital content, and seldom use the library's OPAC. The library retains its traditional services (circulation, reference, and interlibrary loan [ILL]) but adds digital components to them, namely the ability of remote and on-site library users to ask questions via text messaging and the library's homepage and receive prompt responses, engage in self-checkout, and place ILL requests online. The library largely outsources technical services and defines accountability in terms of the amount and quality of service it provides to students and faculty, its support of classroom instruction, and customer satisfaction. The library manages the institutional repository.

The primary motivation for this scenario is comfort with the present and a desire to avoid uncertainty, but a willingness to expand digital services. Undoubtedly the library is wireless, and there might be an information or learning commons; however, these do not affect the service role the library director envisions.

Scenario Two

With the increased digital availability of information resources from an increasing array of service providers, this virtual library sees its primary role as being a mediator of content licenses. To support educational programs, it maintains contracts with vendors or other libraries to provide support service (e.g., digital reference service or full-text, online journals). The library manages the institutional repository.

The primary motivation for this scenario is to acknowledge the need for remote students and faculty to have online access to many materials available in the library. In addition, there is a desire to convert precious campus (library) space to more directly supporting classroom learning and to relieving space congestion on campus. The institution is greatly expanding distance education, defined in terms of Web delivery of content. A major drawback of this scenario might be opposition from program and institutional accreditation organizations that might have a traditional view of a library.

Scenario Three

Embracing an institutional service role, the library is totally restructured. It has greatly downsized its physical collections and traditional services. The physical space emphasizes group study space and sharing space with selected campus support units (e.g., the writing center). Moving beyond the physical setting of the library, four types of service roles for librarians emerge:

1. Embedded specialists supporting faculty research teams and projects, and developing the collection and/or providing access to it. These specialists might preserve and make data sets accessible online that faculty members produce for their research. They might also convert faculty field notes and photographic collections for online access as well as assist faculty in a Web-based sharing of resources with their colleagues at other institutions.

2. Embedded instructional design librarians working closely with academic programs to support mutually agreed-on student learning outcomes that contribute to student learning and faculty teaching, especially in the online delivery of courses and programs. These librarians include visual literacy in their program-level instruction and contribute to the institution's successful methodology for addressing general education learning outcomes.

3. Librarians engaged in special projects such as working with specialists and instructional design librarians to develop digital guides as finding aids and help guides. These librarians do not have a content role.

4. Librarians working in the center for digital initiatives, which produces digital content for use in campus scholarship and teaching, digitizes signature collections from the library's special collections, and offers consultative services to academic units undertaking digital projects.

The same librarians might perform all of these roles or a subset of them, as the library lacks unlimited resources. With this scenario the library assumes an active, nurturing role of information discovery, supporting and advancing teaching and learning pedagogy, and knowledge production for the institution.

To accommodate the service roles, the library further outsources technical services and no longer offers assistance at a traditionally regularly staffed reference desk. Students and others needing assistance in doing research either make appointments with knowledgeable staff members or convey their questions via the library's homepage or text messaging (librarians in type 3 above fulfill this role). The library might also manage the institutional repository.

The primary motivations for pursuing this scenario are (1) the changing information needs and information-seeking behaviors of faculty and students, and (2) the critical role that the library actively plays in student learning. The library has not gained a larger percentage of the institutional budget and is engaged in reengineering operations and staff positions. Given the expectation of program and institutional accreditation organizations, the library has dramatically shifted its attention to program-level assessment for all students, wherever and however they participate. The library advances the institutional mission and how it demonstrates campus-wide support, while still coping with the shift in student use of databases over the library's OPAC. Depending on the extent to which a library assumes the four service roles without having staff engaged in more than one service role, there is likely a need to expand the number of professional staff members, not necessarily librarians who hold the master's degree from a program accredited by the American Library Association.

Scenario Four

Building from either the first or third scenario, the library views scholarly communication as part of its core mission and actively engages in electronic publishing for academic departments and faculty (through the use of the espresso book machine to print books and other resources on demand). The purpose is to expand the library's role as an online publisher engaged in knowledge creation, scholarly access, and preservation. To accomplish this role, the library invests in the technology necessary to engage in publishing, preferring to take a more independent role, and develops both the infrastructure and expertise as an online publisher.

As a complement, the library has an office for digital rights, which advises academic units about choices for placement of their scholarly, research, and classroom teaching materials. The library extends this service to graduate students as well. That office might be part of an office of scholarly communication that integrates the university press, institutional repository, coverage of intellectual property rights, and publishing (online and print). This office is also involved in technology transfer and advises the university on international technology transfer.

The primary motivations for pursuing this scenario are to make the library (1) a more visible partner in scholarly communication and the changing publishing model, and (2) a central campus player in knowledge preservation and production. The goal is to make the library more central to the dissemination and preservation of campus scholarship and research. A concern is the institution's tenure and review process as the faculty move into nontraditional scholarly publishing. To achieve this scenario, the library director may assume a broader institutional role, namely managing the information infrastructure (including information technologies).

Scenario Five

The library has a professional staff specializing in learning pedagogy and partnering with classroom faculty in teaching information and visual literacy competencies (similar here to scenario three), working collaboratively with support services across the campus such as through learning commons, and engaging in evaluation and assessment to improve the quality of the services offered and student learning outcomes. The assessment occurs at the institutional level, with the library participating in the achievement of program and institutional student learning outcomes. To do this, the library redirects staff to work closely with the academic programs. The library combines a technologically advanced learning environment with inviting instructional space, classrooms, and support services (e.g., writing tutors).

The primary motivation for pursing this scenario is to make the library more of an institutional partner that accomplishes the mission and vision that the institution projects. The goal is to make the library an important player in attracting and retaining students and assisting faculty in their teaching and research. Achievement of this scenario might necessitate a professional staff with an assortment of advanced educational degrees.

DISCUSSION

Some of those interviewed view the first scenario as traditional and ignoring trends that enable a library to be a "better institutional partner." As one director comments, if any library is still focused on this scenario in fifteen or more years, that library "is in deep, deep trouble." Turning to the second scenario, one director sees it as more applicable to a small college, where there is a merger of information and instructional technology and the library.

Except for scenario two, the final two scenarios build on the first one, which offers a traditional view of a library as a physical space. Scenarios three and four create more opportunities to blend digital services with the physical space. The future most likely for many institutions will therefore involve components of both scenarios. One participant mentions that,

> We have been pushing the envelope of what the research library is . . . . We are going to be searching for a new head of archives and special collections and one of the requirements will be that he/she has the ability to integrate archival science into the management of data. Our librarians are now being expected to include data management as part of their position requirements as well as information literacy instruction. Librarians no longer work on reference, and are participating in grant research.[29]

One participant speculated that in the future there will be a sharp distinction between the library and librarians. Librarians will not be identified with their setting. Instead, they will be known throughout the institution as faculty members specializing in the concept, principles, and applications of organizing resources and making them accessible. Librarians, as he explains, "are members of the faculty who are associated with library and information science," like faculty known as part of the history or biology department. Although they will be engaged in preserving and maintaining access to datasets, they will still remain stewards of the print collection as they "take those collections into the future"; this means finding a digital presence for them. In addition, libraries will focus on legacy collections. With one exception, the participants see the third and fourth scenarios as adding important roles and responsibilities.

One director is already actively engaged in the fourth scenario and sees it as rich in opportunities for the future. The library has gone beyond maintaining its institutional repository and archiving and preservation of special collections. The goal is to "provide the technology and expertise to enable faculty and departments to meet their needs." For instance, the library converts traditional journals, those with declining subscriptions, an uncertain future, and produced by departments or small societies that have a narrow revenue base, to e-journals and, after a couple of years, places them in an open-access venue.

This director also notes that the library has abandoned some traditional activities (e.g., binding books and journals and engaging in journal check-in) and has shifted priorities to its publishing program. Still, the director encourages the investigators to explore a set of scenarios about the future of reference desk service. Noting that reference desk activity is down 80 percent nationwide, he has reduced the number of staff at the desk and diverted more resources to the provision of digital reference. He wonders what is the proper balance between new and traditional reference service and sees reference in a traditional phase, especially since there is little activity at the desk. Those libraries that have moved away from reference desk service, he points out, provide such service in other ways; in other words, instead of getting rid of the service, they are merely refocusing its provision (e.g., at the circulation desk).

One director at a non-ARL institution thought the four scenarios are too concerned with "gatekeeper/access roles as a way to branch into other areas, many surrounding information literacy education." A fifth scenario emerged to address her vision of a future library, one recognized as an educational enterprise. In her opinion, it would seem that those libraries able to construct a new physical building or renovate the existing one might be better able to achieve the first and fifth scenarios.[30]

Instead of merely creating new scenarios and refining existing ones, further research might examine the type of workforce that will be needed to carry out each scenario. That research might include an investigation of the service vision of managerial leaders. What leadership abilities, knowledge, and skills will be necessary to make either of the last two scenarios a reality? Warren Bennis argues that "the primary responsibility of a leader is to make judgment calls."[31] What are some of the judgment calls that leaders may have to make to achieve a given scenario at their institutions? He believes that "adaptive capability is the most important attribute for success as a leader."[32] How might libraries undergoing transformation take advantage of such capability? Further, research might examine leadership vision and the extent to which that vision is reflected in a preferred scenario.[33]

CONCLUSION

Scenarios such as the ones covered in this appendix encourage managerial leaders to think about their vision of the library and its services. Through discussions with the staff and others within the institution, scenarios are opportunities to gain buy-in to a particular vision. At the same time, one of the challenges is to identify, attract, retain, and nurture the type of workforce that will be necessary to achieve the vision represented in a given scenario. What will be the educational background, knowledge, abilities, and skill set that this workforce must possess? What will be the role of libraries, professional associations, and LIS education in shaping that workforce? LIS education in fact may be less relevant to the future than it has been in the past. Scenarios such as the five presented here and scenario planning are ways to engage communities in discussion of the future and the form it will take locally.

NOTES

1. James G. Neal, "Information Anarchy or Information Utopia?" *The Chronicle of Higher Education* (December 9, 2005), accessed April 29, 2010, http://chronicle.com/article/Information-Anarchy-or/2773.

2. Ibid.

3. Peter Hernon, *Shaping the Future: Advancing the Understanding of the Future* (Santa Barbara, CA: ABC-CLIO, 2010), chapters 10 and 11. See also Stuart Hannabuss, "Scenario Planning for Libraries," *Library Management* 22, nos. 4/5 (2001): 168–76; and Andrew Wells, "A Prototype Twenty-First Century University Library: A Case Study of Change at the University of New South Wales Library," *Library Management* 28, nos. 8/9 (2007): 450–59.

4. Nina W. Matheson, "Perspectives on Academic Health Sciences Libraries in the 1980s: Indicators from a Delphi Study," *Bulletin of the Medical Library Association* 70, no. 1 (January 1982): 28–49.

5. Duane E. Webster, "Scenarios for Contemplating Research Library Futures" (unpublished manuscript, Simmons College, 2009); Duane E. Webster, "Organizational Projections for Envisioning Research Library Futures" (unpublished manuscript, Simmons College, 2010).

6. Jon Cawthorne, "The Academic Library of the Future: The Vision of 2007 Senior Fellows" (unpublished manuscript, Simmons College, 2009).

7. Peter Hernon and Laura Saunders, "The Federal Depository Library Program in 2023: One Perspective on the Transition to the Future," *College & Research Libraries* 70, no. 4 (July 2009): 351–70.

8. Jerry D. Campbell, "Changing a Cultural Icon: The Academic Library as a Virtual Destination," *EDUCAUSE Review* 41, no. 1 (January 2008): 16.

9. *No Brief Candle: Reconceiving Research Libraries for the 21st Century* (Washington, DC: Council on Library and Information Resources, 2008).

10. David W. Lewis, "A Strategy for Academic Libraries in the First Quarter of the 21st Century," *College & Research Libraries* 68, no. 5 (September 2007): 418.

11. Larry Hardesty, "Future of Academic/Research Librarians: A Period of Transition—to What?" *portal: Libraries and the Academy* 2, no. 1 (January 2002): 79–97.

12. Laura Saunders, "The Future of Information Literacy in Academic Libraries: A Delphi Study," *portal: Libraries and the Academy* 9, no. 1 (January 2009): 99–114.

13. Roger C. Schonfeld and Ross Housewright, *Ithaka S+R Faculty Survey 2009: Key Strategic Insights for Libraries, Publishers, and Societies* (New York: Ithaka S+R, 2010), 14, accessed May 25, 2010, http://www.ithaka.org/ithaka-s-r/research/faculty-surveys-2000-2009/Faculty%20Study%202009.pdf.

14. James W. Marcum, "Visions: The Academic Library in 2012," *D-Lib Magazine* 9, no. 5 (May 2003), accessed May 1, 2010, http://www.dlib.org/dlib/may03/marcum/05marcum.html. See also P. Sennyey, Lyman Ross, and Caroline Mills, "Exploring the Future of Academic Libraries: A Definitional Approach," *The Journal of Academic Librarianship* 35, no. 3 (May 2009): 252–59; Maria Anna Jankowska and James W. Marcum, "Sustainable Challenge for Academic Libraries: Planning for the Future," *College & Research Libraries* 71, no. 2 (March 2010): 160–70; and Sue McKnight, *Envisioning Future Academic Library Services: Initiatives, Ideas, and Challenges* (New York: Neal-Schuman, 2010).

15. Denmark's Electronic Research Library, *The Future of Research and the Research Library* (2009), 13, accessed June 1, 2010, http://www.resourceshelf.com/2010/02/26/report-the-future-of-research-and-the-research-library/.

16. "Libraries of the Future," *Inside Higher ED* (September 24, 2009), accessed May 1, 2010, http://www.insidehighered.com/layout/set/print/news/2009/09/24/libraries. See also Daniel Greenstein, "Strategies for Sustaining the University Library," *portal: Libraries and the Academy* 10, no. 2 (April 2010): 121–25.

17. Barbara Fister, "Leaders of Academic Institutions Reflect on the Value and Role of the Library," *Library Journal* (May 1, 2010), accessed May 11, 2010, http://www.libraryjournal.com/article/CA6726948.html.

18. John Dupuis, "Confessions of a Science Librarian: Twenty-nine Report about the Future of Academic Libraries," accessed May 1, 2010, http://jdupuis.blogspot.com/2009/02/twenty-nine-reports-about-future-of.html.

19. Association of Research Libraries, *The ARL 2030 Scenarios: A User's Guide for Research Libraries* (Washington, DC: Association of Research Libraries, 2010), 38, 39.

20. David J. Staley and Kara J. Malenfant, *Futures Thinking for Academic Librarians: Higher Education in 2025* (Chicago: Association of Research Libraries, 2010), 3, accessed June 23, 2010, http://www.ala.org/ala/mgrps/divs/acrl/issues/value/futures2025.pdf.

21. Ibid., 21–22.

22. Dana Mietzner and Guido Reger, "Advantages and Disadvantages of Scenario Approaches for Strategic Foresight," *International Journal of Technology Intelligence and Planning* 1, no. 2 (2005): 233, accessed April 30, 2010, http://www.lampsacus.com/documents/StragegicForesight.pdf. They also note weaknesses to address when developing scenarios.

23. James L. Mullins, Frank R. Allen, and Jon R. Hufford, "Top Ten Assumptions for the Future of Academic Libraries and Librarians: A Report from the ACRL Research Committee," *College & Research Libraries News* 68, no. 4 (April 2007): 240–41, 46.

24. For an introduction to e-science and libraries, see Jake R. Carlson and Jeremy R. Garritano, 'E-Science, Cyberinfrastructure, and the Changing Face of Scholarship: Organizing for New Models of Research Support at the Purdue University Libraries," in *The Expert Library:*

Staffing, Sustaining, and Advancing the Academic Library in the 21st Century, ed. Scott Walter and Karen Williams, 234–69 (Chicago: American Library Association, 2010).

25. David W. Lewis, "Academic Library Staffing a Decade from Now," in *The Expert Library*, 1–29.

26. James G. Neal, "The Hybridization of Library Personnel Resources: New Responsibilities Demand Staff Diversity," in *The Expert Library*, v, vii.

27. Joseph P. Martino, "The Precision of Delphi Estimates," *Technological Forecasting* 1, no. 3 (1970): 293–99.

28. Although the selection of participants is arbitrary, there is a geographical and gender distribution, and the investigators know that each director is a leader.

29. For a similar perspective, see James L. Mullins, "Bringing Librarianship to E-Science," *College & Research Libraries* 70, no. 3 (May 2009): 212–13. Clerical and paraprofessional staff members might handle general reference but make referral to professional faculty as needed. The same applies to digital reference.

30. See Scott Carlson, "A Place to See and Be Seen (and Learn a Little, Too)," *The Chronicle of Higher Education* LVI, no. 27 (June 4, 2010): A16–17.

31. Warren Bennis and Patricia W. Biederman, *Still Surprised: A Memoir of a Life in Leadership* (San Francisco: Jossey-Bass, 2010), 160. See also Noel Tichy and Warren Bennis, *Judgment: How Winning Leaders Make Great Calls* (New York: Portfolio, 2007); and Ronald A. Heifetz, Marty Linsky, and Alexander Grashow, *The Practice of Adaptive Leadership: Tools and Tactics for Changing Your Organization and the World* (Boston: Harvard Business Press, 2009).

32. Bennis and Biederman, *Still Surprised*, 160.

33. See Amanda S. Shipman, Cristina L. Byrne, and Michael D. Mumford, "Leader Vision Formation and Forecasting: The Effects of Forecasting Extent, Resources, and Timeframe," *The Leadership Quarterly* 21, no. 3 (June 2010): 439–56.

Appendix B: Twenty-first-Century Pressures

This case study addresses both evaluation and assessment, while inserting a number of stakeholders and their perspectives into the discussion. Before discussing this complex scenario, we encourage readers to review the problem-solving model developed by A. J. Anderson, professor emeritus, Simmons College. His model, which shows readers how to analyze a case study, can be found in *Shaping the Future: Advancing an Understanding of Leadership*, edited by Peter Hernon (Santa Barbara: ABC-CLIO, 2010), 118–34.

Shortly after the board of trustees had adjourned from their meeting, the library director walked into the administration offices, head hanging, somewhat dejected. It had not been a good day.

The institution's board of trustees had conducted their biannual meeting on campus earlier in the day. For the third year in a row, the institution's senior administrators informed the board's members that cuts were under consideration in the annual operating budgets to reduce the expected gap between revenues and expenses. To save an already stretched staff from additional layoffs in the next fiscal year, nonpersonnel budgets would necessarily absorb the reductions. Although it was wonderful that staff jobs were safe, the library director was concerned about any further erosion to the collections, technology, and support costs such as supplies.

And as if the budget news were not bleak enough, a community leader's presentation to the board provided another blow to university administration, staff, and faculty. The president of the county's chamber of commerce made a presentation about the workforce readiness of the university's graduates. She pointed out several deficiencies, including writing and math skills. Of particular importance to the library director was that graduates had difficulty finding credible information sources for company use in analysis and reports. Graduates "googled" a topic and accepted almost anything they found, apparently not knowing how to evaluate whether or not the source was reliable and credible. "Bad information makes for bad business decisions," the chamber president had concluded.

As the board members were leaving the room, the library director was approached by the provost. She asked about the equipment funds from the operating budget expended to support the library's laptop lending program. "Why," she asked, "is the library purchasing laptops to loan since all of the students have laptops? This is a perfect expenditure to eliminate as part of the cost reductions necessary to balance the budget for the next fiscal year." The provost began to talk with a trustee before the director had a chance to begin a response.

The director recognized these symptoms. Accountability had become an overarching institutional and organizational focus over the past few years. The local businesses expected that the institution's graduates would, in large measure, supply the geopolitical region's needed skilled and educated labor force, from accountants to computer specialists, from nurses to teachers. Internally, the institution pushed for increased departmental cost efficiency and effectiveness. New programs and services would not be funded without a thought-out and vetted proposal; existing programs and services could be called upon at any time to justify their ongoing costs. The laptop lending program had been operational for ten years. A popular service according to its usage statistics, its annual appropriation was level-funded. The program started with 20 laptops and now numbered 100.

"Libraries are not immune from the pressures of twenty-first-century accountability," the director kept reminding herself. "We must demonstrate, not just claim, to support and contribute to the institution and its mission."

WE DO THIS AND WE DO THAT

After the library director summoned the management team, she thought about the overall context she was facing. The library had a strategic plan. As with most plans, however, though it was readily available on the library's Web site, the management team did not use it often except to point out its existence, such as referring to the plan when preparing the presentation to support the request for the operating budget. The plan's numerous goals and objectives were not related directly to the budget. Progress toward meeting the plan's objectives was reviewed and not thoroughly measured when the annual report was being drafted or when a new strategic plan was needed because it was about to expire. The laptop lending program was a service objective, but the director was unsure how much the program actually cost and whether the plan's objective had any measurable outputs other than stating that a laptop lending program would exist.

The director also realized that the businessperson's statement about workforce readiness was an outcome, namely the skills, attitudes, and values that the institution and its academic programs proudly stated graduates possess as a result of attending the university. She also recognized that the stated deficiency—evaluating information resources—was an information literacy skill and included in ACRL's guidelines (see http://www.ala.org/ala/mgrps/divs/acrl/standards/index.cfm). The library had an information literacy program. Well, it was actually an instruction program. The library supported faculty by orienting students about the library and its services and by instructing students how to search its frequently used resources, especially licensed electronic databases of full-text articles used when writing course-required papers. Most of the library's instruction sessions were "one-shots," in which the library provided fifty or seventy-five minutes of library instruction to students in the library's computer-equipped instruction room. Because most instruction sessions were a one-time only event, the library did not measure what the students learned, instead asking them if they understood the concepts taught during the class, usually answered by affirmative head nods. The true measure was faculty satisfaction. Did the faculty view the instruction session as worthy of the class time used by the librarians? That was measured by the number of faculty returning the next semester for another librarian-led instruction.

IT IS JUST A TWO-STEP PROCESS

The management team filed in, taking seats around the oval conference table. The director made a matter-of-fact report on the trustees meeting, focusing on the community leader's statement as well as the brief post-meeting, one-way conversation with the provost.

Less than five seconds passed before the first protest, followed by others. Aggregated, one argument was that "we have an effective information literacy program. We conduct hundreds of sessions each academic year, and many of our sessions are with faculty members who return each semester with their classes. What evidence did this person provide to the board of trustees to back up her claim? If there is a problem with students' searching skills, look at the classroom and the amount of grade inflation. We teach students what they need to know to use the databases and write their papers."

The second discussion was as heated. "The laptop program is one of the most popular services we provide—just look at the circulation stats. At peak times during the day, students queue to check out a laptop. If students do not need them, then why do they check them out? Lots of students do not have computers, and they need us to get their course work done. Reducing or even eliminating the laptop program is a bad idea."

"Okay, okay, I get it. We have to respond to both of these issues, however," said the director as she began to deal with the heated discussion in the room. "How should we approach this?"

Again, aggregating the responses, most of the management team wanted to just ignore the community person's statement to the board. "She did not single out the library. She probably understands that we are doing everything we can to help students get through the paper writing season. The faculty needs to respond, not us." As to the provost, the team was blunter. "She knows how popular the program is. We include statistics every year in our annual report. We need to convince her that we have already cut everything that we can. We have nothing left to cut."

Quietly, a couple of voices rose in dissent. "The boss is right. We need to address both issues. Whether or not we agree with her, this businessperson brought this up in a public meeting. We need to prove to all that we are worth the institutional investment, and we help students succeed." The library director asked all members of the management team to talk among themselves over the few days and reconvene in a week to craft an approach.

The chatter flew within the library as fast as the week passed. Before reconvening the management team, the director set up two tripods with white pads for note-taking during the meeting. During the meeting, ideas for approaches were listed on the white pads, as well as a list of the seemingly endless barriers raised by those attending. It was decided that, because of the nature of the two responses, the management team would be divided into three groups. One group would work with the information literacy issue and the other on the laptops. A third group would meet as requested with the two groups to help. It was agreed that the groups would meet over the next week and then reconvene as a whole.

A week later the three groups reconvened. The approaches from the groups were presented. The information literacy group proposed the following as an approach:

Step 1:   Review the existing information literacy plan.

Step 2:   Talk with faculty about their perceptions of how well students evaluated information sources.

The laptop group also proposed a two-step approach:

Step 1:   Review the statistics concerning the laptop lending program.

Step 2:   Prove the provost wrong.

After the high-fives subsided over the second step of the laptop approach, the director, as part of the third team, asked about the "hows" and "whens." The barriers resurfaced. "How do we talk to the faculty about how they teach students to evaluate sources? It's their classroom, and they may see that as crossing the line onto their turf." When asked to identify a means to measure how well students evaluated information sources, no one responded. "Our two-step approach may sound simple," one manager posited, "but I really don't even know where to start."

The three groups came to a common conclusion. They did not know how to approach either issue. Again, the two groups were given another week to reconsider their approaches.

Before the groups reconvened as a whole, the director met with the oversight group. This third group reviewed the barriers identified so that it could look for solutions. After some discussion, the most significant barrier identified was that staff did not know how to proceed. They did not know how to undertake a study that would help demonstrate their contributions to information literacy or to articulate the value of the laptop program. Bringing in an outside consultant was out of the question; the funds were just not available. The university, however, has a respected Office of Institutional Research. The director was tasked with making contact, explaining the need, and seeking help. A second barrier was the time expected to conduct a study. The library was student-centered, and this project would take time away from directly serving students. Reducing this barrier would require serious commitments from library administration. Another suggestion was to find some practical articles and books to help the groups learn how to undertake internal studies.

When the groups met again, the assistant director for institutional research attended to assist the groups as a whole. She pointed out that two studies were indeed needed because the objectives differed. The information literacy study would be an assessment of student learning outcomes: Did the students learn how to evaluate information sources as a result of library instruction? Direct and indirect measures could be applied to help determine what was learned and how well, as well as how well the instruction served its purpose. What was learned from the assessment study could be used to improve the library's instruction sessions. The laptop issue was actually an evaluation study. This study would learn about the effectiveness of the lending service.

The institutional research officer emphasized that each group would need to design a study approach. Such an approach would need to articulate what study questions they wanted answered and what they expected to learn from the study; identify what data would be needed to answer the questions and how the data would be gathered, compiled, and organized, and by whom; who was going to interpret the data and craft the findings; and how, and to whom, the findings would be reported. To provide some basic assistance, the third group had found a dozen articles and half a dozen books to read and consult as the groups proceeded. The library director promised whatever support was affordable, including a temporary sabbatical from their day-to-day activities for three hours a day. The assistant director for institutional research invited any member to contact her for advice or assistance.

Before they left the conference room, the library director emphasized the importance of their work and asked the groups to involve all members of the staff in the process. Even if a staff member did not directly participate in the studies process, the director asked that the two groups keep all staff informed weekly about their progress.

The assessment group began by reviewing the information literacy plan and instruction program. Its members reviewed the institutional mission and were able to link the general education program to the mission by identifying a shared outcome that graduates would be able to think critically and write effectively. Evaluating information sources certainly fit under that general educational outcome. So far, so good. Upon closely reviewing the information literacy program document and talking with the librarians who taught the library instruction, however, they realized that much of the effort was on the use of library subscription databases and that little time (less than 10 minutes) was allocated in the one-shot, fifty-minute instruction sessions to evaluating either subscription or nonsubscription sources. Based upon observing a dozen sessions, the group came to understand that the session's portion focused on the evaluation of sources was dedicated to reminding students that libraries develop collections based upon professional or peer reviews and subscribe to databases of scholarly articles, and that a ".gov" or ".edu" Web site trumps a ".com" for credibility. Little, if any, time was actually devoted to the mechanics of evaluating the authority or credibility of information sources. To supplement this observation, "clickers" were used in a pre-test to measure what students knew about evaluating sources at the beginning of half of the instruction sessions observed. At the end of these sessions, the pre-test was readministered as a post-test. Analysis of the results showed that there was no improvement by the students in properly evaluating information sources.

Members of the library staff also met with faculty members about their perceptions of information source evaluation. Faculty stated that they did not spend much time on that skill in their classrooms; their perception was that students, usually of native digital age, know how to use a computer, surf the net, and find sources. What students did not know would be taught in the instruction sessions when the faculty brought them to the library. Besides, the faculty said that they required and only accepted peer-reviewed and other scholarly sources in student papers, and therefore, taking the time to teach evaluation of sources would take away from valuable class time. All students had to do was use the library's collections and databases to find and retrieve quality information. The faculty admitted that students turned in papers with questionable sources, but that was because they were too lazy to do proper research and were willing to accept a "C" for barely adequate work.

While the information assessment study had frequent contact with the Office of Institutional Research, the members of the department were less knowledgeable about evaluation than assessing outcomes. As a result, those in the group conducting the laptop lending program evaluation study had less institutional assistance. The group kept to its study plan and first reviewed the statistics gathered about the service. Usage statistics (outputs) were available throughout the program, as well as the number of laptops available (inputs). Using a time series chart, the group graphed the number of laptops available and the number of times the laptops had been borrowed during the past ten fiscal years. A visual review of the time lines showed that, as the number of laptops increased, the number of loans also increased. The steepness of the curve for the number of times lent, however, had begun to level off three years before. A group member suggested a third time series line, the number of loans per full-time equivalent (FTE) student over the same fiscal years. Using that ratio, the ascension was reduced to being a nearly horizontal line for the past three fiscal years. The group surmised that the increase in loans was likely a result of the increased availability of the number of laptops rather than the need for students to borrow a laptop.

The *need* would be answered by asking the students about the laptop program. Because they wanted to gauge need, the group wanted to survey everyone in the student population, not just the users of the laptop lending program. Group members created a short online survey with extensive help and revision from the Institutional Research office and ran it for two weeks. The survey "popped-up" on both the library-owned laptops as well as personal laptops when a laptop connected to the wireless network, and on the fixed desktop computers in the library. It asked students if they were aware of the laptop lending program, if they had borrowed a laptop in the past, and if they were on a library laptop as they took the survey. The students were also presented with a set of checkboxes of reasons they did or and did not borrow a library laptop. The reasons had been gathered beforehand from brief conversations with students by members of the laptop evaluation group. Other questions were demographic-based, such as student major, the number of years at the university, and if they owned a personal laptop.

The analysis from the two-week survey did not match the library staff's perceptions of the use of the laptop lending service. Library staff had expected that the majority of use of the laptops was by students who did not own a laptop. In other words, the laptop lending service helped bridge a gap between the "computer haves and have nots." The results said otherwise. More than 80 percent of the students owned a personal laptop. So why did they borrow a library laptop? The students did not want to carry their personal laptops to/around campus.

The survey comments provided anecdotes about students using the lending service so as not to have to "haul" a laptop around campus in an already-loaded backpack in variable weather conditions. While many students had smart phones (another online survey question), they could not as easily edit papers on their phones as they could by borrowing a library laptop. The group members came to a finding that based upon the number of laptops borrowed and the survey comments, students valued the lending program primarily as a convenience.

Group members then decided to pull together a valuation of the laptops, combining economic value with the anecdotes. After reading several articles and reports on the value of library services, the group decided to develop a valuation of services from two perspectives, of the library and of students. In its library valuation of services, the group based the figure on the value of the laptops times the number of transactions. The library had 100 laptops, and each asset was valued at a replacement cost of $1,000 (hardware and software). The laptops had been loaned 50,000 times in the last fiscal year. The library's value of the service was $1,000 per asset times 50,000 uses to equal $50,000,000. No one, however, expected students would pay $1,000 to the library to support each laptop. To students, it was a usage value, not a replacement value, since they already owned a laptop. The library group then looked at laptop rental costs across its geographic service region. On average, for-profit businesses lent laptops at $15.00/hour. The library, taking a more conservative approach, decided to use $5.00 for each loan, even if the loan was for more than one hour. A laptop loaned for four hours, therefore, would have cost $60.00 from the for-profit business, while the library would value that transaction at only $5.00. The value of the laptop to the student was calculated at $250,000—$5.00 per use times 50,000 uses. The group then took this calculated value another step. They gathered the costs for the program, including the laptops, the necessary maintenance and repairs to keep the laptops available for use, and estimated staff time (labor) to manage and circulate the laptops. The library expended $100,000/year in equipment, $10,000 in maintenance and repair, and $30,000 in library labor costs, including fringe benefits for library full-time staff in the last fiscal year. The lending program cost $140,000 to operate and generated a student-based valuation of $250,000. For each $1.00 expended by the library, it was estimated that the students borrowing the laptops realized a conservative and positive return of investment of $1.79.

LOOK WHAT WE FOUND

The two groups reconvened to share the findings and to plan their next steps. The assessment group went first. Summarizing, the group had found that, though evaluating information resources was covered by library instruction, the focus was on the library's licensed content, which would not be available once a student left the institution. The content was delivered passively in the course and focused on the library's developed collection and subscription databases. Because of licensing agreements, the databases were not available to nonenrolled students. Faculty thought librarians covered information source evaluation during the fifty-minute librarian-led instruction and were reluctant to give up class time to discuss and illustrate a "critical searching process" over course content. In fact, faculty had equated students knowing how to "evaluate sources" with "finding information." The library might indeed be a contributor to the problem identified by the business community member at the board of trustees meeting.

The laptop lending service group then summarized its findings. The service was popular, as illustrated by its outputs. The level of usage of the service, however, was beginning to level out, especially when usage was graphed with the student population as full-time equivalents. In addition, as a result of the survey, the service group found that most students indeed owned personal laptops, but borrowed library laptops as a convenience. Because usage was flattening out when measured using the FTE student ratio, the group instead looked at the value of the service over need. Using two cost estimates, the group found a significant value of the laptop service based on the asset cost and the number of usages. The group also calculated a student user return on investment and found that for every dollar annually expended for the equipment and its maintenance, and the staffing needed to provide the service, the service yielded a positive return.

The third group suggested the next steps. The findings from the two study groups would be presented first to the library staff for review and comment, and then to select members of the university community, focusing on the faculty who used the library's instructional services, the staff of the university's Alumni Relations Office, and members of the student government association. A one-page summary would be handed out at meetings, at which representatives of the three groups and a staffer from institutional research would make a short presentation. The attendees would be asked to comment on the findings and reflect on what the library might do to address them.

TAKING IT FOR A TEST DRIVE

Although attendance was sparse, the attendees were enthusiastic about the studies and their findings. Suggestions were numerous, and the library representatives followed up by exploring the suggestions made. Some suggestions would not be possible to implement. For example, the Alumni Relations Office suggested that the library fund access to the subscription databases for alums. The library found that, with only a minority of vendors willing to provide such access, the annual cost for licensing the databases more than doubled. Even if they could collaborate on the cost, neither the library nor the Alumni Relations Office could afford it. The library staff proposed creating online tutorials, uploaded to YouTube, that focused on how to access and evaluate "googled" information sources. Internally, the staff decided that the library's information literacy program would be improved by increasing the instruction time devoted to discussing the evaluation of information resources, creating an active learning session to support this instruction and content, and developing handouts for the students as checklists for determining author authority and credibility. Using pre- and post-tests would help the library to determine if the revised instruction had a positive impact. Faculty were agreeable to providing a sample of completed student papers so that librarians could review the sources cited, using a rubric to determine the level of student achievement in evaluating information sources. Librarians also stated that once these activities were completed, the process would have to start again so that the library would continually assess its instruction to discover what students had or had not learned.

Student government was much more interested in the future of the laptop lending service than in instruction. Informally polling students, its officers found that it was a valued service that they did not want reduced, much less eliminated. Some students identified a need for the laptops because they did not have one, while the vast majority stated that they did not want to carry their personal laptops around all day. The personal laptops were not often used in class, and some students stated that having their own laptops with them would create a distraction because they would use them to access Facebook or play games. The Student Government Association was not at all interested in the total value of the asset as measured by transactions, but discussed publicly what other university services had a positive measured return on their tuition dollar.

WE HAVE AN ANNOUNCEMENT

Based on the discussions with the various stakeholders, the third group wrote two reports about the information literacy program and the laptop lending service. These formal reports discussed the study's objectives, design, and methodology; data collection and analysis; initial findings; and the comments and discussions generated by the select stakeholders. Both reports were short, relying on a few tables and charts to supplement the text. These reports were forwarded to the senior university administration. The president's office, in turn, provided copies to the board of trustees.

Other reports were also created, focused on specific stakeholders. For example, a one-page, back-to-back flyer was created for chamber of commerce members. The flyer listed the activities that the library would undertake to help support the business community, such as the targeted content and process tutorials on YouTube and Web-based research/support guides publicly accessible from the library's Web site. A two-page report was prepared and distributed to the faculty via e-mail about the changes to the library's instruction program, reminding them about the library's willingness to review student-cited sources in papers. An offer from the library director to visit academic departmental meetings to discuss the changes and any library program or service was included in the e-mail.

The provost received both formal reports as well as a brief, one-page document about the value of the laptop lending service, which had been created for the Student Government Association. While she thanked the library for the studies, she insisted that the laptop lending service be discontinued as a necessary budget reduction.

FOR WHAT IT IS WORTH

At the next board of trustees meeting, the chamber's businessperson again asked to address the board. She commented on the library's study, thanking the library for taking a proactive approach to learning about the issue she had raised. "Frankly," she said, "we had not even linked the library to the problem, but they seriously considered our comments and have come up with some positive ideas of helping us. We have a proposal for the library to consider," she continued. "Would the library be willing to create an information center that would help region-based businesses by providing answers or at least links to answers to our questions? We would propose that business would not only pay a fee for the service, but would pay an annual membership fee to belong to the service." The board responded that they would take this under advisement and asked the library, through a board-approved resolution, to bring such a plan to them at their next biannual meeting.

Later during the meeting, the student representative to the board of trustees asked for time under "other business" to discuss the library's threatened laptop lending service. "Students have enough things to worry about than having to drag a laptop with them every day. The library provides a great laptop lending service that we use, and we ask that the service continue at its current level. We also request that other services for which usage is not as well documented, and which cannot prove a net positive benefit, be considered for reduction or elimination before the laptop lending service is axed." The board agreed to take this issue under advisement and directed the provost to report back at its next meeting with her findings.

And with that, the board chair thanked all in attendance and, after hearing a second, adjourned the meeting.

DISCUSSION QUESTIONS

1. How would you characterize the culture of the library? Was there change over the course of the case study? What was the impact, if any, of the library director?

2. Do you agree with the approach taken by the two groups? What are the strengths and weaknesses of each approach? What alternatives to each approach would you have recommended, and why? Consider the entire study design.

3. Were the findings credible and reasonable from the information/data collected?

4. How would you have managed the discussion of the initial findings and the distribution of the various versions of the reports? Would you have followed the same approach as the library, or an alternative approach?

5. What are the various possible scenarios now that the board of trustees has become involved?

Appendix C: Selecting the Appropriate Data-Gathering Methodology

There are many ways to gather information useful for evaluations. Each method has advantages and disadvantages. This guide highlights factors to consider when selecting the protocol best suited for a specific evaluation, including illustration of types of problems or questions the results may meaningfully address. Consider too that gathering data through multiple approaches will give richer results. Detailed discussions of the methods are found in various chapters. Indications are made here of each method's typical placement within either the quantitative or qualitative research paradigm, or in some cases, the option that the method may follow either approach.

CASE STUDY (QUALITATIVE)

Problems: How does a library function, in detail? Why do people behave a certain way? How does the library's research education program impact learning?

Advantages: Considerable flexibility exists to expand initial questions and pursue unexpected insights. Detailed *deep* descriptions result. All factors do not have to be identified prior to starting the exploration. Practical experience is helpful in preparing the case study, and results are typically easy to understand. The case study is an excellent way to increase familiarity with a problem and to gain a brief awareness of a setting or phenomenon.

Disadvantages: There is high subjectivity throughout the design, implementation, and presentation. Results have limited applicability because they cannot be generalized. It is time consuming and thus expensive, requiring that the researcher learn about the setting. The review and analysis of data take a great deal of time.

CITATION ANALYSIS (QUANTITATIVE)

Problems: How many of the publications cited by campus researchers are available through the library? How dependent are a university's doctoral students on interlibrary loans or services other than the library's collection and licensed electronic resources to prepare literature reviews for their dissertations?

Advantages: Citations provide a profile of a literature and might indicate citation changes in disciplines and fields of study over time. Citation analysis shows what scholars and others cite. Such analyses do not depend on human interaction (and response rates).

Disadvantages: Citations are not synonymous with use or reading habits of those producing the citations. The results should not be judged outside a study's research design (the design indicates the degree of external validity or generalizability). The extent of self-citation might indicate bias. Sources from which citations are drawn might selectively index journals, articles, and other types of publications. There is no assurance that all materials used are cited, or on what basis the decision to cite a work was made. Errors and inconsistencies may prevent bibliographic citations from being complete and accurate.

CONTENT ANALYSIS (QUANTITATIVE AND QUALITATIVE)

Problems: To what extent does the content of strategic planning reports include factors identified as important to the development of the digital library? Do e-mail communications among library administrators reflect issues associated with different styles of leadership? Do YouTube student reports of library experiences capture activities identified with theories of intentional learning? To what extent do student writing assignments demonstrate learning outcomes related to information literacy? What words are used to identify what librarians do?

Advantages: This approach organizes a lot of data into categories that are easier to analyze and draw inferences about. Data gathering and analysis are unobtrusive and can be replicated relatively simply. The researcher fully controls implementation of the process and can be independent of factors such as timing, location, or availability of subjects.

Disadvantages: It is very time consuming, calling for unpredictable amounts of effort to repeatedly review the content, and is subject to errors. Not everyone finds inductive reasoning and formulating or applying coding categories easy. This method is vulnerable to bias and subjectivity of coders, misinterpretation of definitions, or otherwise unclear categories.

ETHNOGRAPHIC OBSERVATION (QUALITATIVE)

Problems: What do people do in the library? How do they behave? What are their research or study habits, and how do they interact with electronic resources and tools? How do they organize their work in physical and virtual spaces?

Advantages: It identifies perspectives and interactions that form stories about the libraries and interactions with them, sometimes uncovering unexpected insights.

Disadvantages: Gaining entrée into the natural setting of participants without creating a sense of intrusion is difficult. The researcher cannot generalize findings to the larger population under study; observing a small portion of a population runs the risk of missing the perspectives of the majority.

INTERVIEWS (EITHER WITH FOCUS GROUPS OR INDIVIDUALS) (QUALITATIVE)

Problems: What future library services or products might be useful in support of research? What equipment or furniture arrangements do faculty expect to have in a library teaching environment? Why are students unsatisfied with the library, as they indicated on a survey? Specifically, what do students not like about staff behavior or the library's Web site? How valuable are electronic reserve services? What works well and does not in presenting library tutorials through the Web?

Advantages: An immediate response is available, with the opportunity to probe for details and clarity; interviews produce rich data about a topic relatively quickly. Group interviews offer added advantages of saving time over conducting multiple individual interviews. The dialog among group members generates broad coverage, triggers recall, and typically covers a topic well.

Disadvantages: Interviews generate a lot of data that have to be sorted, analyzed, and reanalyzed to formulate results. They may be costly and time-consuming for the interviewer to conduct repeatedly. The success of interviews depends on the skills and effectiveness of the interviewer, and if these are lacking, the opportunity to gather data is lost; nothing can be salvaged if the questions are not posed well or responses probed. Focus group interviews are conducted typically in artificial settings and do not offer observation in a natural context. Interviews provide insights into what people think, but they do not identify what they actually do.

MYSTERY SHOPPING (QUANTITATIVE OR QUALITATIVE)

Problems: What is easy or difficult about locating and using a library service? How friendly, courteous, responsive, and helpful are staff members? How reliable are services—does the library deliver, dependably, what it says it will do?

Advantages: Mystery shopping is relatively simple to execute. It uncovers insights into staff performance and library appearance without engaging actual customers.

Disadvantages: Mystery shopping is vulnerable to impressions among staff of "big brother" checking. It is difficult to balance execution without tipping off the staff. There is an ethical and political responsibility to let staff know about the evaluation.

OBSERVATION
(QUANTITATIVE OR QUALITATIVE)

Problems: How many people use library computers? How often are more than two people waiting for service at the circulation desk? How many students use mobile devices for texting, and how many use phones in the lobby?

Advantages: Simply observing people bypasses problems associated with self-reporting (i.e., false reporting or failing to disclose something). It reveals indisputable actions as they occur. It provides a means to check the validity of other data collection methods. It reduces bias (assuming the observer has no investment in the outcome).

Disadvantages: Observation requires a great deal of time and preparation to carry out. The actions observed must be closely defined, interpreted, and coded. There is a possibility of bias in data collection. Careful thought must be given to when and where to conduct the observation. There is a question of whether the observer will be visible or hidden. If the observer "plays to the audience," the results are contaminated.[1]

STANDARDIZED TESTS (QUANTITATIVE)

Problems: At what speed and with what accuracy do people type? What are average SAT scores for students in Freshman English 101, and do they correlate with successful use of bibliographic search engines?

Advantages: Most likely the test has been certified (its reliability and validity have been examined); the data collection form is ready to use

Disadvantages: The use of copyrighted tests may be expensive. The questions may not have been written for (or applicable to) the intended population. Not everyone is good at test taking. Some test instruments cannot be modified. Test taking may be stressful and time-consuming. Tests must be reliable and valid. People may not like to take tests.

SURVEYS (INTERNET)
(QUALITATIVE OR QUANTITATIVE)

Problems: Given a low budget and shortage of time, what are the major concerns faculty have with the library? Who uses the library's electronic resources, and for what reasons?

Advantages: The survey process can be controlled with little effort and cost. Data may be collected continuously. The method is self-administered. There may be opportunities for interaction and follow-up with respondents. The survey reaches a geographically dispersed group. The method is faster than the use of mailed and some other survey forms. The likelihood of a prompt response is high. The data-collection instrument can be visually appealing.

Disadvantages: The population may be unknown or unknowable. Responses are self-reported, and there are risks of a self-selected sample. The response rate may still be low. People may not want to open e-mail attachments. It may be difficult to demonstrate the legitimacy of the study (e.g., the authority of the sponsoring organization or the evaluator).

SURVEYS (MAILED)
(QUALITATIVE OR QUANTITATIVE)

Problems: How satisfied are undergraduate students at your university with library services? What are the highest expectations for excellent library services among faculty? What are the most often cited reasons people give for not using the library? Are freshmen afraid of asking for reference assistance?

Advantages: Surveying a large number of people is relatively inexpensive. Surveys can be self-administered. They should capture study objectives and research questions.

Disadvantages: Surveys produce self-reported data. The data may lack depth in comparison to data generated from qualitative interviewing in which the investigator can probe or ask follow-up questions. There is no assurance that the intended person actually answered the questions. Increasingly there are declining response rates and the need to consider the use of incentives (widgets may be used to encourage higher response). A poorly developed survey is inevitably going to overlook important issues and waste participants' time by asking useless questions. Mailed questionnaires take time to reach the intended audience and for them to respond. The results produce a snapshot of the situation at a particular point in time. It may be time-consuming to analyze and interpret the results.[2]

SWEEPING STUDY
(QUALITATIVE OR QUANTITATIVE)

Problems: What do people do within the library? What do they bring with them to study? What proportion of seats is occupied? How many people work in groups at tables, and how many groups meet in the library? Is there really that much napping going on in the library?

Advantages: Sweeping studies generate a lot of data that indicate what people are actually doing in a physical space without involving human interaction. Analysis of the data offers insights into the behaviors of occupants and detailed descriptions of the setting for these activities.

Disadvantages: It is difficult to remain unobtrusive when walking around with a clipboard and making notations from observations. There is the ethical issue of balancing respect for people's privacy with the objective of observing and recording what they do. It can be difficult to discover exactly what people are doing on their laptops or library computers without asking them. The study represents point-in-time occurrences only. People may not understand what they are observing. It is time-consuming to conduct accurate sweeps. Staff must be well trained.

TRANSACTION LOG ANALYSIS (QUANTITATIVE)

Problems: What is system response time at different times of day or with different levels of traffic? What do people ask through instant messaging (IM) reference service? Are keyword, title, or author searches most often the first query method in using the library's catalog? How often are all the "seats" simultaneously utilized for a licensed electronic resource? Do search strategies differ among students before and after attending library instruction?

Advantages: This method does not involve human interaction. Depending on the number and selection of records, the evaluators can either study a population or generate a probability sample. It provides insights into user communities and areas requiring service improvement.

Disadvantages: The evaluator must be knowledgeable about the datasets and their strengths and limitations. Data extraction can be time-consuming. The data can be difficult to interpret.

USABILITY TESTING (QUALITATIVE OR QUANTITATIVE)

Problems: To what extent do people who use a particular information system, database, or Web site do so quickly and easily to accomplish stated tasks? How easy is it to use a system interface? How does a student approach using the library's Web site, and what does she or he expect when performing each operation of searching it?

Advantages: Usability testing provides direct feedback on how people navigate Websites, databases, and information systems. It indicates their search behavior and expectations.

Disadvantages: Testing may be time-consuming (depending on the study questions and research design used) and expensive (e.g., payment of participants and perhaps the need for special facilities to conduct the testing). Large amounts of data may be generated and complicate analysis and interpretation. Participants may not be at ease during the testing.

VERBAL PROTOCOLS (QUALITATIVE)

Problems: How do people approach tasks? What are they thinking when they search a Web site or use the online catalog? What is their rationale for decisions made or steps taken during interaction with a system interface?

Advantages: Verbal protocols provide rich data about cognitive processes. With data collection over time and repeatedly, it offers insights into changes in knowledge or skills to identify information to complete a task.

Disadvantages: Verbal protocols are very labor intensive. Participants can only report what they are consciously aware of and typically cannot verbalize what they do automatically. Furthermore, participants may filter what they are comfortable reporting.

NOTES

1. For a detailed analysis of unobtrusive testing as a method and how to cope with reliability and validity, see Peter Hernon and Charles R. McClure, *Unobtrusive Testing and Library Reference Services* (Norwood, NJ: Ablex, 1987).

2. For an excellent list of the advantages and disadvantages of different types of survey research, see Creative Research Systems, "The Survey System: Survey Design," 2010, accessed January 6, 2010, http://www.surveysystem.com/sdesign.htm.

Appendix D: Getting Published

People often say that they publish and then note which of their publications have appeared in journals and books. In fact, they are not the publisher but the author; they *are* published, which is not the same thing at all. The exception is self-publishing through vanity presses or by placing content on the Internet. The focus in this appendix is on publication in peer-reviewed journals.

An initial and important question is: "To which journal should I submit my manuscript?" The answer is often to one of the more prestigious journals in the discipline (e.g., library and information science) or field of study (e.g., academic or public libraries or reference service). As a result, a subset of journals dominates the landscape, because potential authors are more likely to submit their papers to them. These journals often have high numbers of citations to some of their articles, and they enjoy high impact factors,[1] are affiliated with prestigious publishers (whether an association, society, or other), are peer-reviewed,[2] have high rejection rates,[3] publish articles that readers are more likely to download,[4] are included in the major indexing and abstracting services, and have respectable total circulation figures (although numbers may be declining as journals become digitally available).[5] The more prestigious journals are likely to have a larger backlog of accepted papers awaiting publication, and the cycle from acceptance to publication may be more than one year. Of course there are exceptions, but on average, for many peer-reviewed journals in library and information science (LIS), the time from submission of the paper to acceptance may be at least three months.

Today publishers usually have automated manuscript handling systems that monitor papers from the time of author submission to the decision to reject or the appearance of papers in print and/or digital form. To reduce somewhat the length of time from acceptance to publication, many publishers release accepted manuscripts online prior to official publication as "uncorrected page proofs."

ADVANTAGES OF BEING PUBLISHED

There are clear advantages to being published, as the authors of this book can attest. In addition to making a contribution to the profession and adding to knowledge and perhaps practice, publications may influence others and lead to recognition of the authors as scholars, experts, and leaders. Recognition might include not only citations but also invitations to contribute to other publications or to speak about their areas of expertise. Finally, research and publication add to a scholar's knowledge and experience.

DEVELOPING A CHECKLIST

As authors prepare manuscripts for submission, they should review the author guidelines for the intended journal. These are usually published in print journal issues and on journal Web sites. Editors report that authors sometimes fail to review guidelines and, for instance, may use the wrong style manual or leave some components of the research process out of the manuscript or submit manuscripts with references in the wrong style. (Editors will often assume in these instances that the manuscript has already been submitted elsewhere and has been rejected.) Authors should review chapter 3, including figure 3.1 (p. 35). For example, the literature review should place the problem statement in the context of previous knowledge, identify variables that previous investigators have found significant or insignificant, and suggest factors to consider in setting the procedures section of a research proposal. The literature review is more than a descriptive list of writings or a set of summaries of the literature. It evaluates and synthesizes past research and alerts the researcher to possible *danger signs* (e.g., previous research has encountered a low response rate to a survey). Knowing this allows the researcher to take corrective action in the methodology section.

A first-time author might ask a colleague to review a manuscript for its written presentation and clarity of thought. It is important to remember that most writings go uncited and perhaps even unread, often because they are poorly written and poorly presented. The author therefore should pay particular attention to the organization and readability of each section of the paper. Here is a portrayal of the typical librarian who examines the professional literature: The reader examines the title of a paper and perhaps reads the abstract. If still interested, the reader moves on to the opening paragraphs and the conclusion. If still interested, the reader may examine more of the content up to the section on findings and may look at of the discussion section. If still interested, the findings section may be next, but sections containing inferential statistics are typically skipped; the reader often lacks the knowledge to evaluate or understand this part of the presentation.

SOME CONSIDERATIONS

Simply stated, editors and reviewers expect the presence and full and correct development of each component of a research study.

Reasons for Rejection

Although written in the early 1990s, the findings of a study of manuscripts submitted to *College & Research Libraries* (*C&RL*) for more than a decade still apply today. Following are the most common reasons for rejection of a paper:

- Little new content/insight is provided (the failure to break new ground).

- There is a lack of generalization.

- The writing is poor.

- The scholarship is poor (meaning poor coverage of the components discussed in chapter 3).

- It is not a good fit for the journal.

- The use of statistical methods is poor.

- It fails to answer the "so what" question.

- It has bad luck.[6]

The category "It is not a good fit for the journal" means that the author probably did not examine past issues of the journal and read the instructions to the author, which include the journal's scope. Often in such cases, editors are likely to suggest more relevant journals. The last category recognizes, for instance, that the editor might have received multiple papers on the same topic.[7]

David R. Krathwohl discusses a "chain of reasoning" that refers to the building of each element of a research study (e.g., reflective inquiry) and contains no weaknesses in the reasoning.[8] In essence, breaks in the chain of reasoning might arise from poor scholarship and poor use of statistical methods. One part of the chain of reasoning is the reflective inquiry (see chapter 3), and failure to match the problem statement *direction* with study objectives, research questions, and hypotheses, if they are relevant, constitutes a break in that chain, as does a lack of generalization, failure to answer the "so what" question, and, by extension, the provision of little in the way of new content or insights. Poor writing applies to the entire chain of reasoning and in itself might form the basis for rejection. Examples of poor writing include

- verb/noun disagreement;

- noun/adjective disagreement;

- dense writing, use of the passive voice and personal pronouns;

- awkward and unclear sentences;

- repetition of a word or phrase in a sentence or paragraph;

- lack of transition between sentences and paragraphs; and

- mismatch between text and bibliographic references.

Steps Leading to Publication or Rejection

Using *Library & Information Science Research* as an example, potential authors submit their manuscripts electronically to the publisher's Web site for the journal. The editors review the papers to ensure they are a good fit. If not, suggestions are made about where they might direct the papers. If the papers are deemed a fit, they are reviewed for layout (e.g., have the components covered in chapter 3) and good writing; there is no review of content. If there are problems in layout or effective writing, the papers are returned to the authors for a first round of revision.

The next step is for one of the editors to select the peer reviewers and to send them the papers electronically to critique. Within three weeks (with some nudging), they return their comments with a recommendation: accept as is, accept with minor change, revise and possibly resubmit to review, or reject. It is rare that a paper is accepted as is; revised papers are reviewed by editors to ensure that reviewer comments were addressed. If they were not, a paper might be rejected at this stage. Once a decision has been made to accept a paper, it is turned over to a copy editor, who makes significant improvements in the written presentation. The changes are returned to the author(s) for review and revision.

Once the editors have the final paper in hand, they schedule it for an upcoming issue and turn over the contents of an issue to the production team at the publisher. The team shepherds the papers for the issue through production and publication. Both the authors and editors have an opportunity to correct final proofs of the paper before publication.

CONCLUDING THOUGHTS

A common assumption is that academic librarians at institutions where there is faculty status are the most likely to seek formal publication in peer-reviewed journals. In fact, there is no single type of faculty status; in other words, publication as a criterion at a number of institutions might be loosely interpreted to include the development of user guides and bibliographies. Nonetheless, it is true that academic librarians contribute more to the published literature than librarians in other settings.

Second, those wanting to engage in formal writing and publication might assume that they cannot think of anything that breaks new ground and will be of interest to a national or international audience. They might benefit from reviewing the research agendas that have appeared in *Library & Information Science Research* or the discussion section on dissertations and published studies that identify topics for further research. They might also examine works such as *The Evaluation and Measurement of Library Services*, which covers a number of topics and provides a good introduction to the literature on those topics;[9] *Academic Librarianship*;[10] and basic textbooks on doing research.[11]

NOTES

1. Impact factor is based on the number of times that articles in a journal are cited in the two years following the year of publication. The impact factor is calculated by dividing the number of current year citations to the source items published in that journal during the previous two years. See the bibliometric data supplied by the *Journal Citation Reports®* (Thomson Reuters), http://thomsonreuters.com/products_services/science/science_products/a-z/journal_citation_reports/.

2. Peer review refers to the decision to accept a paper for publication based on the evaluation conducted by knowledgeable reviewers assigned by the editor. The peer-review process might be blind, which refers to the authors not knowing who reviewed the paper, or double blind, which means that the reviewers also do not know the name of the author.

3. Acceptance and rejection rates are not publicly available. Any data depend on the willingness of the editor to reveal the statistics and to do so accurately.

4. Publishers infrequently release this information and may forbid editors to do so.

5. Publishers also infrequently release this information and may forbid editors to do so.

6. Peter Hernon, Allen Smith, and Mary B. Coxen, "Publication in *College & Research Libraries*: Accepted, Rejected, and Published Papers, 1980–1991," *College & Research Libraries* 54, no. 4 (July 1993): 303–21.

7. Gloriana St. Clair, "Editorial: Improving Quality: An Editor's Advice to Authors," *College & Research Libraries* 54, no, 3 (May 1993): 195–97.

8. David R. Krathwohl, *Social and Behavioral Science Research: A New Framework for Conceptualizing, Implementing, and Evaluating Research Studies* (San Francisco: Jossey-Bass, 1985).

9. Joseph R. Matthews, *The Evaluation and Measurement of Library Services* (Westport, CT: Libraries Unlimited, 2007).

10. Camila A. Alire and G. Edward Evans, *Academic Librarianship* (New York: Neal-Schuman, 2010).

11. For example, Lynn S. Connaway and Ronald R. Powell, *Basic Research Methods for Librarians*, 5th ed. (Santa Barbara, CA: ABC-CLIO, 2010).

Index

About the Authors

PETER HERNON is Professor, Graduate School of Library and Information Science, Simmons College (300 The Fenway, Boston, MA 02115; peter.hernon@simmons.edu), where he teaches courses on research methods, evaluation of library services, academic librarianship, leadership, and government information. He received his PhD from Indiana University, Bloomington, and has taught at Simmons College, the University of Arizona, and Victoria University of Wellington (New Zealand). Besides various activities in New Zealand, he has delivered keynote address in nine other countries: Canada, Denmark, England, France, Finland, Greece, Portugal, Spain, and South Africa.

He is the coeditor of *Library & Information Science Research*, founding editor of *Government Information Quarterly*, and past editor-in-chief of *The Journal of Academic Librarianship*. Professor Hernon is the author of approximately 300 publications, of which 50 are books. He has received awards for his research and professional contributions, including being the 2008 recipient of the Association of College and Research Libraries' (ACRL) award for Academic/Research Librarian of the Year. The first edition of this book, *Assessing Service Quality*, was the 1998 winner of the Highsmith award for outstanding contribution to the literature of library and information science. *Viewing Library Metrics from Different Perspectives*, which he coauthored with Dugan and Nitecki, received the 2010 Greenwood Publishing Group Award for the Best Book in Library Literature.

ROBERT E. DUGAN is the Dean of Libraries at the University of West Florida (John C. Pace Library, Building 32, University of West Florida, 11000 University Parkway, Pensacola, FL 32514; rdugan@uwf.edu). He has worked in academic libraries for more than twenty years in Massachusetts, Delaware, and Washington, DC. Before that he worked on library services and issues at the local, state, and federal levels in public and state libraries as well as a federal agency. His writings cover outcomes assessment, planning, policy implications, the application of information technologies to libraries, financial management, and the federal depository library program. His current interests concern issues of institutional and organizational accountability, metrics applicable to higher education and libraries (such as those metrics reported in *Viewing Library Metrics from Different Perspectives*), and the presentation of these metrics to, and usage by, various stakeholders.

DANUTA A. NITECKI is the Dean of Libraries as well as Professor in the College of Information Science and Technology at Drexel University (W. W. Hagerty Library, 33rd and Market Streets, Philadelphia, PA 19104-2875; danuta.nitecki@drexel.edu). She returned to her graduate school alma mater after nearly four decades and having worked in the libraries of the universities of Tennessee (at Knoxville), Illinois (at Urbana-Champaign), Maryland (at College Park), and Yale. She received her PhD in library and information science from the University of Maryland and a second master's degree in communications from the University of Tennessee. Her research and writings include exploring applications of service quality assessment and of technologies to library services, resource sharing, and design of public spaces in libraries. She serves on editorial boards for *The Journal of Academic Librarianship and Library & Information Science Research*. She edited, or coedited with Eileen Abels, four volumes of *Advances in Librarianship*, and with Curtis Kendrick, *Library Off-site Shelving Guide for High-Density Facilities*.

She has taught research methods and evaluation courses in library science programs at the University of Rhode Island and Simmons College, as well as designed and implemented, with Toni Olshen, *Measuring Service Quality*, a six-week online course for the Association of Research Libraries Online Lyceum. Her current interests focus on evolving the academic library as a learning enterprise, design and assessment of learning environments, and leading change in academic library organizations.